Slaughter of the Dissidents

By Dr. Jerry Bergman

With Introductions by
Dr. D. James Kennedy
Dr. John Eidsmoe

Introductory Chapter by
Kevin H. Wirth

Disclaimer and Registration Information

Legal Notice

The author (Dr. Jerry Bergman) and publisher (Leafcutter Press, LLC) have used their best efforts in preparing this book and the accompanying materials. Though every effort has been made and will continue to be made to ensure the accuracy of what is contained in this book, the author and publisher make no representation or warranties with respect to the accuracy, applicability, fitness, or completeness of the contents of this book. The information contained herein is strictly for educational purposes only. Therefore, if you wish to reference or apply ideas contained in this book, you are taking full responsibility for your actions.

The author and publisher disclaim any warranties (express or implied), merchantability, or fitness for any particular purpose. The author and publisher shall in no event be held liable to any party for any direct, indirect, punitive, special, incidental or other consequential damages arising directly or indirectly from any use of this material, which is provided "as is", and without warranties.

As always, the advice of a competent legal, tax, accounting or other professional should be sought. The author and publisher do not warrant the performance, effectiveness or applicability of any sites listed or linked to in this book. All links are for information purposes only and are not warranted for content, accuracy or any other implied or explicit purpose.

Reading beyond this point constitutes your acceptance of this legal notice/disclaimer. If you do not agree to the terms stated in this disclaimer, then please do not read or reference this book.

Note: If you purchased an electronic version of this book, you were required to register it before you could read it. If you somehow obtained a copy of this book without any registration requirements, then you are reading a pirated copy. If you report the source where you obtained a pirated copy, you will receive a reward. To qualify for a reward, report pirated copies within 10 days of purchase to: sodeditor@gmail.com and include the source internet URL where you obtained it, the download URL, and a copy of the purchase receipt.

Leafcutter Press, Publisher

Leafcutter Press, PO Box 102, Southworth, WA 98386. Published in the United States of America.

Publisher's Note

This book is volume one of a trilogy on the subject of discrimination against Darwin skeptics. The other two volumes, also available through Leafcutter Press, include (volume 2) a discussion of how various groups work against the rights of Darwin skeptics and (volume 3) censorship against Darwin skeptics.

Library Catalog Data

Bergman, Jerry R. (1946 –)
Wirth, Kevin H. (1951 –)

ISBN 978-0-9818734-2-8 (digital)
ISBN 978-0-9818734-0-4 (paperback)
ISBN 978-0-9818734-1-1 (hardcover)

1. Discrimination – United States
2. Education and science – United States
3. Religion in the public schools – Law and legislation – United States
4. Religion and science – United States
5. Evolution (Biology)
6. Intelligent Design
7. Academic freedom – United States

Book design by Lori A. McKee

Dedication

This book is dedicated to those who have paid a high price for the discrimination they have suffered while taking a stand for freedom, with the hope that the lessons learned from their experience will help secure freedom for students, educators, and scientists of the future.

Table of Contents

Acknowledgements

Although some persons whom the writer interviewed are not in harmony with the theistic interpretation of scientific data, nonetheless many were extremely helpful and concerned relative to the deplorable level of religious discrimination in academia today. Of the hundreds of individuals who helped in gathering the data for this book over the past three decades, or who permitted interviews for this book—often at the risk of adversely affecting their careers—a few who had the most significant impact include: Dr. D. James Kennedy of *Coral Ridge Ministries*; Dr. Norman Geisler, Dean of Southern Evangelical Seminary; Kevin H. Wirth, Director of Product Development at *Access Research Network* (ARN); Wilbert Rusch, former President of *The Creation Research Society*; Dr. Duane Gish and Dr. Richard Bliss of *The Institute for Creation Research* in San Diego, California; Dr. Wayne Frair, Professor Emeritus of Biology at *The King's College* in New York; Dr. Robert Kofahl of the *Creation Science Research Center* in San Diego, CA; Dr. George Howe, Emeritus Professor of Science at *The Masters College*, Newhall, California; aerospace scientist Luther Sunderland; Dr. John N. Moore, Professor Emeritus of Natural Science at *Michigan State University*; Professor Harold Armstrong, former editor of *The Creation Research Society Quarterly*; Dr. Norbert Smith, research biologist; Dr. M. James Penton, Professor Emeritus of Church History at *The University of Lethbridge*, Alberta, Canada; Dr. David Menton, Associate Professor Emeritus of Anatomy and Neurobiology at *Washington University Medical School*; Dr. Gordon Melton, director of the *Institute for the Study of American Religion* in Los Angeles, California; Ken Miller, Past Director of Activity Therapy at *The Toledo Mental Health Center*, Toledo, Ohio and currently the Director of Psychology at a large clinic; George Mulfinger, former Professor of Physics at *Bob Jones University*, in Greenville, SC; author Jim Melnick; Paul Ellwanger; Tom Jungmann; John Woodmorappe; Robert Gentry; Dr. Hilton Hinderliter; Mrs. Brian Nelson; Dr. David Warriner, former Professor of Natural Science at *Michigan State University*; Mr. and Mrs. Gary DeYoung; Dr. C. Richard Culp; Dr. Bolton Davidheiser; Jim Pearl; Clifford Burdick; Eric Blievernicht; and David Herbert, Ed.D.

Also many thanks to Dr. Raymond Damadian, teacher Roger DeHart, Nancy Bryson, Ph.D., award winning science writer Forrest Mims, Stanford

University Professor Richard Bube, Professor Dean Kenyon, Ph.D., Samuel Chen, Ray Webster, Bryan Leonard, Irene Herbert, Rodney LeVake, Caroline Crocker, Diliwar Edwards, Attorney Danny Philips, Mark Looy, and Dr. David Phillips for reviewing sections of this book and offering many valuable suggestions, most of which I incorporated into the manuscript. Wayne Frair Ph.D., Bert Thompson Ph.D., Jody Allen RN, Roger Assman, Andrew Lamb, and Clifford Lillo, M.S. reviewed the manuscript and offered many valuable suggestions, most of which were incorporated into the final draft. These were only a few of the scores of persons to whom I am extremely grateful for their help, encouragement, insight and willingness to invest sometimes hours of their time on this now over three-decades long research project.

Also, mention must be made of science teacher David Bulhuis; Dr. Patricia Remington, formerly an anthropology professor at Bowling Green State University (BGSU); Attorney Dr. Steven Ludd, professor of Political Science at BGSU; Dr. Robert Reed, formerly Associate Professor of Education and Chair of the Department of Educational Foundations and Inquiry at BGSU; Dr. Darrel Fyffe, former Associate Professor of Science Education at BGSU; Dr. Robert Simonds, President of the Christian Educators Association; and Dr. Scott Morrow, former professor of Biochemistry at Wofford College, Spartanburg, SC. I want to especially thank Bert Thompson, Ph.D.; Clifford Lillo, M.A.; Rev. Paul A. Bartz; Robin D. Fish; Rev. Ron Boehem; Ernie Johansson, Ph.D., and John Woodmorappe, M.A., and several anonymous reviewers for their comments on an earlier draft of this manuscript. Needless to say, the conclusions in this book are mine alone and the reviewers do not necessarily share them.

Also thanks go to my typists, Nancy Tucker, Sue Schwartz, Melissa Green, Cathy Hern, and Kim Lenz. A particular note of thanks to attorneys, David Latanick, Susanne R. Blatt, Frederick Cloppert, John Allen Eidsmoe (formerly of *Oral Roberts University Law School*), John Whitehead, editor Cameron Wybrow, and John Warwick Montgomery.

Select Quotes

"Restriction on free thought and free speech is the most dangerous of all subversions. It is the one un-American act that could most easily defeat us." - William O. Douglas

"If you will not fight for right when you can easily win without blood shed; if you will not fight when your victory is sure and not too costly; you may come to the moment when you will have to fight with all the odds against you and only a precarious chance of survival. There may even be a worse case. You may have to fight when there is no hope of victory, because it is better to perish than to live as slaves." - Winston Churchill

"A strict observance of the written laws is doubtless one of the high duties of a good citizen, but it is not the highest. The laws of necessity, of self- preservation, of saving our country when in danger, are of higher obligation. To lose our country by a scrupulous adherence to written law would be to lose the law itself, with life, liberty, property, and all those who are enjoying them with us; thus absurdly sacrificing the end to the means." - Thomas Jefferson to John Colvin, 1810

"Do not keep silent when your own ideas and values are being attacked. ...If a dictatorship ever comes to this country, it will be by the default of those who keep silent. We are still free enough to speak. Do we have time? No one can tell." - Ayn Rand, Philosophy: Who Needs It?

"If liberty means anything at all, it means the right to tell people what they don't want to hear." - George Orwell

"Should not the Bible regain the place it once held as a schoolbook? Its morals are pure, its examples are captivating and noble. In no Book is there so good English, so pure and so elegant, and by teaching all the same they will speak alike, and the Bible will justly remain the standard of language as well as of faith." - Fisher Ames (the man who drafted the first amendment)

"Many of the views which have been advanced are highly speculative, and some no doubt will prove erroneous...False facts are highly injurious to the progress of science, for they often endure long..." - Charles Darwin in *The Descent of Man*

Introduction by Dr. D. James Kennedy

To the majority of contemporary Christians religious persecution conjures up pictures of pogroms mandated by insane rulers of antiquity, public "shows" in blood-drenched coliseums, elaborate inquisition torture chambers, and martyred saints being burned at the stake in the town squares of medieval Europe.

But Dr. Jerry Bergman brings the issue of punishment and discrimination and injustice—which he quite properly identifies as outright anti-Christian warfare—up-to-date as he focuses on the Twentieth Century theaters of academia, government, mass media, the courts, and the evolutionary establishment in general.

The nature of the problem, religious bigotry, and the root of the problem, secular humanism, receive the fullest treatment in this comprehensive analysis of the battle between the creation and evolution world views, and its multi-generational spinoff of religious intolerance and suppression.

Like the Nazi threat of little more than a half-century ago, the current penchant for hating individuals because of their religious beliefs concerns not just the immediate targets of scornful persecution but eventually the entire social structure if allowed to go unchecked.

Evangelicals and fundamentalists arouse passions and prejudices more than any other social group or minority, based entirely on what they choose to believe under the aegis of the same Constitution that established liberty for every American citizen.

Something has to be done to ensure academic freedom while there is still time. Dr. Bergman, I believe, brings that imperative to the attention of the reader more effectively than most authors have been able to accomplish.

Introduction by John Eidsmoe

"If there is any fixed star in our constitutional constellation, it is that no official, high or petty, can prescribe what shall be orthodox in politics, nationalism, religion, or other matters of opinion or force citizens to confess by word or act their faith therein. If there are any circumstances which permit an exception, they do not now occur to us." U.S. Supreme Court, *West Virginia State Board of Education v. Barnette*, 319 U.S. 624 (1943).

This is established constitutional doctrine. In the marketplace of ideas, the government must treat all ideas and their proponents equally. It is to aid none, and hinder none. Protestants and Catholics, Christians and Jews, theists and atheists, liberals and conservatives, humanists and fundamentalists, all stand on the same footing before the law. The First and Fourteenth Amendments, with their prohibition of an establishment of religion and their guarantees of freedom of religion, freedom of speech, and equal protection, require no less.

That's the way it's supposed to work in theory. But in practice, one idea has gained the ascendancy and become the official faith, the "established religion" of the state. I refer to evolution, and the religion of Secular Humanism, of which evolution is a cornerstone. Evolution is more than a scientific model. It is an underlying belief-system that profoundly affects the way people think and live. Most, if not all, academic disciplines as practiced today—psychology, economics, political science, sociology, even law and technology—are rooted in evolutionary principles.

Governments spend billions of dollars each year promoting evolution. In most public schools, evolution is taught as fact. Zoos, museums, cultural exhibits, and national parks proclaim the evolution of life as well as rigid uniformitarian geology. Despite pious claims of neutrality and equal access, public television will present Carl Sagan's "Cosmos," along with other evolutionary programs, as fact, while totally ignoring the other side. The public is bombarded with evolutionary thought wherever they turn—much of it disseminated at the taxpayers' expense. Despite First Amendment prohibition against the establishment of religion, evolutionary humanism has become the established religion of America.

Those who do not accept evolutionary humanism may well find their religious freedom infringed. They must pay taxes to support the evolutionary establishment as its disciples conduct their research, publish their findings, and teach and enforce their doctrines at public expense. Compulsory attendance laws force parents to send their children to school, and those who cannot find or afford private schools are compelled to expose their children to evolutionary brainwashing. In any other context but the public schools—the supposed "bastion of American values"—we would call this religious persecution!

But the persecution doesn't stop here. The evolutionary establishment is not content with merely taking the taxpayers' dollars and imposing its views upon a captive audience. As this book demonstrates, those in the evolutionary establishment are engaged in a systematic and determined policy of suppressing those in the academic and scientific community who dare to question their beliefs. Consider and ponder:

> In a nation that prides itself in freedom of religion, an outstanding educator—one who, a few years earlier, had received the Outstanding Educator of the Year Award in his state—was fired for using the two-model approach in teaching theories on origins.

> In a nation that supposedly protects the freedom of speech, a highly competent professor was denied tenure at a state university simply because his colleagues objected to his views published in an article advocating a two-model approach to origins.

> In a state university that piously gives lip-service to academic freedom, a student's doctoral thesis was rejected simply because it supported special creation.

> A student was expelled from class for calling evolution a *theory* while the professor insisted it was a *fact*.

> A group of college professors organized a boycott of all textbooks published by a certain company just because that company had published one small book by an eminent scientist advocating catastrophism instead of uniformitarianism.

Whether the viewpoints these persons advocated may someday prove to be incorrect is irrelevant here. The point at question is the right to discuss a scientific view one believes to be correct and has evidence to support.

In this fascinating and disturbing book, Dr. Jerry Bergman—himself a victim—chronicles the history of modern religious persecution in America. A highly respected, credentialed, and published professor, he was denied tenure—and subsequently fired—admittedly because of his creationist beliefs and writings. Dr. Bergman describes numerous other cases, often concealing names to protect those who do not wish to risk losing their current positions (a common means of persecuting those with minority views).

And these cases, I am convinced, are merely the tip of the iceberg. How many more cases are there in which teachers are not hired or are fired, students failed or their grades lowered, promotions denied, admission to graduate programs refused, theses rejected, books or articles denied publication, or scientific projects denied government funding simply because the evolutionary establishment does not believe in equal rights for creationists? Usually the persecution is more subtle than in Dr. Bergman's case. Reasons are fabricated or frivolous reasoning is substituted. But in more cases than most of us realize, the real reason is religious bigotry.

That's exactly what it comes down to—religious bigotry.

And, I would add, it is hypocrisy to teach only one of the scientifically tenable theories of origins and prate about academic freedom at the same time! Of course, creationists can potentially be bigoted too. But at the moment, the government-sponsored evolutionary establishment has the best opportunity to practice bigotry, and they are showing themselves to be most willing to do so. This book calls for justice, freedom, fairness, and honesty for all sides; it also calls for justice for Dr. Bergman and others like him who have suffered persecution and discrimination for their beliefs. It also calls for freedom for countless "closet creationists" who occupy prominent positions in the academic and scientific communities, but who dare not go public for fear of losing their jobs. This book shows why it is unjust for taxpayers to be forced to subsidize an evolutionary belief-system in which they do not believe, and which they feel undermines the values that they teach their children. Justice also must extend to students who ask that their grades be based on the quality of their work, not upon whether they adopt their professors' ideas and attitudes on evolution. Yet, many civil libertarians claim to believe in freedom of speech and religion, but act as though the First Amendment does not apply to creationists and conservative Christians.

Maybe you're shaking your head incredulously, saying, "This professor's got to be wrong! This can't be happening here! This is a free country!" This *is* a free country. You can believe whatever you wish, if you are willing to pay the price—your job perhaps and even your career. Before you dismiss this problem from your mind, read Dr. Bergman's book and find out for yourself what is happening. Then make your judgment based on facts, not ignorance. Dr. Bergman has done the public a great service by exposing the double standard now practiced by the academic and scientific community.

John Eidsmoe is a retired Air Force Lt. Colonel and Alabama State Defense Force Colonel, Headquarters Judge Advocate, Deputy Chaplain and Training Officer, and a graduate of the Air Command & Staff College and the Air War College. He is Professor of Law at the Oak Brook College of Law and Government Policy, and in his various teaching positions his students have given him the Outstanding Professor Award or Prof of the Year Award 5 times. He currently serves as Senior Staff Attorney for the Alabama Supreme Court. He is an ordained pastor with the Association of Free Lutheran Congregations and serves on the Board of Lutherans for Life, is a constitutional attorney who has defended home schools, Christian schools, the right of students to study the Bible in public schools, and the right to display the Ten Commandments in the public arena. He has authored 13 books, including *Christianity & the Constitution*, *God & Caesar*, and *Columbus & Cortez*, and has produced numerous audio and video lecture albums including *The Institute on the Constitution* and *Here I Stand: A Biblical Worldview for a New Millennium*. He is one of the foremost leaders in the struggle for religious freedom and family rights in America today. A University of Iowa law graduate, he also has an M.A. from Dallas Theological Seminary, and an M.Div. from Lutheran Brethren Seminary. He was also an Adjunct Professor of Theology at Tulsa Seminary of Biblical Languages. A lifelong student of the Crusades, he is a Knight/Chaplain for the Sovereign Military Order of the Temple of Jerusalem (osmth.org). A Third Degree Black Belt with the American Taekwondo Foundation, Colonel Eidsmoe is also a Fifth Degree Black Belt with the Gospel Martial Arts Union and with Black Belts of the Faith International. He is an avid horseman and skier, and tries to get 8 hours of sleep every week. He and his wife Marlene have been married since 1970, have three children (David, Kirsten, and Justin) and live in rural Pike Road, Alabama.

Preface by Dr. Jerry Bergman

This book is not trying to prove or disprove an origins theory, but simply to argue that academics have the right to question Darwinism or some aspects of evolution without losing their careers or being denied degrees. People who have serious doubts about the validity of NeoDarwinism are refered to in this book as "Darwin Doubters." The primary concern is the actions and attitudes towards Darwin Doubters by "ultra-Darwinists" or "Darwin fundamentalists," terms Stephen J. Gould used to brand Darwinists like Maynard Smith, Richard Dawkins, and Daniel Dennett.[1] Academic freedom and human rights issues are key themes of this work.

When deciding on a title for a book, authors and publishers desire to accurately reflect the general contents, yet also draw attention to their work. How does a writer convey the gravity of the situation facing Darwin Doubters without alienating potential readers? Further, if I were to summarize the situation in a quick introductory statement, some readers would no doubt be skeptical. Therefore, I have decided to let the facts speak for themselves—quoting extensively from court cases and the leaders in the struggle in an effort to ensure that Darwin Doubters "have a place at the table" in American society, especially in academia. Currently, they are being excused from that table with alarming frequency and consistency, or are not being seated at all.

Hate Crime on the Rise

As I will document, many of the manifestations of discrimination against Darwin Doubters should, in my opinion, qualify as hate crimes. While usually less violent than many other types of hate crimes, the anti-religious motivation that accompanies many of the manifestations of behaviors against Darwin Doubters is clearly illegal discrimination—at least in the United States, and should be protected under freedom of speech, academic freedom, and religious freedom. I am not suggesting that new hate crime legislation is required to protect victims of the abuse I report here, but that existing laws should be equitably enforced. Many of the same behaviors that define a "hate crime" against other protected groups

---

1   Richard Morris, 2001, pp. 1–2.

should also be applied to actions taken against Darwin Doubters. It seems clear that while the rights of other protected groups in our society are being zealously defend, seem to receive far less attention and protection under the law. This inequity needs to come to an end.

Although there has been much debate over what constitutes a hate crime, some studies have already been undertaken in an effort to understand the scope of this growing problem.

> In a study of law enforcement agencies, the FBI found that 7,163 hate-crime incidents, affecting 8,795 victims, were reported in 2005 to police departments that participated in the study. Estimating incidents involving elements of hate crime during an earlier time period—July 2000 through December 2003—BJS coupled results from victim interviews with additional factors such as offender use of derogatory language or hate symbols to estimate an annual average of 191,000 incidents, affecting 210,000 victims.[2]

As part of the research I did for this book, I contacted over 300 persons, most of whom were active scientists, many of them out-of-the-closet[3] and some still in-the-closet Darwin Doubters. I specifically inquired about whether they faced discrimination in the workplace from either their supervisors or professional colleagues. All of those interviewed had earned at least a master's degree, and the majority held a Ph.D. Several had more than one earned doctorate, and their occupations ranged from students to Nobel Laureate scientists. Their level of involvement in creationism or Intelligent Design activities, such as writing or speaking in favor of these positions, ranged from being very active to having little or no involvement.

All of the out-of-the-closet Darwin skeptics, without exception, reported that they had experienced open and often severe discrimination because of their position on origins. Their experiences ranged from open derision from their colleagues—being made the brunt of jokes—to being outright fired and even physically assaulted. Many of these situations, in my opinion, qualify as hate crimes. Some of these cases were tragic in their extent, blatancy, and the consequences on victims and their families. It's important for readers to know that the

---

2   Shively and Mulford, 2007.
3   For a partial list of over 2,000 such individuals see: http://www.rae.org/darwinskeptics.html

case studies presented in this work do not represent the most extreme instances of discrimination, but are in fact typical of what Darwin skeptics commonly experience. Several cases from each category of discrimination (see below) were selected to demonstrate the effects the widespread problem of academic and religious discrimination had on the lives of those who were affected.

Forms of Discrimination Exercised against Darwin Doubters

In this section I attempt to set forth, in summary form, the main types of discrimination experienced by those who have openly criticized, or even expressed doubts about, some aspect of Darwinian evolutionary theory. Each of these forms of discrimination will be explored in greater detail in the case studies presented later in this book. The following summary of how discrimination against Darwin Doubters is most frequently manifested will serve as a useful point of orientation.

1. Derogatory and Inappropriate Comments

Examples range from minor events, such as the placing of obscene cartoons on the victim's desk (e.g., one that showed a creationist as having a pea-sized brain, and an evolutionist as normal-sized brain), to the more serious constant inundation of insults and name-calling aimed at a Darwin Doubter's scientific or personal religious beliefs, especially if they are sympathetic with (real or alleged) "creationist" or Intelligent Design (ID) concepts. In an employment situation, courts have ruled such name-calling is considered illegal harassment since it produces a hostile work environment. As will be documented, such comments can have a devastating effect on one's career and professional life. Many students and educators were also asked questions about their religious orientation. Aside from these queries being potentially illegal, information gain from them has been used against both students and educators seeking to secure a degree or a tenured faculty position.

2. Denial of Admittance to Graduate Programs

Candidates for Graduate programs have in some cases clearly met admission criteria, having high GRE scores, 3.5 grade point average, etc., but letters of recommendation advised against admission because of the applicant's doubts about Darwinism or evolution, religious beliefs, or history of involvement in a religious organization. This seems to be clear evidence that these students' denial of admittance was, or may have been, decided inappropriately. The effect of this action has resulted in blocking entry of Darwin Doubters into a science related profession at the very earliest stages. It effectively serves to curtail career advancement for an individual viewed as unfit for work in various types of environments (such as academia or in the biological sciences, for example).

3. Denial of Degrees

In some cases, students met all legitimate degree requirements, but were denied degrees anyway. It can reasonably be assumed that the student was denied the degree solely, or largely, because of his or her perspective on the origins issue. The discriminatory comments for those cases we examined were frequently in writing and were usually verified by interviewing others, often non-creationists or others who rejected ID arguments. The impact of this type of discrimination on individuals, who have put a great deal of work into preparing for a career, was (and still is) significant, and has prevented many from ever entering their chosen career.

4. Denial of Deserved Promotion

Many competent and qualified Darwin Doubters have suffered the loss of career advancement because of their views. Non-promotion of individuals that clearly meet all the requirements for promotion (had earned high student ratings, achieved more than an adequate number of publications, etc.), is evidence of bias, especially in cases when other individuals of equal or lesser accomplishment were promoted. Comments by faculty such as, "all persons who deny Darwinism are incompetent—and if you weren't tenured, we would terminate you," are evidence of bias against Darwin Doubters.

5. Censorship of Darwin-Critical Works from Libraries and Schools

Where large libraries have dozens of books promoting Darwinism, yet few or no books promoting creationism or Intelligent Design, or even some of the better published work critical of Darwinism or aspects of evolution, this can reasonably be viewed as an indication of censorship. In some cases, works critical of Darwinism have been donated to libraries, but never made their way to library shelves.

6. Firings, Terminations, and Denial of Tenure

A significant number of the cases that I have examined involved open firing or termination as a result of publishing articles on creationism, Intelligent Design, or the weaknesses in Darwinism or evolution – even though many times these publications were not directly associated with their job or career positions. These cases frequently involved individuals who met or exceeded the criteria for continuing employment in terms of a sufficient number of acceptable, relevant, and even peer-reviewed publications and who demonstrated adequate or better ability, comprehension and understanding of knowledge required for their jobs or teaching performance, yet they were terminated. Where clear evidence of religious bias existed in these cases, it constitutes reasonable evidence (or, in legal terminology, "probable cause") that the termination was due to the individual's religious orientation, even when their religious views were not known or fully understood, and even if their dissent focused on science, not religion.

Furthermore, loss of a job or a career has often resulted in significant financial difficulties, even bankruptcy and loss of one's home on top of a means of earning a living. Some former professors, most with nine years (on average) of education in the sciences, were forced to take whatever work they could find including driving taxicabs or trucks, becoming part time teachers or entering an entirely different career, often having nothing to do with their degree or university training. The stress associated with these changes has often produced financial, family, and other problems often ending in divorce, moving to different cities and/or states, adverse effects on children, and even suicide.

7. Demotions

A number of educators in evolutionary biology have been removed from courses they previously taught and instead were made to teach introductory biology courses, or were reassigned to courses outside of the biology department altogether. In such cases, the rationales for such moves were often determined to be based on the expression or allegations of doubts about Darwinian theory, the presumption that the educators were proselytizing or teaching their students about creation or ID, or for other religious or philosophical reasons. Demotions can also be defined as placing someone into an administrative position—anything to get them out of the classroom.

8. Threats and Personal Intimidation

Some critics of Darwinism have experienced blatant threats and personal intimidation including death threats. Such threats not only produce fear and stress, but often affects family relations, career advancement, self esteem, and student-teacher or professor relations. Some of these threats have been acted on, resulting in hospitalizations, surgery and permanent, ongoing health problems.

Various Motives for Discrimination against Darwin Doubters

Why are Darwin Doubters discriminated against in the manifold ways enumerated in the previous section? There appear to be a number of reasons, including the following:

1. Objections by the majority of practicing scientists to the real or alleged weaknesses in the scientific arguments offered by Darwin Doubters;

2. The natural defensive response of any intellectual or academic establishment against challenges to the dominant theory within a discipline, in this case biology;

3. The connection of Darwinism, in the minds of many scientists, with an atheistic and or secular humanist world view which they find more congenial than one allowing "religious" views;

4. The association of any criticism of Darwinism with "creationism," "Intelligent Design" or other alleged "pseudosciences" which are also termed "religious" and are therefore considered unacceptable since religion and science are separate areas of inquiry;

5. Unwillingness to concede that any valid philosophical or scientific arguments exist with regard to Intelligent Design.

Alleged Weaknesses in the Science of Darwin Doubters

Many scientists oppose Darwin Doubters because they believe that their science is disingenuous, weak, or non-existent. They often point out that there are no "Designer Labs" studying and testing the tenets of Intelligent Design or publishing results in peer-reviewed journals (although as long ago as December of 2006, the Biologic Institute, headed by Dr. Douglas Axe in Seattle, has begun publishing papers of their findings at least one peer-reviewed journal).[4] Darwin skeptics respond by noting that many Darwinists have themselves written about the numerous and specific concerns they have about Darwinism and evolution. Many Darwinists acknowledge that much controversy exists, but stress that such concerns are not about whether evolution has in fact occurred, but rather that some mechanisms or evidences of evolution remain to be discovered or more fully articulated. Both Darwin skeptics and other scholars respond that poorly defined mechanisms clearly lead to more questions about the validity of the extrapolations of evidence used for some evolutionary explanations, such as from micro to macro evolution. For example

> without greater proofs, microevolution cannot be automatically expanded to support the idea that Darwinism accounts for the appearance of all living things across the major divisions of nature. The distinction should not be blurred, microevolution is based on fact; macroevolution is based on faith.[5]

Others in the Darwinian camp claim science must be "methodologically materialistic" or "methodologically naturalistic." Many Darwin Doubters do not

---

4 Axe, et al., 2008. See also Anika Smith, 2008 at
http://www.newscientist.com/channel/opinion/mg19225824.000-intelligent-design-the-god-lab.html
5 Addicott, 2002.

agree with this approach, but argue that science can be divided into two areas; empirical science, which deals with evidence that can be evaluated by using the scientific method as commonly defined (formulate a hypothesis, collect data, reject, revise, or accept hypothesis), and historical science, which cannot be replicated or falsified empirically. Neo-Darwinism (defined as evolution from organic chemicals to humans via a common ancestor), creationism, and ID all involve interpretations of historical science which cannot be directly replicated, but requires the extrapolation of information to the past, and thus cannot be falsified.

As a result, the speculations of Darwinians are viewed as "science," but the speculations of Darwin Doubters are labeled as necessarily "religious" and are therefore inadmissible for serious scientific discussion. A common claim by many Darwinists is that neither ID nor creationism are falsifiable, a trait considered by Karl Popper and other philosophers of science to be a critical factor in determining what is science. As Ronald Numbers has documented, however, many critics argue that both ID and creationism are unfalsifiable—and then argue they have been falsified![6] Clearly, Darwinists cannot have it both ways.

The Natural Resistance of Intellectual Establishments to Change

As Thomas Kuhn has documented, many persons—especially scientists—resist new paradigms, and when the defense of a paradigm becomes so fanatical and unreasonable it actually threatens scientific progress.[7] Thus, when Michael Behe's and Michael Denton's biological work, and William Dembski's mathematical work are dismissed out of hand partly because they don't fit the reigning paradigm of biology or evolutionary theory, doctrinaire rejection of their views effectively becomes a "science stopper," and blocks the development of new knowledge. Ronald Numbers documents that "establishment defensiveness" results in the persecution of those who oppose the new model competing with the dominant model, producing an "embattled minority."[8] The establishment model is often overturned by the establishment retiring or dying, and the new generation taking over with new ideas. Or when overwhelming evidence is

---

6   Numbers, 2006, p. 276.
7   Kuhn, 1970.
8   Numbers, 2006, pp. 274–275.

produced, a scientific revolution results,[9] such as in the case in medicine when it was proven by numerous studies that the major cause of ulcers was the bacteria *H. pylori*, not stress or diet as was assumed by the medical establishment for generations.

The Religious Objections to Darwin Doubters: Naturalism versus Theism

The metaphysical, religious, philosophical, and political bias coming from biologists, the media, and the general educated intelligentsia, clearly favors Darwinism and is used to block any serious attempt at criticism that might open the door to any hint of theistic or religious interpretations of nature. The primary conflict arises between the "naturalistic" world view, which maintains that all of reality can be explained by natural law, time, chance, mutations and natural selection, and the "theistic" world view, which concludes that everything cannot be solely explained by that criteria. Although the basic charge against Darwin Doubters is generally that they are religiously motivated, the fact that not all Darwin Doubters are openly theists seems to elude the notice of many Darwinists. Examples of non-theistic Darwin Doubters include David Berlinski, Michael Denton, Periannan Senapathy, Chandra Wickramasighe, Murray Eden, Marcel-Paul Schützenberger, Herbert Yockey, Stanly Salthe, Christian Schwabe, Gerald Kerkut, Professor Lima-De-Faria, Pierre Grasse, Soren Lovtrup, David Stove, Fred Hoyle, John Davison, and many others who have disagreed with one or more aspects of Darwinism or evolution. These and many other scientists cannot be placed into the typical philosophical constraints defined by critics of Darwin Doubters.

The dissent from these and other scientists clearly demonstrates that this issue is not grounded in promoting a religious view, but involves philosophical and scientific disputes that have no basis in theistic arguments. Yet critics of Darwin Doubters continue to conveniently ignore this fact. These and many other Darwin dissenters have no "religious" axe to grind. These scientists do not want to substitute "theism" for naturalism, but simply want to raise the question about whether Darwinism, or even naturalism, is an adequate method of interpreting the scientific evidence. As of July, 2008 over seven hundred scientists

9   Kuhn, 1970.

(most of them with Ph.D.'s) have signed a "dissent list" with Discovery Institute affirming their agreement with the statement that "We are skeptical of claims for the ability of random mutation and natural selection to account for the complexity of life. Careful examination of the evidence for Darwinian theory should be encouraged."[10] In a healthy, democratic society where freedom of thought and speech are highly prized, it is necessary for these ultimate questions about nature, science, and God to remain open to review, debate and criticism rather than being stifled by eliminating from the academy those who harbor doubts. Too many intelligent and qualified dissenters exist, and to dismiss them all as irrelevant or 'religiously motivated' (as many critics of Darwin Doubters do) is not only ridiculous but also clearly demonstrates a greater concern for controlling the discussion than for going where the evidence leads.

Many scholars who have been denied degrees (or lost their positions) were forced to move to other communities and had to start over. Their hope has been that they would be able to successfully hide their doubts about Darwin conclusions and survive "in-the-closet." Unfortunately the internet has made this somewhat difficult. Several persons the author interviewed were not hired based on internet searches that uncovered their creationist or Intelligent Design leanings. To be open about one's beliefs now is often possible only in openly Christian institutions, and even many of them are not secure places of refuge.

I have personally interviewed many of those directly involved with the cases cited here but have, whenever possible, relied upon published sources for additional verification (all of the cases I mention at length in this book have been reported elsewhere). Many persons who were only indirectly involved with certain cases were hesitant to discuss them with me, but agreed to so only because of long personal acquaintance and the assurance that specific information about them would not be revealed. To this condition, I have willingly consented. I have endeavored to contact the person of interest for all the cases I present here and, in a few instances, they have argued that my write-up was in some way inaccurate. In these cases I have tried to sort out the information and make the best judgment given the information I had as to what actually happened.

---

10   Discovery Institute's dissent list may be found at: http://www.dissentfromdarwin.org/ or http://www.discovery.org/scripts/viewDB/filesDB-download.php?id=660 (as of 05/03/08).

I have also endeavored to extensively research both sides of each case cited in this work. In most cases, original sources, including court transcripts, affidavits, internal memos, and other information was obtained. In addition, where possible, individuals on both sides were interviewed. In most of the cases researched, the agency that discriminated against an individual usually claimed that its actions were due to other valid reasons, and these reasons had to be researched. It is often not easy to prove a discrimination claim beyond reasonable doubt, and other factors that I may not have evaluted could have been involved in some of the cases discussed here. In addition, some of the cases cited in this study may not, in fact, have been textbook cases of discrimination. However, it should be noted that generally, wherever a Darwin skeptic was denied equitable treatment among peers (i.e., denied advancement, tenure, degrees, etc.), yet met or exceeded the requirements for the same recognition and advancement afforded their peers—when the only recognizable difference was their dissent over Darwinism—discrimination was inferred.

In most of the situations I researched, the reasons given for the discrimination were found to be totally vacuous. The routine response in these cases is to simply deny that religion was the reason no *matter what the evidence*. In one of the most well-documented cases, that of Forrest Mims III, *Scientific American* adamantly denied religious discrimination had anything to do with his termination. This claim was made in spite of the fact that the editor who terminated him specifically gave religion as the reason in a published transcript.[11] The same is also true in the case of Guillermo Gonzalez. Emails exchanged among his colleagues seem to indicate a clear concern about his alleged religious beliefs. The publication of his work "The Privileged Planet" (co-authored with Jay Richards) leaves the door wide open for those who read the book or view the video to become positively influenced in the direction of being open to the possibility of an Intelligent Designer at work in the universe.

In most of the cases cited here, the evidence for discrimination was overwhelming, but nonetheless denials, often made under the advice of an attorney, existed for virtually all of them.

---

11   Bergman, 1993a.

I am aware of only one credible critique of the concerns discussed in this book, by Ronald Numbers.[12] Numbers' attempt to critique these conclusions in fact eloquently supportes them—and for this reason his work will be quoted extensively. The two most common responses to the information presented here are that a) the type of illegal discrimination I document *should* occur (because this is allegedly a dispute over allowing flat-earth-believing crackpots teach our children), or b) that illegal discrimination is not occurring because valid reasons have existed to deny degrees or terminate the Darwin Doubters in question.

This work is especially prone to attack because, as is often said, every story has two sides. I have made every effort to contact both the victims and their critics in compiling the case studies you are about to read. It may be that one of the case histories might be seized upon as partially inaccurate by claiming someone else interviewed a person involved in the case and heard a different story. A critic who obtained a different account might attempt to impugn one of the case studies I've presented, claiming it is inaccurate.

Minor inaccuracies, or alternate stories about some cases, do not detract from the basic premise of this work, and in no way negates the overall indictment illustrated by the remaining cases, not to mention the untold thousands of other cases that I have not recounted here. Unfortunately, in many instances critics did not respond to my requests for their perspective, and where they have, I always took into consideration their comments and arguments. Some case histories were dropped from the final edition of this work because of feedback received from critics.

In other cases, the discrimination account was modified to accommodate the claims made by those who disagreed. In cases where I received no feedback whatsoever, I could only assume my review was correct. One can hardly respond otherwise when the other side does not provide any information. Of course, they might not have responded for valid reasons. Nonetheless, I could only make conclusions on the basis of the information I was able to obtain. In many cases, I relied heavily upon written documentation as well as my personal knowledge of the person and the circumstances of their case.

It has been my experience that when I sent a paper to a critic for feedback on a case, I received either no information or vague, uninformative responses.

---

12   Numbers, 2006.

However, when these case studies are published, I expect critics will provide helpful feedback—some of which may turn out to be accurate and helpful. Additional information will be carefully considered for revisions to future editions of this work. For most case histories presented here, the person of interest reviewed the write-up of their case for accuracy.

Those who doubt the validity of the theme in this work are welcome to produce a book documenting that hundreds of out-of-the-closet Darwin Doubters sailed though graduate school, published widely, achieved tenure and promotion regularly and with little contest, and became successful in their fields. Some cases (such as Mortimer Adler, Ernst Chain, Raymond Damadian, and others) do exist, but they clearly are the rare exception, not the rule. It is also clear, judging from my publishing experience in this field, that I likely will be on the receiving end of vicious, mostly unfounded attacks. No matter how extensive or accurate my documentation, and whatever my conclusions might be (although I have no doubt errors exist in this work), some will respond with contempt directed against me because they believe those I am defending *should* have their rights truncated.

Like most victims of discrimination, many of those I communicated with exhibited various types of apprehension about relating their experience. Many expressed a great deal of concern about being "found out." Ruination of a career is no minor matter—it often means years of schooling and many thousands of dollars are lost. This was less true with tenured faculty or those whose careers were well established in research, writing or in other areas. Even some of these individuals, though, were cautious. Many wanted to discuss their case but hesitated due to fear of repercussions.

Some prominent scientists and teachers claimed that they have experienced discrimination but those who had information to collaborate their claims were not willing to come out of the closet due to a well founded fear of retaliation or other related reasons. Of those I interviewed, however, almost 70% claim they have faced open prejudice, and about 40% possessed evidence of clear discrimination against them directly because of their ID or creationist beliefs. Discrimination against Darwin Doubters is widespread and is often irrational and may involve physical violence. About 12% of those I interviewed stated that they had received highly emotional non-verbal feedback or irrational verbalizations against them. The situation was stated well by Paul Bartz:

A couple of years ago the Soviets said that creation materials and thought were the most dangerous tools against communism ever brought into the Soviet Union. Once, in the United States, it was only a few wild-eyed radicals who echoed such thoughts. But in the last few years major newspapers have compared conservative Christians to Germany's Nazis and used this and similar justifications to suggest that conservative Christians—sometimes they even used the word "creationists"—do not have a constitutional right to the freedom of speech. Some have even called for laws to control traditional Christians because they are a threat to society. Now a Harvard professor has had difficulty in finding anything wrong with crowd violence against a conservative speaker...one anti-creationist arsonist set fire to a printing company which prints creation materials, telling police he burned the business because it prints creation science materials. The arsonist also warned the printer not to reopen! While most conservative Christians have paid little attention to these very serious threats to their civil rights, the number of Christians who are becoming alarmed is growing. This is happening because more and more Christians are finding themselves on the receiving end of such bigotry.[13]

The Need to Stand Up for Our Rights

The 1995 U.S. Supreme Court five-to-four *Rosenberger vs. The University of Virginia* decision eloquently verifies the thesis of this book. The court ruled that a public university does not violate the Establishment Clause when it grants access to its facilities on a religion-neutral basis to a wide spectrum of student groups, even if some of those groups use the facilities for devotional exercises. In this specific case the court ruled that the University of Virginia violated the First Amendment rights of Christians by denying them the same funding resources for their magazine that was available to secular student-run magazines. Civil rights attorney Jay Sekulow called this case a "critical threshold in the fight for religious liberty."[14]

---

13 Bartz, 1987b, p. 1.
14 *USA Today*, June 30, 1995, p. 8A.

Even though the arguments of many Darwin Doubters does not rely on "religious" doctrine, in almost all cases critics tend to whitewash their dissenting views as "religious" or "religiously motivated" and therefore deserve to be dismissed as invalid in a "scientific" discussion. Critics often use the religious preference of an individual as evidence of their inability to conduct scientific inquiry. They prefer to focus on the "no aid to religion" principle, while ignoring the dissenter's scientific work or denying their freedoms.

Historically, the pendulum on many issues swings back and forth. Even many in the secular community recognize that the pendulum has swung too far away from a reasonable center and against Christians who take their faith seriously. This work documents a partial history of that swing, and is a plea that readers and supporters will work to move the pendulum toward more tolerance and accommodation of Darwin skeptics in line with the principles of a free and just society. It is my hope that at some point this work will no longer be a call to action, but will instead merely recount the history of a bygone era of intolerance and repression of thought. Even though the rise of the Intelligent Design movement during the 1990s seemed to signal a swing of the pendulum towards more tolerance of dissenting views, academia and the media have in fact actually become much more inflamed. Increasing public awareness of the plight of Darwin skeptics as detailed in this volume will aid in the pendulum's move toward more tolerance and accommodation.

This work is intended to reveal the need for greater support of religious liberty, academic freedom, freedom of speech, and human rights. Most Americans think these rights are secure, but this book documents an alarming and broad disregard for those freedoms, as reflected in one headline, "Limits on Religious Liberty Widespread in 1985."[15] A United Methodist task force concluded that religious liberty issues in America and the world "are significant and need to be addressed."[16] The situation is now, over two decades later, much worse. The cover story for the July 9-15, 2005 issue of *New Scientist* titled "The End of Reason: Intelligent Design's Ultimate Legacy" implied that a dark age is upon us if people are allowed to believe that God had a role in history.

---

15   Beck, 1986,
16   Beck, 1986, p. 3.

The Modern Growth of Anti-Christian Sentiment in America

The modern creation-evolution debate has come a long way since its origins in Europe in the middle 1800s. The first step was for Darwinists to argue that it was unreasonable to teach only creationism—the world view usually taught up until the turn of the century—in many American public schools. Both creation and evolution should be taught, many evolutionists argued. Consequently, Darwinism was gradually introduced into the public schools. Because of the controversy surrounding this issue in the 1930s, though, many school textbooks and teachers of the time elected to cover neither view. The appearance of Darwinism in school texts slowly became more and more prominent—especially after 1957 following the Soviet Union's launch of the Sputnik satellite—until it eventually became the only view usually taught in the public schools today.[17]

Beginning in the 1970's, Darwin Doubters began to protest that this totally one-sided instruction was open indoctrination.[18] Evolutionists countered that presenting only evolution in public school science classes was proper because it is the only valid scientific view,[19] and that presenting creationism or Intelligent Design amounted to a violation of the establishment clause of the US Constitution on the grounds that they are "religious" views. On the other hand, even opponents of creationism often stressed during this time that creationism had a valid place in the school curriculum as part of social studies, literature, or comparative religion classes.[20] In an effort to discredit all Darwin Doubters, opponents have mischaracterized their views as just another version of Biblical creationism.[21]

The next step was to discourage any favorable coverage of creation in science classes. Soon, school authorities began to terminate teachers who were allegedly teaching creationism in science classes, or at least many schools threatened to do so.[22] In many cases, the school authorities *did not know* exactly what a teacher was covering in class, but only that the teacher *personally* did not accept evolutionary naturalism; consequently, they assumed that creationism could have

---

17 Herbert, 2004, pp. 104–105.
18 Beckwith, 2003; Whitehead and Conlan, 1978.
19 Eldredge, 2000.
20 Buderi, 1989, p. 219; Eldredge, 2000.
21 Dembski, 2004.
22 Bergman, 1984a.

crept into their classroom lessons. At first, usually only science teachers were affected, but later, even social studies and English teachers who were attempting to present a neutral agnostic viewpoint became victims (see the Ray Webster case in this volume). All out-of-the-closet Darwin skeptics were now threatened and many faced problems.

The next and last step—which is now being aggressively pushed—is to call on American courts to require that neither creationism nor Intelligent Design be favorably presented *anywhere* in any public school— or even in Christian school science classes. Baptist Liberty University's accreditation was threatened in its struggle to determine its own science curriculum. In a compromise, which I will document in the third volume of this trilogy (focusing on censorship), the school elected to teach creationism in the religion department, and the science department was allowed to teach only evolution. One of the Christian colleges targeted for similar restrictions was the *Institute for Creation Research* (ICR) Graduate School. As its name implies, ICR was established to focus on creation research; thus the school obviously taught this view. The state officials formally and openly objected to this focus, arguing that *only* Darwinism could be taught, and that all discussion and all evidence in support of creation must be censored.[23] In a compromise, the state at first agreed to allow the college to teach creationism in a *separate period* involving the student's free time. Suspicious that this was not enough to render their creation teaching ineffective, the state then decided to force the school to close. The situation was summed up well by Russian scientist, Dmitri Kuznetsov:

> In a time of *perestroika*, the academic freedom in Moscow and Leningrad looks better than in California. We have a real opportunity to carry out biological research in the creationist field, to organize public debates, scientific meetings, publications, lectures, and even to teach creationism as a *scientific subject* in newly formed colleges supported by churches and independent Christian associations...my old friend and opponent Dr. Kirill L. Gladilin, a Head of Laboratory of Evolutional biochemistry of the USSR Academy of Sciences Institute of Biochemistry (Moscow, USSR) usually supports my efforts in organizing debates between creationists and evolutionists at his institute, which is the most famous evolutionist institute in the world. At least

---

23   Looy, 1990; Larry Gordon, 1989, p. 34.

this means that prominent evolutionists in the USSR consider creationists scientific opponents.[24]

I will document the ICR case in detail in the third volume of this series on censorship, including the great legal costs incurred by ICR. They eventually prevailed in court and their graduate degree program in science was fully approved by the state of California.

A key agenda of many leading ID advocates seems to be all but ignored in the controversy over how to manage better science education, and that is what I call the "full disclosure" approach to science. Rather than seeking "equal time" presentations for their views, many IDers are content to simply see an expansion of the scientific evidence presented on the topic of evolution to include a discussion of the theory's potential problems and contrary evidence. For example, the Discovery Institute has stated that

> Instead of mandating intelligent design, Discovery Institute recommends that states and school districts focus on teaching students more about evolutionary theory, including telling them about some of the theory's problems that have been discussed in peer-reviewed science journals. In other words, evolution should be taught as a scientific theory that is open to critical scrutiny, not as a sacred dogma that can't be questioned. We believe this is a common-sense approach that will benefit students, teachers, and parents.

Attacks on Individuals

Increasingly, Christian teachers have been prohibited by court order from even mentioning their own world view, even during their free time, anywhere on school grounds (see the Bishop case in this volume). The situation has escalated to the point where firing (or demotion) of teachers and professors whose only crime was that they personally were creationists is becoming more common.[25] As I have documented, many individuals have been terminated not for what they did (i.e., they did not teach 'creationism' or 'ID' to their students), but for

---

24 Kuznetsov, 1990, p. 3.
25 Bergman, 1995b.

what they believed. Others have been terminated merely because they added optional reading from respectable peer-reviewed science journals to the curriculum they were required to present to students. Meanwhile, educators teaching in other disciplines are free to add their suggested reading material to students without comment, challenge, or similar restrictions. And the American courts have *consistently failed to support* the rights of teachers who are Darwin Doubters.[26] This problem is documented more thoroughly in a chapter found in the second volume of this trilogy.

Darwin skeptics of all stripes are often fired or discriminated against based on accusations of "teaching creationism" in their classrooms, which (it is claimed) violates the separation of church and state doctrine. The fact is, surveys have found that scores of thousands of American public school teachers continue to "teach creationism" in our public schools, as long as they argue *against* the creation view.[27] The reality is that teachers are required to present *only* naturalistic evolution—which is at least more consistent with atheism than any opposing view. Surveys, including one I am currently working on, have found that many science educators teach that God is the who, evolution is the how, and therefore no conflict exists between these two views. This, though, is clearly teaching theology which the courts have ruled is impermissible in a science class. Typically, teachers who oppose teaching evidence that challenges evolution do not *directly* teach blatant atheism because this could cause problems. Indeed, there is no need to be overt about an atheistic approach, since they teach that everything is fully explainable by natural causes (life, love, religion and everything else in the universe). They have, in essence, put an Intelligent Designer out of a job and made him permanently unemployed.

Additionally, many educators who are Darwin Doubters but not creationists or Intelligent Design advocates encounter problems due to the mere suspicion that they are teaching some form of creationism or Intelligent Design, accusations that are rarely defined or supported by evidence. As Johnson argues,[28] the allegation that a person was fired for teaching creationism is often specious—they were usually fired not for what they did, but for who they were or what they believed.

---

26 Bergman 1984a; Eidsmoe 1984.
27 see Berkman et al. 2008.p. 124.
28 Phillip Johnson, 1995b.

Discrimination often depends upon *which side of the debate school authorities and one's fellow teachers assume a teacher favors.* If they assume the teacher will firmly lecture *against* some form of creationism or Intelligent Design, there is rarely any problem. If they come to believe that the teacher may be presenting information challenging evolution or *in favor of* design, difficulties often result. In virtually all of the cases that I researched, the problems encountered were usually not because of what someone was doing (teaching or writing, etc.), but because *of what the victims personally believed.* Even writers and teachers who agree to espouse only atheistic evolution in their writing and teaching experience trouble. An excellent example is the Mims case, in which an award winning science writer was terminated from Scientific American because he questioned Darwinism.[29]

In spite of the widespread scope of this problem, extensive legal research I conducted has revealed that neither creationist nor ID educators have *ever prevailed in an American court in a single employment discrimination court case.* Indeed, other than cases involving "reasonable accommodation" in employment, I was not able to locate a single religious discrimination case where an American court decided in favor of any theistic religious minority. This is not because of a shortage of cases—crimes based on religion have been in some years identified as the second most common hate crime category according to F.B.I. reports.[30] This ranking fluctuates from year to year (in 2005 it was the 6th most commonly reported hate crime)[31] but is still a major problem. Nor is it due to the alleged difficulty of proving these types of cases. Rather it is a result of bias on the part of the courts. A review of court cases such as that presided over by Judge Jones in the 2005 Dover, Pennsylvania case indicate that many Judges are trained by secular professors, and thus tend to manifest the same brand of intolerance against Darwin Doubters as do many professors. Judges who are unsympathetic to Darwin Doubters are apparently not inclined to apply the rule of law as vigorously as they seem to do on behalf of other protected groups. For these and other

---

29 Bergman, 1993a.
30 *USA Today*, June 29, 1994, p. 3A.
31 Harlow, 2005, p. 3 (also available at www.ojp.usdoj.gov/bjs/pub/pdf/hcrvp.pdf).

reasons in *all* academic discrimination suits, faculty members end up losing in court.[32]

Many clear-cut accommodation-of-conscience cases have been decided in favor of religious minorities. Examples include the right to collect unemployment if terminated for refusal to work on weekends for religious reasons, refusal to print pornographic material, and refusal to transfer to the tobacco or defense divisions of one's employer. Much of this litigation does not deal strictly with discrimination issues but with very carefully defined questions such as: "Can an employer force an employee to work on Saturday against that employee's conscience, based on religious scruples, regardless of the need for his services on this day?" The rulings in most of this litigation conclude that the employer must try to make "a reasonable accommodation" to the objecting employee's conscience, philosophical beliefs, value orientation, or religious training.

As of this writing, many atheists have prevailed in employment law cases. One of many examples involved a bank teller who the Fifth Court of Appeals ruled was discharged because of her atheism. Her company's mandatory monthly business meeting started with a short devotional; so she walked off her job. The bank argued that she quit and was not fired, but the court ruled that once the teller's lack of religious beliefs became known to the bank, it had a duty to "accommodate" them; therefore, she had been "forced" to resign.[33] I can find no similar cases where a ruling of accommodation for Darwin Doubters has been upheld.

Surveys and EEOC files indicate that thousands of job loss cases occur each year in which the victim feels clear evidence of religious discrimination exists. Given this number, it is both astonishing and disheartening that evidently *none* of these cases have been adjudicated favorably by the courts. I can hardly believe that none of those cases reflected situations where actual religious discrimination occurred, yet this is what the record would have us believe. The only conclusion that one can draw from this is that the American government is generally not as interested in enforcing the civil rights of Christians as it appears willing to pro-

---

32   McMillen, 1987a, p. 1.
33   *Young v. Southwestern Savings*, EEOC release No. 74.1306; see *American Atheist Magazine*, Sept., 1975, p. 19.

tect other groups.[34] In an extensive study on this problem, the U.S. Commission on Civil Rights concluded that the courts *are not adequately protecting the rights of Christians to practice their religion.*[35] Evidence of this problem is seen in the epidemic of intolerance and persecution against Christians today by secularists who dominate our courts and institutions of learning.[36]

Although some of the stronger religious discrimination cases or claims may have been settled out of court (and one is forced to rely on published court opinions, since out-of-court settlements are hard to study), employers are nevertheless often fully aware that they can exercise even blatant religious discrimination with little or no fear of reprisal. A former president of *Bowling Green State University*, Dr. Hollis Moore, indicated to me that the university could terminate a professor *with impunity* for any reason, legal or illegal. Also, as I recall, he further stated that a university can "justify" or cover the termination merely by claiming that it was because the professor does not, in their "professional judgment," qualify for a new contract. The university feels it is on secure ground, especially if the "secret ballot" voting system is used. Moore stressed that the courts are extremely hesitant to intervene in university affairs, especially on issues regarding personal decisions. They rarely scrutinize the colleges' judgment even if the terminated employee can clearly demonstrate illegal discrimination. As I recall Dr. Moore telling me: "We can cover our tracks." And they usually do.

Universities often have been able to successfully hide behind secret tenure votes, and the courts usually rule that voting colleagues need not reveal how, nor why, they voted.[37] Thus, in the case of universities, justifying someone's termination is often unnecessary if the individual did not receive a positive two-thirds vote which is a "requirement" for continued employment as a tenured faculty member. If we are going to reduce the scandalous level of religious discrimination in state colleges and universities, the trend to fire by a secret vote must be eliminated in favor of fully visible standardized requirements and universities in all cases must provide valid, documented, relevant reasons for every employee's

---

34 Limbaugh, 2003; Sunderland, 1983.
35 See *Christianity Today*, November 25, 1983, p. 35.
36 McQuaid, 2003.
37 McMillen, 1987a; Metzger, 1955.

termination.[38] A California lawsuit called the "Open Files Case" argued for just this right.[39]

In 1990 the U.S. Supreme Court finally ruled that universities do not hold a first amendment or common law privilege against disclosure of peer review materials.[40] Unfortunately, the seven-to-two Supreme Court decision in *Edwards vs. Aguillard* has greatly exacerbated this problem. Journalist Joseph Stowell opines that

> evolutionists will become more "militant and aggressive" in their views as a result of the decision. A "Scopes-in-reverse" could be the next legal front in the continuing battle between creation and evolution, Keith says. John Scopes was the biology teacher who in 1925 was convicted of teaching evolution and became the focus of the famous "monkey trial." Keith, who is now president of the Creation Science Legal Defense Fund, says he has more than 100 documented cases of teachers who have been denied tenure, promotions, awards, and grants; harassed and even fired because they taught creation science. Several of those could make powerful cases if pressed into court, he says.[41]

The situation has become far worse since the "*Edwards*" case was decided. The concern in this work is not the validity of various positions such as Intelligent Design, creationism, deism, or even the position that a transcendent God is ultimately the author and sustainer of the universe. The concern here is primarily academic and religious freedom, and the necessity to clearly delineate between the illegal suppression of dissent and the legitimate rejection of a view that is impossible to empirically falsify. The biggest concern is academic freedom and first amendment rights, issues that an untold number of persons have died for and wars have been fought to preserve and maintain. As Evelyn Beatrice Hall once wrote, "I disapprove of what you say, but I will defend to the death your right to say it."[42]

---

38 Bergman, 1984a.
39 McMillen, 1987a, pp. 16–18.
40 Flanigan et al., 1995.
41 Stowell, 1987, p. 93.
42 Or at least this quote is attributed to her (not Voltaire or Patrick Henry).

Chapter 1: A Context for Discrimination Against Darwin Skeptics by Kevin H. Wirth

It's an inescapable fact that we live in an age dominated by science and technology. Many of us make our living using the wonderful tools that have resulted from recent discoveries derived from the scientific enterprise. Concurrent with the blessings of these new scientific advances, our culture is also the beneficiary of another, much older inheritance—one that many scientists and educators believe no longer fits with our new age of scientific progress. The worldview that preceded our modern age of science held that we owe our existence to a Creator. This view still persists today, despite the efforts of many secular scientists, philosophers, and academics to replace it with what they believe to be a much more rational approach to apprehending the universe, naturalistic materialism.

The battle for the philosophical heart and soul of science, in the view of many, revolves around the theory of evolution. And ground zero for that battle has been, and continues to be, our academic institutions. Academia is the gateway in our culture where we determine who qualifies and who is allowed entry to practice in a scientific venue or educate our young people about the principles of science. And, academia is where we are currently witness to a grave injustice, often a purging, of students and educators who are skeptical about one or more aspects of Darwinian evolution. A contentious result of this intellectual carnage is the abrogation of a host of freedoms; freedom of speech, freedom of thought, academic freedom, and freedom of religious expression, to name a few.

Educators, scientists, and students who are skeptical of many claims made by neo-Darwinism as taught in our biology classrooms have been discriminated against in various ways for their dissenting views, resulting in countless stories of ruined careers, a few of which you are about to read. And, the discrimination is often based upon the religious beliefs of those dissenters.

What this book chronicles is the extent of this shameful injustice that has plagued and claimed many thousands of victims. These victims are *not* people who are anti-science, or who reject science as a way of understanding the universe, as many of their critics often eagerly allege. Rather, these are people of conscience who have not been able to reconcile the facts of science with one or more evolutionary conclusions, and who insist that evolution is an inadequate explanation for the incredible complexity of life we are just now beginning to understand.

In America, we are supposed to be protected against acts of discrimination based on gender, age, race, sexual orientation, religion, or handicap. Yet, as Dr. Bergman documents, within academia religious freedoms are being distorted and discarded in the name of protecting the nearly sacrosanct status of evolutionary naturalism. What's worse, this practice seems to be gaining a growing cultural acceptance, and little is being done to correct it.

According to Dr. Bergman, it doesn't matter if an educator can demonstrate his competency in an area of science – if he is also religiously oriented in any way, he is at high risk of losing not only his current position, but also an entire career.

This book is the first installment of a trilogy written by Dr. Bergman on this issue, and will focus on a series of case studies relating how a number of victims have been discriminated against for their evolutionary skepticism. The second volume will address in some depth many of the concerns related to this issue, and some of the means by which discrimination is carried out against dissenters. Finally, the third volume will focus on just one aspect related to this issue: censorship. In combination, these three volumes will provide readers with a thorough top-to-bottom rundown of discrimination as practiced against those who question evolution.

I would say the primary value of this first volume is that it brings into focus the extent of the deplorable practice of discrimination it exposes. In practical terms, what you'll find here is how freedom of expression is being stolen from those who dare to dissent. And, notably, this issue has somehow managed to linger under the radar of the news media and public awareness until recently with the release of the movie "Expelled." When was the last time you heard a report on your nightly news of an educator who had been denied tenure for being a Darwin Doubter? Yet it occurs with frightening regularity. While this type of discrimination has been reported in print media over recent years (just scan the bibliography…), it hasn't been given the attention it merits. The impact of the discrimination you are about to read is significant: it reflects a widespread drain from academia of skilled and competent educators needed to challenge and inspire the next generation of scientists and educators. While Darwin Doubter dissidents are tolerated, and even welcomed at some universities, they are effectively being purged wholesale from major institutions within our national academic environment.

Dr. Bergman understands first-hand the abuses he documents here, having been the victim of a rather protracted and incredibly unjust denial of tenure and court trial himself. His experience and research on other victims of discrimination in academia ranks him as one who is eminently qualified to address this issue. Essentially, Dr. Bergman reveals a category of hate crime that is seldom discussed in a public forum. This book has been created as part of an ongoing effort to bring this travesty into the sphere of broader public awareness.

A much smaller version of the theme covered in this volume was originally published by Dr. Bergman in a 1984 book titled *The Criterion*. Even before then and ever since, Dr. Bergman and I have discussed many of the case studies you are about to read—and beyond that—we've agonized over how many people have suffered at the hands of individuals and groups who don't seem to think twice about derailing, obstructing, or ruining the careers of countless people who in good conscience could not come to terms with some aspect of neo-Darwinism. The reasons for their objections and dissent is often not based on their 'religious' views, but on a rational consideration of the scientific evidence. And worse, if they conclude that the evidence indicates an intelligent agent was responsible for life, their alleged "religious" beliefs are often ultimately viewed as the reason for their inability to perform their scientific or academic duties.

This book tells the story about what has been going on behind-the-scenes in recent decades as students, professors, and science professionals have been systematically harassed and eliminated from their professions for harboring skepticism about Darwinism. These activities are all the result of what writer Denyse O'Leary refers to as "academic fascism," that poses a serious threat, not only to freedom of speech and academic freedom, but also sends a chilling message about a pernicious agenda in academia and science as a whole.

Different Types of Darwin Doubters

In this work we often refer to evolutionary skeptics as "Darwin Doubters." Darwin Doubters don't typically insist that others accept their views, or that their views are the only viable ones, but they do often insist on their right to be respectfully heard. Many Darwin Doubters would be happy to present their arguments without any of the trappings of "religion," but Darwin Defenders are often adamant in their insistence that any criticism of evolution or design-oriented counter arguments are necessarily 'religious' and, therefore, cannot be heard in any science venue or context.

Darwin Defenders typically miscast, misconstrue, and lump all Darwin Doubters into one big family they call "Creationists." They typically make no allowances for the differences across these groups, nor their scientific objections, and simply refer to all of them as people with a "religious" agenda because in their view, anyone with a *truly* scientific orientation can only arrive at the inevitable conclusion that the history of life was shaped by a strictly evolutionary influence. And, as you will see in the case studies Dr. Bergman presents, anyone who falls into any of these four classes of Darwin Doubter is subject to attack, persecution, and discrimination.

Creationists

Creationists unabashedly state that they believe that the God of the Bible created life pretty much as we know it, though there are a variety of groups within this class who have different views about how He did it. They make no bones about their belief that they are basing their opinion about the origin and development of life using Biblical revelation as a key piece of evidence for their arguments.

Many creationists would love to see creationism taught alongside evolution in our public schools – though many would disagree with this approach. This group would include, among others, progressive creationists, young earth creationists, old earth creationists and others.

Intelligent Design Advocates

ID advocates conclude that the scientific evidence supports a modified interpretation of many neo-Darwinian principles (such as the conservation aspect of natural selection, rather than the creative ability typically ascribed to it by most evolutionists), and an intelligent cause without any need to reference what we would commonly refer to as Biblical or other religious texts or beliefs. They question the evolutionary assumption that natural causes by themselves can account for the complexity of life on planet Earth, and conclude that an intelligent agent may have been involved in the process (note: you don't need to be "religious" to make this deduction). ID suggests that the likelihood of life having evolved via chance natural processes flies in the face of all applicable probability scenarios. ID advocates do not typically promote the notion that we need to teach creationism or any religious views in our public school classrooms (a claim that is often made by their critics), but many of them would be content if better science were taught. ID arguments may be consistent with some common religious beliefs, but no religious texts or views are used as evidence for any of their propositions. Their approach is science-centered, and addresses mathematical and probability arguments, plus an examination of the philosophy of science. They advocate that teaching evolution should also include a solid review of the difficulties with the theory.

Darwinians

Darwin Doubters are generally viewed by their more certain brethren within the Darwin camp as misguided traitors and almost as off-center as any Creationist or ID advocate. Darwinians who are skeptical about some aspects of Darwinism are reported to be rare, but I suspect only seemingly so since they tend to keep a low profile about their doubts, knowing full well what the consequences could be for their career if they openly shared their real feelings about this subject. This group would include, among others, theistic evolutionists, agnostic and even atheist Darwinians.

Skeptics who are not married to any of the first 3 views.

This is perhaps the smallest of the four groups mentioned here, and are a 'catch-all' class of individuals who have no religious or scientific predispositions, but who are nevertheless skeptical of Darwinian conclusions, and do not fit into any of the other groups just described.

Defining the Context of Discrimination

As with any book where claims of misconduct are alleged, it's helpful to provide a framework within which to consider what you are about to read. Discrimination against Darwin Doubters does not occur in a vacuum, but in the context of several ideas that shape public perceptions of who they are and the alleged dangers they pose to science and academia. There exist a few basic factors that contribute to the climate we see both within academia and elsewhere. Attorney Jeffrey Addicott notes that

> Perhaps the best way to capture the power of evolution's *Weltanschauung* (world-view) is to view the matter as a function of three interrelated factors. First, there is an unwillingness to separate the portion of the theory of evolution that is correct and factual from the portion which is purely theoretical. Second, Darwinian thought has been completely institutionalized in western science and culture as the dominant paradigm. Third, many adherents of evolution possess an unrelenting religious-like faith in Darwinism.[43]

What follows is an elaboration of the issues hinted at in these factors that work together to create an environment that facilitates the types of discrimination many Darwin Doubters find themselves facing today.

1. ***Where we are as a culture.*** The current climate of intolerance in academia against people holding religious views is the logical outcome of where our culture has been headed, at least philosophically, for several decades. Attorney and former Berkeley professor Philip Johnson[44] and philosopher Francis Schaeffer,[45] for example, warn about this at length in their writings.

---

43 Addicott, 2002.
44 See especially Johnson, 1998.
45 See especially Schaeffer, 1985.

What we are seeing today in the discrimination documented here is the predictable and logical outcome of the preference for secular philosophical premises so widespread in our culture today, especially among our more formally educated citizens.

2. *The issue of Freedom.* This debate isn't just about evolution and creation or Intelligent Design. The prevailing pro-Darwinian attitude within academia is a lightening rod used to challenge many of our most basic and cherished freedoms. The debate over the problems related to evolution are one matter; our freedom to challenge it is quite another. And, based on what you are about to read, you will see that those freedoms are currently being savaged. The primary mission of this book is not to address the validity of Darwinian evolution, creation, or Intelligent Design, but to call attention to the incredible abuse of those freedoms and to urge the readers participation in providing and supporting remedies to reverse this trend.

Some of these case studies describe instances where the victims sought relief from our courts. That process reveals yet another layer of obstacles for the victims: they usually do not prevail in court, even when there is clear evidence of discrimination. The courts have tended to focus on the role and responsibility of government to ensure that the first amendment tenet of separation of church and state is rigorously upheld. The more challenging side of the first amendment coin also deserves the same rigor, however, while it seems that the government typically gets all the protection it needs, the victims often get the leftovers.

Activist groups have joined the fray in an effort to steamroll Americans with cries of "separation of church and state" whenever a brave educator dares to suggest to his students that there are problems with Darwinism or that an intelligence may be behind the complex marvels of life we see every day. Many of these groups pretend to be experts on the true meaning of the First Amendment, but their lopsided focus ignores both the intent and the balance implicit in that phrase:

> *Congress shall make no law respecting an establishment*
> *of religion, or prohibiting the free exercise thereof;*
> *or abridging the freedom of speech, or of the press; or the*
> *right of the people peaceably to assemble, and to petition*
> *the Government for a redress of grievances.*

Freedom of religious expression is clearly a protected right for every American—including educators on school property. I say this knowing full well what many of our Courts have ruled in recent years. Fortunately, some of those rulings include a refreshing breath of sanity. In a rare rebuke of the ACLU's repeated argument of the separation of church and state, 6th Circuit Judge Richard Suhrheinrich wrote:

> [T]he ACLU makes repeated reference to "the separation of church and state." This extra-constitutional construct has grown tiresome. The First Amendment does not demand a wall of separation between church and state. *See Lynch*, 465 U.S. at 673; *Lemon*, 403 U.S. at 614; *Zorach v. Clauson*, 343 U.S. 306, 312 (1952); *Brown v. Gilmore*, 258 F.3d 265, 274 (4th Cir. 2001); *Stark v. Indep. Sch. Dist., No. 640.*, 123 F.3d 1068, 1076 (8th Cir. 1997); *see also Capitol Square*, 243 F.3d at 300 (dismissing strict separatism as "a notion that simply perverts our history"). Our Nation's history is replete with governmental acknowledgment and in some cases, accommodation of religion. *See, e.g., Marsh v. Chambers*, 463 U.S. 783 (1983) (upholding legislative prayer); *McGowan v. Maryland*, 366 U.S. 420 (1961) (upholding Sunday closing laws); *see also Lynch*, 465 U.S. at 674 ("There is an unbroken history of official acknowledgment by all three branches of government of the role of religion in American life from at least 1789."); *Capitol Square*, 243 F.3d at 293-99 (describing historical examples of governmental involvement with religion). After all, "[w]e are a religious people whose institutions[46] presuppose a Supreme Being." Zorach, 343 U.S. at 313. Thus, state recognition of religion that falls short of endorsement is constitutionally permissible.[47]

Courts are not infallible. And no court, however learned or well informed it may consider itself to be, has the right to abridge the protected freedoms

---

46   No. 03-5142 ACLU of Kentucky, et al. v. Mercer County, Kentucky, et al. p. 14
47   *ACLU v. Mercer County*, 2005. http://www.ca6.uscourts.gov/opinions.pdf/05a0477p-06.pdf

of Americans, and it is the solemn and simple duty of every American to rise up and respectfully refuse to yield to any efforts seeking to diminsh or recast them. When those freedoms are challenged, as they often are in the cases of Darwin Doubting educators, we need to stand with them, encourage them, and let our voices be heard loudly and clearly in support of their *right* to express dissent without having it labeled as inadmissibly "religious". In most instances, the freedoms of educators have been denied because of the complaints from groups that are vigilant in their opposition to our freedoms. There needs to be a corresponding, or better yet, a more *overwhelming* show of support for those freedoms from the rest of us. In several instances we know of where such support was provided by students and the public, discrimination ceased and decisions were reversed (I'm thinking of the Francis Beckwith and Nancy Bryson cases, for example). Failing such action on the part of those who support freedom, we will continue to see more of the same types of sad case studies Dr. Bergman has presented here. Note: if you would like to be alerted whenever we learn of an instance where an educator is being unjustly discriminated against, and would like to consider possibly sending an email supporting them, please go to www.slaughterofthedissidents.com and sign up as a free subscriber to our notification service. If you are an educator who has been the victim of discrimination, please contact us via email at sodeditor@gmail.com.

I am not suggesting that in every case cited by Dr. Bergman the victims acted completely appropriately in every way, or that there were no genuine issues that the government rightfully needed to address. But, I do think many of these cases clearly demonstrate patterns of gross misunderstanding, injustice, and inappropriate discrimination. I also regard what is happening to Darwin skeptics in academia today as the modern equivalent of the canary in the coal mine when it comes to our freedoms. Freedom is the canary. If we let it die for one group, then we allow it to die for us all. When one class of citizens has their freedoms denied, it is an attack on the rest of us because we *all* share these same freedoms. None of us will escape the fallout of allowing freedom to be snatched or stolen from any class of Americans, especially those protected freedoms owed to us all.

Based on what you are about to read, I would say that there also appear to be some very clear violations of basic freedoms proscribed under the protection of the U.N. Universal Declaration of Human Rights[48] (specifically, Articles 5, 12, 18, and 19).

3. ***Critics claim dissent is religious.*** Even though religion is the not the primary rationale used by many Darwin Doubters to explain their reticence to fully adopt the commonly accepted conclusions of neo-Darwinism (claiming their dissent is based on scientific merit alone), their adversaries have been insistent that their primary motivation, more than anything else, is based on their religion, and not science.[49]

This tactic of categorizing the dissent of Darwin skeptics as necessarily religious is then used to declare that the opinions of Darwin Doubters are therefore inappropriate, or impermissible in an academic institution. In fact, many opponents of Darwin Doubters go even further, classifying the views of skeptics as "anti-science," owing to the alleged "religious" bias of dissenters. Though Creationists do reference Biblical texts in support of their views, many other Darwin Doubters do not (such as ID advocates). Many Darwinists assiduously refuse to regard this distinction as having any merit, and insist that *all* Darwin Doubters rely on a 'religious' basis for their arguments. Claims from ID advocates about the non-religious nature of their arguments often fall upon deaf Darwinian ears. William Dembski makes an all but ignored distinction between a design inference and the design argument.[50] Legal Scholar Francis Beckwith examined how the courts have tended to view religions, and has summarized the non-religious nature of ID rather succinctly:

> ID is not a conventional religion and thus is not a paradigm case of a religion. Rather, it is a point of view based on philosophical and empirical arguments. The purpose of ID is to provide answers to the same questions for which the

---

48 http://www.un.org/Overview/rights.html
49 Dembski, 2002 p. 367 notes: "Design is detectable; we do in fact detect it; we have reliable methods for detecting it; and its detection involves no recourse to the supernatural."
50 Dembski, 2004a, p. 77

evolutionary paradigm is said to provide answers. That is, design theory and naturalistic evolution are two conflicting perspectives about the same subject. Admittedly, if the ID arguments are plausible, they do lend support to the metaphysical claims of some conventional religions such as Christianity, Judaism, and Islam. However, as Justice Powell wrote in his Edwards concurrence, "a decision respecting the subject matter to be taught in public schools does not violate the Establishment Clause simply because the material to be taught 'happens to coincide or harmonize with the tenets of some or all religions'"... if a point of view is religious because its plausibility lends support to a religion or a religious point of view, then we would have to conclude that naturalistic evolution is as much a religion as ID, for it lends support to some nontheistic and antireligious perspectives recognized as religions by the Court.[51]

What this means is that Darwinists should take care whenever they insist that ID is clearly a 'religious' perspective, since making such a claim could eventually backfire on them. The Supreme Court has yet to fully address the definition of religion in the context of the debate between evolution and Darwin Doubters, but when that does occur, it could go badly for ardent evolutionists.[52] And, as mentioned previously, many critics prefer to paint *all* Darwin Doubters using the same broad brushstrokes without making any distinctions (i.e., they are *all* religious, they are *all* anti-science, they *all* promote pseudo-science, etc.). What is worse, those who attempt to articulate the different distinctions between various Darwin Doubters are often called liars because their critics have already presumed they are all a) cut from the same religious cloth, and b) believe and operate essentially the same way.

Of course, this is a most convenient position for critics of Darwin Doubters to take, since the courts in *Epperson*, *McLean*, and *Edwards* have rejected Scientific Creationism, partly because it was determined to be based largely on, and to also impermissibly advance, religious views. But to suggest that all Darwin Doubters fit neatly into the definition of Scientific Creationism is the equivalent of suggesting that all evolutionists are advocates of punctuated equilibrium. Not all evolutionists agree with punctu-

---

51 Beckwith, 2003, p. 149.
52 Addicott, 2002 – see especially text footnoted from 338-360.

ated equilibrium in the same sense that not all Darwin Doubters agree that we need to be using the Bible as a reference point for an investigation into the key issues related to this debate. There exists some significant diversity among Darwin Doubters concerning how they go about interpreting and analyzing both the scientific and theological evidence. This refusal to acknowledge such differences needs to change if an honest appraisal of Darwin Doubters is to be undertaken. And it is partly due to mistaken views like this that harsh antagonism and eventual discrimination against Darwin Doubters persists within academia.

The result of insisting that all Darwin Doubters view the scientific evidence for the history of life through a religion-only filter has resulted in what can only be described as a battle over the religious freedoms of Darwin skeptics on the one hand, and the right of academia to insist on removing religiously oriented educators on the other—*often regardless of what an educator may actually practice in the classroom*. Witness the fact that once a Darwin Doubter has been branded 'religious,' he or she frequently stands little chance of avoiding discrimination or even surviving in academia. Many educators find themselves victims of discrimination even when they have not expressed any religious views with their students or colleagues, or when what they have expressed is protected speech.

Increasingly, merely admitting to harboring doubts about any aspect of Darwinism is often sufficient to initiate a special inquiry into what and how an educator is teaching his students (or worse, making assumptions about it *without* any serious inquiry). This frequently results in everything ranging from murmuring to open hostility among faculty colleagues and students, often culminating in the removal of science educators from their position. Though often not stated in such terms by those within academia, we believe that a close and independent examination of many case studies presented here warrants reaching such a conclusion. We urge readers to make their own determination.

4. ***Critics claim religious people are not qualified to teach or practice science.***
Believe it or not, this claim is made frequently and emphatically today
among faculty and administrators in many academic institutions throughout the U.S. This pervasive attitude is also reflected in numerous blogs. For
example, critic P.Z. Myers has remarked that

> I don't think the religious are necessarily stupid, and I most definitely do not
> believe they are born stupid. *I do believe they are saddled with a set of foolish
> misconceptions that can throttle their intellectual development and send them ca-
> reening off into genuinely weird sets of beliefs*, but this doesn't make them stupid.
> I also think that IQ tests are written by people who promote an implicitly
> scientific perspective (which is a good thing!), and it's therefore not surprising
> that a group in which a significant fraction of its membership actively reject
> science will do poorly on such tests… *accepting the handicap of faith might lead
> to poor performance on non-faith-based tests and scientific thinking.*[53]

This clearly articulated bigotry against people of faith (by a college professor, no less) reveals more than just an undercurrent in our culture—it
reflects a widespread antagonism that is growing by leaps and bounds,
particularly among young people. Not only that, but commentary like this
grossly ignores the thousands of scientists who were and remain people of
faith and who have also contributed significantly to scientific discoveries.[54]
We are well beyond the point where polite discussions over disagreements
on the issue of evolution in academia and elsewhere is the norm (as this
book clearly documents).

Out of the closet Darwin dissenters are automatically suspect and the reaction to them is quite often to deny them a role as an educator or scientist, or
deny them a degree if they are a student. This is *clearly* the response offered to
thousands of educated faculty in our universities (both secular and religious)
all across the U.S. The religious views of dissenters should not be a factor
with regard to their competence as educators and scientists or their qualification to receive a science degree, but many opponents of Darwin Doubters

---

53   Myers, P.Z., 2008 (emphasis added)
54   http://tektonics.org/scim/scientista.html

maintain that religious views are grounds for disqualification, insisting that one's religious persuasion necessarily infects one's perception of how science should be conducted. The message is often made very clear: educators or scientists with religious views don't belong in academia or the scientific community. Such a position ignores the great many world renown scientists and educators who were and are creationists or ID advocates, and who have made incredible contributions to science, as you will see in chapter 14.

5. *The Myth of Religious 'Neutrality'.* The issue of 'religious neutrality' as defined by our courts has created concerns among many who seek to ensure the protection of religious liberties. Although the courts have upheld laws that require teachers to refrain from wearing any clothing, garb or insignias indicating a religious affiliation because "the preservation of religious neutrality is a compelling state interest,"[55] maintaining religious neutrality is not achieved by the complete removal of religion or religious symbols from academia. Of greater interest to the courts should be the preservation of the freedom of religious expression. As attorney Philip Johnson points out

> For at least the last twenty-five years the dominant principle (occasionally ignored in practice) has been that neutrality means "no aid" to religion.[56]

This "no aid" policy has had a debilitating effect on the lives of the victims of viewpoint discrimination. As Johnson also points out, "religion-free secular knowledge… is anything but neutral on religious questions."[57] I am not suggesting we need to advocate religious proselytization in science education, but merely point out that a growing number of Darwin Doubter educators have experienced an alarming increase in the number and type of discrimination by students, their colleagues, and their employers. It's quite clear from reading many of the case studies in this volume that a religious witch hunt was undertaken against many victims who then rightly responded in an attempt to defend themselves against bogus charges. Invariably, once the religion issue enters the picture, even when it was not established to have ac-

---

55 *U.S. v. Board of Education*, the 3rd Circuit
56 Johnson, Philip, 1998, p. 109 (see especially ch. 11 – The Law & Politics of Religious Freedom)
57 Johnson, Philip, 1998, p. 111

tually played any role in what an educator taught his students, it was usually held against them.

It's a misnomer to think that religious neutrality is achieved by eliminating any and all reference to religion. Courts and advocates concerned with protecting against establishment clause incursions also need to consider the *outcome* of court rulings upon those who are equally entitled to protection under the free exercise clause. If the outcome of a ruling infringes on free exercise rights, then it should be corrected to provide proper accomodation rather than allowed to remain on the books and and cause further harm. Americans should not be expected, nor can they afford, to suffer the loss of protected freedoms based on the failed experiments of lopsided jurisprudence favoring establishment cause rights at the cost of free exercise liberty. Until the current interpretation of religious neutrality is somehow balanced to include better protections for religious expression, then our culture will continue down a secular path where our students are taught the false notion that religion needs to be muzzled because it is anti-science, or that people of faith have no business in science or academia. Clearly, such an outcome is contrary to the spirit and intent of the first amendment free exercise clause. While secularists are constantly pushing the 'separation of church and state,' button, those who have an equally valid expectation of protection for the 'free exercise' of their religious liberties need to become just as insistent for reasonable accommodation without the encumbrance of 'no aid' laws and court rulings that remove or restrict them in the public forum and generally erode their protected rights.

6. ***The tenure review process is broken.*** The tenure review and approval process in academia today facilitates discrimination without accountability. Dr. Bergman's experience and research shows that there is a strong need for reform in the academic tenure process. Secret ballots are used as a means of ensuring that, even if an educator meets or exceeds all other requirements defined by a university, tenure can still be denied on the basis of the faculty vote *alone*. And if enough tenured faculty agree that an untenured professor's religious or philosophical perspective does not align with their own, they can

simply vote him out of a job, or more often, a career. They can base their vote on misinformation, prejudice or bigotry. This must change to ensure that faculty are granted tenure based on a fair and balanced set of criteria. The faculty vote should count only as one part of the overall requirements for gaining tenure, and other requirements should carry much more weight. The emails that were exchanged between colleagues of Guillermo Gonzalez (see the Addendum at the end of chapter 13) before his tenure denial is just one of many examples of why this is necessary.[58]

7. ***Allowing the opposition to set the alleged 'religious' agenda.*** The government (i.e., academia and our courts) has often allowed organizations and other entities that are hostile to people of religious persuasion to set the agenda and define the nature of the dissent from Darwin skeptics, as well as what constitutes religion and religious practice in their domains. Even though many Darwin skeptics do not intend to impermissibly promote their religious views, the insistence by their opponents that they do places them in a defensive mode on the issue of their religious liberties. The government has been all too agreeable in permitting opponents of Darwin Doubters to inaccurately define the nature of the harm caused by people of faith, even when the testimony of Darwin Doubter expert witnesses clearly counters the characterizations offered by their critics. This approach is like permitting a software pirate to design the security protocols for unlocking software products on a CD – *of course* he's going to shrewdly design such protocols with a back door to his advantage.

For example, critics often characterize the philosophical viewpoint of Darwin Doubters as religion-first rather than science-first. ID advocates insist it's the other way around: they want to see better *science* taught. This focus on religion is a convenient approach for ID critics to take, and they strongly promote it, since school districts can and usually do direct teachers to "refrain from expressions of religious viewpoints in the classroom and in certain school related settings."[59] Defining the views of Darwin skeptics as

---

58   You can also download screenshots of the actual emails from Gonzalez's colleagues by going to http://www.slaughterofthedissidents/cases/gonzalez/emails./zip
59   *Bishop v. Aronov*, 926 F. 2d 1066, 1077 (11th Cir. 1991).

necessarily religious is therefore in the interest of secularists, but *should* it matter? Should it really be a point of contention if Darwin Doubter science educators hold religious views? Should Darwin Doubter educators be prevented from challenging their students to consider the scientific problems with evolution – even those raised by respected scholars within the scientific community? Critics of Darwin Doubters would typically answer "yes" to all of these questions, but many Darwin skeptics would not. For example, one might adopt any number of ID positions without holding to any conventional religious persuasion. Other Darwin skeptics may indeed hold religious beliefs, but that should not matter, especially in America, where one's religious persuasion is a constitutionally protected right. Leading ID advocate William Dembski speaks to this issue directly when he says

> For the record, therefore, let's be clear that the opposition of design theorists to Darwinian theory rests in the first instance on strictly scientific grounds. Yes, we are interested in and frequently write about the theological and cultural implications of Darwinism's imminent demise and replacement by intelligent design. But the only reason we take seriously such implications is because we are convinced that Darwinism is on its own terms an oversold and overreaching scientific theory.[60]

And what about Darwinism - could it be considered religious? Many wonder if a court would ever uphold such a determination. In spite of repeated denials by many Darwinians, some solid evolutionists who disagree with the views of Darwin skeptics admit that evolution in fact contains elements of a religion. Philosopher of science Michael Ruse notes that

> Evolution is promoted by its practitioners as more than mere science. Evolution is promulgated [by its adherents] as an ideology, a secular religion—a full-fledged alternative to Christianity, with meaning and morality. I am an ardent evolutionist and an ex-Christian, but I must admit that in this one complaint...the literalists are absolutely right. Evolution is a religion. This was true of evolution in the beginning, and it is true of evolution still today.[61]

---

60   Dembski, 2001b, p.12
61   Ruse, 2000, p. B3

Critics of Darwin Doubters claim that their religious views render them incapable of practicing or teaching good science. That's a lot like saying that because I'm a good baseball player I can't also work the night shift in a print shop where baseball cards are made. One activity does not disqualify me from effectively doing the other. Yet this is exactly what many critics of Darwin skeptics are saying: if you're religious, or if you have doubts about Darwinism, you can't practice good science – and you should not be given the opportunity – because your 'religious' motivations disqualify you. This junkyard argument is one that most people (except many in academia) are quick to recognize as outright bigotry.

A key distinction: the source of an idea v. its effect

But let's play devil's advocate for just a moment as we consider how the agenda is being set by Darwinians. There is another important distinction that needs to be made, and that is the difference between a religious source and a religious effect.

a) An idea or argument can come from a religious source and also have an impermissible religious effect.

b) Conversely, an idea or argument can come from a religious source and have no impermissible religious effect.

Darwinians often make the distorted claim that any ideas promoted by Darwin Doubters are necessarily religious because they come from a religious source, and are therefore inadmissible in a scientific venue. But are they? Let's break this down.

If the *effect* of an idea or argument is to promote religion in a way that secures exclusive privileges for its adherents over and above everyone else, or advances sectarian religious or antireligious beliefs, *that* would be unconstitutional. But if an argument is derived from a 'religious' source, or is even religiously motivated, yet does not have the *effect* of promoting religious views in the manner just described, then the 'religious' source of such an an idea is totally irrelevant, and should *not* be grounds for automatically dismissing it. Quoting Supreme Court Justice Lewis Powell:

> The Establishment Clause is properly understood to prohibit the use of the Bible and other religious documents in public school education only when the purpose of the use is to advance a particular religious belief.[62]

Which then begs the question: then under what circumstances is the use of the Bible *not* to be understood as advancing a 'particular religious belief'? This is a distinction that many vocal advocates of 'separation of church and state" fail to make. It seems clear Justice Powell is not saying that the use of "religious documents" (or ideas) is wholly inappropriate in a school setting, but that their use is inappropriate only *under certain circumstances:* such as when the "purpose of the use" is to impermissibly promote "a particular religious belief." In other words, teachers can *educate* but not *indoctrinate* in government funded schools.

It's a lot like the difference between describing what a car can do versus trying to persuade you to buy it. If I describe all the features of a car without asking you to make a purchase or giving you any indication that your life would be much better if you did purchase it, then it's not considered promoting or selling (i.e., "endorsing"). It's an important distinction. Just because I talk about what a car can do or how it's built or what equipment it comes with doesn't mean I'm trying to urge you to buy it. Likewise, when an educator discusses criticisms of evolution with his students, it does not automatically mean he is promoting or proselytizing a particular religious view. Quoting Judge Suhrheinrich once again:

> [T]he ACLU erroneously–though perhaps intentionally–equates recognition with endorsement. To endorse is necessarily to recognize, but the converse does not follow. *Cf. Mercer County*, 219 F. Supp. 2d at 789 ("Endorsement of religion is a normative concept; whereas acknowledgment of religion is not necessarily. a value-laden concept.") ... If the reasonable ob-

---

62   *Edwards*, 482 U.S., 605 (Powell, J., concurring), quoting *Harris v. McRae*, 448 U.S. 297, 319 (1980), (quoting *McGowan v. Maryland*, 366 U.S. 420, 442 (1961)). http://www.law.cornell.edu/supct/html/historics/USSC_CR_0482_0578_ZC.html

server perceived all government references to the Deity as endorsements, then many of our Nation's cherished traditions would be unconstitutional, including the Declaration of Independence and the national motto. Fortunately, the reasonable person is not a hyper-sensitive plaintiff.[63]

Many critics of Darwin Doubters often abuse the 'separation of church and state' clause and make a mad rush to judgment when they *suspect* the intentions of Darwin Doubters *might* be religious. In fact, the mere *existence* of any religious views held by a science educator is often all that is needed to kick into motion disciplinary proceedings and other actions designed to restrict whatever information he presents to his students (or remove him from teaching). This is a wholly inappropriate (not to mention illegal) response. Since many academic institutions take the position that criticism of Darwinism is equivalent to promoting religion, such criticisms from an educator are frequently not welcomed or are viewed as inappropriate. This flawed perspective among academics fails to make the proper distinctions, and does not respect the right of all American educators to hold whatever religious beliefs they may choose.

Put another way, critics of Darwin Doubters often fail to understand the difference between (a) the right of educators to hold and even describe their religious views to students, colleagues, or anyone else and (b) the promotion (endorsement) of religious views in ways that impermissibly establish religion. Describing one's religious views is not the same as promoting them, nor is such an expression an act of proselytizing. Expressions related to "(a)" are permitted under the free exercise clause of the first amendment, while expressions related to "(b)" are not allowed under the establishment clause. No academic or other institution has the right to suspend, abridge, or deny any American their free exercise rights anywhere or for any reason, including the fear that such expressions might be perceived as the views of the university or the state. The first amendment was not intended to curtail the freedom of religious expression among Americans to protect against feared governmental establishment of religion, which is how it has

---

63   *ACLU v. Mercer County*, 2005. http://www.ca6.uscourts.gov/opinions.pdf/05a0477p-06.pdf

come to be understood by many. We are never to deny freedom of expression, even with the intent of protecting the unlawful establishment of religion. Freedom of religion and religious expression is an inviolable right of Americans, whether Darwinists like it or not. A university does not have the right to terminate educators who hold religious views just because it's somehow repugnant or inconvenient for them. The first amendment specifically prohibits such an action by the state (or university).

There is an even finer point to add to this: if an argument offered by a Darwin Doubter is *merely consistent with* a religious view, but does not include any reference to religion or religious texts, it should not be considered religious nor prohibited. Many critics of Darwin Doubters often fail to make this distinction and even often equate arguments that are merely consistent with some religious views as actually *being* religious. This is a **huge** misnomer and a stumbling block for many Darwinists – and when they hear ID educators denying the claim that they are teaching religion in their classrooms, this twisted reasoning is why they are often called liars. In actuality, IDers *are* telling the truth – the problem is with those who misunderstand these key distinctions. Consistency with religious views does not mean an idea is necessarily religious. Once again, Justice Powell wrote in his *Edwards* opinion

> A decision respecting the subject matter to be taught in public schools does not violate the Establishment Clause simply because the material to be taught "'happens to coincide or harmonize with the tenets of some or all religions.'"[64]

The source of an idea doesn't matter

The bottom line here is, *it should not matter* where an idea comes from – a religious text, a media report, daydreaming, or an educated guess. What

---

64   *Edwards*, 482 U.S., 605 (Powell, J., concurring), quoting *Harris v. McRae*, 448 U.S. 297, 319 (1980), (quoting *McGowan v. Maryland*, 366 U.S. 420, 442 (1961)). http://www.law.cornell.edu/supct/html/historics/USSC_CR_0482_0578_ZC.html

really matters is how well an idea, once formulated, is able to stand up to scientific scrutiny, as even many critics of Darwin skeptics will attest. For example, ID critic Robert Pennock notes that

> When a scientist puts forth a new hypothesis about how the world is…it is typically an *educated* guess, but it does not have to be even that, and may have been thought of at random or in a dream. The real scientific work consists in taking this hypothesis and checking to see whether it can survive the rigors of logical and empirical testing.[65]

I concur with Pennock on this point. To be consistent, critics of Darwin Doubters need to get synchronized about their argument – they can't have it both ways. Either a new idea is acceptable regardless of where it comes from, or it isn't. If critics are saying scientists can produce ideas that come from *anywhere* as long as they are put to the test of the scientific method, but do not allow ideas into the discussion if they are derived from (alleged) religious sources, then religious discrimination is clearly afoot. The point here is that ideas submitted from *any* source should be subject to the *same* standard of scientific scrutiny for Darwinians and skeptics alike, not one standard for 'scientists' and another standard for 'religionists.'

8. ***Not all Darwin skeptics approach this issue the same way.*** Critics of Darwin skeptics have lumped creation science and intelligent design advocates into the same kettle, referring to ID as "stealth creationism," or "creationism in a cheap tuxedo." PBS, on their "Evolution" web site has even defined "creation science" as

> An assortment of many different, non-scientific attempts to disprove evolutionary theory, and efforts to prove that the complexity of living things can be explained only by the action of an "intelligent designer."[66]

While such blended and highly abbreviated definitions might be very convenient for critics of creation science and ID, it strays considerably from

---

65   Pennock, 1999, p.174 (emphasis in original)
66   http://www.pbs.org/wgbh/evolution/library/glossary/glossary.html

how ID and Creation science groups would define their own views. The key concerns of ID proponents are very different than that of creation science. Creation science freely uses biblical passages as reference points for much of what they claim while ID advocates do not.

William Dembski, a prominent leader of the current ID movement, has documented the difference between Scientific Creationism and the Intelligent Design argument, but few critics seem to be listening and don't seem to be too concerned about making any of the following key distinctions between the two groups.

Scientific creationism is committed to the following propositions:

a) *SC1: There was a sudden creation of the universe, energy and life from nothing.*

b) *SC2: Mutations and natural selection are insufficient to bring about the development of all living kinds from a single organism.*

c) *SC3: Changes of the originally created kinds of plants and animals occur only within fixed limits.*

d) *SC4: There is a separate ancestry for humans and apes.*

e) *SC5: The earth's geology can be explained via catastrophism, primarily by the occurrence of a worldwide flood.*

f) *SC6: The earth and living kinds had a relatively recent inception (on the order of thousands or tens of thousands of years).*

Intelligent design, on the other hand, is committed to the following propositions:

g) *ID1: Specified complexity and irreducible complexity are reliable indicators or hallmarks of design.*

h) *ID2: Biological systems exhibit specified complexity and employ irreducibly complex subsystems.*

i) *ID3: Naturalistic mechanisms or undirected causes do not suffice to explain the origin of specified complexity or irreducible complexity j)* *ID4: Therefore, intelligent design constitutes the best explanation for the origin of specified complexity and irreducible complexity in biological systems.*

A comparison of these two lists shows that intelligent design and scientific creationism differ markedly in their approach. Scientific creationism takes the biblical account of creation in Genesis as its starting point and then attempts to match the nature of the data to the biblical account. Intelligent Design, by contrast, starts with the data of nature and from there argues that an intelligent cause is responsible for the specified complexity in nature. Intelligent Design shares none of scientific creationism's religious commitments.[67]

9) ***The influence of the 'reputation' of evolution.*** Another key obstacle facing Darwin Doubters is what I call the influence of the 'reputation' of evolution. I say reputation because that is largely what most people reference when they think about the credibility of evolution. A good many educated people are confident that science has firmly established the incontrovertible evidence for evolution when in fact a) a great deal of what is promoted in support of the theory is speculative and b) advocates of the evolutionary theory have not effectively dealt with many of its most embarrassing failures (including a *lack* of compelling evidence). Yes, there is evidence for microevolution. But the evidence for macroevolution is not solidly built upon unambiguous evidence, but *speculation about the evidence* extrapolated from microevolution.[68] In fact, the use of speculation in the context of evolution is so pervasive that it not only competes with but overshadows most of what is scientifically falsifiable about the theory. It is the heavily promoted *reputation* of the evidence and its speculative interpretations that most people (often unknowingly) base their understanding of evolution upon. Anyone who takes the time to investigate the evidence for historical evolution soon discovers that there is a nearly endless supply of inference, speculation and extrapolation designed to depict the evidence in the most positive evolutionary light imaginable. Yet, no matter how well constructed these "just-so" stories may be, they never offer more than

---

67   Dembski, 2004a. pp. 42-43.
68   http://darwinstories.blogspot.com/

possibilities (as opposed to confirmations) of alleged evolutionary history. The general public, however, is of the impression that these "stories" purport to be much more than that, and are in fact offered as reliable evidence of how evolution actually took place. The distinction between the stories about the evidence and what we really know is rarely made crystal clear by evolutionary advocates, who of course want their theory to be considered a) completely impervious to assault by Darwin Doubters, and b) unquestioningly reliable.

Darwin Skeptics charge that supporters of evolution either gloss over the problems with the molecules-to-man theory of evolution, dismiss them as irrelevant, or set them aside for future discoveries to confirm. For example, trilobite eyes,[69] which are among the most complex eyes known, appeared abruptly and *very early* in the fossil record. The optics of trilobite eyes are anything but primitive, and would have required eons of time to evolve, but alas, there are no clear and unequivocal ancestral precursors. Not only that, but trilobite fossils are so numerous and diverse (so far, 17,000 species have been identified[70]) that they are by far one of the best known and documented extinct arthropods on the planet. Yet, for all the thousands of trilobite fossils we've uncovered, we have not seen *any* of the predicted and unambiguous fossil evidence for any step-by-step evolution from more "primitive" ancestors leading up to the first trilobite. Instead, what we see is lots of variation *after* they appear and predictably, this is what evolutionists tend to focus on. As two trilobite experts have opined:

> The introduction of a variety of organisms in the early Cambrian, including such complex forms of the arthropods as the trilobites, is surprising ... The introduction of abundant organisms in the record would not be so surprising if they were simple. Why should such complex organic forms be in rocks about six hundred million years old and be absent or unrecognized in the records of the preceding two billion years? ... If there has been evolution of life, the absence of the requisite fossils in the rocks older than the Cambrian is puzzling.[71]

69   Bergman, 2007c http://www.create.ab.ca/articles/trilobite.html
70   Hartmann, 2007.
71   Kay and Colbert, 1965, pp. 102-103

Yet, as many others have concluded, "the variety and structural complexity of trilobites found near the base of Cambrian rocks surely indicates a very long antecedent existence of animal life..."[72] Just exactly what that antecedent existence was, no one has thus far been able to discover. Evolutionists simply shrug their shoulders and move forward, trusting that the appropriate evidence will someday show up[73]. The problem with this approach is, it makes an unsupported *a priori* assumption that evolutionary theory is accurate *in spite of* the missing (but nonetheless required) evidence. Even though the evidence remains undiscovered or unconfirmed, many Darwinists assert that making assumptions about Trilobite evolution is not unreasonable in light of extrapolations derived from other evidence. Finally, another observer has noted that

> The evidence [for the origin of trilobites] is neither clear nor unambiguous. The fossil record is spotty, but suggestive, and only some remarkable sites such as Chengjiang, Kaili, and the Burgess Shale reveal the rich diversity of non-calcified arachnomorph arthropods. The fossils of the Precambrian reveal some bilaterian diversity, among them a few species that *might be* candidates for trilobite ancestors.[74]

Not only is the absence of trilobite ancestors "puzzling," other experts have noted that trilobite origins remain "cryptic,"[75] and have a "prior evolutionary history of which we know nothing."[76] Yet, evolutionary scientists insist that trilobites somehow "must have" evolved by an as yet unknown process from an as yet unconfirmed ancestor. Here is where the 'reputation' of evolution comes to the rescue once again:

> Stratagraphic sequence does not present an unequivocal narrative of early trilobite evolution, and there *must have been* events in that evolution of which we have no record in the rocks.[77]

---

72 Moore, Raymond et. al. 1952.
73 Johnson, 2001, p. 100 - Johnson notes that "Even the most crushing disconfirmation of the Darwinian story (like the Cambrian fossil record) is met with a shrug."
74 Gon, 2007 (emphasis added).
75 Fortey, et. al., 1996.
76 Lipps and Signor, 1992, p. 345
77 Lipps and Signor, 1992, p. 345 (emphasis added)

The inability to sort out the ancestors for Trilobites is not an isolated example. Paleontologists continue to be frustrated with their inability to reach consensus regarding the unambiguous origin of the vast majority of ancestors for nearly all vertebrates.[78] Here we see how the reputation of evolution is such that whenever scientists are unable to fully explain how a life form evolved, it is assumed that it 'must have', even though we can't explain how just yet. We are given numerous assurances that scientists *will* eventually discover the evidence needed to explain how it all happened someday in the future.

It is one thing to *suggest* that, based on conjectural conclusions, we can assume trilobites evolved just as many Darwinians have suggested. But it's a different matter when Darwinists insist that we must agree with them (or suffer dire consequences), given the nature of the evidence available to support such a conclusion. There is no compelling evolutionary history available for the first trilobites when it should be screaming at us from the fossil record. But the evolutionist plods on, undaunted and certain that even though the missing evidence should be present in nothing less than hundreds of thousands of examples, trilobites still *had to have* evolved. Such is the persuasive force of evolutionary theory on many scientists today, even in the face of zero or contradictory evidence. It seems to never occur to them that the missing ancestral evidence is not just a minor bump in the road or a mere inconvenient fact: this *should* be viewed as a potentially *huge crater* in evolutionary theory.

But it's not. Why is that? Well, ironically, it's because trilobites are just one part of a much larger mystery. The trilobite is just one of several *thousand* other critters that suddenly appear in the fossil record at about the same time in history, *with no trace of who their ancestors were.* Add to that the fact that field observations by trilobite specialists indicate incredible stasis (i.e., little to no change) within the various trilobite sub-species over eons once they did appear.[79] Scientists can't explain this puzzling phenomenon, but

---

78   Valentine, et al. 1991, p. 284
79   Eldredge, 1985, ch. 3

they keep on working up new evolutionary explanations (just-so stories) until they figure out an answer that fits into their worldview.

Many scientists and educators remark that we shouldn't focus on what we don't know, but rather on what we think we do understand about evolution. That's a nice spin but everyone who has read much about evolution knows how famously fond Darwinians are for creating numerous "just-so" stories about the evidence.[80] These stories often contain massive doses of what they consider to be 'reasonable' extrapolations. This practice is employed to a greater or lesser extent in nearly all accounts of evolutionary history, described by expert scientists who skillfully weave in a little conjecture here, and a smidgen of extrapolation there, to convincingly depict how evolution "must have" or "most likely" occurred.[81] But in situations where no imagination should be required, when the incredible super-abundance of fossil evidence should also include numerous examples of ancestors (as should be the case for Trilobites), but does not, it is more than reasonable to be skeptical about evolutionary assumptions.

Educators have a right and an obligation to pose such dilemmas to their students as part of an honest and full appraisal of evolutionary history without having to face the accusation of being an incompetent crackpot guilty of promoting a 'religious' idea. One cannot, for example, read an honest appraisal of the evidence for vertebrate evolution without encountering numerous admissions of where evolutionary confirmation falls short, where inferences abound, or the numerous debates concerning how different clades supposedly evolved for jawed fishes, birds, and mammals (for example).[82]   Many experts affirm and assume the fact of evolution by keeping us hooked with "progress reports" of our increasing understanding of evolution based on new fossil discoveries and molecular data, when in fact they are simply promot-

---

80   http://darwinstories.blogspot.com/
81   Stahl, 1974. Stahls book is literally overflowing with admissions of how we are unable to link up evolutionary relationships among vertebrates
82   Stahl, 1974, Anderson and Dieter-Sues, eds., 2007, Fedducia, 1999.

ing the latest and greatest evolutionary stories scientists have come up with. The stories change based on new evidence, but the results remain essentially the same: numerous evolutionary dead ends, heated debates among experts, new models and stories (and the correction of older stories), gaps in the fossil or molecular evidence between critical groups of animals, confirmation bias related to the interpretation of evidence, and so on. These are real issues and represent just a handful of notions that students should be given exposure to when they are taught about evolution.

Darwin skeptics, and the public at large, are often told that the vast majority of scientists accept the tenets of evolution as sufficient to explain the development of life. But they typically have nothing much to say about those irritating "non-religious" professionals in academia and the scientific community who have taken the Horatio Cain approach and followed the evidence wherever it leads—and have found what they consider to be serious problems. These people did not consult tea leaves or any religious text to reach their unconventional conclusions—they did it by following well established empirical and logical deductions using a naturalistic approach. Arriving at a conclusion that there are problems with evolution is anathema to many evolutionists and Darwinists who insist that such "conclusions" could *only* be reached by those who harbor *a priori* assumptions of a religious nature. As philosopher of science Paul Nelson notes

> ...as many evolutionary biologists have come to realize, natural selection does not serve as a placeholder where the real evidence has stepped away for a moment. Rather, it is precisely because the evidence (of large-scale heritable variation) is *wanting* that natural selection indeed explains nothing. Thus, those biologists who argue, like the Austrian evolutionary theorist Gerhard Müller, that "the origin of new morphological characters is still unexplained by the current synthetic theory," have not neglected to read Darwin or Dawkins. Rather, they have gone there, weighed natural selection for what it truly is – a simple deductive formula – and come away empty handed.[83]

---

83   Nelson, 2001, p. 143.

10. *'Reasonable' Extrapolation.* A distinction also needs to be made between evidence and what is considered 'reasonable' inference from that evidence by Darwinists. Many Darwinians claim that it is perfectly "reasonable" to extrapolate large scale macro-evolutionary events from the smaller micro-evolutionary changes we see both in the lab and in nature. ID critic Eugenie Scott suggests that the examples of natural selection seen in the world today mean that "it is not *unreasonable* to extend their operation into the past."[84] Did you catch that? She did not say we have tons of *evidence* to back up such claims What she said is that it is not *unreasonable* to extrapolate the evolutionary operations we see today to explain historical evolutionary events. This subjective metric of 'reasonableness' is a widespread concept shared by many pro-Darwinian scientists and scholars. As paleontologist Niles Eldredge notes:

> The assumption (and it seems a perfectly reasonable one) is that artificial selection in the lab and barnyard mirrors a process in nature pretty well. But we cannot test the hypothesis that 50 million years of horse evolution, in which the average size of horses increased, as did the relative length of the face and height of the cheek teeth, and the number of toes diminished, was the product of "adaptation through natural selection."[85]

Note how the reputation of evolution once again fills in for evidence. In fact, the theory could be said to actually rely on the ability of its own reputation to convince others of its extrapolative and speculative explanatory power. I refer to this practice as evolution 'coasting' on its own reputation. To recap: all explanations promoted by Darwinists of putative past evolutionary events rely on "perfectly reasonable" assumptions based on speculation and extrapolation. As such, they can never lay claim to being a fact of science no matter how many educated people buy into this assumption. And they do buy into it in spite of the fact that many experts plod through vertebrate history and admit to the extreme difficulty, if not utter failure, of making evolutionary connections between one family after

---

84 Scott, 2004c, p. 19 (emphasis added).
85 Eldredge, 1985, p. 143.

another.[86] Where alleged evolutionary lineages of vertebrates are described, massive amounts of imagination and contingencies are required. But this is not viewed as problematic by most Darwinians:

> Darwinists shrug off the extrapolation from small-scale to large-scale evolution, arguing that it is a failure of imagination on the part of critics to appreciate the wonder-working power of the Darwinian mechanism when given vast time scales to operate.[87]

These subjective speculations are not a solid foundation upon which to construct a truly compelling case for evolution. Therefore, it is at least *equally reasonable*, in the view of many who are qualified to speculate as much as any evolutionist, to suggest that perhaps an intelligent agent was responsible for the intricate construction of life we see all around us. After all, many Darwin skeptics would suggest, one speculation could be equally as valid as another. Who's to say that Darwinists have the corner on "reasonable" speculation? Well, Darwinists do, of course. I hope you're seeing clearly that this is where "faith," not evidence, comes into the picture for many Darwinists. This heavy reliance on speculation is one of the key reasons why most people continue to question the validity of evolutionary proclamations. Whenever Darwinists offer "reasonable" explanations to justify the larger aspects of their theory where evidence is consistently absent or not falsifiable, they are in fact demanding that others agree with their subjective speculations. This is an example of why many Darwin Doubters are convinced that key portions of evolution are masquerading as science.

And it is one reason why dissidents are so important in science – they shift the focus of possibilities away from the conventional views and assumptions that nearly everyone else operates under. Though many Darwinians cry foul and proclaim that such actions destroy scientific integrity, in fact it is a healthy approach recognized by those within their own ranks.

---

86   Stahl, 1974, Anderson and Dieter Sues, 2007, Fedducia, 1999.
87   Dembski, 2004a, p. 283.

Multiple hypotheses should be proposed whenever possible. Proposing alternative explanations that can answer a question is good science. If we operate with a single hypothesis, especially one we favor, we may direct our investigation toward a hunt for evidence in support of this hypothesis.[88]

Such comments underscore the danger of confirmation bias (see item 17 in this chapter). The no-other-option approach championed by many Darwinians leads scientists down a path of seeing exactly (and oftentimes *only*) what they want or expect to see.[89]

11. ***Transcripts and letters ensure skeptics are blackballed.*** Darwin Doubters are often singled out for special treatment, such as when it comes to letters of recommendation and transcripts. I have seen this pattern emerge time and time again, beginning with my 1983 interview of Thomas Jungmann's professor who wrote in a letter of "recommendation" for Tom that "certain [of his religious] beliefs may interfere with [Tom's] ability to objectively deal with certain academic subjects…" to the 2002 case of Associate Professor of Biology Michael Dini[90] at *Texas Tech*, who required his students to "truthfully and forthrightly affirm a scientific answer" to the question: 'How do you think the human species originated?' before they would receive a letter of recommendation from him. Of course, Dini maintains that the only truly 'scientific' answer was unflinching support for Darwinism. Dini's stance resulted in a complaint being filed by Micah Spradling, one of his students, which in turn drew the attention of the Justice Department, which set off an investigation. The inquiry into Professor Dini's actions was eventually dropped when he agreed to remove his adherence to evolution policy. Both of these are blatant cases of religious discrimination that have become much more commonplace in recent years.

I ran into this same attitude in a 1983 exchange with (then Professor of Materials Science [now emeritus] at Iowa State University) Dr. John W. Patterson, who wrote:

---

88   Campbell, Neil et. al, 1999, p. 14
89   Broad and Wade, 1982, p. 108; Hartwig and Nelson, 1992, p. 9
90   Kitchen, 2003.

> Suppose the student gives the correct scientific answers in his or her science course and suppose he/she also knows and gives the correct scientific arguments and reasons for the follow-up questions, but still insists on rejecting all this for reasons of incompatibility with his/her religious beliefs? In this case, I would prefer to pass the student strictly according to the usual scoring criteria **but with the proviso that his religious reasons be noted on his transcript of grades.**[91]

I believe this type of behavior also falls into the category of illegal discrimination. One is entitled to hold whatever religious beliefs one cares to – and should be able to do so without fear of being encumbered in the manner described by Patterson.

The point worth noting here is that any state or federally funded institution needs to make sure its employees are in compliance with laws regulating discrimination on the basis of sex, age, religion, etc.

> "A biology student may need to understand the theory of evolution and be able to explain it," said Ralph Boyd Jr., the Justice Department's assistant attorney general for civil rights, in a statement. "But a state-run university has no business telling students what they should or should not believe in.[92]

Anyone who completes the requirements for a degree in a field of scientific study and demonstrates a thorough and competent understanding of the principles and issues related to that discipline, regardless of whether they fully agree with all of the ideas they were taught, has earned the right to a degree just as atheists or agnostics – with no provisos, comments, or strings attached. There should be no special labeling applied to dissenters.

12. **How refereed journals enforce a 'no dissent' policy.** A key part of the rationale used to justify the crusade against Darwin Doubters is the value of the refereed "scientific literature" that Darwinists submit as Exhibit A. This, they argue, affirms that evolution deserves its place as the crown

---

91   Thompson and Harrub, 2002 (emphasis added).
92   AOSA Newsletter, June 2003. (P.O. Box 25907, Tempe, AZ 85285). www.PuritanHope.com/AOSA

jewel of science because every scientist who is qualified to render an opinion about evolution and has done so, producing a body of writing that is "overwhelmingly" in favor of the theory. Bottom line: many Darwinists confidently and repeatedly assert there is no debate in science about the 'fact' of evolution. This is a big part of what supports the reputation of evolution I mentioned earlier. Ignore for the moment the related 'fact' that 98% of the papers allowed for publication in the vast majority of premier Western science journals are only those favorable to a Darwinian perspective. A moment of reflection on this point should be enough to suggest to most observers that the deck is stacked in favor of evolution. Active censorship eliminates dissenting views, but a reasonable explanation is usually offered (such as "well of course we only publish *scientific* papers, not pseudoscience or religion"). If you were to submit a paper challenging some aspect of Darwinism to most of these journals, chances are very high that, unless reviewers were asleep at the wheel, it would be summarily rejected without so much as a second glance.

This is like the candy company with a world-wide monopoly on selling *only* peppermint sticks. Since this is the only type of candy sold to anyone on the planet, *does this mean the candy company can legitimately brag that their product is the **favorite** of candy lovers everywhere?* Or that everyone agrees it is the *best* candy on the planet?

Well sure—like black was the favorite color of Henry Ford's early automobiles (they were all black). If you don't have a choice, it's a bit disingenuous to say everyone agrees it's the best thing going.

Yet this is *exactly* how Darwinian views are promoted using the tactic of publishing almost exclusively pro-evolution papers in the majority of the predominant mainstream refereed science journals. This tactic goes a long way towards ensuring that Darwinism is generally perceived to be *the* only valid way of viewing the history of life on planet earth. So is it any wonder that there appears to be such widespread support for Darwinism within many fields of science? How could it *possibly* be otherwise? Fortunately, critics of Darwinism have resorted to publishing books and reports outside the mainstream to get the word out about Darwinism's problems.[93]

And, not only are critics denied access to the leading science journals, but what they *do* publish is often referred to as unacceptable as well. Many critics of Darwin dissidents claim that their books, videos, and other publications have no scientific or scholarly merit. However, an inquiry into the review process itself uncovers some rather interesting questions about its value.[94]

Criticisms of evolution or Darwinism promoted by Darwin Doubters are a matter of grave concern to many unyielding Darwinians who *insist* on an exclusively evolutionary view of history. Lawyers, judges, educators, scientists, and laymen of all stripes have come together in a loose coalition, supporting the common cause of making sure that the *only* message taught in our public schools regarding the origin and development of life is a Darwinian one. Questions or doubts about the legitimacy of Darwinism, while allowed from within the ranks of orthodox Darwinian scientists, are typically _not_ viewed as acceptable topics of debate within our public schools, since such discussions (it is widely alleged) could create confusion among easily influenced students. It is this type of excuse-laden rhetoric that alarms students and educators alike.

13. *No conflict between religion and science.* One other thing this book does is underscore the hypocrisy of the scientific establishment, the courts, and media who have engaged in a significant but largely ineffective crusade to convince the general public that there is no conflict between science and religion. The "no-conflict" assurance is the face presented by many Darwinians who seek to assure the public that science and religion are perfectly harmonious, and that evolution is good science and dissent by Darwin skeptics is not reasonable. The reality is that while they publicaly claim that there is no conflict, they are extremely predatory as they engage

93   For a broad range of books and reports challenging the Darwinian view, visit **Access Research Network** online at www.arn.org
94   Tipler, 2004.

in a systematic practice of eliminating as many Darwin Doubters and dissenters as possible from the theatre of science and academia. Nor will they often tolerate the 'infection' of allowing educators with dissenting views of Darwinism to practice science or teach our children. Admitting that you have religious views AND that you question any aspect of Darwinism is often a sure-fire way to get yourself excommunicated from the halls of academia and some areas of science. Often the only time there is no apparent conflict with religion and science is when people with religious views accept neo-Darwinism.

14. ***The claim that skeptics are pushing for religion in science classrooms.*** One of the most common misconceptions about this debate perpetrated by critics of Darwin Skeptics is that creationists and ID advocates are working hand in hand to try and push their pseudoscientific and religious views in our public schools. A couple decades ago in some states the debate over 'equal time' was raging, but this is not true today of the leading creationist and ID organizations (including *Answers in Genesis, The Discovery Institute, and Access Research Network*). In fact, many national organizations who support Darwin dissenters simply want to see better <u>*science*</u> taught in our schools. And that includes a more robust presentation of not just the affirmative evidence for evolution but also that which may suggest some aspects of the theory warrant closer examination. Critics seem to conveniently overlook this when they make the overly broad claim that <u>*all*</u> Darwin Doubters are on the same page when it comes to what they want to see taught. A strong tendency exists among critics to portray many leading ID and Creation Science groups as being united in a conspiratorial effort to do everything possible to get their brand of so-called pseudo-science taught in our public school science classrooms. This myth persists despite the clear and unambiguous statements to the contrary.

One of the premier ID organizations in the U.S., the Discovery Institute, has made its views well known on this subject. They have stated:

Don't Require The Teaching of Intelligent Design

All of the major pro-intelligent design organizations oppose any efforts to require the teaching of intelligent design by school districts or state boards of education. The mainstream ID movement agrees that attempts to mandate teaching about intelligent design only politicize the theory and will hinder fair and open discussion of the merits of the theory among scientists and within the scientific community.

Teach More About Evolution

Instead of mandating intelligent design, the major pro-ID organizations seek to increase the coverage of evolution in textbooks by teaching students about both scientific strengths and weaknesses of evolution. Most school districts today teach only a one-sided version of evolution which presents only the facts which supposedly support the theory. But most pro-ID organizations think evolution should be taught as a scientific theory that is open to critical scrutiny, not as a sacred dogma that can't be questioned.[95]

A well-known U.S. creationist group, *Answers in Genesis* (AiG), was misrepresented by the editors of the Cincinnati Post in 2002 regarding their alleged efforts to "champion the teaching of options to Darwininan [*sic*] evolution in schools...."[96] But in fact AiG has never advocated anything of the sort. AiG's then CCO Mark Looy responded to the Post's inaccurate claim with the following comments:

> One would think that the Post, after years of reporting (often critically) on Answers in Genesis and our future Creation Museum, could write an informed editorial about us and the teaching of origins in public school science classes. This was not true on August 7.

> The Post described AiG as an organization that "champions" the effort to teach alternatives to evolution in science classes. We must once again point out to the Post that AiG has never lobbied legislatures, gone to court, dis-

---

95 http://www.intelligentdesign.org/education.php
96 Cincinnati Post, "The Evolution of Kansas," August 7, 2006, p. 12A.

tributed petitions, pressured school leaders, or backed political candidates to force creation or intelligent design to be taught in schools. Although AiG does agree with efforts by others to remind teachers that they can legally talk to their students about the grave problems with evolution (academic freedom certainly allows this), we are not an activist organization (or "advocacy group," as the Post called us).

Moreover, and as we have repeatedly told Post reporters over the years, we think it is actually counterproductive to mandate that instructors teach creation or intelligent design in schools. Forcing them to teach something they may not believe in (much less be equipped to teach) will not work, for such instructors will probably teach creation/ID poorly.[97]

Even leading ID advocate Phillip Johnson makes this clear when he says "I do not myself think that such advocacy groups ["biblical fundamentalists"] should be given a platform in the classroom."[98] The message here is amazingly consistent, but is just as consistently ignored or misreported by most of the local and national news media and critics of Darwin Doubters. In spite of having made their position on this issue crystal clear, those who oppose Darwin skeptics continue to persist in a campaign outlining the alleged 'religious agenda' of many national "creationist" organizations that are constantly thinking up new ways to "get their religious views into our schools."[99] This charge is then used as a reason to demonize these groups as anti-science and pseudo-science know-nothings who should be stopped wherever they show up. The outcome of promoting these erroneous claims is the creation of a highly charged atmosphere and intolerance of educators who exhibit the slightest amount of dissent over any aspect of Darwinism.

One final example: in 2007 a bill was introduced in the Montana state legislature, as reported on the *The National Center for Science Education* (NCSE) web site, claiming that a "*a number of national fundamentalist*

---

97   Looy, 2006.
98   Johnson, 2004, p. 39; Johnson, 2001, p. 76
99   Even university presidents make this erroneous claim, such as Cornell's Hunter Rawlings III, who stated "'Teach the controversy' has become the rallying cry of the Discovery Institute and others in the "I.D." camp." http://www.cornell.edu/president/announcement_2005_1021.cfm

organizations [are] seeking to force local schools to adopt a science curriculum that conforms to their particular religious beliefs":

> *House Joint Resolution 21, introduced by Representative Robin Hamilton (D-District 92) on January 26, 2007, in the Montana House of Representatives and referred to the Committee on Education, would, if enacted, express the Montana legislature's recognition of the importance of separation of church and state and support of the right of local school board trustees to adopt a science curriculum based on sound scientific principles. The resolution refers to "a number of national fundamentalist organizations seeking to force local schools to adopt a science curriculum that conforms to their particular religious beliefs and that includes theories commonly referred to as creationism, creation science, and intelligent design theory" and describes their efforts as undermining "a community's local control, a teacher's academic freedom, and a student's opportunity to receive quality science education" as well as the separation of church and state.[100]*

A review of the facts shows nothing whatsoever indicating any so-called national "fundamentalist" groups have undertaken such efforts as reported by the NCSE. Such unsupported charges should result in the bill being dismissed on sight for failing to provide any substance to back up such false claims. Fortunately, this bill died on April 27, 2007.

The bottom line here is: Darwin Doubters want accountability in science education. This includes evaluating the assumptions made by scientists, and making sure students come away with an honest understanding of what those assumptions are and why they are held. Assumptions like the ability of evolution to account for the creation of new information content (not just the rearrangement of existing content), or the assumption that micro-evolutionary processes are a sound basis for extrapolations of historical macro-evolutionary events, or why scientists believe naturalistic assumptions about how life evolved are the only credible ones. Darwin skeptics would simply prefer to shift the focus of a few concepts in ways that would encourage students to start thinking about what's inside the box of evolutionary constraints. This is a positive step in science because,

---

100　Anti-creationist legislation in Montana, NCSE web site:
http://www.ncseweb.org/resources/news/2007/MT/15_anticreationist_legislation_in_1_30_2007.asp

as Philip Johnson said, "You can't rationally decide whether you are on the right road unless you are willing to consider the possibility that you are on the wrong road."[101]

15. ***The notion that Darwin Doubters completely reject all evolutionary evidence.*** Another misperception about Darwin Doubters is that they reject evolution entirely. This is not accurate. For example, as William Dembski noted:

> Intelligent design can accommodate plenty of evolutionary change and allows for natural selection to act as a conservative force to keep organisms adapted to their environments... On the other hand, intelligent design utterly rejects natural selection as a creative force capable of bringing about the specified complexity we see in organisms.[102]

Statements like this make it clear that while Darwin skeptics do not ascribe the full range of capabilities to evolutionary mechanisms that evolutionists do, the disagreement is often about how many evolutionary mechanisms actually work rather than a wholesale rejection of them, as claimed by many creation and ID critics.

16. ***Reluctance of Darwinians to be critical.*** Many Darwinists seem to have an aversion to even consider the proposition that life is so complex that it is likely not the result of evolutionary mechanisms. They also resist criticizing evolutionary theory beyond acceptable limits. There are reasons for this resistance, and none of them are good. A good scientist is willing to consider and explore contrary notions and evidence, even if it does go against current assumptions or the ruling scientific paradigm. But unfortunately, that's not how things work in the world of evolutionary science. Educators and science practitioners alike come up against an extremely hardened reticence to question established orthodoxy. This renders the claim that all reputable scientists affirm evolution as similar to the claim that all members of a chain gang are free to escape at any time. Of course, if they do, they will be hunted down and likely shot for attempting their

101 Johnson, 2000, p. 145.
102 Dembski, 2001.

escape. This is exactly what often transpires when Darwin Doubters express their dissent, only instead of bullets, the establishment uses a variety of other tactics designed to suppress or eliminate the dissenter. Allow me to explain this concept a bit further.

Leading Darwinians are provided with little or no incentive to be critical of evolution, for they know full well that if they do, they lose everything - prestige, reputation, (funding!) and other benefits associated with their position. So *of course* they all agree with one another. It's not because the scientific evidence is so compelling (though they will insist all day long that it *is*) -- there is simply no return on their vested interests if they do not fully support evolution. The case studies presented in this book stand as solid testimony to this fact. Think about it for just a minute. After reading this book, would you dare to dissent if you had any honest doubts about evolution? I wonder if Colin Patterson, for example, would dare to reiterate the doubts he expressed on Novemner 5, 1981 if he had the chance to do it all over again.[103] It's a big deal when someone of Patterson's stature in the scientific community admits to having doubts about any aspect of evolution. Why is that? Edward Sisson explains:

> ...no leader of a major American scientific institution can publicly abandon the paradigm of unintelligent evolution and yet retain his position of leadership. As in any human organization, the people who most effectively advance the interests of the scientific establishment are the ones chosen to lead the establishment. Those who impede the achievement of the establishment's ends are rejected. Thus, there is simply no purpose for scientists to take the time to consider the challenges to the paradigm and develop an individual response, because if that response is a rejection of the paradigm, the scientist must either suppress it (and violate the rule that scientists should be sincere) or else express it (and likely end his career). Everyone below the top on the hierarchy ladder knows that to question unintelligent evolution will mean the end of career advancement; so for them, too, there is simply no incentive to consider that the challenges to unintelligent evolution might be valid. On the contrary, there are very

---

103   http://www.arn.org/docs/odesign/od171/colpat171.htm

strong incentives *not* to consider those challenges in any way that might lead to accepting them.[104]

This is a fairly stunning rebuke against the integrity of science as well as the often touted claim that reputable scientists everywhere agree that naturalistic evolution is a fact. If there is no incentive to say or do otherwise, and if in fact there are strong pressures *not* to voice dissent, then how can we possibly rely on the credibility of the scientific or academic consensus? I would suggest, for these and other reasons, that crowing about a consensus maintained under the threat of severe punishment is hardly a stance worth bragging about. Even members of a chain gang understand never to push the "Man" to the limit unless they want a taste of his whip. Similarly, educators and scientists generally understand where most of the boundaries are for disagreement, and they typically don't rock the boat beyond those limits for fear of ending up as another case study in future editions of this book. In fact, we know of many within both academia and the scientific establishment who do *not* support some aspects of evolution, but their fear of reprisals prevents them from openly stating their dissenting views. So whenever I hear the claim that "scientists all agree that evolution is how life on earth progressed," I take a look at some of the case studies in this book and remind myself how much stock I ought to place in such a claim. If all the Darwin dissenters have been eliminated, the claim that all good scientists agree about evolution is hardly an argument we should listen to.

17. ***Competency isn't enough.*** Many Darwin Doubter science educators currently teach in our universities, but they often remain in the closet -- keeping their views to themselves because they understand many of their colleagues, students, and administrators are intolerant of their concerns about various aspects of Darwinism. These people have degrees and solid reputations as educators -- and stable careers. Clearly, they are viewed as competent in their roles as educators, however based on many of the case studies we know of, all that would be turned upside down and inside out literally overnight if their doubts became known. In academia to-

---

104   Sisson, 2004, p. 88 (emphasis in original).

day, many science educators are deemed incompetent if they fail to *believe* wholeheartedly in Darwinism. In many instances, they could know everything relevant about Darwinism -- and competently teach it better than any of their peers -- but if they don't *believe* in evolution, they stand to lose everything. Belief is therefore compelled upon many science educators, and is the defacto litmus test of their competency. They can possess numerous awards, have a list of published articles as long as your arm, but if they are not true Darwinian believers, it counts as next to nothing if their doubts become known. Educators working in other academic disciplines who have unusual or unconventional views are much more readily tolerated as nonconformists or even a bit odd, but not the Darwin Doubter. Suddenly, the formerly competent educator has been transformed into something hideous. Once they become tagged as a non-believer, they are regarded as religious heretics, and worse -- incompetent traitors who don't understand a thing about science. I'm not exaggerating when I say that we have seen educators who are held in the highest esteem, are published in some of the best peer-reviewed science journals, who produce work that is respectable, admired, and even the cause of envy among their peers, who have been tarred and feathered overnight and without mercy when they let it be known they are a Darwin Doubter.

18. *Confirmation bias.* There is one last part of the context I need to mention here. Many Darwinians view the key pieces of evidence used to defend evolution with what can only be called "confirmation bias." What is Confirmation bias?

> It refers usually to unwitting selectivity in the acquisition and use of evidence. The line between deliberate selectivity in the use of evidence and unwitting molding of facts to fit hypotheses or beliefs is a difficult one to draw in practice, but the distinction is meaningful conceptually, and confirmation bias has more to do with the latter than with the former ... for the purposes of this discussion ... confirmation connotes evidence that is perceived to support—to increase the credibility of—a hypothesis.[105]

---

105   Nickerson, 1998, p. 175-176.

Confirmation bias is rampant among Darwinists. Most Darwinians assume that all evidence of life affirms evolution, even when there is no way of confirming it, or when experts can't imagine how it occurred, and even when contradictory evidence exists. Darwinians are supremely confident that future evidence or explanations will eventually appear to provide whatever solutions are needed to give us a more accurate view of what happened in evolutionary history. Meanwhile, because they believe the evidence will eventually confirm evolution *somehow*, Darwinians feel free to speculate *ad infinitum* on how it 'might have' or 'must have' occurred historically.

Confirmation bias is both powerful and insidious because it leads scientists down a path of inquiry where they reject, ignore, or discount any evidence (or interpretation of the evidence) that seems to contradict or is not quite in alignment with evolutionary assumptions. Instead, because the perspective of Darwinians is tainted with evolutionary bias, they see what they expect to see in *all* of the evidence they come across. This is true even in situations where good judgment suggests insurmountable problems for evolution. Many will put the assumption of evolution ahead of evidence that seems incompatible with the theory simply because it is the accepted and dominant explanation of the scientific establishment. The result is, Darwinists are compelled to find a way to force square evidence into a round hole. Even when there is no conceivable way to understand how to make the evidence fit within the framework of evolutionary theory, the final conclusion of this often frustrating exercise is that we simply haven't been imaginative enough to figure out how evolution transpired rather than admit that perhaps there is a problem with the theory itself. Darwinists simply *refuse* to consider this as a viable possibility, and have no incentives to do so, but plenty of incentives not to.[106]

Confirmation bias poses problems for many science educators and practitioners who are expected to not just understand how evolution works, but also view all the key evidence (from the fossil record, comparative anatomy, and

---

106   Sisson, 2004.

the jump from micro to macroevolution) through the lens of evolutionary assumption or face the threat of losing their job and/or career. Confirmation bias effectively places a stranglehold on the integrity of scientific inquiry when it comes to evolution, and those who refuse to bow their knee to conventional wisdom almost always come out on the losing end.

Summary

These contextual issues are representative of what Darwin Doubters find themselves up against as they seek a hearing for their criticisms of evolution. Once their doubts about evolution become obvious, misrepresentations about who they are and what they seek to do begin to circulate, which often results in a climate of near hysteria whenever their presence becomes known on the faculty of a university, or when they are seeking a degree as a student. The resulting rush to judgment is frequently based on falsehoods, distortions, and misperceptions about who they are. What happens to a Darwin Doubter educator or scientist once their views become known is often very predictable.

The views of Darwin skeptics are labeled 'religious', and they are often presumed to have been proselytizing their students or poisioning their minds with unfounded criticisms of evolution. As their motivations become suspect, colleagues and supervisors confront victims with accusations of misconduct and/or require them to explain their behavior and curriculum. Efforts may be undertaken (even if only temporary token gestures) to define corrective actions to ensure that victims are not behaving inappropriately (even if they never were). Students and teachers may find themselves excluded from activities offered to their colleagues. But all of these actions typically occur within a phased process I refer to as the Degrees of Discrimination.

Degrees of Discrimination

In addition to the fact that discrimination against Darwin Doubters does not occur in a vacuum, but in the context of the many issues just described (and others as well), it is also manifested in degrees. Discrimination involves a variety of tactics with different degrees of severity. What's more, each level of severity can, and often does, eventually escalate into a more severe level. What may start out as tiny mutterings can often escalate to the construction of elaborate schemes which eventually do great harm to the victims. The phased process for what happens to many Darwin Doubters once they become known, looks something like this:

1. *The questioning phase*. Discrimination often starts out with questions like "what religion are you?" (that's also an illegal question in the workplace...), or "do you really believe that stuff?" and "where did you learn that?"

2. *The name-calling phase*. Colleagues, former friends, the media, blogs, and your supervisors begin making remarks like "we really have a problem here with a fundamentalist nutcase on our staff" and "we need to get rid of this IDiot creatard." This is also where colleagues may begin to discuss ways of getting rid of the victim or at least minimizing the "damage" he may cause to students and more importantly, the reputation of the school or university. Colleagues also begin talking with others in an effort to determine what kind of dirt they can dig up on the victim that would provide a legitimate basis for eventually dismissing them.

3. *The accusation phase*. This is where informal complaints or accusations show up describing the activity and/or alleged religious beliefs of victims or other reasons why their presence is no longer required. Many times, accusations are made about the victims that are not based on facts or are based on distortions or exaggerations. The skepticism of the victim is labeled religious, and victims are often assumed to have been proselytizing their students. Colleagues and supervisors confront victims with accusations of misconduct and/or require them to explain their behavior and curriculum. Efforts may be undertaken (even if only temporary token gestures) to define corrective actions to ensure that victims are not behaving inappropriately (even if they never were). Students and teachers may find themselves excluded from activities offered to their colleagues.

4. *The formal charges phase*. This is where formal charges are levied against the victim, requiring them to take corrective action to ensure that they are acting in full compliance with the wishes of their superiors. The actions proscribed to them are typically not required of other educators. The charges are frequently fear-based rather than fact-based (i.e., based on suspicion and allegation rather than actual documented misbehavior).

5. *The removal phase*. This is where the denial of degrees and tenure kicks in, and/or removal from the classroom. It does not matter if the student or educator has demonstrated competence and skill in their knowledge and understanding of the subject matter – their 'religious' views, it is often charged, have tainted their psyche and disqualified them from teaching or practicing good science, and so they will not be awarded the degree they have earned, or will not be allowed to teach science again, or they will be denied tenure. If they already have tenure, they will often be reassigned to teach other classes where they are less likely to corrupt young minds with the cancer of their doubts. They are often punished based on charges that are false, misconstrued, or exaggerated. Tenure is often denied to educators based on their failure to secure the requisite number of positive faculty votes, and no reason is usually required to justify those votes.

6. *The legal phase*. This is where victims decide to fight the charges leveled against them. It is extremely rare for victims seeking relief in the court system to actually achieve the justice they seek, and many academic institutions both know this and count on it to work to their advantage.

Keep in mind that Darwin Doubters are often taken to task for doing things other educators are freely allowed to do without question, such as provide their students with additional reading materials that were not pre-approved by their university administrators or department heads.

This brings me to a final point. Darwin Defenders of many stripes will no doubt suggest that it is perfectly legitimate to remove Darwin Doubters from our universities and halls of science, especially if they hold to any designer oriented view of the universe. In their minds, eliminating them is just as legitimate as removing a cancer from healthy tissue. Conversely, then should we also remove all of Issac Newton's discoveries from our universities simply because he also studied alchemy? Or because he was also motivated by "religious" views? Who would dare claim that this was not a great man of science? And what of creationist Raymond Damadian, inventor of the MRI (just one of many case studies presented in this book). Should we say that he is not entitled to practice science because of his "religious" beliefs? Should we get rid of all the MRI machines in the world today because the person who invented them could not possibly be a scientist? Or should we have prevented former Surgeon General C. Everett Koop from obtaining his medical certifications, and thus prevent the scores of people he was responsible for helping? Or what about Dr. William S. Harris, who has been conducting scientific research for the last 20 years, and has been awarded about $3.5 million in research grants and has over 70 published scientific papers to his credit? Or Guillermo Gonzalez, an astronomer who has scores of peer-reviewed published papers under his belt, has discovered planets, but was denied tenure at Iowa State because his colleagues didn't agree with his pro-ID position? These and many other highly credible Darwin Doubters somehow managed to achieve important scientific accomplishments while holding views that many Darwin Defenders maintain are incompatible with good science. So much for that bigoted claim.

Many science educators and professionals today face a host of Christophobic, theist-adverse colleagues and administrators in academia who seek to malign their intentions, talents, and abilities and vigorously act to restrict or prevent them from functioning within the scientific and academic fraternity on the basis of their alleged "religious" inclinations – *especially* if they also dissent over any aspect of widely held evolutionary assumptions. It seems that conformity is the gold standard that determines acceptance within these communities, and certain types of dissent are conveniently labeled "anti-science," as a means of ensuring that only those who adhere to the conventional wisdom are allowed to remain members.

As this book will show, Darwin Defenders frequently use thug-like tactics to remove, discredit or restrict the influence of dissenters within their ranks. This is nothing less than an abridgement of freedom and an assault on true scientific inquiry. We maintain that the motivations, assumptions, or conclusions reached by Darwin skeptics should not count against them or be found as reasons to exclude them from their careers. Especially when a great many clearly intelligent and qualified scientists and educators have been pointing out problems with evolution for decades. Make no mistake – the victims chronicled in this book have had their careers and freedoms stolen from them simply because they dared to deviate from what amounts to established scientific dogma. Those who persecute and discriminate against Darwin skeptics believe freedom of opinion belongs exclusively to those who agree with an evolutionary explanation of the evidence, and have missed the point about what it means to be free. If we truly are a free society, then all of us will stand for nothing less than freedom of expression, and will open up a listening ear to Darwin Doubters, and will defend their right to dissent. And if we all fail to defend the freedom of these dissenters, then you should consider what impact this will have on *your* freedoms. I often recall the quote Dr. Bergman mentions elsewhere in this volume from Martin Niemoeller:

> They came after the Jews and I was not a Jew, so I did not object. They came after the Catholics and I was not a Catholic, so I did not object. They came after the trade unionists, and I was not a trade unionist, so I did not object. Then they came after me, and there was no one left to object.

Chapter 2: Intolerance Against Darwin Skeptics

The debate about creationism and Intelligent Design often degenerates to attacking the Darwin Doubter in some way, even when Darwin critics are ostensibly concerned primarily or solely with science. Dr. Richard Culp summarized his experience, noting that while the "evolutionist expects tolerance of his teaching [and ideas]... he is intolerant of the concept of special creation."[107] To support this assertion, he cited several cases, including a horticulture professor in Nebraska who debated a creationist—and reportedly lost. The defeated professor responded by endeavoring to impede the activities of a local church involved in creationism. Professor John Hand noted, under the subheading "the desperate attempt of evolutionists to crush all opposition to their doctrine," that to make yourself unpopular in

> worldly society, just announce that you do not believe in evolution...you will get the raised eyebrow treatment immediately. You will see the sly, smirking smile exchanged between your hearers, and you will be politely snubbed and avoided as if you were a leper no matter what your qualifications, otherwise, may be. You can deny anything else in the book, but never evolution.[108]

Hand then quotes from Thomas Dwight of Harvard, who opined: "The tyranny in the matter of evolution is overwhelming to a degree of which the outsider has no idea."[109] And University of Chicago professor Paul Shoray wrote that "there exists no cause so completely immune from criticism today as evolution," and that:

> An ambitious young professor may safely assail Christianity, or the Constitution of the United States, or George Washington, or female chastity, or marriage, or private property, or defense of his native land—but he must not apologize for Bryan [the famous creationist].[110]

---

107 Culp, 1975, p. 141.
108 Hand, 1972, pp. 81-83.
109 Thomas Dwight, quoted in Hand, 1972, p. 83.
110 Paul Shoray, quoted in Hand, 1968, pp. 83-84.

Many reasons exist for this discrimination in colleges.[111] Wood and Jackson[112] found that professors tend to "consolidate their power, trying to fire all those department members" who they believe are opposed to their worldview or policies, and retain only those who go along with their viewpoints and decisions. They then discuss examples, such as a "highly qualified" teacher from Austin, Texas, whose contract was not renewed after it was discovered that she held "unpopular" beliefs.

Intolerance Began Almost a Century Ago

Open persecution of creationists has been with us at least since at least the beginning of the 20th century. Byron Nelson[113], author of the classic *After Its Kind* (first published in 1927, with a revised edition still in print), experienced numerous problems due to his creationist beliefs. Despite close to a perfect 4.0 grade point average, he was denied his Master of Science degree in genetics at Rutgers University.[114] His Master's committee argued that, as a Darwin skeptic, Byron could not do science. In a letter to the author, Byron's widow, Anita, who at the time was nearly 90, stated that during the

> early days of struggle with evolutionary concepts ... my husband and I met in our college days at the University of Wisconsin (1915-16) [and] also with our church board (1925) which turned down the first manuscript of *After Its Kind*. The book was "rescued in time" by a chance (?) visit to our parsonage in New Jersey by the secretary of the church (Dr. Lorhre). It was a lifetime—50 years (1920-1970)—of battling for...creation as we saw it. Byron almost constantly faced rejection and ridicule. Even our children at college felt under a cloud—and were embarrassed by their father's position.[115]

Nelson—not one who might be termed a conservative creationist—concluded that Adam and Eve were literally created, but that this event occurred about a million years ago. He also accepted long periods of time for the geologi-

---

111   LaNoue and Lee, 1987.
112   Wood and Jackson, 1982, p. 176.
113   No, not Byron Nelson the golfer (sorry). Question: Is Byron Nelson related to modern-day philosopher of science Paul Nelson? Answer: Yes!
114   Letter from Anita Nelson to Jerry Bergman, July 5, 1982.
115   Letter from Anita Nelson to Jerry Bergman, July 5, 1982.

cal ages (as did William Jennings Bryan), but still experienced serious problems with intolerance.

Historian Ronald Numbers indicated that Nelson's problems did not involve the usual claims of personality conflicts. Nelson did have some evolutionist friends. For example Numbers related the story of Nelson's visit with a friend who was then head of the Rutgers University zoology department. At his friend's invitation, Nelson enrolled in a genetics course "taught by a notoriously anticlerical professor," Alan A. Boyden (1897-1986). Nelson's account of his experience is as follows:

> From time to time Boyden would say nasty things about ministers. At the end of the semester I chanced to sit beside him at a lecture. He asked me, "By the way, what is your business, Mr. Nelson?" When I told him I was a Lutheran minister, his face got as red as a beet. Then he urged me to join a seminar class [involving breeding]... fruit flies by the thousands, attempting to bring about mutations by feeding them arsenic. While in this advanced class I was invited to join the whole faculty once a week and take my turn lecturing to the bunch. One day I was absence (sic) and the whole faculty divided on evolution—encouraged by my taking a stand. The Nelsons and Boydens became very friendly—fellowshipping at picnics etc. He helped me to make some improvements in After Its Kind. Boyden had several copies put into the university library.[116]

A few years later Dr. Boyden was Wayne Frair's doctoral dissertation advisor. Dr. Frair, an active creationist, noted that when he studied under Boyden several years later, Boyden by that time had major reservations about certain aspects of evolution theory.

Antagonism Against God

A major aspect of the intolerance towards Darwin Skeptics is that many professors appear to take issue with the notion of God. Shapiro concluded that too many professors "enlighten students to the purposelessness of their own existence" by teaching that God does not exist or, if He does, is "uninvolved in the world." As

---

116   Byron Nelson, in Numbers, 2006, p. 298.

a result, humans take the place of God because, as Princeton University Professor of Bioethics Peter Singer (who also seems to condone the practice of bestiality[117]) asks:

> "If we don't play God, who will? There seems to me to be three possibilities: there is a God, but He doesn't care about evil and suffering; there is a God who cares, but He or She is a bit of an underachiever; or there is no God. Personally, I believe the latter."[118]

Singer's book *Rethinking Life and Death,* has been referred to as "the *Mein Kampf* of the euthanasia movement, in that it drops many of the euphemisms common to pro-euthanasia writing and acknowledges euthanasia for what it is: killing."[119]

Stanford University's John McCarthy, one of the nation's leading artificial intelligence scientists, stated that "the evidence on the god question is in a similar state to the evidence on the werewolf question. So I am an atheist." *Hunter College* Professor James Wright calls Jesus a "half-crazed logician," adding, "I don't believe in God." University of Maryland Professor Corey Washington opines that "it is more probable that God does not exist."[120] University of Texas Professor Steven Weinberg opined:

> I think in many respects religion is a dream—a beautiful dream often. Often a nightmare ... But it's a dream from which I think it's about time we awoke. Just as a child learns about the tooth fairy and is incited by that to leave a tooth under the pillow—and you're glad that the child believes in the tooth fairy. But eventually you want the child to grow up."[121]

On the whole, naturalistic evolution is the dominant and almost universally acceptable position among the modern academic cadre. As Will Provine observed: "the great majority of modern evolutionary biologists are atheists or something very close to that."[122]

---

117   Singer, 2001. http://www.nerve.com/Opinions/Singer/heavyPetting/main.asp
118   Peter Singer, quoted in Shapiro, 2004, p. 85.
119   DeMarco. 2003.
120   All quoted in Shapiro, 2004, p. 85.
121   Steven Weinberg, quoted in Shapiro, 2004, p. 85.
122   Provine, 1987, p. 51.

The intolerance leveled against Darwin Doubters is often intertwined with their religious or perceived religious views. Attacks against such skeptics often have a broadly anti-Christian (as opposed to a purely scientific) motive. Shapiro opined that most Christians and Jews believe that there exists "no implicit conflict between science and religion." Examples of harmony he cites include the priest Gregor Mendel and Sir Isaac Newton. He adds that it was Albert Einstein who said that God does not play dice with the universe and that "Science and religion bolster one another. The more we learn about the world in which we live, the clearer it becomes that there must be a divine Planner."[123]

Many professors, though, disagree, concluding that science and religion are completely at odds with each other because orthodox science believes that God is not a master designer; rather,

> everything is an accident... Perhaps the perceived dichotomy between science and religion explains the lack of faith among scientific faculty. While the percentage of Americans who believe in God remains between 85 and 95 percent, the percentage of scientists who believe in God is less than 40 percent. The main battle between science and religion takes place in the field of evolutionary biology, where professors demonize creationists as archaic relics in the Dark Ages. Creationism isn't just wrong, it's intellectual sin, they say, despite the fact that 45 percent of Americans believe in Intelligent Design.[124]

Numerous studies have documented that many professors actually lecture against belief in creationism and ID in class and make use of readings that include indoctrination in naturalism.[125] For example, one biology textbook reads: "many adaptations seem more easily explained by natural selection than by God's design because the design is imperfect and God presumably could have 'done better.'"[126] The text also derides creationists as people who attempt to "portray themselves as scientists, calling their new approach 'creation science' even though they have never conduct experiments or tested hypotheses."[127] Actually organizations such as *The Creation Research Society* have been publishing creation research for over a half a century.

123 Shapiro, Ben, 2004, p. 89.
124 Shapiro, Ben, 2004, p. 89.
125 Berkman et al., 2008.
126 Minkoff and Baker. 2004, p. 146
127 Minkoff and Baker. 2004, p. 143

Other examples include Professor Timothy Shortell of *Brooklyn College*, who espouses the idea that religious people are "moral retards," intellectually immature, incapable of moral action, and are "an ugly, violent lot."[128] This is hardly a value-free evaluation of the beliefs of 90 percent of Americans, especially for a sociologist. Professor Paul Ehrlich of Stanford University wrote that "American neoconservatives promote creationism because, as their own statements reveal, they apparently fear an educated population and see the theory of evolution as a threat." Shapiro adds that sterotypes Ehrlich believes include "conservatives are out to lynch blacks and enslave the poor," and that many professors believe that creation science is "foolish":

> "They could just as well talk about Kumulipo," the Hawaiian creation chant, scoffs Professor Pauline Chinn of the University of Hawaii. "Creationism isn't science, it's faith," nods Hawaii Institute of Geophysics and Planetology Professor Gerald Fryer. "The big lie is that there's something to (creationism)," sneers Professor Victor Stenger, also of the University of Hawaii.[129]

Writer Paul Bartz relates an experience involving a chemistry professor on the faculty at a major state university who was an evolutionist until a few years ago. When the professor first became convinced of the validity of the creationist perspective, he experienced very few problems. He had a good discussion with his evolutionary colleagues. However, "as he became active in publishing some technical articles which underlined points which are scientifically damaging to evolution, he found less and less acceptance among his colleagues at the university." According to Bartz:

> He reports that he is no longer welcome in the offices of certain of his colleagues at the university. While no accusations of wrong-doing or inadequate science have been made, there had been a concerted effort to harass him. For example, while he has been active in his church both at the local and national level, often on issues surrounding his creationist beliefs, he has been informed that he does not participate in "community service" projects as much as should be expected by a faculty member... he is no longer regarded to be as acceptable a faculty member as he was before he accepted and began publishing creationist articles. He is a soft-spoken, uncontentious sort of

---

128   Timothy Shortell, quoted in Horowitz, 2006, p. 327.
129   All quoted in Shapiro, 2004, pp. 89-90.

person whose personality is not the cause of this kind of reaction. However, his position itself could ultimately be at stake. [130]

The most *common* consequence facing tenured faculty when they accept the heresy of creation is reassignment so that they will not be in a position to further influence students toward their view. (Of course, without the protection of tenure, most would probably also lose their teaching position altogether.) Another professor who has raised questions about evolution, G. Lawrence Vankin of *Williams College* in Massachusetts, had his students read "two articles from the prestigious *Journal of Theoretical Biology* that questioned the plausibility of evolution by random processes." The result was that the Williams biology department had the library cancel its subscription to the journal, and that Vankin was reassigned to the history of science department.[131]

Because *San Francisco State University* Biology professor Dean Kenyon concluded that "a scientifically sound creationist view of origins is not only possible but is to be preferred over the evolutionary view," he was reassigned to other courses, "apparently when he began to raise questions about the subject."[132] Bethell notes that Kenyon, who has a doctorate in biophysics from Stanford University, is the co-author of the 1969 book, *Biochemical Predestination*. This case will be explored in detail in a later chapter. These cases are mentioned here only to provide the reader with a background of the extent and type of common conflicts.

Hatred of Christianity

It is well documented that there exists a general dislike of conservative Christians among society's elite. Evidence also exists that the persecution of creationism and ID is a lightning-rod manifestation of that general dislike, and therefore smacks of religious intolerance despite many protestations that it's really only about the poor science peddled by creationists or ID advocates, or the need to keep religion and science separate.[133]

---

130   Letter from Paul Bartz to Jerry Bergman, June 16, 1983.
131   Bethell, 1986, p. 32.
132   Bethell, 1986, p. 32.
133   Many leading critics of Darwin skeptics no longer refer to their theory as non-science, but "bad science." See John Campbell, 2003, p. 79

Steinberg summarized some of the problems that can occur when public school administrators involve themselves in Christian social programs. One such case includes an administration that tried to fire a principal because he assisted in a Christian program that dealt with the problems of drugs, sex, and crime. Parents in the Detroit suburb where this incident took place

> angrily demanded that the school board take immediate action... The superintendent ordered the monitoring of the activities of the principal of the offending high school... Supporters ... for the Christian group claimed that Youth for Christ [involvement] cuts down on drugs, sex, and crime by the students. The ADL and the American Civil Liberties Union made it clear that [they thought] there had to be a better way to deal with [those issues][134]

Although Christians experience most of their difficulties in the higher levels of academia, those in scientific research (and teaching in general) also encounter problems. A biologist ran a tissue culture lab at a cancer research center, earning excellent recommendations during most of his six years. The director asked him several times if he wanted a lab assistant. Feeling he could manage on his own (which he could), he consistently declined. When the director learned of his position on creationism, the work load mysteriously became heavier, forcing him to work up to 55 hours a week. All requests for an assistant were now refused, and the pressure became such that he soon felt that he had no choice but to resign. (The victim's identity has been withheld to protect him from additional discrimination.)

Paul Ellwanger has three decades of experience in science-related fields, including ten with the Atomic Energy Commission and six in college work. He concluded from this experience with the scientific and academic community that, in certain academic fields,

> there exists a subtle but rigidly controlled discrimination that is steadily growing in intensity. It has destroyed the academic professional careers of a number of persons and has been the cause of job deprivation, including persons not directly employed as a professional in the academic community. This discrimination involves the subject of origins. The two predominant scientific positions for explaining origins and their complex ramifications are the evolution and the creation models. Both of these are fraught with metaphysical and unnatural ele-

---

134   Steinberg, 1984, p. 9.

ments; both frankly coincide with a number of religions. But to my knowledge, only persons favoring the creation model have been made victims of discrimination that has resulted in deprivations of their civil and human rights.[135]

This reaction results not just in response to theism, but to a whole series of issues that today have divided the nation, including abortion, school prayer, war, and similar concerns.[136] John Indo, writing in *Free Inquiry* (a magazine whose contributing editors include such academic luminaries as Albert Ellis, Antony Flew, Sidney Hook, Thomas Szasz, and other scientists and university professors) in an article about Christians who took their faith seriously, wrote that the government should require a class in logic for them, but

> then we would face another problem in making them respond to it. Logical thinking is antithetical to ... [them]—except, of course, when it is used to propound their strictly ad hoc arguments ... this is what is so hideous about them. Their limited little minds function only in support of parochialist stupidity. Frankly speaking ... we must stop them at all costs. Otherwise disaster will be the result.[137]

What disaster will result if they are not stopped, Indo does not say. Nor does he say how they should be stopped—yet action is clearly called for to avoid a Christian inspired "disaster."

Membership List Kept Confidential to Protect Creationists

Problems such as those experienced by Nelson have caused many creationist organizations, early in their history, to keep their membership lists private. Wilbert Rusch, when he was the Secretary of the *Creation Research Society* (CRS), noted that the reason for strictly guarding the membership list was that even in the early days of CRS clear evidence existed that "membership in the Society might be a hindrance to young members in the pursuit of a career in science, for example in admission to advanced degree programs." He also noted that:

---

135   Letter from Paul Ellwanger to Jerry Bergman, June, 1983, p. 1.
136   Trager and Dickerson, 1999.
137   Indo, 1981, p. 3.

There were also reports from members that a belief in creation had served as a possible cause for the denial of tenure or promotion. In some cases, the fear of outright dismissal from an institution was expressed. Since there is no evidence of any change in this state of affairs today, the custom of not producing a membership list or directory is a CRS policy to this day. Certainly the history of the actions of some scientists toward those who held views contrary to the party line has been amply documented.[138]

The British creationist organization, *The Biblical Creation Society*, had a similar rule in effect. Their number 14, 1983, *Newsletter* stated that the list of members and others supportive of creation is confidential: "... for obvious reasons ... we are not able to let [outsiders] have a copy."

For the same reason, some scientists who publish articles on creationism wisely use a pseudonym. Bartz notes that he knows four scientists who publish creationist materials under assumed names because they are aware, from personal professional contacts, that to publish under their real name would mean almost immediate loss of position. One scientist, who does medical research at a nationally known school of medicine, said:

> discussions on the entire creation-evolution issue have revealed an attitude of absolute intolerance of any scientifically trained person accepting creationism among this individual's superiors and peers. An electrical engineer who works in research and development for a nationally-known corporation also published creationist material under an assumed name because he, too, feels that his superiors would not be tolerant of his creationist beliefs. His position [on this topic] ... could keep him from job advancement.[139]

Do Anti-Design Advocates Promote Hate Speech?

To determine if the anti-design movement promotes "hate speech," we need to examine what the courts have said in this regard. The U.S. Supreme Court[140] "recognizes" hate speech as "a category of low value speech that does not warrant

---

138 Rusch, 1983, pp. 2-3.
139 Letter from Paul Bartz to Jerry Bergman, June 16, 1983, p. 1.
140 *R.A.V. v. City of St. Paul*, 505 U.S. 377 (1992)

full First Amendment protection."[141] Unfortunately, the Supreme Court has not yet explicitly defined hate speech, but in general defines it as "speech that demeans or discriminates against individuals based on race, color, gender, national origin, age, sexual orientation or other inherent characteristics or deeply held convictions, such as religious belief."[142] Legal scholars have argued that hate speech goes beyond offending—it involves "threats or fighting words" that are "inherently harmful to those targeted and to social cohesion generally." Furthermore,

> name-calling, epithets and hate-filled diatribes not only fail to contribute to enlightened discourse and to the enhancement of social well-being; they silence their targets and harm the marketplace of ideas the First Amendment is designed to protect. Hate speech does not convey abstract principles; it acts to debase, threaten, and intimidate. From this perspective, hate speech abuses the powerless and embodies systemic discrimination that violates the constitutional principle of equal protection under the law.[143]

The Supreme Court has also indicated that "speech falls outside constitutional protection only when it is directed at and intended to immediately threaten or harm a specific individual or individuals."[144] As I have documented in this book, much of the rhetoric against Darwin skeptics is openly designed to deprive them of a living, schooling, and other opportunities in society. At the least it has these effects, and for this reason it's often quite reasonable to view the rhetoric against Darwin Doubters as hate speech. References to design advocates as "IDiots" or "creatards" and similar vulgar expressions are becoming more common, and are used to justify repression against them, as we will document in the following chapters. Moreover, these expressions of hate commonly translate into discriminatory actions and behavior. An example is the threats of violence against the creation museum in Kentucky that are taken seriously: the Museum now employs an elaborate security system, a full time police department, three explosive-sniffing dogs, and state of the art high-tech security systems to protect the property.[145]

---

141 Susan Dente Ross, 2004, section 7.1.
142 Susan Dente Ross, 2004, section 7.1.
143 Susan Dente Ross, 2004, section 7.1.
144 Susan Dente Ross, 2004, section 7.1.
145 Hopkins, 2007, p. 1.

Paul Oles, an astronomer and program director with the prestigious *Buhl Planetarium* in Pittsburgh and writer of a science column for the *Pittsburgh Press* since 1969, said he "decided to go public with his creationist conclusions about the origin of the universe."[146] As a result, "The Christian community responded to this column with support, but opponents exploded with boiling letters and vehement phone calls. Some reacted [to him] irrationally and violently."[147] Not long after, the paper canceled his popular column.

The mere belief that God exists can cause problems for those in higher education, but to claim additionally that *He might have actually created something in the past* could put one's job on the line—and maybe even one's life.

The opposition to Intelligent Design has stiffened in recent years, and demonstrates a substantial increase in hate speech. Barry Lynn, of Americans United for Separation of Church and State, has publicly threatened lawsuits against school districts that allow Intelligent Design to be objectively discussed. "The Supreme Court has rejected the idea of balanced treatment between science and pseudoscience," he said. "And it would cost school boards a tremendous amount of money to fight this." Such threats have attended attempts to criticize highly debatable aspects of Darwinian theory. Hundreds of books and articles have been written in an effort to discredit Intelligent Design, many focusing on its alleged philosophical illegitimacy and the supposed religious motives of its leading proponents. Those who oppose Intelligent Design retain immense power – in scientific organizations, university departments, the media, and the legal system. Virtually every official science organization has felt compelled to issue some denunciation of Intelligent Design, and especially of its anticipated impact on science education.[148]

Threats of Violence

I have documented in my research many examples of threats and some actual instances of violence against Darwin skeptics. One example is the case of scientist Chandra Wickramasinghe of the University College in Cardiff, Wales,

---

146 Gabler, 1982, p. 50.
147 Gabler, 1982, p. 50.
148 Richards, 2004, pp. 50-52.

a co-worker with Fred Hoyle, then one of the best-known living astronomers.[149] Prof. Wickramasinghe felt that creationists had some valid points and, although he disagreed with several common creationist views, he bravely spoke out publicly in favor of two-model teaching. For his audacity he received death threats which the police were "taking very seriously." *Discover Magazine* said, "Wickramasinghe has been receiving chilling letters and taped telephone calls for months." A recent letter read, "We mean business. You have three weeks to get out of Cardiff or you and your family will regret the consequences."[150]

When one Darwin Doubter debated Professor Jim Paulson, Paulson's associate became furious and stormed off of the stage, then "grabbed the microphone and began yelling (the crew quickly cut off power to the mike) ... the guy ... just wanted to rant and rave."[151] When Dr. Duane Gish lectured at Michigan State University several years ago one "evolutionist threatened to become physically abusive and had to be restrained."[152] When William Dembski lectured at the University of Oklahoma about "30 questioners grilled Dembski over the course of more than two hours... I had expected Dembski's talk to get a warm reception... Instead the room had almost a carnival atmosphere [and] Dembski was heckled repeatedly..."[153]

Jack Cuozzo, in his book *Buried Alive*, discusses the "violent reaction" that his research into Neanderthal man caused, providing another illustration of the extreme reaction that can result from Darwin Doubters. In this case there were seven witnesses to the events—two adults and five children.[154] The year was 1979 and "it all began when I started to question the evolutionary record of fossils in 1976."[155] The antagonism resulted from his attempt to study the original Neanderthal skeletal material housed in several Paris museums.

Several persons were evidently trying to destroy some incriminating radiographs that Cuozzo had taken of the Neanderthals with a portable cephalometric x-ray machine developed by General Electric Corporation for use in fossil research (at the time there were only two portable cephalometric

149   "Seeds of Terror" *Discover Magazine*, March 1982, 3(3): 81.
150   "Seeds of Terror" *Discover Magazine*, March 1982, 3(3): 81.
151   Letter from Dave Sack to Jerry Bergman, dated May 19, 2003.
152   Letter from Doug Sharp to Jerry Bergman, dated Feb. 9, 2004, p. 1.
153   Dickson-LaPrade, D. 2008. p. 7.
154   Cuozzo, 1998, p. 13.
155   Cuozzo, 1998, p. 17.

x-ray machines in the world). Fortunately, as Dr. Cuozzo details in his book, he was able to elude those who pursued him and his family around Paris in a dramatic high-speed car chase and even tried to break into his apartment in France. He finally arrived safely back in the United States with his radiographs intact. The pursuers were not able to destroy his x-ray photographs, which turned out to produce important new information about Neanderthals that was detrimental to Darwinism, showing that many textbook measurements were incorrect. In this case, some of the people who cooperated with Dr. Cuozzo (who were themselves not Darwin Doubters) were also threatened and, Dr. Cuozzo believes, one died under very suspicious circumstances and was possibly murdered.[156]

Although the incriminating details surrounding the attempts to destroy his radiographs are unclear, it is well established that someone did everything in their power to prevent him from collecting data on Neanderthal fossils once they found out that he was a Darwin skeptic. Before he was outed, he had the full cooperation from leading evolutionists. After he was outed, things changed drastically. For example, the detailed letters from Darwinists in answer to his questions stopped, and he has not been allowed in some museums to do his ongoing research. His book documents in detail, including names, dates, and places, how Darwinists have done everything in their power to block any research he attempted to complete.

In another revealing example, when William Dembski attempted to reactivate interest in the field of apologetics at Princeton Theological Seminary, including support for Intelligent Design and critiques of Darwinism, he faced two lawsuits and was "threatened with physical violence, accused of racism and sexism, denied funding that other campus groups readily received, had posted signs destroyed and removed, and [was] explicitly informed by faculty that membership in the Charles Hodge Society [established to study apologetics] jeopardized [his] academic advancement."[157]

Yet another example, typical of the scores I have reviewed, was a hate letter sent to anti-Darwinist Ken Ham, calling him insane. The writer added:

---

156 Cuozzo, 1998, p. 61.
157 Dembski and Richards, 2001, p. 26.

> People like you need to be exterminated. I hope some group or individual does their part to rid people like you from society. It may take one year, two years, five years, or ten years, but hopefully something awful will happen to you and your family. You could do everyone in the USA a favor and hop in your car [and drive] ... to the nearest river, lock the door, leave the windows open halfway, drive into the river.[158]

One of the worst examples of threats of violence is extensively documented by Dr. Vernon Grose. Grose, former Curriculum Commissioner for California Public schools, was personally threatened with physical violence by, among other persons, "the dean of one of the largest universities in the world" for his work to ensure that Darwinism is taught non-dogmatically.[159] In another case, after a Midwestern university professor came out of the closet, he claimed that his colleagues began threatening him in various ways. For example, he "was physically assaulted twice [once by a professor striking him with his fists], the second time requiring surgery from complications resulting from the assault [due to a broken nose]." He writes:

> I reported the assault to the campus police. The dean told me he could understand why my ideas made them mad, and, in my opinion, he condoned the whole affair and did nothing. The police filed a report, but otherwise did nothing.[160]

Research in which I am currently engaged has also resulted in both physical threats and physical violence such as those described in the paragraphs above. These threats are no doubt inflamed by rhetoric such as that of Purdue biologists Deyrup and MacDonald,[161] who said that creationists are an "insidious threat" to education, or Harvard's Richard Lewontin's blast that creationists are "know nothings."[162] One reason for the violence is because hate speech or inflammatory rhetoric, such as the following statement by Fredric L. Rice, is now common:

---

158 Anonymous Letter to Ken Ham dated June 28, 2005, p. 3.
159 Grose, 2006, p. xiii.
160 Interview of Midwestern university professor by Jerry Bergman, Apr. 23, 2004.
161 Deyrup and MacDonald, 1982, p. 245.
162 Lewontin, 1981, p. 559.

I've yet to meet a creationist that appeared to be even marginally sane, all of which absolutely hated freedom of speech. Creationists appear to be on the whole either pathological liars or else suffering from massive cognitive dissonance. Even as *Talk Origins* ... solidly debunks Creationist occultism and points out these cults' lies, the solidly documented truth isn't enough to make these insane cults refrain from their public exhibitions.[163]

Based on these and even more examples of physical violence threats and action, plus the increasingly open calls for such action (especially on blogs), I predict that violence against Darwin Doubters will continue to increase unless firm action is undertaken to curb the escalating discrimination tactics employed by those who are intolerant of their views.

Intolerance Acknowledged by Scientists

Even many non-creationist or anti-ID scientists admit that the intolerance Darwin Doubters face is deplorable. Carl Sagan apologized for the shabby way in which the scientific community treated another dissident, Immanuel Velikovsky, with the following words, "My own strongly held view is that no matter how unorthodox the reasoning process or how unpalatable the conclusions, *there is no excuse for any attempt to suppress new ideas—least of all by scientists...* Therefore, I was very pleased that the AAAS agreed to" hold a discussion on *Worlds in Collision*, in which Velikovsky took part.[164]

Unfortunately, though, the meeting was designed so that the majority of papers were very negative toward all of the work of Velikovsky, and many felt that his views were very unfairly represented. This same situation occurs frequently in instances when creationists or ID advocates are "allowed" to present their views in formal professional forums—and even when they are permitted to speak, a storm of protest often results. A good example is the 63rd AAAS symposium (1983) held at the University of California at Santa Barbara, which resulted in protests by a number of professors who objected to the presence of Darwin Doubters attending the conference. More recently the trend is to prohibit Darwin Doubters of all stripes from presenting any papers at conferences such as AAAS. One scientist

---

163 Rice, 2004, p. 1.
164 Carl Sagan, 1977, p. 45, emphasis added.

reported that his paper, which was based on empirical evidence his research team collected, was rejected because, as one reviewer stated

> It is obvious where this research is going and for this reason I object to this paper being presented at the ... conference. The authors have identified a major problem with neo-Darwinism then imply that their evidence argues against the theory. I object to this approach. If the authors have evidence against neo-Darwinism they should present it, then deal with it by explaining how the evidence does not argue against the theory. At the least they should present possible research ideas that will deal with the evidence presented in harmony with neo-Darwinism. I agree that this study presents a major challenge to neo-Darwinism but any theories not based on naturalism are not acceptable. The researchers have presented a problem and should solve it in harmony with the prevailing naturalism paradigm. Any other approach is not science.[165]

At another debate at a science conference, one professor, who up to that point was "comfortably distant" in his academic and professional environment "from creationists and other Bible-mad deviants," wrote:

> However, a distressing episode recently revealed to me the extent of their grasp...I attended an AIA [*Archaeological Institute of America*] session titled "Time and Chronology: Contrasting Views of Creationists and Evolutionists." The title alone, indicating a doctrine or point of view was to be discussed, rather than ... science, lowered my respect for this otherwise excellent professional organization. The speakers were father and son, H. M. and J. D. Morris, of the Institute for Creation Research (a leap of the imagination— what is there to research?). What really bothered me was ... the fact that they were ... addressing such a group. It was mind-boggling—not only to me ... but to people who came away overwhelmed by ... the presentation. I talked to one archaeologist who was foggy enough to accept the creationists' terms of debate and felt they deserved equal time for their "science." I have written the president of the AIA to register my complaint...[166]

---

165 Neither the name of the professor who submitted the paper nor the lab can be revealed due to the professor's concerns about his career. It can be stated that he does not live in America. The blind peer reviewer's name is not known.
166 Elinor Wright, 1987, pp. 3-4.

Professor Christopher Toumey cites a case of a creationist research scientist who worked in a biology lab at a major government research facility in the Research Triangle Park, the largest research park in the United States, located near Durham, Raleigh, and Chapel Hill, in North Carolina. The scientist reported that his supervisor was extremely hostile toward creationist views. Toumey wrote about this event:

> This creationist had a Ph.D. in a scientific field and was especially articulate on scientific issues, so that the local creationist group wanted him to be their president, which would make him their public spokesperson. He declined, however, citing his fear that his boss would harass him if it were known that he was a creationist. Instead, he agreed to be the vice-president, which would allow him to assume some leadership but remain discreet about his creationist affiliations.[167]

Sometimes counter examples are noted that seem to indicate creationists are intimidated in academia less often than many reports imply.[168] In one such case, after a speaker reviewed the problem of intolerance in academia and the difficulties religious persons experience, a creationist in the audience stated that he had just received tenure in a large state university biology department without problems. He added that his department members on occasion made a few negative comments about his religion, but he did not experience the problems discussed in the lecture, adding:

> I have freely shared my faith with both my students and my colleagues, and have had only a few people voice any objections. In fact, my department chair, who is a highly respected historian, is an evangelical Christian and makes no bones about it. He has chaired the department for over twenty years.[169]

---

167 Toumey, 1994, pp. 230-231.
168 For example see Grant, 2007. pp 171-175.
169 Letter from Anonymous to Jerry Bergman, September, 2006. The author did not want his identity made public.

To this the lecturer responded, "Your department chair is an evangelical Christian? This is a good case of the exception proving the rule. I wonder how circumstances would fare if your department chair was not an evangelical Christian?"[170]

Intolerance Against Non-Scientists

One case illustrates the problems creationists and ID advocates encounter in non-science situations quite often. Russell P. Reach, a Harvard Law School graduate, scored a perfect 800 on the law school examination test (extremely rare). He achieved an outstanding academic record in spite of the fact that he worked full-time to support a family while attending Harvard Law School. He was also an active conservative Christian and a creationist. Harvard Law School graduates experience about a 50 percent job offer rate for each interview (a person who interviews for two positions usually receives one offer), and the vast majority of Harvard Law School graduates receive offers before they graduate. Mr. Reach had about two dozen interviews, no second interviews, and not a single offer. He eventually received an offer from a Texas Christian law firm. In spite of his outstanding academic record, he was close to the last hired.

Potential employers would likely have known of his religious faith because his undergraduate work was completed at *Bob Jones University*, a red flag to those who are informed about the alleged danger of the "new right." Reach accepted Christianity, including a rejection of Darwinism, because of his own personal study and convictions, not because he was indoctrinated into this worldview as a child. (His father was a well-known liberal and former president of Owens College in Ohio, a state school that now enrolls over 20,000 students.) Reach currently works for a Christian law firm in Atlanta, Georgia.

Attorney John Whitehead warned that so rampant are civil liberty violations against Christians by our secular society that every believer is now on a collision course with the government. Some of those who are at the forefront of this collision are stressing that to break the present "religious apartheid" we need protests, letter-writing campaigns, involvement in politics and the like in order

---

170   Letter from Anonymous to Jerry Bergman, September, 2006. The author did not want his identity made public.

to continue practicing our historic Christian religious convictions.[171] A society that permits such undiluted hatred is neither free nor just.

The irony is that propagation of hate against ID advocates, creationists, or Christians in the employment and educational arena is illegal, yet is almost totally ignored by a government that claims to be concerned about human rights. Francis Schaeffer, in his book *The Christian Manifesto*, says he would not rule out civil disobedience—and his son, Franky, goes even further in his book, *A Time for Anger*. Such responses do not appear to be "over-reacting" when one realizes that the goal of many secular humanists, as openly stated by Edelman, goes beyond the separation of church and state and to what they call separation of "fantasy and reality" as a "precondition for producing mentally healthy and responsible citizens." He concludes that no nation today:

> can afford mass insanity, not with the kind of weapons man is capable of producing... laws in most states ... prevent the insane and the feeble-minded from having or raising children. [This is not true – J. B.] Since no one but a moron or a fanatic can believe ... the Christian religion ... one wonders why believers are excluded from such prudent legal restrictions. I question the right of the insane to perpetuate insanity however numerous they may be ... I am for keeping religion out of the schools [and] ... out of the churches and the homes; in fact I am for abolishing it all together, because nothing but harm can come from believing in a lie or a delusion, as the whole history of religion amply demonstrates. The young should be trained to face reality, not to be hopelessly dependent on a religion that is little better than alcohol or morphine.[172]

This is hardly an informed opinion, and is essentially emotional propaganda. The tragedy is that the U.S. government holds itself up as an example of respect and a beacon for human rights, but in fact has an incredibly poor record of protecting the rights of those it is sworn to uphold. Admittedly, the situation Darwin skeptics face in other countries is often the same or even worse. Kosta Radisavlijavich, a Yugoslavian-born physicist, active in developing highly sensitive infrared detector materials in the USA, recently visited his home country. He noted that Christians there could not understand how he could be a believer

---

171 John W. Whitehead, 1995, p. 38-53
172 Edelman, 1984, p. 28.

and a scientist at the same time. It was very difficult for out-of-the-closet Christians in his country to be practicing scientists. Those who became Christians, if they were found out, often soon lost their positions. Before the end of the cold war, in order to be hired in most Soviet-bloc universities a candidate must have signed a doctrinal statement professing to be an atheist![173]

A teacher in a religious school in the British Isles, James Watson, was dismissed because he taught creation along with evolution in his science classes. Watson soon left England for the United States, where he assumed that he would experience fewer problems. He did not; so he returned home.[174] Attorney John Whitehead notes that if religious people are unable to "regain their free speech rights in public schools" and public places in general, then "religion will be totally privatized." He goes on to say:

> There must also be legal precedent strengthening the Christian teacher's right, at the least, to express his or her honest opinion on the Creator or Christ... If these precedents and freedoms are not forthcoming, those Christians in public education are faced with two possibilities. Either they *leave the system or resist*. Again, *resistance and civic disobedience will result in penalties and perpetrators of such must prepare to suffer the consequences.* Consequences could range from the firing of a teacher to suspension of students. These penalties should be met with lawsuits in carefully selected test cases. Millions of children sit entombed in an educational system that, in most instances, omits any serious references to God.[175]

This concern was discussed by Mims, who noted, "I've tried to turn the other cheek for now, but at some point I've got to ... put a halt to this kind of discrimination before it gets too advanced. If Christians don't act now, it may be you who doesn't get a job next time."[176] McDowell and Hostetler agree

> that it is now time for Christians to respond. If we do not, our freedoms will be increasingly eroded and our children's faith will be increasingly undermined, our culture will crumble all around us, and our churches will be destroyed from within. But for that response to be effective in defusing

---

173   Melnick, 1982.
174   Case history in Jerry Bergman's files.
175   Whitehead, 1986, p. 203 (emphasis added).
176   Forrest Mims, quoted in McDowell and Hostetler, 1998, pp. 81-82.

the new tolerance and preserving the faith for us and our children, we need to do more than simply defend our civil and religious rights... We need a strategy, a plan. We need a positive response that will not only defend but also advance the kingdom of heaven.[177]

We expected the old Soviet-bloc nations to persecute religious believers, yet this is exactly what has happened in the United States. The previous examples portend not only what may become more common in this country, but what is *already* occurring here.

It is eerie and depressing to read of such persecution in these former communist countries, and realize that so many similar acts are still occurring in this country with the awareness or approval of our government. If the names and the nations were excluded from these reports, one would often be at a loss to identify whether they happened in a totalitarian nation or the United States. Test yourself: which nation is spoken of below?

Graduate students [were] ... refused admission if it were known that they did not accept evolution. Teachers have threatened students with failing grades if they do not profess a belief in evolution. Advanced students have even been denied earned degrees when it was found out they were not evolutionists.[178]

The author is not speaking about the old Soviet Union, but the United States. At least in the former communist nations, the governments were often open about their discrimination. Former Cuban leader Fidel Castro openly admitted that "Christians are not welcome to join the Cuban Communist party," and that "if I were questioned as to whether there exists a form of discrimination against Christians, I would have to say, yes, that is something we have not yet overcome."[179] In America, those who most often decry bigotry—the professors, intellectuals, and politicians—are often the most intolerant of Christianity. Thus, Anderson noted, it is ironic that one of the most frequent clichés in this debate is that "fundamentalists are intolerant," yet "these Christians, and their

---

177 McDowell and Hostetler, 1998, pp. 81-82.
178 Hand, 1972, p. 53.
179 Fidel Castro, quoted in Rafferty, 1987, p. 14.

leaders, are often victims of a bigoted and intolerant crusade championed by those concerned about fundamentalist intolerance."[180]

Conclusion

This chapter documents the fact that intolerance against Darwin skeptics is a problem in America, is often tied to the religious beliefs of those dissenters, and can lead to verbal and physical assaults. Another factor related to this form of intolerance is the relationship between creationism and Christianity. This chapter also refutes Brown University Professor Ken Miller's claim that "creationists are not being persecuted by scientists; they have deliberately *avoided* the scientific community."[181] Out of the closet Creationists and Intelligent Design advocates want very much to be an active part of the academic scientific community, and have earned that right, but as one revewer has stated, this goal has recently proven nearly as likely as a African American being allowed to sit anywhere on a public bus in the South before the civil rights movement.

---

180 Kirby Anderson, 1987, p. 12.
181 Kenneth R. Miller, 1982, p. 12.

Chapter 3: Denial of Earned Degrees

A frequent claim of many Darwinists is that no Darwin Dissenters hold earned degrees, and that none of them have published in refereed science journals. The irony of this is that in many cases, this is true, but only because of the systematic practice of discrimination that denies earned degrees or publication to Darwin skeptics based solely on their questions about evolution, Darwinism, or their perceived religious beliefs. In particular, graduate students who openly express their reservations about Darwinism experience problems in completing their degrees. This insidious practice, with its horrific toll in broken promises and ruined careers, has been allowed to run unchecked in America for decades, with no apparent end in sight. In fact, the failure to remedy this situation has served to embolden those who engage in such practices to continue.

Though the discrimination associated with this issue is all but invisible when it comes to media coverage, it has become a key *de facto* grassroots flashpoint of the culture war in America. One of the reasons why this is true was discussed by Duffy, who suggests the public school curriculum from K through 12 and even at the college level:

> maintained a Protestant bias up through the 1960s, even though the theology was watered down to a nominal level in most schools. Over the past thirty years, what little Protestant bias remained has been replaced by a different bias—called secular humanism. The public school curriculum of recent history rejected Protestant presuppositions and the accompanying worldview. Suddenly, the former majority who seemingly dominated the education system found themselves in the role of the disregarded minority. Protestants have realized what the Catholics realized in the 1800s—it does make a difference who controls education. And it makes a huge difference to minorities and to those who disagree with the majoritarian worldview.[182]

Examples of this bias are found everywhere in America today. In an excellent discussion of the problem of survival in academia professor Olasky writes that many people

---

182   Duffy, 1995, p. 30.

who refuse to ignore God in their work never get through the ideological pounding of graduate school, never get a university job, never get tenure. There is, after all, a culture war going on throughout the United States, and it is becoming ever more vicious in our academic hothouses. Discerning alumni and taxpayers should ask whether the universities they support have a policy, "No fundamentalists allowed." Christian students and professors should not allow themselves to be shut up, slammed down, and forced out without a fight. When they are attacked, they deserve the full support of Christian alumni, taxpayers, and the entire church community.[183]

In some cases, students are allowed to complete everything required to earn a degree, and after spending thousands of dollars and investing years of effort, are at the last moment denied what they have rightfully earned. Frank Manheim details a very revealing experience that occurred when he was a Harvard undergraduate:

> I am pretty orthodox in my thinking about evolution. Yet, I feel that the ongoing campaign against creationism and creationists is counterproductive and unwise. These thoughts have roots in an experience early in my undergraduate study at Harvard, when I took a biological survey course. The young professor hammered on two themes: evolution and challenging authority. I was doing "B+" work, and when the time came for our term paper, I took him at his word. What would more challenge authority than to critically examine the theory of evolution? Of course I thought it would be hard to find much counter material. But when I went into the stacks at Widener Library, I found—to my astonishment—that the problem was extraordinarily complex. There were many solid reasons to question the evolution theory. In fact, Darwin himself acknowledged problems with his theory and, by the 1880s, was castigated by burgeoning Darwinists for his weakness.

> I worked hard on my paper and eagerly awaited an "A" and my professor's approbation for my imaginative and authority-challenging research. Imagine my shock when my final grade came out as a "C" and my term paper as a "D-." Taken aback and puzzled, I asked the professor what happened. I explained that I had tried to follow his guidance in challenging authority at the highest level. Of course, I mentioned almost in passing that I didn't personally doubt evolution theory. "Oh you don't?" said my

---

professor, realizing I had taken an intellectual debater's position rather than becoming an apostate to evolution.[184]

Manheim reports that once the professor knew what he personally believed, his grade was changed on the spot to an A! This episode elegantly demonstrates that what is of concern in the origins debate all too often is about *beliefs*, not one's ability to accurately understand and articulate the issues. This experience was Manheim's first introduction to the "objectivity" of modern scientists. His narrative continues:

> Later it was underscored that the universally praised "challenge authority" in science and academia is only advisable if it's not the cherished theories of your own professor or the establishment you are challenging, or if you are in an independent position to do so. And as for the permanence of the strongly espoused geological and cosmological theories I was taught as an undergraduate—virtually all are gone now! ... remembering the hypocrisy of my early professor and the fallibility of many noted scientists, I have been chagrined by the arrogance and vituperation with which the creationists have been treated... intolerance and absolutism—no matter how sure we are of our case—are not really consistent with the scientific method and give science a bad image. Indeed, if there had been less militancy and more humility and good will in the educational and scientific community, I doubt whether the fundamentalist groups would have felt themselves isolated and the object of contempt, hence needing to mobilize politically to counter what they view as anti-religious prejudice in schools.

He asserts that "it is unscientific to censor alternative views about creation, or anything else, in our society," adding that:

> The Scandinavian countries have not emasculated their textbooks of pertinent and appropriate reference to religion as we have done or attempted. Yet they have no known problem with "creationism." We don't have to give up our principles to restore a sense of genuine humility that would serve the science establishment well and help it achieve a more balanced role in society.[185]

---

184   Manheim, 1993, p. 4.
185   Manheim, 1993, p. 4.

Dr. Eugenie Scott disagrees, claiming that it is not an issue of religious discrimination but discrimination "on the basis of science" to deny degrees to those are "so at variance with what we consider standard science."[186] To this, paleontologist Professor Fastovsky responded that depriving a student a doctorate because of religious beliefs is wrong: "we are not here to certify the religious beliefs of students."[187]

Another case involved a candidate for a doctorate in zoology at the University of Virginia. Although the examiners probed his religious beliefs, the candidate refused to respond—which, Richard Culp notes, irritated his examiners—but he was awarded the degree.[188] The lesson, according to Culp, is that hiding one's personal beliefs reduces problems.

Culp also relates the example of Mr. Zumstein, a botany doctoral candidate at *Purdue University* (the school where Culp earned his degree). Zumstein, an excellent student, had finished all of his requirements for a Ph.D. except for the oral examination given at the end of the Ph.D. program. Culp recounts the case as follows:

> I knew well the members of his examining committee. One was the head of the department, who had written in my defense to the University of California; another was professor of plant physiology ... the third was the notorious professor in plant anatomy for whom I then worked. The oral examination proceeded smoothly while the first two professors questioned the candidate, and they intended to pass him. When the third professor had his turn, however, he wasted no time in demonstrating his dislike for the candidate. The candidate's [religion] ... was against him. The veteran agnostic fired one question after another ... until he became confused and made some errors. The professor seized upon these and insisted that he could not pass such a man.[189]

Culp concluded that "a Christian who is a candidate for the doctor's degree may find his entire work ... destroyed, in the name of science, by an intolerant evolutionist" a fact that "helps to explain why there are not more outspoken Christians with advanced degrees in the biological sciences."[190]

---

186 Quoted in Dean, 2007, p. A19.
187 Quoted in Dean, 2007, p. A19.
188 Culp, 1975, p. 142.
189 Culp, 1975, p. 143.
190 Culp, 1975, p. 143.

Erville Clark, in spite of possessing above-average qualifications that earned him an excellent academic record, was denied his Ph.D. in biology at *Stanford University*. He was finally able to complete his doctorate at Oregon State University. The department chair there, in evaluating Clark's admission papers, contacted Stanford and learned that Mr. Clark was denied the Ph.D. because he was a creationist. Numbers comments about this case:

> In recounting the bitter incident, Clark himself expressed far more uncertainty about how much weight to assign to his creationist views. Early in his program he had taken a course on evolution with Paul R. Ehrlich (b. 1932), from whom he received a *B*. Later, when Clark attempted to defend his dissertation *on the ecology of a single county in northern California, Ehrlich zeroed in, quizzing him on ecology around the world, about which the young biologist admittedly knew relatively little.* From what he later learned, four of the five committee members voted to pass him, but the department required a unanimous decision. The next year he retook the examination with the same results, which led to automatic termination... Determined to earn the doctorate his father never possessed, Clark later enrolled in a general science program at Oregon State University, from which he received a Ph.D. in 1971 for a dissertation on radiation biology.[191]

It is clear that the one member of his Ph.D. committee who made sure that Clark would fail his oral exams was Ehrlich.

George Mulfinger was a physics professor at *Bob Jones University* in Greenville, South Carolina, until his untimely death. He was denied his Ph.D. in physics at *Columbia University* in spite of his outstanding academic record (*summa cum laude* and straight A's in all graduate work prior to that time). His interdisciplinary program included approximately equal physics and chemistry content. When he progressed to his research stage his advisor told him that he was "no longer welcome" in the program. He later found out that a student whom he had once spoken to about his belief had informed his advisor about his creationist convictions. He did not contest the decision because, without his advisor acting as his advocate, he felt that little could be done. Consequently, he was never able to complete his Ph.D.

---

191   Numbers, 2006, pp. 299–271, emphasis added.

Admission Problems

Discrimination often occurs even before one becomes a student, scientist, or educator. The problem is most common in programs directly related to Darwinism, such as physical anthropology. Warriner related the case of a former missionary who had applied for admission to a major university as a doctoral candidate in anthropology. During his interview, he was asked by the department chairman if he had

> accepted the theory of organic evolution, to which he replied that he had not. He was then told that they accepted no doctoral candidates who were not evolutionists; that the nearest they had come to doing so was to accept one master's degree candidate who was not an evolutionist. Thus, they can say, "No anthropologist denies evolution!" Why? Because no one who denies evolution is allowed to become an anthropologist![192]

Admission problems even occur in areas having nothing to do with human evolution, such as the medical field. A student with outstanding grades and recommendations applied to *Washington University* Medical School in St. Louis, Missouri. After reviewing his credentials, the admissions board noted that one of his former professors stated in his written recommendation that the student was a creationist and therefore "could not do scientific research." Several of the board members mentioned that they agreed with the adverse recommendation and, for this reason, the candidate should not be admitted to medical school. If he was, one member stated, the student would not achieve a passing grade in *his* class, no matter how high the quality of his work, ensuring that this student would not graduate.

Several other comments were made along the same vein, indicating clear prejudice against this applicant. One might wonder how many thousands of times this same scenario has been played out by admission committees, grant advisory boards and hiring committees. Culp relates another outcome:

> A physician friend recently told about his interview with the admission committee at the Indiana University Medical School. Three times he was

---

192   Warriner, 1975, p. 54.

asked how he would answer an examination question involving evolution. Each time he told them that he would say that it is only a theory. He was accepted, he felt, only through the grace of God.[193]

The Tom Jungmann incident

A young scholar and M.A. graduate at San Jose State, Tom Jungmann ran into problems when he applied to a Ph.D. program in biology. He discovered the true colors of one of his thesis committee members when two letters of "recommendation" were accidentally mailed back to him. One of these letters, written by Professor Gregor Cailliet, stated that Tom's "religious views" could be a "major barrier" to his earning a Ph.D. Cailliet said of Tom:

> He worked very hard and completed the thesis, despite the questions and reservations expressed by me and the other members of his committee. During this time it became obvious that Tom was quite determined to complete his thesis, but that he was more interested in achieving the degree goal than in finding something out of an interesting scientific nature.[194]

And what exactly was this "scientific" element that Tom was unwilling to pursue? In an interview with Cailliet, Kevin Wirth and student Tom Jungmann heard him say that "[Tom] did a good job doing what he did, but the scientific part of it, which is to interpret what that means in some context, was lacking"[195] When Wirth then asked if Cailliet was concerned that Tom was not interpreting his data in an evolutionary context, Cailliet responded:

> Yeah, but I told him that he didn't have to do that, that he can get a [MA] degree this way, but that's as far as I want him to go with it.[196]

---

193 Culp, 1975, p. 143.
194 Letter from Gregor M. Cailliet to Dr. Clifton A. Poodry, dated March 28, 1983
195 Interview of Gregor M. Cailliet by Kevin Wirth and Tom Jungmann, October 19, 1983 at Moss Landing Marine Lab, CA
196 Interview of Gregor M. Cailliet by Kevin Wirth and Tom Jungmann, October 19, 1983 at Moss Landing Marine Lab, CA

Meaning, because Tom was unwilling to include in his thesis a write-up of the evolutionary implications of his data, Cailliet didn't want Tom to pursue a higher degree. That's because, according to Cailliet, the data Tom collected needed a context (and according to Cailliet, it should be an evolutionary one).[197] But the most damning part of Cailliet's letter came when he wrote in his 'recommendation' for Tom that

> ...his committee and I realized that the major barrier to his understanding and accepting his suggestions as constructive to his project, were related to his religious beliefs. Therefore, *since he did not believe in evolution, and had other associated religious constraints,* we suggested that he include the clustering or similarity analysis and avoid the phylogenetic aspects of the analysis he had undertaken. Once we had finally approved the writing in his thesis, we made it clear that we passed him under the condition [or assumption?] that the Master's was a terminal degree and that we assumed that he would not further seek an additional graduate degree.[198]

Cailliet's claim that the "other members of his committee" had reservations about Tom might be construed by the reader to be all-inclusive, and that all other members were in agreement that Tom would not pursue a higher degree because of the "major barrier" posed by his "religious beliefs." However, it's interesting to note that Tom's main thesis advisor (and also thesis committee member), Dr. Robert Hassur, wrote a letter of recommendation (just days before Cailliet wrote his) which stated in full:

> Tom is a very bright, well trained, and intensely interested biologist. I was a member of his M.A. thesis committee and worked closely with him on the electrophoresis aspects of his study. Tom is a very diligent worker and is very self-motivated; he requires almost no supervision to get the job done. He is not easily discouraged, so when confronted by a challenge he will devote enormous energy to master it. Although he is a bit shy and reserved at first, his friendly and pleasant personality soon shows. I feel that he has all the qualifications to perform well in your graduate program and that he will be a credit to both our institutions.[199]

---

197 Junbgmann, 1983. Note that Tom somehow managed to publish his findings anyway, without an evolutionary context.
198 Letter of recommendation for Thomas Jungmann written by Gregor M. Cailliet on March 28, 1983.
199 Letter from Robert Hassur to Dr. Clifton A. Poodry, dated March 22, 1983

This letter doesn't sound like it was written by someone who agreed with Dr. Cailliet that Tom should have been held to a "terminal" M.A. degree.

Jungmann protested that he never brought his religious beliefs to bear on the science related to his thesis, but it proved to be of no avail even though he was granted his M.A. degree and also managed to get Dr. Cailliet (under threat of a discrimination lawsuit) to write a letter retracting the statements in his letter of "recommendation".

One final note about letters of recommendation. In Tom Jungmann's case, and that of many other graduate students, the right to view such letters is often waived by the student. When Tom waived his right to view these letters, Dr. Cailliet evidently felt free to write exactly what he thought about Tom. And, rather than recommending Tom as he said he would, he did his very best to ensure that those who read his letter clearly understood that Tom was not a fit candidate for graduate work in any academic institution that held evolution in high regard. He even went well beyond that by specifically singling out Tom's religious beliefs as an impediment to his ability to do good science.

Students beware – if you sign a waiver rescinding your right to view a letter of recommendation from members of your thesis committee – this is what you might get instead. Tom's case illustrates just two of the many tactics employed within the academy to weed out undesirable candidates who fail to be a "good comrade"[200] when it comes to evolution: bargaining for a "terminal" degree, and sending out letters of 'recommendation' designed to sabotage a student's future education opportunities. Writing warning letters or attaching notes to a student transcript is nothing new, as we shall see when we examine the case of Dr. Dini later in this chapter.

Problems Encountered While Taking Classes

Sometimes a degree is not denied to a Darwin skeptic, but problems still occur when taking classes. An honor student majoring in microbiology made a comment about Intelligent Design on a paper and was docked two letter grades with the following remark written on the paper: "I think you should seriously consider changing your major. It is ludicrous for you to major in biology. Pick

---

200   See the movie "Expelled," starring Ben Stein (released in the U.S. on April 18, 2008).

another major where personal opinions are all that matter. I suppose my remarks will feed your martyr complex, but so be it."[201]

A young Christian man at a university in the Southwest wrote several "politically incorrect" editorials in his campus newspaper. As a result he was the only student with a 4.0 GPA *not* selected for the Honors College. This made him ineligible for the scholarships that he needed to continue his education.

Margaret Pieczonka, a college student in Poland, openly stated in her college biology class that she did not accept Darwinism and, as a result of this admission, she failed the class.[202] This action put her a year behind in her university studies. What is ironic is that in Poland the university could not just expel her, an honor student, without encountering legal difficulties, yet in America she would not likely have had this type of protection.

In some parts of the world specific bans against Christians attending higher education have existed for years. In an article about the former East Germany, *Time* stated, "Christian children are often barred from higher education."[203] That a similar trend exists in America, a nation that has staked its reputation on freedom of religion and freedom of speech, is a surprise to many Americans who are not actively involved in mainstream academia or the scientific enterprise. It is almost as if this form of discrimination has been ignored, accepted, or viewed as something not worth bringing into public view. This ongoing practice is one that responsible citizens should resist in every possible way.[204]

Non-Science Majors' Experiences In Courses and Graduate Degrees

Similar stories can be repeated *ad infinitum*, and the discrimination is even common among students who are not enrolled in life-science studies. This section reviews evidence that Darwinism has become dogma in other fields as well, and many students face difficulties in academic areas having nothing to do with biology. An example is Don McDonald, Assistant Professor of Human Resource Management at *Troy State University* in Alabama. He states that his sociology professor managed to work atheism into his very first lecture, exclaiming that

---

201 Interview of microbiology student by Jerry Bergman. The student who did not want his identity revealed.
202 Interview of James Parkinson by Jerry Bergman, 1982, p. 1 of transcript.
203 *Time*, April 23, 1984, p. 61.
204 For example, see the movie *Expelled*, starring Ben Stein.

"There's no such [expletive deleted] thing as god!" McDonald was shocked by this and as a result his

> respect for him as a scientist dropped. It is of course unscientific to state anything with such certainty, especially in regard to what *isn't* there. Later another professor went even further: "You can not be a good sociologist and believe in god." I came to understand that for many sociologists the models or theories were not simply pictures of the way things work, but actual attempts to explain the way things are. Such professors think the models are the real thing (a position I now know to be called "methodological naturalism"). Many others believe that nothing can exist beyond what can be measured in a material world. I read the theories. I regurgitated them back on exams and in papers..." Still, I didn't have to agree with the specific theory... that it is possible to logically explain virtually all experience without God.[205]

The issue that seemed to cause the most problems in Dr. McDonald's college career was Darwinism. Based on his experience he learned that one should never

> *argue with your professors.* Once when my committee was meeting to discuss my dissertation progress, I happened to take issue with a certain theory held strongly by one of my committee members. It was a theory that ... was not even relevant to my hypotheses. Believe it or not, it had to do with Darwinian evolution. I am not even sure why it came up. All progress stopped as my committee discussed what should be done... They agreed that I would meet with one of the committee members and review the literature on the matter... I reported to his office at the appointed time, and from the beginning of our conversation it was clear to me that I understood the theory and its ramifications better than he. The second revelation took longer—he was supposed to win. Eventually I said, "Oh, I see what you mean. Thanks." Does the above scenario bother you? It bothers me... Now as a professor I let students know of my faith in Christ; it is a matter of intellectual honesty that I let them know where I am coming from. They may not choose to believe, and I don't ask them to make that choice in class, but neither will they have cause to doubt that I believe.[206]

---

205 Don McDonald, 1999, p. 7.
206 McDonald, 1999, p. 9.

Dennis Cheek, a law student over halfway through his J.D. degree at the University of Maryland, wrote a paper on the legal aspects of teaching about creationism. As a result, he ended up with a failing grade in a required course (in contrast to his exceptional grades in all of his other courses). Forced to take this same instructor again because this required course was taught only by her, he failed the course again and was expelled from the law school (failing two courses means automatic expulsion regardless of one's grades in all other courses). Several glowing letters written by other professors on his behalf failed to reverse the decision. When the grades were released, he was not even allowed to finish the term, but was curtly told to pack his books and leave immediately. He later went back to school to complete a Ph.D. in a science field.[207]

Another student completed a degree in the humanities at Harvard University with honors, and sat for the Rhodes scholarship. His professors told him that he would be a "shoo-in"—his grades, performance, and total record were clearly outstanding. At the scholarship examination, his examiners noticed on his vitae that he was involved with *Campus Crusade for Christ*. Interrogation about this involvement led to questions about his beliefs in naturalism and how he would respond if he located evidence that appears to contradict his theistic views. When it became clear that he was a creationist, he was told that he could not receive the Rhodes scholarship. After this incident, he completed his Ph.D. at a major University and became a professor, but has wisely stayed firmly in the closet (and for this reason would not give me permission to reveal his name, degrees, or current employment).

Research shows that this type of discrimination is also prevalent even at elite colleges. One *University of Texas* professor related his personal experience with what he calls academic bigotry as follows:

> During my first year in graduate school as an atheist and a communist, professors at the University of Michigan called me a genius: they were wrong. When I left as a Christian and a conservative, one professor believed I had become a moron: he also was wrong, but he tried to keep me from receiving a Ph.D. and probably would have succeeded but for the intervention of the one outspoken conservative on campus. Ever since then I have been very sensitive to ideological bias in grading... [from] what students have told me and shown

---

207   Dennis Cheek intervire with Jerry Bergman July, 1982

me concerning other courses . . . such bias occurs elsewhere. This is not to say that I'm a more virtuous grader than others; since I work in hostile territory and know that everything I say or do is examined critically.[208]

A telephone survey completed at one Ivy League school specifically asked, "Does religious bigotry exist at Brown University?" It found that of the 305 respondents, fully 50% thought that religious bigotry *did indeed exist* at this so-called liberal university but, unfortunately, the *specific* type of religious bigotry existing at Brown was not part of the question.[209] These results are surprising only because active Christian students are generally thought to be far more aware of this problem than others. Clearly, even many non-Christian students are aware of the anti-Christian bigotry, and are sensitive to the problem.

Cases of Closet Darwin Skeptics

Many of the cases in my files are from individuals who do not want their name revealed because they were trying to stay in the closet and complete their degrees wherever they could. One example is a University of Michigan zoology doctoral degree candidate who was asked during his Ph.D. examination if he believed in naturalistic evolution. After replying in the negative, he tried in vain to explain his views. His examiners concluded that they "could not recommend anyone who put his own personal views above the voice of the entire scientific world," and they subsequently denied him his degree because of his "religious beliefs." These exams should be designed to evaluate knowledge and understanding *only*, not personal religious beliefs.

Another example is a chemistry graduate student in an Ivy League college who was assigned a term paper and, to help with the topic selection, the professor provided a list of possible subjects from which to choose. Intrigued with the "Chemical Evolution" topic, the student completed a paper titled *The Impossibility of Chemical Evolution* which, in the judgment of several other professors, was clearly a scholarly paper and deserved an "A" or "A+" grade. However his professor marked points off for only one section of the paper. Otherwise it was void of critical remarks, yet was given a "C"—an unacceptable grade in graduate school.

---

208   Olasky, 1997, p. 58.
209   Hinds, 1983, p. 28.

Even if one is able to graduate, work critical of Darwinism in graduate school can cause problems in one's career or when attempting further graduate study. A college professor, whose credentials include a B.S., M.A., and M.S. in chemistry, taught high school and college chemistry for 22 years. His master's thesis at Columbia University, titled "Evidence for God in the Creation" caused him to be blackballed from several good Ph.D. programs (and he was barely awarded his master's). Isaac Asimov even once wrote to the director of the first college where he taught trying to get him fired because of his beliefs. The student did his thesis as a result of his own doubts about chemical evolution, using only reference materials that were available on the subject in the *Columbia University* Library.

These examples illustrate the validity of Numbers' observation in his study of the history of the modern creation movement:

> Over the years a number of creationists had reportedly been kicked out of secular universities because of their heterodox views, and leaders had warned graduate students to keep silent "because, if you don't, in almost 99 percent of the cases you will be asked to leave." Several graduate students [to protect their identity] took to using pseudonyms when writing for creationist publications.[210]

Robert Baldwin, of Toledo, Ohio, was denied his doctorate in education (curriculum major and higher education minor) at the *University of Toledo* in the late 1970s primarily because of his outspoken Christian beliefs. The questions on his written examination were designed by his advisor so that Mr. Baldwin, if he answered them honestly, would be forced to admit his Christian commitment. For example, when asked who, in his opinion, was the greatest philosopher who ever lived, he answered "Jesus Christ." This question was evidently asked solely to bring up his religion as it did not directly relate to his field of study. In discussions of his exam results by those who graded him, it was clearly stated that he would have to "change" his religious beliefs in order to receive his degree. His inquisitors openly expressed anger at his beliefs and Christian values. He realized that to obtain the degree would require either lying or changing his beliefs, neither of which he was willing to do; thus he dropped the goal of completing his doctorate. Jerry Rabbit, a friend of Baldwin, was also denied his doctorate

---

210   Numbers, 1982, p. 543.

from the *University of Toledo* in mathematics education at about the same time because of his Christian commitment and creationist beliefs.[211]

The Case of Arthur Custance

In one of the better-documented cases, Canadian creationist Arthur C. Custance (considered by some creationists to be among the "pantheon of anti-evolutionist martyrs"), was denied a Ph.D. in anthropology from the University of Toronto because of his religious beliefs. Numbers recounts a highlight of the case as follows:

> Despite some problems over unexcused absences from classes, he thought he was doing well until the oral part of his comprehensive examinations, when a professor asked, "Do you believe Adam and Eve were real people?" When Custance answered in the affirmative, one of the committee members reportedly threatened to resign if they "put through a man for a Ph.D. who believes in this kind of crap." Concluding that Custance's lapse in judgment reflected "insufficient scientific training"—and unwilling to have him represent the department as its first Ph.D.—the faculty strongly encouraged him to withdraw, which he eventually did.[212]

Soon after he left Toronto, Custance became head of the Human Engineering Laboratory for the Canadian Defense Research Board. Still wanting to complete his doctorate, he was able to take some evening and weekend courses at the *University of Ottawa* School of Psychology and Education. He submitted a previously written thesis titled "Does Science Transcend Culture?" and in 1959 received his Ph.D. from *Ottawa University* for this work.[213]

Another case involves a Ph.D. student doing his thesis in English literature on evolutionary themes found in the works of American writer Kurt Vonnegut. His subject had caused him such serious trouble with one thesis advisor that he was forced to totally abandon the thesis because of his critiques of evolution. Recently, he was able to recruit someone else on his committee, and it seemed he could salvage his several years' worth of work. Actually, the thesis should have

---

211 Interview of Jerry Rabbitt by Jerry Bergman.
212 Numbers, 2006, pp. 299–300.
213 Numbers, 2006, pp. 299–300.

been accepted months ago, but he is now in trouble again. He recently received the following note from his new "friendlier advisor" which said:

> I have gone through the first two chapters of the dissertation…. As I read it, however, I am developing some serious concerns about the direction your argument seems to be taking. You need make it clear that it is not the theory of evolution that you are critiquing, but the misinterpretation of it, and the way some people have converted it into an unscientific myth. I am also disturbed by some of your sources, especially Philip Johnson, who is a creationist polemicist, and whose works have no scientific or scholarly value. As for the writing itself, I have made comments on the document. In general I suggest that you need to be more careful about making overly definitive assertions that are not well supported, and that you should try to make your thesis less repetitive.[214]

Even in the field of literature it seems one must not question Darwinism. Furthermore, to quote someone does not mean that you agree with them (of course, I strongly suspect that if the thesis was critical of ID he could quote Johnson all he wanted without any repercussions). As of this wrting it appears that he will not be awarded the degree. As a result of this struggle, his marriage has suffered greatly.

When I was teaching in the college of education at *Bowling Green State University* in Ohio, several of my colleagues mentioned that, if they discovered a student was a creationist, they would fail him or her. One professor showed me a paper that a graduate student had written on the topic, "My Philosophy of Teaching." The student had included in his paper many Scripture citations and freely discussed the religious motivations that were his reason for being a teacher. After stressing that teaching was his ministry, he proceeded to support this philosophy in the paper. My colleague stated that he gave him a "C" for both the paper and the class. He admitted to me that the paper was well-written, but because it clearly revealed the student's religious orientation, it was judged "not acceptable" by the professor—and, as a result, the student failed the class. The student did not prevail on appeal, because the university held that it was the professor's prerogative to assign whatever grade on whatever grounds he wished,

---

214 Letter quoted by English student sent to Jerry Bergman dated June 2006. The student has requested anonymity to protect his career.

as long as his standards were *consistently applied*. The professor's judgment was held to be absolute in this area (which is usually the case).

On the subject of Ph.D. examinations, Culp warns that out-of-the-closet Darwin Doubters can often expect "intolerant opposition" in their oral examination for a Ph.D. degree:

> This examination culminates a period of arduous study and research usually lasting seven or eight years, three or four of which are on the graduate level. His investment of time and money represents a sacrifice that is drawn out over years. His inquisitors can ask anything about his field... It can be very subjective and the prejudices of the examiners can influence considerably their questions and evaluation of the answers... The Christian must not only know the secular material as well as the other candidates, but also must be prepared to defend his conviction that God created the universe...[215]

Bryan Leonard: Intolerance at Ohio State

One of the most extreme examples of a doctoral student being denied his Ph.D. degree due to his concerns about dogmatic Darwinism is Hilliard Davidson High School biology teacher Bryan Leonard. Davidson is a large public school near Columbus, Ohio. Mr. Leonard was not even accused of teaching creationism, but only of non-work related activities that support critical teaching of Darwinism, such as helping to draft Ohio's plan calling for "critical analysis of evolution" in high-school science classes. He was appointed to the curriculum-writing committee—an honor in itself—which drafted the model lesson plan that the Darwinist establishment is now up in arms over (specifically, those who object to the committee's decision to allow criticism of Darwinism). The committee consisted of highly qualified research scientists, college professors, high school biology teachers, and even a veterinarian.

Leonard also testified before the Kansas Board of Education, which was considering a similar proposal. Leonard has a B.S. in Biology, an M.S. in Microbiology, and has completed all of the course work for his Ph.D. in science education at *Ohio State University*. He also has six publications in refereed scientific

---

215   Culp, 1975, p. 142.

journals, including one of which he was the primary author (very rare for a high school teacher).

Leonard's problems began when he spoke out, on his own time after school, in favor of exposing students to the scientific challenges of macroevolution. Intelligent design—which Candisky defined as the notion that life is too complex to be explained by natural forces alone and therefore a higher power must have been involved—was not at issue.[216] As a result of discussing his views, Bryan Leonard's June 6, 2005, *Ohio State University* dissertation defense, required for his doctorate in science education, was postponed by his advisor in order to allow the university to evaluate the barrage of complaints against him by Darwinists.[217] It now appears that the opposition is so great that he will not graduate.[218]

The trigger for his problems was when mathematics professor Brian W. McEnnis, anthropology professor Jeffrey K. McKee, and biology professor Steve Rissing (a well-known active opponent of anyone who questions Darwin) wrote a letter claiming that "There is evidence that Mr. Leonard's dissertation committee has been improperly constituted and that his research may have involved unethical human-subject experimentation." The letter was sent to Carole Anderson, interim dean of Ohio State's graduate school, in a clear effort to prevent Bryan Leonard from earning his doctorate at OSU.[219] The "experimentation" the letter refers to is actually Leonard's state-approved instruction to his high-school student class! The objectors also claimed that the "panel is stacked with creationists and the research might be unethical." Professor DiSilvestro, who is on the committee, responded to this charge as follows:

> Lynn Elfner, of the Ohio Academy of Sciences, is quoted as saying that the dissertation committee members "are not qualified to judge science. They are avowed creationists." Actually, none of us call ourselves creationists. I have written on Intelligent Design, but that hardly makes me unable to judge science.[220]

---

216 Candisky, 2005, p. 1C.
217 Stokes, 2005, p. 12.
218 Interview of Ohio State official by Jerry Bergman. Official's name withheld to protect his career.
219 Annie Hall, 2005.
220 DiSilvestro, 2005, p. 8.

Catherine Candisky noted that the three objectors had not even read Leonard's dissertation and based their comments solely on their perception of the testimony that he presented before the Kansas Board of Education! Or, in Stokes's words, they based their opinion "on clues" in his testimony before the Kansas State Department of Education in May of 2005.[221]

The main question that Leonard researched for his dissertation was: "When students are taught the scientific data, both supporting and challenging macro-evolution, do they maintain or change their beliefs over time? And what empirical, cognitive and/or social factors influence students' beliefs?"[222] This concern is of much interest to science teachers, and is a question some people would much prefer remains unanswered by scientific research. Leonard's dissertation topic has produced a storm of outrage from some Darwinists.[223] Mark Bergin concluded that curious college students can face grave consequences for researching the results of teaching the weakness of Darwinism:

> Three Ohio State University professors recently launched a public smear campaign against graduate student Bryan Leonard, whose dissertation studied the effects of teaching Darwinism's weaknesses alongside its strengths. The professors accused Mr. Leonard of unethical behavior for challenging evolution, but they did not refute Mr. Leonard's thesis. Nor did they read his dissertation.[224]

As of June 20, 2005, 42 pages of mocking name-calling against Leonard appeared on the anti-creation web site Panda's Thumb—and it's likely that none of the mockers have even bothered to read his thesis. This rhetoric included the following comment:

> There are no valid scientific data challenging macroevolution. Mr. Leonard has been misinforming students if he teaches them otherwise. His thesis presents evidence that he has succeeded in persuading high school students to reject this fundamental principle of biology. As such, it involves deliberate miseducation of these students, a practice we regard as unethical."[225]

221 Quoted in Candisky, 2005, p. 1C.
222 Stokes, 2005, p. 12.
223 Hoppe, 2005.
224 Bergin, 2005, p. 23.
225 Quoted in Candisky, 2005, p. 1C.

However, much scientific evidence does in fact challenge the claims of *macroevolution*, and many parents, students and administrators are very supportive of Leonard's research. Additionally, the lesson Leonard used is consistent with both the state and his school academic standards for science. Leonard was simply doing his job as a teacher and conducting his research according to established policy. Furthermore, the claim that Leonard's dissertation "pits evolutionary science against Intelligent Design" and involves exposing high school students to the question "whether evolution should be taught, alongside Intelligent Design" is false.[226] In fact, the dissertation never mentioned Intelligent Design, but instead

> evaluated high school students' reactions to a state approved curriculum presenting data supporting and challenging macroevolution. Although one reaction to the challenges could be Intelligent Design, so is saying the challenges are weak or are covered by theory modifications such as punctuated equilibrium. The students were not even presented with Intelligent Design as an alternative.[227]

The critics also cried foul because Leonard's research focuses on the teaching of evolution, yet they falsely claim that no member of his dissertation committee is a science educator or an evolutionary biologist.[228] His faculty adviser, Paul Post, is an assistant professor in the College of Education. On the committee is entomology professor, Glen R. Needham, of the College of Biological Sciences, and professor of human nutrition, Robert DiSilvestro, from the College of Human Ecology. Dissertation committees usually consist of a student's faculty advisor, another professor in the student's major field of study, a professor in the department from which the degree is being sought, and a representative of the graduate school. More important, however, is the selection of persons interested and knowledgeable about the students' thesis.

Ohio State director of research communications, Earle Holland, said the controversey forced the graduate school to review the dissertation panel "to ensure its membership is qualified and appropriate." One member of the thesis committee responded to the incorrect procedural charges by noting the dis-

---

226 Stokes, 2005, p. 12.
227 DiSilvestro, 2005, p. 8.
228 Jaschik, 2005.

sertation defense was actually postponed due to a college policy violation—the withdrawal of the "thesis ombudsperson." Furthermore, the student's committee initiated the postponing because they wanted an explanation for the

> highly irregular, last minute removal of the Graduate School representative affected without the representative's input. The policy issue, which was raised only after the postponement, involves a small university subdivision. The issue is subdivision affiliation distributions of the committee. If a mistake was made, it was duplicated by other committees, and was fostered by two university governing groups who advised on and approved the committee composition.[229]

What exactly did Darwinists find so upsetting about Leonard's thesis? It could be his findings that 89 percent of the 350 students who responded to his survey said they wanted to learn information both supporting and challenging macroevolution. In response to the case, Jody F. Sjogren opined that "evolutionists appear to be trying to shut down debate because they can't win and are quick to label anyone who challenges them as a religious fundamentalist. I think people trying to hamper academic freedom are going to find themselves swimming upstream against public preference."[230] Sjogren's group, created to defend teaching evolution objectively, was formed during the Ohio State Board of Education debate on teaching evolution.

Darwinian fundamentalists are actually trying to claim that the issue is not academic freedom, but academic and professional responsibility! Lynn Elfner, head of the Ohio Academy of Science, even claimed that "By virtue of his testimony in Kansas, he [Leonard] is trying to influence public policy with research that has not passed muster in graduate school."[231] If his critics have their say, his work will be censored regardless of the validity of his findings.

The charge that his thesis committee was "stacked" is also disingenuous: all thesis committees are stacked in the sense that the committee members all have good will toward both the project and the candidate or they would not be on the committee. To require a thesis committee to include people hostile to the candidate is counterintuitive, and irresponsible. Furthermore, it is improper

---

229 DiSilvestro, 2005, p. 8.
230 Quoted in Candisky, 2005, 1C.
231 Quoted in Candisky, 2005, 1C.

at such a late stage to debate basic foundational questions about the design of his research. At a university, a student in the dissertation defense stage has been given approval for each stage of his thesis, and to claim at the end of this long process that his work is unacceptable is virtually unknown in academia. To claim after four to six years of successful work that a student cannot meet the requirements is also problematical.

The real issue in this case is that people with political motives who are not on the committee (and have not even read the thesis) are improperly interfering in a student's degree process. Fortunately, many people have seen through this thinly veiled attempt to censor Leonard. As Charles Mitchell asked, "even if Leonard's thesis *did* question evolution" should not the dissertation be "judged on its reasoning and analysis, not its point of view?" Mitchell argued that even if Leonard's thesis was on Intelligent Design:

> Ideas and theories are made to be questioned—mine certainly were in college, and I am stronger today because of it. The purpose of the academy (theoretically) is the search for truth, and Leonard thinks he has found it in Intelligent Design, just as most others think Darwin found it in evolution. Such disagreements are what it's all about—they are positive steps toward finding the truth, not problems to be squelched... some people at OSU don't think a thesis can even be *discussed* because it studied (not even praised, but studied) a topic they've ruled "out of bounds" and was written by someone known for holding views they regard as wrong-headed.[232]

Mitchell concluded with these remarks:

> Evolution may well be the absolute truth... But why is it not open to question and debate? At a secular university, nothing ought to be sacrosanct—not diversity, not evolution, and not even God. As Alan often says on campuses, religious students are often asked to bear any number of indignities and insults to their faith in the name of freedom.[233]

This case has allowed many more people to observe the draconian techniques employed by Darwin fundamentalists. Evolutionist Steve Rissing claims

---

232 Mitchell, 2005, p. 1.
233 Mitchell, 2005, p. 1.

that Intelligent Design is "a brand of evangelicalism that has to have a personi-fied enemy," when in fact ID is relentlessly attacked from every angle, and is only trying to assuage its opposition.[234]

Pat Shipman, in an article titled "Being Stalked by Intelligent Design," actually suggests that Leonard's ability to nearly earn a Ph.D. at Ohio State proves that ID poses a "threat" to science. She adds that his case prompted her to "take ID seriously" adding that "this movement scares me," and it created a sense of fear for her, like "a jogger in the park at night who realizes that she is far too isolated ... Now I know that I and my colleagues in science are being stalked with careful and deadly deliberation. I fear that my days are numbered unless I act soon and effectively."[235] Her concern was not over the intolerance that Leonard experienced, but rather that he did not experience *more* intolerance, and *sooner!* Shipman should be reminded that it is not Darwinists who are being denied degrees, tenure, and grants right and left, but Dar-win Doubters. Shipman's rant is typical of the derision heaped on Leonard.

Two of the professors who were on Leonard's committee are now also be-ing threatened. An Ohio State Board of Education member obtained an e-mail written by Professor Jeffrey McKee which admitted that:

> DiSilvestro and Needham have become viewed as parasitic ticks hiding in the university's scalp, who just got exposed by a close shave. I learned in Boy Scouts to twist the ticks when taking them out, so their heads don't get embedded in the skin. Others prefer burning them off. What fate awaits OSU's ticks remains to be seen.[236]

Attorney Robert Crowther wrote that this e-mail

> reveals the mindset of so many Darwinists: they are not tolerant of those who dissent from their views. So dogmatic are they that they not only op-pose the teaching of the views of scientists who dissent from Neo-Dar-winism, but they refuse to co-exist with them in the university setting. So much for academic freedom and collegiality. If there were any doubts about Darwinist dogmatism, this lays them to rest.[237]

---

234   Stokes, 2005, p. 13.
235   Shipman, 2005, p. 501.
236   Quoted in Crowther, 2006, p. 1.
237   Crowther, 2006, p. 1.

The E. Norbert Smith Case

The E. Norbert Smith case illustrates the problems Darwin Doubters commonly experience in academia as students. After Smith had served four years in the Air Force, he worked in the electronic field for several years in the Dallas, Texas area. To further his education, he enrolled at Southwestern Oklahoma University (SOU) as a Biology major. In only the second week at the university he met Dr. Hobart Landreth, who had just received a major grant to study rattlesnake migration. To follow the patterns of the reptiles he was researching, Landreth required a specially designed small radio transmitter. When Smith learned of this need, within a month he designed a unit for Landreth.

From the outset, Smith was open and honest and informed Landreth that he did not accept Darwinism. Landreth said that this would not be a problem and that Smith would be respected solely on the basis of his work. They worked closely together over the next three years. Smith's radio transmitters enabled Landreth to follow rattlesnakes and successfully complete his research project. Shortly before graduation, Smith had the opportunity to speak briefly about scientific evidences for Creation at a local civic club. A university Dean was present and later told Dr. Landreth that Smith had "bad-mouthed evolution." That very night, Dr. Landreth came to Smith's home and, in front of his family, informed him that he would not recommend him to graduate school due to his rejection of Darwinism.

Dr. Landreth also mentioned that he had talked to the other Biology faculty, and none of them would write letters of support for him. Smith was devastated, but his excellent record soon earned him a slot for graduate study at Baptist *Baylor University*. His graduate research and course work were both exemplary (he was one of very few Baylor biology students who, as a graduate student, had published several scientific papers in peer-reviewed journals). Smith's master's thesis research was accepted for publication even *before* he graduated.

As a result of Smith's experience at Southwestern, he stayed in the closet about his creationist views at Baylor and earned an M.S. in Zoology in two years without problems. Two months after his graduation from Baylor, a paper of his was published in the *Creation Research Society Quarterly*. His major professor found out and was outraged. He informed Smith that, had anyone known of his creationist beliefs, he would *not* have been accepted at Baylor for graduate study!

Smith then applied to UCLA to complete a Ph.D. in biology. Smith notes that his extensive exposure to creation and evolution helped him do well on the UCLA entrance exams used to place students in the correct courses. He was the only one of about ten incoming doctoral students that year to totally pass all of his qualifying exams without needing any additional course work. Many of the questions on the UCLA Zoology Department qualifying exams were about biology in general, and physiology in particular, and fully 80 percent of the questions dealt in some way with evolution, a topic Smith understood well. Even though additional course work was not required, to earn the doctorate at UCLA still required seven years beyond his Master's. Because Texas Tech did not have this requirement Smith chose to complete his doctorate at Tech. Dr. Fred White, the co-chairman of his graduate committee at UCLA, and another professor, Dr. Bartholomew, both remained on Smith's graduate committee and were at Texas Tech for Smith's successful defense of his Ph.D. dissertation.

Years later, while he was teaching at ICR, Dr. White (who was the Research Director at Scripts) and Dr. Smith arranged a field trip for his ICR students. Dr. White gave the students a first-class tour and spent an entire day with them. At the end of the day, White had the students assemble in his office, which was adorned with evolution flow charts and "family trees." Dr. Smith was hoping the students would be impressed with Dr. White's research and that his experience might help to motivate some to go into research.

Two weeks after Smith completed his doctorate in Zoology at *Texas Tech University* he once again found himself in a firestorm similar to the one he had experienced at SOU. A paper of his was published in the *Creation Research Society Quarterly*, and a graduate student saw it and showed it to his major professor, Dr. Francis Rose. Dr. Rose was outraged and actually formed a committee in an effort to annul Smith's doctorate! The committee was unsuccessful and he retained his Ph.D., but Smith was unable to obtain letters of support for employment (and still has a strained relation with his alma mater).

At Texas Tech, Smith had four scientific papers from his dissertation research accepted for publication, plus several smaller articles, before he graduated. His ability as a student was never at issue, nor was his ability to do research and publish. The only problem was his rejection of Darwinism. Smith concludes from his experience that "in graduate school and beyond, one can get in deep trouble for simply asking the wrong questions. Science is, in many ways, objective, but scientists as people are not. We are all influenced by our beliefs."[238]

The Bill Keith incident

Although many of the case studies in this chapter focus on discrimination against students in higher education, the problem also exists at lower levels as well. I have documented many horror stories from high school students about confrontations with dogmatic high school science teachers trying to ram Darwinism down the throats of their students. All too typical is the following account, as related by Bill Keith:

> One evening when I arrived home from work, my wife, Lowayne, told me a very bizarre story. It concerned our twelve-year-old son Richard and his science teacher. ...his science class had been studying the subject of origins. On that particular day the teacher directed her very first question to our son, asking him how the world was formed. His answer reflected the opinion of most twelve-year-old boys or girls when he said, "It was created." Somewhat startled, the teacher asked him if he had read his textbook assignment. "Yes," he replied. "What did your textbook say?" she asked. "The textbook said we came from monkeys," he answered. "But I don't believe it—I believe we were created." The teacher could have just smiled and said something like, "Well, there are different ideas about how the world came into being."[239]

Instead, she ridiculed and harassed him in front of his peers and

> ordered him never to say that again in her classroom or she would take him to the principal for discipline. My wife was in tears as she concluded the story. It shocked and angered me. At that time I thought we still had academic freedom in this land. That the public schools were a marketplace for ideas. Apparently that was no longer true.[240]

Keith added that, ironically, he was still an evolutionist when this incident took place and that he believed in evolution because his "teachers in high school

---

238 Letter from E. Norbert Smith to Jerry Bergman, dated July 24, 2005.
239 Keith, 1982, p. 3.
240 Keith, 1982, pp. 3–4.

told me it was true and my college professors confirmed it."[241] Keith noted that several questions greatly troubled him about what had happened to his son:

> Should my son be required to be an evolutionist in order to get along with his teacher? Should he be encouraged to believe in evolution just because his father and his teacher believed it was a rational explanation of origins? Did he have the right to choose for himself? How could he choose for himself if only one concept was presented to him?[242]

He concludes that this single event in a public school science classroom revolutionized his life:

> I began to study the subject of origins. My search opened up a new world of understanding, not only about origins but also about academic freedom and scientific integrity.[243]

Keith eventually was elected a Louisiana State senator where he served with distinction.

The Michael Dini Affair

Few cases illustrate the discrimination within the academic community as well as the Michael Dini incident. A professor of biology at Texas Tech University, Dini wrote that before he would write a letter of recommendation, the student must set up an appointment, where he would ask the student:

> "How do you think the human species originated?" If you cannot truthfully and forthrightly affirm a scientific answer to this question, then you should not seek my recommendation for admittance to further education in the biomedical sciences. ... The central, unifying principle of biology is the theory of evolution, which includes both micro- and macro-evolution, and which extends to ALL species. How can someone who does not accept the most important theory in biology expect to properly practice in a field that is so heavily based on biology?... physicians who ignore or neglect the Darwinian aspects of medicine or the evolutionary origin of humans can

---

241   Keith, 1982, p. 4.
242   Keith, 1982, p. 4.
243   Keith, 1982, p. 4.

make bad clinical decisions... If modern medicine is based on the method of science, then how can someone who denies the theory of evolution—the very pinnacle of modern biological science—ask to be recommended into a scientific profession by a professional scientist?[244]

The problem developed when a premed student needed a letter of recommendation from a biology instructor to apply to Southwestern University Medical School. Taylor notes that:

> The student, a devout believer in creationism, stated he had no problem learning about evolution but had to draw the line when informed that to receive a letter of recommendation from Dini he must "truthfully and forthrightly" affirm belief in evolution. The student felt he was being discriminated against because of his belief in biblical creation.[245]

An investigation by the State Department concluded, in the words of Ralph Boyd, Jr., assistant attorney general for civil rights, that "a biology student may need to understand the theory of evolution and be able to explain it. But a state-run university has no business telling students what they should or should not believe in."[246] Chief Counsel of the Liberty Legal Institute, Kelly Shackelford, wrote that "Students are being denied recommendations not because of their competence in understanding evolution, but solely because of their personal religious beliefs."[247]

Marvin Olasky commented that Professor Dini's attempt to stop careers before they get started reminded him of his own experience years ago. He notes that:

> Since I was a Communist when I entered graduate school in 1973, my professors were impressed by the Marxist dialectic I spun in seminars. They penned enthusiastic recommendations for me; I still have one from the chairman of my program at the University of Michigan, Marvin Felheim, who wrote in 1975, "Marvin Olasky has made the most distinguished record of any of our graduate students in recent years." That recommendation sits in a folder along with angry letters that Prof. Felheim sent me in 1976, when he was chairman of my dissertation committee but—since he hadn't

---

244 Document dated February 4, 2003. Copy at http://www.scienceagainstevolution.org/v7i5n.htm
245 Larry Taylor, 2003, p. 6.
246 Quoted in Larry Taylor, 2003, p. 6.
247 Olasky, 2003, p. 36.

taught me since my first year in graduate school—did not at first realize that my views had changed.... He was angry when he read a draft of my dissertation and saw that I was no longer a Marxist. He wrote plaintively, "I thought you were one of our most intelligent students." Apparently, moving from atheistic left to biblical right causes brains to fall out. Like Prof. Dini this year, Prof. Felheim 27 years ago tried to abort an academic career: He refused to write any further recommendations and, crucially, resigned from my dissertation committee two weeks before I was scheduled to take my final Ph.D. examination. My university prospects were saved only by the support of the one conservative at that time in the Michigan history department, Stephen Tonsor, who saw Prof. Feldheim's bigotry and came on to chair my dissertation committee. One of my tasks is to remember Prof. Tonsor's boldness so that I will go and do likewise.[248]

Often students run into difficulty gaining acceptance into graduate school in the first place, as the following case history illustrates. It tells of a student who wanted to complete a Ph.D. in anthropology and had already developed a preliminary bibliography containing a couple hundred pertinent references for his thesis. He contacted a professor who was very interested in his work and then began the registration process including sending his

graduate and undergraduate transcripts and completed the required GRE test. I hadn't even got the results from the GRE test back when a letter came in the mail informing me that I was not accepted in their Ph.D. program. The university had been aware of my grades when I talked to my potential thesis advisor and my GRE test results had not even arrived yet (I scored 660 verbal, 560 quantitative, and 580 analytical) so their rejection had nothing to do with the relevant criteria. The freedom of information act allowed me access to my file which seemed in good shape. I had the distinct impression that my potential thesis director had made a phone call to the school where I completed my masters degree and learned about my creation beliefs. I have information that my advisor where I earned my masters said that, once I graduated, I might make trouble as a professor (which always had been my ultimate goal). The University where I did my B.A. and M.A. had a 3 inch thick file on me. Once, during a heated discussion during my masters committee meeting, my thesis adviser asked me why I didn't do my thesis in the theology department. He was a diehard Marxist (and since then had become involved in the Occult). I have made about 4 or 5 other attempts

---

to do a Ph.D. at other institutions, but in most of these other cases there was insufficient professorial experience there to properly direct my work. Unless someone makes a deathbed confession, I don't expect I'll ever know this side of heaven what happened. Since then I have been forced to make a very painful career change and leave the academic world, a career change that did NOT get me a stable job, but that's another story.[249]

John W. Patterson's Call for Discrimination Against Students

According to many well-known science educators, even those Darwin Skeptics still in the early stages of doubt should be discriminated against before they have a chance to formulate and solidify their views. These educators endorse the position that a professor should have the right "to fail any student in his class, no matter what the grade record indicates," and many even advocate "retracting grades and possibly even degrees, if [a person espouses creationism] after passing the course or after graduating."[250] Some professors, including former (now emeritus) engineering professor John W. Patterson of *Iowa State University*, actually believe that *it is the university's responsibility* to terminate creationists and rescind their degrees! Even students with excellent grades who produce highly regarded work should be denied their degree, he advocates, and should be expelled from the university if it is discovered that they are Darwin skeptics.

The problems Darwin Doubters experience are not accidental, flukes, or rarities, nor are they "mere coincidences." Witness the following excerpts from an interview with Patterson:

"If a faculty member observes a spectacular display of incompetence [such as doubting Darwinism], whether in class or out, he should no more pass that student than should a quality control engineer at General Motors pass along engine blocks after observing gaping cracks in them."

This is not an abstract educational issue...students who espouse creationist views have passed science courses whose subject matter [Patterson believes] shows that creationist arguments are scientifically untenable...professors in the life sciences have given stamps of approval (passing grades and diplo-

---

249   Confidential case history from the 1980's, in Jerry Bergman's files.
250   Fezer, 1984a, p. 22.

mas) to students who have publicly rejected the idea that biological evolution has ever occurred... He calls such cases "spectacularly embarrassing" and has said they "could eventually ruin [the university's] credibility" just as much as if a geophysics department passed students who maintain that science proves that the earth is flat. A university, says Patterson, owes it to society not to further unfounded notions... [and] universities should strongly support their faculty in implementing such a policy...[251]

Patterson concluded professors should have the

right to fail any student in his class, no matter what the grade record indicates... Moreover, I would propose retracting grades and possibly even degrees if such gross misunderstanding are publicly espoused after passing the course or after being graduated. [And]...the decision to retract grades and/or degrees should not be made solely on the basis of one's assertions, but also on the arguments he advances to support his assertions. Resorting to arguments based on religious commitments...would not be acceptable defenses; however, logically coherent argument based on scientifically valid evidence would be."[252]

Furthermore, many educators have stated in print that they feel it is irresponsible for a university to grant Darwin Doubters a Ph.D. degree. Flacks openly remarks that it is a "pathetic commentary on our universities that grant doctorate degrees...without fully determining a candidate's true understanding of universal knowledge and logic... The alleged concept of 'scientific' creationism is not only an illogical contraction in terminology but an absurd fiction."[253]

Patterson also argued that grades do not necessarily measure competency: A student can memorize material and be able to discern the "correct" answers on tests, yet still hold views that are "incorrect." Thus, Patterson and others argue such students should be failed or denied a rightfully earned degree or, if one was previously awarded, it should be retracted.[254] Kevin Wirth responded that this proposal "...is nothing less than gross religious discrimination... A student's command of a subject in science *can* be disassociated from his religious beliefs.

---

251   John W. Patterson, quoted in Fezer, 1983, pp. 2–3.
252   John W. Patterson, quoted in Fezer, 1983, pp. 2–3.
253   Flacks, 1985, p. 28.
254   Quoted in Zuidema, 1984, p. 17.

In other words, someone with religious beliefs can function as a scientist."[255] Is this view common? Begley,[256] in answer to the questions "can a creationist be a good scientist?" and "can a good scientist be a creationist?" concluded that mainstream researchers have answered with an emphatic "no," because no one naive enough to believe the arguments of creationists could possibly do good science.

Many of the letters written in response to this interview, published in the spring 1984 issue of *Liberty*, focused on the question, "Should a student fail because of openly advocating a creation world view." Ironically not many persons would be left to judge Darwin Doubters, in view of the fact that at least 44% of the population already claim to belong to this group, and 38% lie somewhere in between creationism and theistic evolution—only 9% believe the orthodox view that naturalistic biological evolution is an adequate theory. Quammen observes that the

"most startling thing about these poll numbers is not that so many Americans reject evolution but that the statistical breakdown hasn't changed much in two decades. Gallup interviews posed exactly the same choices in 1984, 1993, 1997, and 1999. The creationist conviction—that God alone, and not evolution, produced humans—has never drawn less than 44 percent. In other words, nearly half of the American populace prefers to believe that Charles Darwin was wrong where it mattered most."[257]

Even among college students, Webb noted "the Creationist view of science is the majority view, even among the educated portions of society."[258] Also, a question that needs to be answered in this debate is, "What arguments are clearly religious?" In sorting out these issues, Fezer noted that Professor John Patterson

suggested, "Decisions as to what is logically coherent or what is valid [nonreligious] evidence would have to be made by appropriate faculty experts or panels who might also be called to task if their rationale reflects academic irresponsibility or scholarly incompetence.".. One avowed creationist presenting nonsensical scientific arguments had been dismissed from an evolution course by the professor teaching it, but he had been reinstated by the university. The student [an honors student in zoology], Patterson says, "is as incompetent about evolution as a person can be..."[259]

---

255   Quoted in Zuidema, 1984, p. 17.
256   Begley, 1996, p. 82.
257   Quammen, 2004, p. 6.
258   Quoted in Kim McDonald, 1986, p. 6.
259   Fezer, 1984a, p. 22.

Patterson also advises that passing creationists in science courses

is virtually indefensible from both a scholarly and a scientific point of view. This is especially troublesome when the professor is made fully aware of the student's commitment to...creationism because it "gives a rubber stamp of approval to their misrepresentations of the facts of biology, geology, and physics." By discouraging the dismissal or failure of such students in science classes...the university subtly pressures faculty members "to betray their best professional judgment"—to, in short, lie about the scientific competence and scholarly trustworthiness of their students. When a faculty member yields on this point, says Patterson, he jeopardizes his own credibility as well as that of the university, because too many have come to rely on grade transcripts when evaluating the quality and trustworthiness of graduates...I suggest judging competency on his arguments—which, by the way, is where the incompetence of creationists becomes undeniable.[260]

In the two decades since this material was written this theme has been echoed hundreds of times in the popular and scientific literature, especially on the internet where the rhetoric has become far more strident, and often nasty, as will be documented in this book. One example from "scienceblogs.com" is "Creationists have to know what to cover up and or fabricate in order to make their lies complete. They are dirty liars, or simpletons" and for this reason should be denied degrees and fired from their jobs.[261]

Additional Case Studies

Although students can sometimes "believe" in God without major problems, if they openly advocate that He has done something meaningful in the past, problems could well result—and often do. Patterson's views are not unique, as is reflected by the fact that when many Professors realize that a student is seriously skeptical about some major aspect of evolution, problems *often* develop as we have noted occurs with faculty. One graduate assistant, according to Richard Culp, was rather blunt, stating: "We teach evolution here at this university and, if you don't believe in evolution, you shouldn't be here!" Culp explained his own situation as follows:

---

260   Fezer, 1984a, p. 22.
261   http://scienceblogs.com/pharyngula/2008/02/are_there_no_intelligent_creat.php

During my undergraduate years at Purdue University, I learned how... [the evolutionists'] intolerance could affect a creationist's career. In my sophomore year, the professor of plant anatomy, an agnostic, asked me to work with him in my free hours...The work involved preparing microscope slides for laboratory classes. The professor drilled me in the proper techniques of cutting, straining, and mounting ultra-thin plant sections. I thoroughly enjoyed the work and the professor decided to recommend me for a scholarship in the botanical sciences to a friend of his at the University of California, where I could obtain the doctor's degree. I was not a Christian then, and this had a tremendous appeal.[262]

Culp notes that his research and the work with his professor went well until he became a Christian. Then, he says, his professor's attitude toward him completely reversed:

Before, he had boasted that I was "better without a course in microtechnique than students with the course," but now he rationalized that I was more of the scholar type who was not as adept with the hands; on another occasion, he downgraded my intelligence, inferring my grade average was high because I was a bookworm [Culp graduated *summa cum laude* in biology from Purdue]. I explained that I worked up to thirty hours per week apart from my studies and often had time to read over my lesson only once. He [now also felt] ... that he could no longer recommend me for the scholarship. This bombshell fell in my senior year (about one year after my conversion), when scholarships were scarce and we were still feeling the effects of the depression... Fortunately, the head of the botany department knew the situation and wrote the professor in California. My overseer, under pressure from his superior, finally relented and recommended me for the scholarship, which the gracious California botanist offered. This vindicated me, but by that time I had already accepted an assistantship at the University of Michigan.[263]

Some students try to compromise, yet still fail to earn their degrees. A creationist working on his Ph.D. in zoology from a major university was successfully able to hide his beliefs as an undergraduate, and thus was admitted to the Ph.D. program without problems. He completed his course work with almost straight A's, still successfully hiding his beliefs (most of his professors were

262 Culp, 1975, pp. 141–142.
263 Culp, 1975, pp. 141–142.

not even suspicious that he was a creationist). Toward the end of his program, the chairman of his thesis committee discovered his serious reservations about evolution. Not knowing exactly how to deal with the student, he discussed his concerns with the student's committee after his oral Ph.D. thesis defense.

It was decided that they would permit the student to graduate *only* if he took four more courses specifically in evolutionary biology. The student agreed, and the agreement was formalized in writing. After completion of the extra courses, the thesis committee asked if he now "believed in evolution." When he responded, "No, I am more firmly convinced of the validity of creationism than ever before," the thesis committee reneged on their agreement and decided not to grant him the degree. Litigation failed to rectify the situation. The problems that creationists experience are clearly due to their conflict with the dominant paradigm in science—widespread acceptance of evolutionary naturalism.

In another case a student completed course work for a degree in evolutionary biology and was still denied the degree when he expressed skepticism about Darwinism. The student, Dirk Ronhaar, was attending *Rice University* and had nearly completed his Ph.D. in evolutionary biology, specializing on insect reproductive behavior. Although his GRE's in biology were exceptionally high (770), as were his grades, his committee removed him from the university because his skepticism about Darwinism surfaced while he was studying for his candidacy exam. He expressed his concerns in a meeting with his professors and students on Friday, September 7, 2001, and since then his professors have openly refused to support him.

However, his concerns were not new, because he had expressed some of them to his professors four years previously when he came to Houston to complete his interview. Despite his statements, he was accepted into their Ph.D. program, but evidently they felt he would eventually conform to a more compatible Darwinian view over the course of time. The repetition of his concerns after four years of study caused his advisors to decide to end their academic relationship with him. He tried, through grievanced procedures, to complete his degree in the department of Evolutionary Biology but, unfortunately, all three grievance committees ruled against him, and informed him that the University was justified in expelling him from the program.

Now that *Rice University* no longer supported him, he has tried *in vain* to finish his Ph.D. at another university. He has been studying the subject for his thesis, i.e., the evolution of sociality in insects, for almost five years (partly in order to obtain his M.S. degree) and does not want to lose the large amount of time and money that he has invested in his research. His thesis is a critique of Hamilton's theory, which forms the backbone of the evolutionary explanation for sociality in insects. Completion of his degree requires mainly completing a literature review on this subject.

Sometimes tenacity is all it takes to deal with intolerance. A 20-year-old Anthropology student I know of earned a zero grade for speaking against evolution. He claimed that the professor required him to select a topic that was

> relevant to the class, and, of course, evolution was a big part of the class. She made horrible comments on my paper, even though she promised that she wouldn't hold our beliefs against us. I went to her personally first when she tried to fail me in the class by saying that I did not do the major assignments and projects, but I was smart enough to make copies. I sent them to her and I said if you still have objections about what I deserve then I will personally go to the head of the department. I received my grade promptly, a 4.0 GPA.[264]

The experience of this student reveals yet another tactic often used against Darwin skeptic students who are deemed unfit to graduate – that of losing or misplacing their work. Wise students will make sure that all the work they produce is date and time stamped and signed when handed in.

Conclusion

As this chapter documents, the often blatant discrimination against Darwin Doubters often begins before one is even able to enter a professional career. The representative cases reviewed here are only a few of hundreds that I have uncovered and researched. They are also only the tip of the iceberg. The end result is those who question Darwinism are often not ever able to enter their chosen career, or soon learn that they must remain firmly in the closet. This is one reason why the true number of scientists who reject orthodox Darwinism remains largely hidden.

---

264   Interview of anonymous Anthropology student by Jerry Bergman. The student did not want his name revealed.

Chapter 4: The Public Lynching of Roger DeHart

The ACLU claims to champion the rights of all Americans, but in fact its members appear to be very active in suppressing the civil rights of certain groups. Sears and Osten wrote that the ACLU uses their 176 million dollars in assets and over 1,000 attorneys to "engage in an ongoing campaign of legal intimidation, misinformation, and fear" especially to suppress the rights of Darwin skeptics.[265] The ACLU's attack on religion is also well-documented in David Bernstein's book *You Can't Say That.*[266] Bernstein observes that anti-discrimination activists, including the ACLU, now often have "little regard ... for civil liberties" of certain groups, especially of conservative Christians.[267]

One of the ACLU's most common targets is Darwin skeptics of all stripes. In the words of Carl Sommer, the "ACLU has been in the forefront of the battle to eradicate any trace of scientific creationism" and also, as of late, any criticism of Darwinism in public schools. ACLU lawyer, Robert F. Smith, after closely following Darwin skeptic literature, lectures, and debates for several years, made this frank confession almost 30 years ago:

> Based solely on the scientific arguments pro and con, I have been forced to conclude that scientific creationism is not only viable theory, but that it has achieved parity with (if not superiority over) the normative theory of biological evolution... creationists have been scrupulous to adhere to strict discussion of science alone. Not religion! Statements to the contrary are false. Contrary to the allegations ... no creationist professors are seeking to "require public schools to offer courses and textbooks that support the literal Genesis account of creation." Nor can it be legitimately suggested that scientific creationists are "disguising fundamentalist religion in scientific jargon," or that they are working for some covert "advancement of sectarian religion."[268]

Unfortunately, the quote is still very true today. The ACLU has ignored the advice of its own attorney, and has continued to pursue a policy of intimidation, harassment, and outright suppression of Darwin skeptics of all types. This

---

265 Sears and Osten, 2005, p. 4.
266 David Bernstein, 2003, pp. 145–153.
267 David Bernstein, 2003, p. 144.
268 Smith, Robert 1980, p. 24

behavior supports Fox News talk show host Bill O'Reilly's oft-stated claim that the ACLU is now the most dangerous organization in America. The following case study documents the events of a high-school teacher who was targeted by the ACLU in Washington State a decade ago. Most of the comments from Roger DeHart in this chapter were prepared by DeHart for this chapter and, as is true of all case studies in this book were reviewed by the subject of the chapter.

From Teacher to Martyr

Since 1987 Roger DeHart had taught biology and environmental chemistry at Burlington-Edison, a small rural town about an hour due north of Seattle between Puget Sound and the northern Cascade Mountains. On a hot summer day in late July of 1997, Roger was starting his tenth summer as a smoke jumper (one who fights forest fires) in eastern Washington State, when Paul Chaplik, the superintendent of the school district where he taught, called. The superintendent said: "Roger, we have received a complaint against you from the ACLU. It involves your teaching of evolution. It is nothing to get excited about. I just need you to respond to the charges in writing when you return to school."[269]

Roger liked Dr. Chaplik. Roger also liked the school system where he taught, which was the first school district in the state of Washington to deal with the serious drug abuse problem by requiring drug testing for all students involved in extracurricular activities. The unit Roger enjoyed teaching most was the two-week origins unit, which he usually presented late in the school year. This unit was a required part of the biology class. He would start this unit by showing *Inherit the Wind*, Hollywood's version of the famous 1925 Scopes Monkey Trial. DeHart recognized that the film was "historically inaccurate" and openly ridiculed Christians at every turn, but he thought the film was useful because it engaged the students and produced good discussion. DeHart then helped students to understand that learning about differing interpretations of the evidence was useful in their education.

In the film the defense attorney asked to have a phrase posted above the courthouse that read "read your Bible daily" replaced with "read your Darwin daily." This led to excellent discussions regarding how science and religion are

---

269   DeHart, 2004.

different. DeHart concluded that the most significant point of the film occurred when the defense attorney told the court that the trial was really about the "right to think." He would then ask students about the current situation in education: did they think that all points of view were allowed to be presented and discussed? DeHart discovered that the "brighter students would realize that only one interpretation was being allowed today and how the situation was now the complete opposite of what the film was portraying as happening in 1925." He describes the rest of his teaching procedure as follows:

> I would then teach the two chapters from the text in a straight-forward manner (I did not teach the last chapter on human evolution but neither did the other biology teacher). The last day of the two weeks I would use about 15 minutes to list the 5 strongest arguments presented by the book for evolution and then list 5 arguments given by other scientists who questioned evolution. I would then hand out a section from a chapter of the book *Of Pandas and People* written by San Francisco State University biologist Dean Kenyon.[270]

He continues, noting that he had the class read articles and then answer a series of questions about them. DeHart then gave students the option of writing a position paper or participating in a debate. The paper required students to discuss the three best evidences that supported their stance and the three that opposed it. While students were writing papers, those who had chosen to debate would meet with others supporting their viewpoint to work on their arguments. DeHart would make sure that there were an equal number of presenters on each side, and that each side had equal time to present their case. The students would then debate and the class would discuss the debate. It is important to stress that these debates were religiously neutral. DeHart writes:

> I was careful never to mention God or the Bible in any of my presentations but would try to steer students away from using the Bible or making religious arguments. I would caution them that using the Bible would open up the debate as to whether or not the Bible was true. We did not have time to do this and it was not the goal of this class. I tried to maintain neutrality throughout the unit. When students would ask me what I believed I would

---

270 DeHart, 2004.

often respond that it was not critical to the debate. It was better that they decide for themselves, free from my influence.[271]

DeHart noted that "Sometimes the debates would get heated. I would caution students to maintain a respectful attitude toward one another and encourage presenters not to take the debate personally."

The Complaint

The charges from the ACLU represented the first complaint that DeHart had received in over a decade of teaching the unit on Darwin.[272] He later discovered the complaint was made by Emma Height, a student whose parents were both attorneys. The complaint claimed that DeHart was setting aside the approved district curriculum and replacing it "with the teaching of the religion of creationism" from the "creationist book" *Of Pandas and People* and was proselytizing students. When fall classes started, DeHart met with Dr. Chaplik and explained to him in detail what he covered in class. Dr. Chaplik then conducted his own investigation, including interviewing several pupils, and found no evidence of impropriety. In fact, students with differing viewpoints on origins went out of their way to say that they felt DeHart covered the topic in a fair and equitable manner. Dr. Chaplik then relayed the results of his investigation to the ACLU lawyer, who seemed determined to stop at nothing short of getting DeHart fired. The ACLU then demanded that the district provide copies of all materials that DeHart gave to his students, including his teaching outline. Shortly thereafter the Darwin advocacy group, *The National Center for Science Education*, notified the school district that

> evolution and only evolution should be taught in the public school classroom and to discuss anything else would be advocating a religious view. It went on to say that no real scientist debates whether evolution occurred and then enclosed a damning review of "Of Pandas and People" stating that it has no place in a science classroom because it offers a supernatural explanation of nature and that is outside the realm of science.[273]

---

271 DeHart, 2004.
272 Foster, 2000a.
273 DeHart, 2004.

Another ACLU correspondence titled *Illegal Teaching of Sectarian Religious Views at Burlington Edison High School,* directed the district to discontinue using these materials and inform "present and past students of DeHart and their parents that unauthorized objectionable materials were used and that these materials prevented students from properly learning about the scientific theory of evolution which is the foundation for understanding more advanced science."[274] DeHart explains that the tenor of subsequent letters became more and more threatening:

> I got a sense early on that this situation was not going to go away. I soon felt the need to seek legal counsel. I called several of the well known Christian legal groups and was amazed at the lack of concern or cooperation that was expressed to me. I was basically told 'you're on your own'. Finally, someone suggested the Rutherford Institute who put me in touch with a local attorney, Rick Sybrandy. Rick became a good ally and was a Godsend.[275]

The importance of the ACLU involvement was critical. The local school board unanimously backed DeHart when the approach he used to teach origins first became public in 1998, but "the threat of a lawsuit by the American Civil Liberties Union—on the grounds that 'Intelligent Design' is religious and therefore illegal to teach—changed all that."[276]

In the spring of 1998, the ACLU evidently started intimidating DeHart by contacting the local papers to spread their allegations concerning DeHart's teaching.[277] The ACLU appeared determined to first try the case in the local press, and in the following six years at least fourteen front-page stories resulted. The outcome of these articles, DeHart stated, was that he learned what being tried by the media was like. First the *Seattle Times* ran an article on the complaint that led to several Seattle television stations running news stories on the Burlington situation. DeHart stated he knew he needed to be cautious concerning the media, but had no idea to what extent:

> One of the most dishonest pieces of journalism occurred when Channel 5 came to Burlington and interviewed several of my students. None of the

---

274   Email from Roger DeHart to Jerry Bergman, dated April 29, 2008.
275   DeHart, 2004.
276   Savoye, 2000, p. 1.
277   Pearcey, 2000a, p. 23.

students interviewed felt that I was doing anything inappropriate. It was then out of desperation to present a controversy that the reporter cornered a special education student and asked him if religion should be taught in a biology classroom. Of course he answered that it was inappropriate to do so. The interview when aired gave the impression that the student was in my class and that he felt I was teaching religion.[278]

About this time a group now called "Science or Myth" found out that DeHart was a "fundamentalist" (their term, and one that DeHart feels is name-calling; DeHart is a Baptist and prefers to be referred to as such) and seemed determined to get him fired. The May 30, 1998, *Skagit Valley Herald* filled the entire front page of the Saturday paper with three articles on the controversy. The headlines were anything but neutral, with one even proclaiming: "Teaching or Preaching?" The *Herald* services about 50,000 people, and the editor, with whom DeHart corresponded several times, was a member of a local evangelical church. DeHart felt he was more accurate in reporting the controversy than those who were less sympathetic.

The editorial page of the paper published scores of letters on both sides for the next four years. Many letters were from students, nearly all concluding that DeHart was very fair and balanced, and did not offer personal opinions in his teaching, but allowed students to think for themselves. The editor received so many letters that he claimed his day "was filled with reading letters to the editor and selecting those that would be printed."[279] The editor also claimed that he had even received letters from scientists across the United States about the case, but his policy was to print letters only from *local* residents.

Many of the letters were vicious personal attacks on DeHart. An opposition group of atheists, local humanists, and college professors soon formed an organized letter-writing campaign designed to try DeHart in the press. Some names would be seen over and over, even though contributors were limited to just one letter per month. Their stated goal was both to shape public opinion and remove DeHart from his teaching position. Many claimed that he was teaching religion, although students consistently testified that he did *not* teach

---

278   DeHart, 2004.
279   DeHart, 2004.

religion. In fact, students could not even tell what religious position he held.[280] Soon, full-page ads appeared that unscrupulously attacked DeHart.

Kelley, in a study of this case, concluded that the early support by members of the school board for DeHart was unanimous and that, according to the letters they had received, most of the community appeared to support Dehart.

> "If this was something out of line with the philosophies of the district, then the board would take exception and direct the building administrator to deal with it," said school board member Mark Leander. "But that isn't the case here." The question is, is he teaching the district-adopted curriculum? The answer is yes," Leander said. ...to approve the supplemental materials DeHart gives his class ... would be unneeded micro-management of teachers. ..... David Hansen, Burlington board member, said his district is not about to give in to the ACLU on this matter.[281]

Of course, they eventually did "give in."

A group formed in support of DeHart included a local physician, Paul Creelman, and businessman, Jerry Benson. Both considered themselves to be theistic evolutionists before hearing of DeHart's situation and the arguments on both sides. They both put their reputations on the line to support him. Later, in 2002, after Dehart had resigned from the Burlington school district, both ran for the Burlington School Board (one won a seat, the other lost his bid), and the defining issue became their support for teaching Intelligent Design.

Before the end of the 1997/1998 school year, two events would be pivotal in DeHart's life. The first was a letter from biologist Jonathan Wells, a scientist with two doctorates (one from Princeton, the other from Berkeley) espousing support for his position, and expressing a desire to meet with him. The second was a meeting with DeHart's school board at the end of the school year. At the school board meeting DeHart was asked to present the materials that he used in his two-week unit on origins. Several board members had children in his class and after reviewing his material, *the board expressed unanimous support for his teaching methods and curricula.*

---

280 Pearcey, 2000a, p. 23.
281 Kelley, T, 1998, p. 1.

DeHart's attorney, Richard Sybrandy, also attended, and gave the board a well-written and thorough legal opinion stating that the board had little to fear if faced with a lawsuit. This board meeting was also to be the last for Superintendent Dr. Chaplik who would retire at the end of the school year. His successor, Dr. Rick Jones, was at the meeting and listened intently to the discussion. Jones then asked a question that raised a red flag in DeHart's mind (and also showed Jones' lack of knowledge of the issues):

> "Why can't we also teach about the Indians' views of origins as well as other religions?" I was quick to answer that there are only 2 scientific answers to the question of origins, either life is the result of a purposeful design or it is the result of nature and its chance randomness producing merely the appearance of design.[282]

The next fall, DeHart was asked to attend a meeting with Beth VanderVeen, the principal, and the new superintendent Rick Jones. In the meeting, DeHart was presented with a letter stating that the district was denying his right to the use of any supplemental materials—even articles from *Science* and *Nature*! DeHart was to teach using the textbook contents *only*. He "responded with shock," and stated that he was unsure whether or not he could abide by this decision. DeHart soon came to realize that the new superintendent also had problems with his teaching philosophy. Dr. Jones brought in new legal counsel and got a new legal opinion on the case.

Problems next surfaced at the first teacher in-service meeting at, of all places, a Lutheran camp in the neighboring city of Bellingham. The meeting, for the high school staff (around seventy persons), was led by the new superintendent. Soon after it began, Dr. Jones stepped away from the podium, moved to a position behind DeHart and placed his hands upon DeHart's shoulders and stated that one of his goals was to improve communications in the district and the place to start was with DeHart:

> He complimented me on my record as a teacher but went on to say that a lot of people in the room probably had questions about what was going on. He stated that they would be reading about it in the evening paper. Basically

---

282   DeHart, 2004.

I was being censored because what I was doing, no matter how well-intended it was, was illegal. The school district did not have the funds to fight 2 potential court battles, the other being the drug testing. He went on to say that not only was the school district at risk of a lawsuit but that each school board member could personally be found liable. At that moment I felt very alone. I responded to both Dr. Jones and the principal that they were merely giving their opinions and that legally there was a debate. The principal even went on to caution the teachers about giving opinions on *any* subject discussed in class. Immediately 2 of my teacher friends raised their hands. Charlie Herzberg stated that he had held debates on environmental issues in his class of seniors. He commented that an intelligent, politically liberal student was asked to defend a position that was contrary to her beliefs in one of these debates. She did such a good job on the debate that Charlie asked how she learned to do that. She replied "in Mr. DeHart's class." An English teacher, Ken Tallquist, then commented that he was not in favor of the ACLU dictating what was (or was not) taught in the district.[283]

As a result, a heated debate on the ACLU ensued, an agenda that continued for the rest of the day during side conversations. That evening the headline in the local paper read "Creationism out of B-EHS classroom."[284] In response to the media coverage, DeHart admitted that he had no problem admitting that he was a creationist, but that creationism was not what he had taught in the classroom. He went on to remark:

> I also cringed at the "ism" suffix, implying a philosophy or a belief. It quoted Dr. Jones saying "We're going to stick to the teaching of science." I never thought I was doing anything but teaching science. In another article Dr. Jones stated "Science is not about beliefs. Science is about what we know at this time." That was also interesting since Darwinists are always quick to give us promises about what science will discover in the future about the fitness of naturalistic methods. He went on to say "As teachers, we encourage students to seek their own truth through their church or parents." He really didn't mean truth. Science in most people's minds is the search for truth, religion is a nice belief but subservient to science.[285]

---

283 DeHart, 2004.
284 "Creationism out of B-EHS classroom." *Skagit Valley Herald* August 28, 1998.
285 DeHart, 2004.

About this time DeHart received a call from The Discovery Institute. They arranged a meeting between DeHart, his attorney, his family doctor (for moral support), and Dr. Jonathan Wells. DeHart learned that there was a local group of over 40 Ph.D.'s, writing, researching, and sharing information about the many problems with Darwinism. It was then decided that the four of them would meet with Discovery Institute leaders on the following Friday evening. DeHart commented: "I remember the meeting well. I was humbled to think that these academics were interested in my situation. As a result of the meeting, the Discovery Institute made a pledge to help me."

A meeting was arranged in October, 1998, with the superintendent, the principal, DeHart's attorney, Dr. Wells, David DeWolf (a member of the Discovery Institute and a professor of Law at *Gonzaga University* in Spokane, Washington), and DeHart. The Intelligent Design advocates presented a formidable case based on their greater experience and familiarity with the legal issues surrounding biological origins. The superintendent and principal, for the most part, listened and took notes. The result of the meeting was a compromise requiring DeHart to submit a list of supplemental materials for official approval by the district. He had not done this previously, and neither had any other high school teacher.

On his list were articles from *Time, Scientific American, Science*, as well as sections from *Darwin's Black Box, Of Pandas and People*, and the *Access Research Network*[286] website. None of the articles mentioned God, the Bible, or creation. A meeting was set up between the school attorney, Dr. Jones, and Rick Sybrandy with David DeWolf. The consensus was that DeHart's methods were all legally defensible and that to censor him might, indeed, be a breach of his academic freedom, which could place the school in even more of a legal bind.

In May of 1999, principal Beth VanderVeen again attempted to reduce De-Hart's academic freedom and limit further the material critical of evolution that he could use in his class, allowing him to use only a four-page excerpt from *Pandas* to

> introduce students to the concept of irreducible complexity. She added that he was not to use the words "God," "creation," "designer," or "Intelligent Design," and he was required to include for balance a pro-evolution article

---

286 www.arn.org

responding to irreducible complexity: "If he wants to show the ongoing controversy and debate, then he needs to do so in a balanced manner. Both sides are to be discussed openly and fairly."[287]

DeHart says he "was feeling pretty good at this point" because he could at least teach the controversy (which is all he ever wanted to do), but this was soon to change as the administration soon implemented a new strategy. Instead of the principal approving the materials, she passed them on to a newly formed "curriculum committee" that was dominated by two card-carrying ACLU- member teachers. These two specifically sought positions on the committee so that they could vote on the materials that DeHart was introducing. The committee stalled, and waited for five weeks to make a decision. Eventually, the committee ruled that *none* of DeHart's supplementary materials could be used in his classroom. The reasons cited included the claim that the materials he wanted to use on evolution to balance the textbook would "overshadow the existing curriculum" (in spite of the fact it was made clear that this was just a possible list of materials). This reason was repeated in spite of the fact that the biology text he wanted to "balance" contained over 150 pages written from a strictly Darwinian perspective.

Other reasons included the allegation that some students might be swayed into thinking that Darwinism was not true—which the curriculum committee felt would be "unfortunate." DeHart concluded that the committee actually did not care if Darwinism was true; it was the curriculum that the school had adopted; so only it could be taught. One real concern of the committee was that the district might face a lawsuit if DeHart used *any* materials critical of Darwinism, even those from the leading two science journals in the world, *Science* and *Nature*! Making such a determination was not the role of the curriculum committee, but was a question for the attorneys to decide. Numerous alternatives had been discussed whereby the district could seek legal clarification through the courts without ever being held legally responsible.

The committee's decision surprised DeHart, because a few committee members had earlier privately expressed much appreciation for DeHart's teaching. For the decision to come back unanimously in opposition to him was a

---

287   Quoted in Forrest and Gross, 2004, p. 218.

harsh setback. In a follow-up meeting with the principal, fearing a lawsuit, De-Hart again made a compromise agreement: He would no longer be allowed to show the *Inherit the Wind* video or even hold class debates on Darwinism. Nor was he allowed to introduce Intelligent Design. He could, though, criticize Darwinian evolution, but for every article that used that was critical of Darwinism, he had to give to his class an article that countered the criticism:

> Apparently the 150 pages of text supporting evolution were not persuasive enough for the students. I chose to stick with a four page section from *Of Pandas and People*. The article relayed problems in mutations as being the mechanism for evolution, differentiated between micro and macroevolution, and told of the integrated package of adaptations contained in a giraffe. As balance, I handed students a copy of an outline of the evolutionary theory that I had downloaded from the internet. This compromise did not satisfy the Darwinists in the district. On Saturday, June 5th, headlines read "Teacher gains OK to use creationist text." This was another example of a charged headline and one that stuck in the craw of the local humanists.[288]

By July of 1999 DeHart was told in writing that he was to teach Darwinism only as proven fact, and was not to "introduce terms such as God, Creation, Intelligent Design, or a Designer into your presentation."[289] This response was ironic because DeHart estimates that over 70 percent of his students were very open to Intelligent Design by the end of the unit. As Gibeaut notes,

> The sailing was smooth for DeHart, whom students on both sides of the controversy describe as a popular, easygoing teacher who sometimes breaks up the classroom tedium with stories about his summer experiences as a smoke jumper for the U.S. Forest Service in eastern Washington.[290]

In the fall of 1999 several events added to the already highly charged atmosphere. A formal complaint was filed with the school district, and DeHart was forced to meet with a couple of hostile parents. DeHart "was becoming a big target." He also received a cryptic letter written by a biology professor at Evergreen

---

288   DeHart, 2004.
289   Letter from Beth C. VanderVeen to Roger DeHart, dated July, 1999.
290   Gibeaut, 1999, p. 53.

State College in Washington State who had learned of DeHart's "interesting teaching style" and asked if he would furnish him with a copy of his lesson plans. DeHart did not send the material that he used because he knew this professor wanted only to discredit him.

About twenty years earlier he had attended a debate between that professor and creationist Dr. Duane Gish. The professor later spoke at an evening gathering held at the high school where he painted DeHart as a "misguided teacher who was leading students back into the dark ages." Furthermore the local community college claimed without evidence that students coming from DeHart's high school "lacked basic scientific knowledge." This, of course, was a direct attack on DeHart based solely on ideology, since no test had been administered to DeHart's students to evaluate such claims.

DeHart's situation was also beginning to catch the attention of the national media. In October of 1999, American Bar Association journalist John Gibeaut flew in from Chicago, claiming that he was impressed with how DeHart had approached the topic, and wanted to write a fair and balanced article. DeHart concluded that the published article was about as balanced as the Jerry Springer show. The article claimed that DeHart was "using a back door approach to sneak creationism into the classroom." and that he was "a creationist who for 12 years has cleverly used euphemisms and pseudoscience to illegally push the biblical version of human origins on his public high-school biology classes in northwest Washington state."[291] One source for the article was an ACLU member on the curriculum committee, who was also a math teacher at the high school who ate lunch with DeHart almost daily. DeHart knew that his son had been in DeHart's biology class and that this teacher did not appreciate his teaching approach. DeHart comments:

> The article quoted the teacher as saying that he and his wife had spent sleepless nights after learning that their son had come home after the origins unit believing that there was indeed an Intelligent Designer... the article failed to mention that this son and an older brother, both of whom were very bright and had good futures ahead of them, had been suspended from school for drug use and had actually ended up missing a large portion of the school year because of being in drug rehab programs. Also mentioned in the article

---

291   Gibeaut, 1999, p. 50, 53, 55..

were two sisters who I had supposedly ridiculed in class for their Darwinist beliefs; neither I nor any other student remembered that happening. The girls had experienced, what had been described to me, as one of the most ugly and hateful divorces... and lived with their father -- he was one of the parents who had filed the official complaint against my class with the district. Interestingly enough, their mother happened to be my attorney's secretary and she supported my teaching methods.[292]

As a result, DeHart was relentlessly attacked in the media and even by the public. Distortion, sarcastic remarks, and claims that those who question Darwin are ignorant, stupid or worse were all common.[293] One of the more vicious attacks occurred on November 24th when DeHart and his wife were out shopping. A middle-aged woman approached DeHart with concern on her face, and asked if he had read the evening paper. DeHart had not, so bought a paper. He recounts on page seven that he found an entire one-page ad had been taken out by the local opposition group and was devoted to the controversy. The large bold headlines read "We're not in Kansas, but science education is under attack in Burlington too." The reference to Kansas referred to the firestorm created when the Kansas state board of education contemplated removing questions about macroevolution from the state exam:

> The article went on to totally distort my situation. It stated I was questioning basic science from the perspective of conservative religious doctrine and that I was propagandizing children at taxpayer's expense. It warned that creationists like me reject not only basic principles of biology, but geology, astronomy, chemistry and physics. The next three-quarters of a page was filled with over three-hundred and fifty signatures that had been gathered throughout the neighboring towns and at the bottom was a form soliciting contributions for the Burlington-Edison Committee for Science Education. The editorial page was also getting nasty with letters calling for my resignation and that the school district should send me "packing."[294]

On October 20, 1999, *Skagit Parents for Truth in Science Education*—a group organized to support DeHart—sponsored a lecture by Dr. Wells to show

---

292 DeHart, 2004.
293 See, e.g., Downey, 2002.
294 DeHart, 2004.

support for DeHart. At the lecture, when Wells "told the audience that DeHart deserved a round of applause, DeHart received a standing ovation."[295] Then, in December of 1999, CNN News came to film a story which was broadcast in early February. DeHart was still not accustomed to the nearly unanimous misrepresentation by the press, but was still surprised to learn that the story was again presented as a science versus religion issue; and even though he was assured that the story would include interviews with students from both sides of the debate, he found that "only the discontented students were saved from the cutting room floor." He also noted that "the film crew was obsessed with the fact that my family actually held hands and prayed before our meals."

On May 2 of 2000, DeHart submitted a list of four articles to the principal for consideration as supplemental materials. The first was a book review from the prestigious British science journal, *Nature*, written by *University of Chicago* evolutionist Jerry Coyne about the peppered moth. The second article, written by the late Stephen J. Gould, appeared in *Natural History*, and discussed irreducible complexity. The third article appeared in *The Scientist*, and also dealt with the peppered-moth controversy. The fourth article was published in the *American Biology Teacher*, and pointed out the misleading use of Haeckel's embryo fraud common in biology texts.

In May of 2000, the district verbally informed DeHart he could not give copies of these articles, all available at any good library, to his students.[296] DeHart also claims that he was criticized for showing these articles to the principal "past the deadline" for supplemental materials even though no deadline existed for handing them in. Because DeHart had stopped using the Panda text, he assumed that these four articles would be approved without problems. Three weeks later, on May 26, 2000, he received a letter denying the use of *all four* articles. DeHart stated that he was shocked and dismayed:

> The main reasons given for the rejection were that the materials detracted from the teaching of evolution. Since the pictures of embryos didn't have Haeckel's name attached to them, it would be a distraction to look at the history of the drawings. It was also stated that the topics require a level of sophistication that does not further the goals of a basic biology course. Fi-

---

295 Forrest and Gross, 2004, p. 218.
296 Forrest and Gross, 2004, p. 219.

nally the principal stated that she also agreed with all the reasons given the previous year in rejecting my materials... It was a helpless feeling knowing that all of the reasoning in the world was not going to change this situation... The manner in which my supplemental materials were evaluated also highlighted the fact that I was being singled out like no other faculty member. My materials were submitted for approval not only to the principal but also to the science department and to selected members of the public. This was unprecedented. The administration all along had tried to drive a wedge between the other science teachers and myself and now they had accomplished their goal. We had in the past worked together very well. We were all seasoned and competent teachers. We never had any harsh exchanges but from then on there was always tension when we were together.[297]

DeHart noted that it was also a trying time in the classroom. He had scheduled the start of the origins unit in mid-May, a full two weeks after he learned of the principal's decision, and the students knew what was going on and could sense his frustration. DeHart walked into class and placed the biology text on the front desk in front of the students. He then explained to his students that, although science must question and test all ideas, they were forbidden to question Darwinism. They must accept everything in these three chapters, even though articles in scientific journals exist that directly contradicted parts of the text chapters.

DeHart recalls that several memorable events occurred that fall, including Jonathan Wells's presentation to a crowd of several hundred gathered at Burlington High school. According to DeHart, Wells showed an excellent PowerPoint presentation highlighting the scientific misinformation presented in our adopted textbook. Then in October, Ken Tallquist, the English teacher who had spoken up at an earlier meeting, asked if DeHart would come into his senior English class and discuss the controversy.

He said he was devoting four class sessions to hearing presentations on the subject. He was having the superintendent of schools and a professor at the local community college present the opposition side. Tallquist asked if I could get Jonathan Wells from the Discovery Institute to speak along with myself to present the affirmative position. The students were then to write

---

297   DeHart, 2004.

position papers: Tallquist told me later that all twenty eight students had taken the position that I.D. should be taught in biology classes.[298]

On December 13th of 2000, DeHart submitted his set of supplemental materials for the second semester of the 2000/2001 school year. This time he left out all articles written by Jonathan Wells—even those published in major science journals—and submitted the articles well in advance of the deadline the school had given him. DeHart again submitted an article from *Nature* by biologist Jerry Coyne on the peppered moth and one from *Natural History* by Stephen J. Gould that were critical of the use of Haeckel-like drawings of embryos still used in biology textbooks. The third article, authored by Intelligent Design advocate Fred Heeren, had previously appeared in the *Boston Globe*, discussing several new Cambrian fossil finds in China. DeHart also included diagrams from Jonathan Wells's newly published book *Icons of Evolution* depicting "the theorized atmosphere of the early Earth, Haeckel's embryos, a diagram showing the development of the Corvette sports car, and homology."

DeHart added that the school district then maneuvered to widen the split within the science department so as to not seem "like the bad guys":

> This time my materials were distributed to each of the department members as if these articles were to be adopted by the school. I answered that I did not expect any of the other teachers to use these materials; these were intended only to supplement my course. This was an intentional blurring between supplemental materials and adopted materials. I also replied that I had not been asked to review any of the materials used in marine biology, chemistry, or physics, [so] why should the members of the science department have a say in my materials?[299]

Of the "scores of letters school officials received on the subject, an overwhelming majority of them supported DeHart."[300] The school did not seem to be influenced by this support because on Thursday, March 22, 2000, DeHart's principal informed him that she was denying him use of *all* supplemental materials! She stated that the materials had been reviewed not only by her and the

---

298   DeHart, 2004.
299   DeHart, 2004.
300   Gibeaut, 1999, p. 3.

science department, but also by the biology faculty at nearby Western Washington University. Furthermore, she had received a letter from Jerry Coyne of the University of Chicago, who did not want his review that was published in *Nature* to be used in the class:

> "Let me get this straight," I said, "a biologist publishes an article in a professional scientific journal and then protests when a high school biology teacher wants to present his findings to his class?" ... Most school districts would be applauding a teacher who keeps current with the scientific literature.[301]

Regarding the censored materials, DeHart wrote:

> I also could not figure out how material used in over 130 districts was not suitable for our district. It surely was not illegal as were none of the other articles that I had used. *The controversy had now moved away from the question of legal culpability to one of downright censorship.* I still had the right to verbally share all that I was learning through my studies, or so I thought.[302]

A short time later DeHart received a call from Ron Thompson, the Seattle curriculum writer who said that he was writing a letter expressing approval of the district's denying the use of DeHart's materials as supplements in his class:

> He went on to ask me not to mention him or his materials in any correspondence that I might have with the media. I pressed him on his decision. He said that when the professors at Western Washington University had reviewed his material they sent out a warning to all biology teachers, calling them stealth creationist materials. He said he was going to rewrite the unit and replace it with a more traditional approach. He also was going to burn all back copies. I could not believe my ears. I suggested to him that he was caving in to the pressure and that this was not about the science but about a political agenda.[303]

Then the Sunday *Los Angeles Times* printed a front-page article titled "Seeking Science to Support Teaching of a Created World."[304] DeHart felt the article

---

301 DeHart, 2004.
302 DeHart, 2004.
303 DeHart, 2004.
304 Watanabe, T. 2001 p. 1.

was both well-written and well-researched. It accurately discussed the Burlington events, but more importantly, discussed the Intelligent Design debate in a "favorable light," accurately quoting Phillip Johnson, Mike Behe, and William Dembski. The same article ran Monday evening in the local paper. Nonetheless, in the article, the principal questioned DeHart's motivation. DeHart notes that "she thought that I was trying to get religion into the public school," and pondered on this misinterpretation:

> The problem with this reasoning is that it does not see Darwinism for what it is. It is distinctly irreligious. It misleads one into thinking that Darwinism is unbiased science and any evidence that points to design or the inability of naturalistic processes to produce the complexity of life must be religion. How far have we come since the days of Bishop Paley? I contend that Darwinism is anti-religion masked as science.[305]

On March 26, 2001, DeHart received a letter from the principal in which she tried to claim that DeHart's beliefs prevented him from teaching the adopted materials, and that he should consider another teaching assignment. She also requested a scripted outline of the evolution unit, and when DeHart had completed the outline, he was required to obtain approval from the science department chair. On March 26, 2001, DeHart responded in writing that he

> had never contended that I could not, nor did not, teach the adopted materials. I also questioned her as to what parts of the text I could correct as new scientific information was made available. Could I share with students the recent discovery that there were only 30,000 genes in humans instead of the 100,000 genes stated in the text? Or was it just the evolution units of the text that I was not free to correct information? I also wanted to know my parameters in answering student questions about Intelligent Design and evolution.[306]

DeHart concluded that his classroom had become a one-sided lecture in which Darwin's theory must have the last word due to "the scientific community's apparent reverence for Darwinism."[307] On Monday, April 30th at a meeting

---

305   DeHart, 2004.
306   DeHart, 2004.
307   Quoted in Foster, 2000a, p. 1.

between DeHart, the department chair, and the principal, as in all previous meetings, not once was the accuracy of DeHart's interpretation or the accuracy of the materials presented questioned. Instead they asked him what he was "trying to do" by using these materials:

> Some had accused me of seeking notoriety and a place in history. This was far from the truth. I am by nature not one who seeks attention. In staff meetings I generally sit quietly. I never notified any of the news agencies of any breaking information.[308]

He added that he does not shy away from controversy if he feels it has educational value and that by not responding he was allowing the media to print whatever they wanted. DeHart concluded that "the meeting was a farce. They were trying to trap me into saying something they could use as leverage to reassign (or, better yet, fire) me." On May 4, the principal wrote a letter outlining the concerns she had expressed, including the fact that DeHart had not yet provided a scripted outline of what he was going to teach. The scripted outline she had in mind was not really an outline but a word for word narrative of what he was going to say for the two week unit. DeHart concluded that this was "an unreasonable request that I doubt has ever been asked of any student teacher let alone one with 23 years of teaching experience." The letter denied him the right to verbally mention anything that was written in the supplemental materials:

> This was the breaking point. The district was actually going to muzzle me. They were telling me that I could not even share what Stephen Gould had written in a science magazine. I knew things were coming to a head. This was definitely a very low point in my life. My wife and I spent evenings discussing our future. I could not in good conscience teach evolution as the text presented it.[309]

Writer Nancy Pearcey, in her review of this case, concluded that the school by its actions was condoning the teaching of "false or misleading information" so long as that information supported Neo-Darwinism."[310]

---

308   DeHart, 2004.
309   DeHart, 2004.
310   Pearcey, 2000a, p. 23.

DeHart felt the only strategy left was to make the district's latest actions public, hoping that public pressure on the school district would force a policy change. On May 16, the local paper ran what DeHart concluded was a very accurate story highlighting the current situation. It listed the district's reasons for its denial and DeHart's rebuttals. It also notified the public that there would be a forum on the topic held at the high school performing arts center that evening. Three persons were to make presentations at the May 16, 2001 event, which was referred to as *Banned in Burlington*. Flyers were printed and displayed in prominent places around town, and several local radio stations announced the "banned" meeting.

About six hundred people attended the meeting, which included Power Point presentations by Jonathan Wells, David DeWolf, and DeHart. The president of the Discovery Institute, Bruce Chapman, set the tone for the evening with a brief introduction. Jonathan Wells spoke first, and reported on several of the icons of evolution that appeared in the school's adopted biology textbook. He showed how this evidence was being distorted and how accurate information was omitted from the adopted text.

The next talk was delivered by attorney David DeWolf. He summarized a *Utah Law Review* article[311] that he had co-authored documenting the fact that the law does not prohibit a teacher from presenting evidence criticizing Darwinism. Quoting from a law review article written on the east coast that had mentioned DeHart by name, DeWolf commented that its author had also come to the same conclusion. The U.S. Supreme Court in *Edwards v. Aguillard* clearly ruled that the Court ruling does not:

> *imply that a legislature could never require that scientific critiques of prevailing scientific theories be taught.* Indeed, the Court acknowledged in Stone that its decision forbidding the posting of the Ten Commandments did not mean that no use could ever be made of the Ten Commandments, or that the Ten Commandments played an exclusively religious role in the history of Western Civilization. In a similar way *teaching a variety of scientific theories about the origins of humankind to schoolchildren might be validly done with the clear secular intent of enhancing the effectiveness of science instruction.*[312]

---

311 DeWolf, Meyer, and DeForrest, 2000.
312 DeWolf, Meyer, and DeForrest, 2000, p. 14 (emphasis added).

DeWolf also noted the court held that

requiring schools to teach creation science with evolution does not advance academic freedom. *The Act does not grant teachers a flexibility that they did not already possess to supplant the present science curriculum with the presentation of theories, besides evolution, about the origin of life. Indeed, the Court of Appeals found that no law prohibited Louisiana public schoolteachers from teaching any scientific theory.*[313]

DeHart presented the articles that he had submitted to the school district for approval, and gave a brief history of his experience. He spoke in a calm, unemotional, rational manner. After a short question and answer period, a contingent of the opposition spoke, some wearing t-shirts that on the front read, "I.D. Intelligent Design equals Intentional Deception," and on the back read, "DeHart, teach real science. Stop wasting our money. Stop lying. Better yet resign."

Charlie Herzberg, one of DeHart's allies and fellow teacher, asked his class the following day if any of his students had attended the forum. One student raised his hand, and related that he had worn one of the stop DeHart tee-shirts. He then stated that at the end of the presentation that he took off the shirt and was now embarrassed that he wore it.[314]

DeHart did not know if any serious pressure was put on the members of the administration, but he learned that they felt more needed to be done to silence him. Early in June of 2001, DeHart learned through a counselor friend that the scheduling board had put DeHart in all physical/Earth science classes. DeHart sent an e-mail on June 4 to the principal to verify this information. The principal replied that no decisions had yet been made. A new part-time science teacher had yet to be hired, and the administration was not yet sure what DeHart's teaching assignment would be. At Burlington, physical/Earth science was traditionally a class taken by non-college bound students, and with it came more discipline problems.

---

313   DeWolf, Meyer, and DeForrest, 2000, p. 8 (emphasis added).
314   DeHart, 2004.

The physical science courses were usually taught by the newly hired science teachers and the physics teacher. On July 15 of 2001, DeHart received a form letter written by the principal and sent to all faculty listing all teaching assignments for the 2001/2002 school year. As he suspected, DeHart was assigned to physical/Earth science, and was not assigned to a single biology course. The new teacher hired to teach biology, a former student of DeHart's, did not have any teaching experience. His degree was in physical education (he was the assistant baseball coach), not biology. DeHart had asked him why he had chosen a PE major, and he responded that he started out in biology but found that it was too rigorous for him.

On July 22 the local paper carried the story. The district would not admit that DeHart's reassignment was based on ideology, likely because it could open them up to litigation. Yet it was no secret why he was reassigned. As Lightcap put it, in Earth science "the intellectual insurgent could keep his rebel theories to himself."[315] The official reason given was that changes in biology enrollment had prompted their decision. DeHart was then faced with a very difficult decision. Biology was his real interest (he graduated with a B.S. in biology and had taught it for twenty-three years). The school had already become a hostile work environment, and to be reassigned to earth science would greatly add to that stress. He did not want to look for a job in another area and move his daughter out of her senior year of high school. He also knew that, in view of the negative media coverage, it would be very difficult to find another teaching job in the region.

At this point he received a phone call from his English teacher friend, Ken Tallquist. Tallquist had left the district and taken a vice-principal job in a town about 30 miles to the south, at the largest high school in the state (about three thousand students). Tallquist mentioned a biology/physical science position that was open. He had told both the principal and vice-principal about the controversy that had surrounded DeHart, but they seemed unconcerned about this Issue, and encouraged DeHart to apply for the position. DeHart applied, and was notified that he was a finalist. The interview went well, but he was surprised that no questions had been asked concerning his past. A week later, DeHart received a call offering him the position. At this time he felt obliged to discuss his past and asked them if the district had any problem with his teaching criticisms of

---

315   Lightcap, 2004, p. 30.

Darwinism. DeHart was informed that this approach would be "good science" and welcomed. On August 9, DeHart notified Burlington schools that he would not be returning because he had accepted a position at Marysville.[316] Then, on August 10, an announcement of this appeared in the paper. Dehart recounts:

> The next day I received a voice message on the phone welcoming me to the Marysville school district and that my teaching assignment would be teaching junior high Earth science. I immediately called the Marysville administration to find out what was going on. No one in authority would talk to me and, in fact, I was told that the superintendent was on the phone that very minute with the media about my hiring. I was told that no one in the administration could answer any questions about my teaching assignment. I would have to wait for a week before the head of human resources could talk with me.[317]

After he hung up, he received a call from a reporter with the *Everett Herald*. They had heard of his hiring and wanted to do an article about his new job. It was then that he had learned that the superintendent stated to the paper the reason for his assignment change

> I was transferred so there would be no temptation to teach something that is not part of the state curriculum. In other words, I was being reassigned due to my beliefs. While Burlington had been dishonest, Marysville had come right out and stated the real reason. Headlines in the Everett paper read "Marysville on edge over the hiring of new science teacher." This prompted another Sunday front page article on Intelligent Design. After the articles ran, my attorneys went to work drafting a letter to the school district. The letter was explicit in relaying the potential legal problems that the district would be in for if they continued with their course of action. The letter was delivered to the school board president as well as the superintendent and head of human resources.[318]

The following week, when DeHart met with the head of human resources, the first words out of her mouth were, "why are you such a trouble maker?" She stated that the district had the right to put DeHart into *any* teaching assign-

---

316   Parr, 2001, p. 1.
317   DeHart, 2004.
318   DeHart, 2004.

ment that it chose. Because DeHart had not yet signed an official contract with the district, she also threatened not to hire him if he did not go along with her demands. DeHart reported that the next morning all new teachers and administrators were to meet at an Indian reservation headquarters as was their custom for "getaways." DeHart arrived early and was met at the door by Ken who, with a big smile, said he was glad to have DeHart on board:

> Apparently, the announcement had graced the front page of the morning paper. It stated that my teaching position would be at the high school and would be biology. Later in the week the superintendent's office called requesting another meeting. It was suggested that I bring representation. I called Rick Sybrandy and he cleared his schedule to accompany me to the meeting. As we entered the meeting room the superintendent, who I was meeting for the first time, became irate. She looked at Rick and said "who are you?" When Rick answered she told him that he was not welcome and he was to leave. Apparently, the district's idea of representation only meant a member of the teachers' association, not a real attorney. In the meeting the superintendent stated that she had received many e-mails and phone calls expressing displeasure at my hiring.[319]

Evidently the local atheist and humanist organizations had waged an active letter-writing and phone-calling campaign against DeHart. The superintendent stated that she had never heard of Intelligent Design, and didn't ask for an explanation. She only wanted to inform DeHart that he was to use *only* the adopted curriculum and, if he was to use *any* supplemental materials, they were to be cleared with her well in advance. DeHart agreed to comply with her request, but still encountered the same problems in this school district. The fact is, they did not like him—clearly due to his religious beliefs and not because of something he had done. This soon became obvious because the "first returning science teacher of the eleven member staff that I met was not happy with my hiring" and the "National Center for Science Education (of which he was a member) had contacted him about DeHart's hiring." This teacher added that he would be "keeping an eye" on DeHart and that "there was not going to be any teaching of ID in Marysville." Otherwise the first semester was uneventful. DeHart was

---

disappointed because the school population was so large and the administrators did not have much experience:

> It was not the quality of education that I was used to at Burlington. Another difference was that biology was only one semester long at Marysville. I later found that one of the school board member's children had been placed in my class. Apparently, I had passed the muster. What I hadn't anticipated was a change in my teaching assignment at the end of the first semester. Whether or not I was intentionally assigned to teach all physical science is a matter of controversy. However, I had one of the science teachers come and ask if I would be willing to switch assignments with him. He had a physics degree and was assigned to teach three sections of biology. He had never taught biology and would rather teach physical science. I loved the idea and the principal seemed agreeable to the suggestion. However, the superintendent's office was not in favor of the move.[320]

At this point that DeHart knew he could not trust the administrators in this district either; nor did he want to remain there. The lynching had started anew, and he recognized he would soon face the same problems all over again. The ACLU's intimidation tactics had worked. His case made the front page of *The Los Angeles Times*, and he was featured in *The New York Times*, on CNN News, and in scores of regional dailies. Often in these articles he was slandered in the vilest terms with a total disregard for the facts. Mr. DeHart taught for a year at MPHS, again earning top reviews from administrators and students, but not wanting to face this nightmare again, DeHart decided he had no choice but to resign, and did so in May of 2002.

In his quest for academic freedom, after his resignation from Marysville, he took a job in Southern California at Oaks Christian, about an hour north of Biola University where his daughter would be attending college.[321] Moving was very difficult because the DeHart family had deep roots in the community; he had built a home, had a good church family, his children were receiving a good education, and he had many close friends in the area. He continues to write and is now able to objectively teach the controversy in a private school setting.

---

320 DeHart, 2004.
321 DeHart, 2004.

DeHart was fortunate to find another biology teaching position. He now is finally out of the clutches of the ACLU's hate campaign and, finally, has the freedom to criticize Darwinism. This case illustrates how antagonistic the public schools can be to those who question Darwinism. DeHart, as of this writing, is in his fifth year at Oaks Christian, says he is very happy to be there, and is still active in helping students evaluate Darwinism, but has not yet escaped his "lightning-rod status":

> In May, Mr. DeHart was scheduled to debate origins on National Public Radio (NPR) with a pro-evolution biology teacher. Hours before the program, NPR canceled Mr. DeHart's appearance, but allowed the Darwinist teacher to speak unchecked. "Certainly, this idea that science and education is this tolerant search for truth doesn't hold true from my experience," he says now. "You'd better tow the party line. If you speak out against the orthodoxy, [the party] is going to deal with you."[322]

Conclusion

This whole DeHart controversy was unnecessary because the law at the highest court level is fairly clear. A summary of the law (titled "Religion in the Public Schools: A Joint Statement of Current Law") by 12 major organizations, including the ACLU and People for the American Way, and endorsed by 23 major religious and secular civil rights organizations, said of the recurring controversy surrounding evolution:

> Schools may teach about explanations of life on earth, including religious ones (such as "creationism"), in comparative religion or social studies classes. In science class, however, they may present only genuinely *scientific critiques of*, or evidence for, *any explanation of life on earth*, but not religious critiques (beliefs unverifiable by scientific methodology). Schools may not refuse to teach evolutionary theory in order to avoid giving offense to religion nor may they circumvent these rules by labeling as science an article of religious faith. Public schools must not teach as scientific fact or theory any religious doctrine, including "creationism," although *any genuinely scientific evidence for or against any explanation of*

---

322   Vincent, 2004, p. 30.

life may be taught. Just as they may neither advance nor inhibit any religious doctrine, teachers should not ridicule, for example, a student's religious explanation for life on earth.[323]

These directives fully endorsed DeHart curriculum and no evidence was ever presented that he was teaching religion, yet this fact was ignored. The controversy in which DeHart found himself was, according to Vincent, "a reverse Scopes Monkey Trial":

> Clarence Darrow and William Jennings Bryan had in 1925 slugged it out in court over whether teacher John Scopes could teach Darwinian evolution, but Mr. DeHart and the ACLU had from 1997 to 2001 slugged it out over whether Mr. DeHart could teach anything except evolution. Specifically, could he teach Intelligent Design?[324]

Actually, DeHart only wanted to objectively teach Darwinism. Even Dr. Eugenie Scott admitted that the "debate between theism and materialism is legitimate."[325] This is not what the ACLU wants. It appears to want only blatant indoctrination in Darwinist philosophy—and nothing less seems to satisfy them.[326]

323 Vincent, 2004, p. 30
324 Vincent, 2004, p. 30.
325 Quoted in Savoye, 2000, p. 3.
326 Bernstein, 2003; Hardaway, 2001; Johns, 2001.

Chapter 5: Professors Richard Bube and Dean Kenyon

It does not require much experience in academia to realize that although objectivity, tolerance, academic freedom, and an unbiased search for the truth are all touted as sacred virtues, universities regularly (and routinely) violate these ideals, often with impunity.[327] In the origins controversy the net is widening and attacks are increasingly being leveled even against individuals in academia who hold to some form of theistic evolution (i.e., believe that God directed evolution), as well as those who support Intelligent Design (i.e., believe that the complexity of organisms implies design by an intelligent agent), or who merely doubt that the Darwinian mechanism of differential survival of organisms produced by mutations can explain the existence of all life forms.

Numerous examples exist, and many writers have justified these attacks by arguing that theistic evolutionists are even *more* dangerous than those who accept six-day creation. Theistic evolution is more acceptable to mainline scientific naturalism orthodoxy, and thus is felt to be a more palatable approach to sneak God into the public schools.[328] This is true in spite of the fact that theistic evolution has been the ruling orthodoxy for most major Christian denominations since not long after Darwin.

The critics conclude that since this approach is more successful in breaking past the wall keeping anti-Darwinism out of the public schools, in the long run it is *more* dangerous. It would be harder to openly allow an obvious poison like arsenic to pollute the environment, but one may permit a less-dangerous poison in the environment at higher levels—which may eventually prove to be even more dangerous. Numerous organizations in the United States, such as the National Academy of Sciences (NAS) and the National Center for Science Education (NCSE), are actively endeavoring to ensure that public schools allow only nontheistic (actually atheistic) evolution, or at least functionally atheistic evolution (where God exists, but has no role in creation). These groups are especially active in opposing theistic evolutionists and Intelligent Design theorists. This chapter reviews the case studies of one theistic evolutionist, Richard Bube, and one Intelligent Design advocate, Dean Kenyon.

---

327 Dickman, 1993, pp. 181-202; Sykes, 1988, pp. 134-139.
328 Pennock, 1999 p. 26-39.

The Case of Richard H. Bube

Among the examples that could be cited to illustrate the trend of increasing intolerance toward not only the creationist world view, but also the broad view of intelligence (as opposed to chance and accident) at work in the universe, is that of Stanford University professor Richard H. Bube. Dr. Bube received a Bachelor of Science degree in physics from *Brown University* in 1946, and his Ph.D. in physics from *Princeton University* in 1950. Between 1948 and 1962, he was a member of the research staff at the RCA David Sarnoff Research Laboratories, Princeton, New Jersey, and section head for photo-electronic materials. He joined the faculty of the Department of Materials Science at Stanford in 1962. From 1975 to 1986, he served as chairman of the Department of Materials Science, the same department that was at one time ranked third in the nation by a *U.S. News and World Report* survey of professors. In September 1992, Bube became emeritus professor of materials science and electrical engineering after 44 years of continuous involvement in scientific research, and has continued to be active in the department.

Dr. Bube is a fellow of *The American Physical Society*, *The American Association for the Advancement of Science*, and *The American Scientific Affiliation*, a member of the editorial advisory board of *Solid State Electronics* (1975 - 1994), and past associate editor of *Materials Letters* (1982 - 1989). He is also a life member of the *American Society for Engineering Education* and the American division of the *International Solar Energy Society*. He is an internationally known scholar in the field of solid-state electronics, specifically on the photo-electron properties of materials—a topic on which he has written over two hundred scientific papers. His many scientific books include *Photoconductivity of Solids*, *Electronic Properties of Crystalline Solids*, *Fundamentals of Solar Cells*, *Photo-electronic Properties of Semiconductors*, and *Photovoltaic Materials*, all published by leading academic publishers, including Academic Press and Cambridge University Press. His other scholarly achievements include associate editor of *Annual Review of Material Science* from 1969 to 1983, and an editorial advisor of *Solid-State Electronics*.

Bube's Concern with Science and Christian Faith

Dr. Bube is also a recognized authority on the interaction between science and Christianity, and he has written five books in this feld, published over 324 research and scientific reviews relating science and Christianity, presented 148 papers, and spoken at over sixty college campuses in this country and abroad on the interaction between science and Christianity.[329] Dr. Bube also has the honor of having been invited as a Stanley distinguished Christian Scholar Lecturer, is listed in *Who's Who in Theology and Science*, and since 1992 has been a member of the editorial board of *Christians in Science* located in Leicester, England. He was also an InterVarsity Christian Fellowship faculty sponsor at *Stanford University*, and is a past member of the Board of the International Students Christian Outreach at Stanford. He has served as the editor of the *Journal of the American Scientific Affiliation*, a group of scientists interested in Christian issues mentioned above. Among the many important lectures that Bube has presented was a major address at a conference on science and Christianity at *Oxford University*. Bube was also an adjunct professor of theology and science at *Fuller Theological Seminary*. His lectures on science and Christianity have been presented on the campuses of over sixty colleges and universities since 1962.

Bube, a scientist of international repute, is widely known for his prodigious scholarly science writing as well as his commitment to his faith.[330] He also led a popular seminar at Stanford titled *Issues in Science and Religion*. This credit class, which focused on the conflicts and concerns related to science and Christian faith, was offered by Dr. Bube at Stanford for a quarter of a century. The course was a seminar, a format where the students read articles and books and then discussed the contents in the seminar. In effect it was a discussion session for college credit. The seminar covered a wide variety of topics related to the theme of science and Christianity, such as the Galileo affair, the Bruno case, the creation evolution controversy, the role of religion and science in society and their intersection and the nature of science. Each seminar involved between fifteen and twenty-five students, usually "with some personal involvement in Christianity" who "then passed their enthusiasm to the next generation of Stanford students."[331] In spite of the fact that

---

329   John Templeton, 1996.
330   Hearn, 1974, pp. 53-59; Bube, 1971.
331   Bube, 1989, p. 206.

the seminar was well received and no one complained about the course (it was an elective) or the instructor, for reasons unknown to Dr. Bube it was unexpectedly and without explanation cancelled. This is the story of the seminar cancellation and Bube's struggle to reinstate it.

Cancellation of Bube's Seminar

The seminar was regularly monitored, and received the "general approval and encouragement from the university office responsible." As an elective, it was not imposed upon any student. It maintained rigorous ivy-league academic standards, including numerous reading assignments and two written papers. In early 1988, without giving so much as one valid reason the seminar director suggested that it be offered as a freshman/sophomore class only, and not open to all undergraduates as previously. Bube countered that it should be open to all undergraduates, because he felt the maturity of juniors and seniors added an important ingredient to its success. In the spring of 1988, a new committee was formed to administer these seminars, but before the spring 1988 quarter started, the seminar was cancelled without explanation.[332] The committee's weak attempt to give "reasons" for the cancellation pervasively illustrated that the correct reasons could not be articulated, and those that were provided could not be defended.

The students became concerned about whether the seminar would be offered and, consequently, Bube was "bombarded by students." Bube, also concerned that it might not be offered, called the director on February 24, 1988. The director then informed Professor Bube that the committee had refused to approve the seminar because of its "lack of balance." Bube learned latter that the committee knew that Bube was an Evangelical Christian and were fearful that he may favor Intelligent Design or creationism in directing seminar discussions. They had absolutely no evidence for this view but, as we will discuss, their actual concerns were with Bube as a person, and who he was, not what he did. He did nothing objectionable and they never presented evidence that he did. Unfortunately, except for the faculty member he met with in December of 1988, Bube never learned the identity of those on the committee who cancelled his course.

---

332   Bube, 1989, p. 207.

The very next morning, Bube was in the director's office to discuss with her the reasons for its cancellation. She related that the committee (two faculty members, two students and the undergraduate dean) concluded that the seminar was "unsuitable" because it openly discussed the "relationship between only the Judeo-Christian tradition and science." They indicated that his course "would be suitable in the religious studies curriculum or under the auspices of [Stanford's] Memorial Church, but not in the committee-sponsored program for academic credit."[333] This decision must be evaluated in view of other undergraduate seminars that have been offered in the past, which included "Hindu Mythology," "Women's Literature of the Holocaust," and one that purported to shed light on the "principles of the American Conservative Movement."

Failing to obtain a valid response to his concerns, Bube then penned a letter in which he noted that the class did not focus on creation versus evolution, or Darwin versus design, but a wide range of modern science topics, and the ethical dilemmas posed by them, as related to the Judeo-Christian tradition. He also questioned the conclusion that a religious perspective "should not be espoused or defended in an academic course," arguing that no college course at Stanford (or anywhere else) "could really teach about ethics, values, morals, etc., without 'being religious in some fundamental sense—[meaning] without some kind of set of values chosen and defended on faith, whether that set of values is derived from a form of religion or from a secular world view."[334] Since Stanford is *not* a state-supported school, but an independent, private university, it is not constrained by church-state separation issues.

The director's reply of March 9, 1988 denied Bube's observation that "almost every course at Stanford espouses a religious perspective" but admitted that it is "almost impossible to teach about ethics, values and morals without engaging in a religious activity." The committee concluded that *only* a "critical examination of the religious perspectives was permissible." Could one assume by this that they meant only a position that is *critical* of religion (i.e., "negative") was acceptable in a college course?

Bube responded on March 14, 1988, in a letter stating that this seminar did, in fact, involve a critical examination of religious perspectives on sci-

---

333 Bube, 1989, p. 207.
334 Bube, 1989, p. 208.

ence, specifically noting that the course examined the insights "obtainable from authentic science on a particular issue, distinguishing them from its religious counterpart 'scientism'." The committee also concluded that Bube must add "a plurality of perspectives" to his seminar. In response, Bube noted that one cannot conclude that plurality means that "intellectual respectability is reserved *only* for an approach that treats *all* perspectives as equally viable, or for a situation in which one would attempt to treat every possible religious and non-religious position in one seminar."

He also asked: "How could one [properly and fairly] lead a seminar on science and religion issues [only] from a non-religious perspective?" Bube next wrote to Stanford's chapel dean, asking, "Can it be that Stanford has come to the point where it is being argued that the opportunity to integrate one's scientific insights with insights from the Judeo-Christian tradition is not an 'intellectually respectable' activity?" The director then suggested yet another approach: have someone with "well established academic expertise in science and religion" review Bube's course outline. An "objective third party with genuine expertise" was found to review the seminar curriculum and affirmed the objections raised by the committee!

The outside review was grossly superficial, and apparently was made primarily on the basis of a collection of handouts that Bube had used in a past seminar he had taught. The reviewer's main concern seemed to be that information favorable to the Christian moral viewpoint would be presented in the seminar. In response to this, Bube provided the committee with a list of books that he used as background readings for the seminar, which included a number of authors who reject the view that the "God theory" is a viable alternative for understanding science and the physical universe.

The irony of this case is that it would be difficult to find someone with as high a level of knowledge and understanding of the integration and conflicts of various aspects of science and Christianity as Professor Bube.

Bube Attempts Again

Bube decided to revise the syllabus again and send it to the committee for review. They responded on October 10, 1988, with the recommendation that Bube explain at the onset his "religious point of view" on the disputes that he would cover in class. It was also suggested that he include "readings from the secular humanist perspective rather than (or in addition to) Wooldridge's 'Mechanical Man'," and include major writings against creation and for evolution, such as Stephen J. Gould's *Panda's Thumb*.

In response to this recommendation, Bube called the director and requested a meeting. On December 16, 1988, he met with the dean, the director, and one of the faculty members of the committee, an assistant professor of philosophy. They again stressed that they felt the seminar should cover *other* perspectives on science not linked to Christianity, and that "human responsibility, chance, freedom and free will" topics all should be dropped, presumably because these behaviors are contrary to orthodox Darwinism.[335] The committee also brought several readings and guidelines that they prepared, and that they felt should be included in the seminar.

On February 7, 1989, the director gave Bube four book titles which he was to read and incorporate into the course by the February 17, 1989 deadline for the revised syllabus (ten days later). Reading four scholarly books in a mere ten days, Bube pointed out to the director, was an impossible request. Bube also noted in the revision that there was not sufficient time for a thorough discussion of many topics in a two-hour-per-week course. The purpose of the seminar was merely to *lay the foundation* for further exploration on the topics presented to the students. Other changes in the seminar were made in an effort to respond to the committee's other recommendations.

As a result of this new revised syllabus, the seminar was "approved," but only for freshmen and sophomores, not undergraduates in general, and only twelve students were "allowed" to sign up, while the others were placed on a waiting list. The committee also requested that professor Bube give them his social security number, his resume, and his current address—a very bizarre request for an academic committee! He also was informed that he would receive only a

---

335   Interview of Richard Bube by Jerry Bergman, 1990

"temporary teaching appointment" as preceptor. Over twenty students came to the first meeting, and seventeen students out of thirty who attended at least one meeting finally registered.

Lacking a valid reason to cancel the seminar, the committee came as close as possible to saying that what they actually objected to was what they *perceived* to be professor Bube's religious viewpoint (which they did not want presented in the classroom), and that they preferred the material be presented by a professor of different beliefs than Bube, specifically an evolutionary naturalist. They likely realized that they were on shaky ground in unilaterally banning a highly successful seminar with a twenty-five-year history, so they indulged in what could only be classified as intimidation and harassment.[336]

It is clear from reading through the various letters, notes, and extensive correspondence related to this case that an exorbitant number of hours were expended on it. Bube benefited from this large time investment, though, because in 1990 his seminar was finally approved without comment. Even though Bube did not focus on origins, the Darwinists still gave him a hard time!

The Dean Kenyon Case

Among the many well-documented cases of university professors who encountered conflicts with their colleagues because of their skepticism towards evolution is that of Dean Kenyon, a professor emeritus of biology at San Francisco State University.[337] This case is important because the issues involved have been clearly articulated, and neither party has alleged other reasons for the conflict. Often in cases in which the major issue is differing religious and world views of the department and the professor in question, the real reasons are covered over, or other totally superfluous reasons are alleged.[338] The case is also important because Kenyon's situation demonstrates the "intolerance bordering on hatred" heaped upon those who question Darwinism.[339]

Dr. Kenyon, known as a quiet, hard-working, highly respected professor, has numerous publications and over two decades of teaching experience. He is

---

336 Interview of Richard Bube by Jerry Bergman, 1990.
337 Holden, 1993, pp. 1976-1977.
338 J. Bergman, 1993b; Bube, 1989.
339 Johnson, 1994, p. 7.

now professor emeritus of biology at San Francisco State University, where he was first appointed in 1966. Kenyon received a Bachelor of Science in physics (Phi Beta Kappa) from the *University of Chicago* in 1961, and a Ph.D. in biophysics from *Stanford University* in 1965. He has been a National Science Foundation Postdoctoral Fellow at the *University of California at Berkeley*, a visiting scholar at *Oxford University*, and a postdoctoral fellow at the National Aeronautics and Space Administration (NASA) Ames Research Center. He is the co-author with Gary Steinman (Professor of Biochemistry at Pennsylvania State University) of *Biochemical Predestination* (McGraw-Hill, 1969), one of the two best-selling advanced-level books on chemical evolution. The book expounds "what was arguably the most plausible evolutionary account of how a living cell might have organized itself from chemicals in the 'primordial soup'."[340] He is also co-author with Percival Davis of the book *Of Pandas and People—The Central Question of Biological Origins*.[341] His many scientific articles have appeared in major peer-reviewed journals such as *Nature, Science,* and *Journal of Molecular Evolution*, and as chapters in books such as *The Origin of Life and Evolutionary Biochemistry*[342] and *Molecular Evolution and Protobiology*.[343]

Kenyon's Intellectual Journey

A committed evolutionist throughout most of his career, Dr. Kenyon began to question the evolutionary viewpoint only much later in his life. Part of the reason for his "conversion" was that his research caused him to conclude that it is impossible for chemicals to become arranged into complex information-bearing molecules by natural processes alone. He concluded that "perhaps a directing intelligence has played a role."[344]

In 1974, Kenyon went to *Oxford University* as part of a sabbatical leave from San Francisco State and spent his time reading and interviewing professors, both evolutionists and theistic evolutionists, on science and faith issues. He also read the works of evolutionist Teilhard de Chardin, whose writings were then very popular at Oxford. Then, in 1976, one of Kenyon's students back at *San*

---

340   Haughton: Dallas, Texas, 1989.
341   Davis and Kenyon, 1989
342   Dose, K., 1974.
343   Koichiro, 1984.
344   Meyer, 1993a, p. A14.

Francisco State gave him a book titled *The Creation of Life: A Cybernetic Approach to Evolution* by A. E. Wilder-Smith. The book argued against the conclusions of Kenyon's book *Biochemical Predestination*, the theory that chemical bonds and forces make it inevitable that life will evolve. Professor Kenyon realized that Wilder-Smith's arguments were largely valid and soon began reading other books critical of Darwinism.[345] After much reading and study, Kenyon realized that he could no longer accept modern orthodox neo-Darwinism. Using what he understood from his clearly prodigious and respectable scientific background, he then began to reassess his teaching and research program.

Problems Begin

Kenyon relates that his conflict first began in 1977, when his colleagues discovered that he was discussing the evidence against evolution in his course:

> My faculty colleagues reacted with shock, dismay, disbelief. Several faculty meetings were held and I was asked to explain myself. I was thoroughly quizzed about my beliefs about how life got here... I don't think I will ever forget the look of shock on the faces of many of my colleagues when I explained some of my views. The first response was an effort to cap the amount of time students in the evolution class would be exposed to arguments against the standard view—the amount of time I would be allowed to discuss negative evidence. The amount was fixed at five percent of the course. The next move was to have me reassigned out of the evolutionary course. I haven't taught it since 1981.[346]

As Jackson reports, as far back as 1980, the science department at San Francisco State was in an uproar because of Professor Dean Kenyon's teaching, specifically at the time when

> Kenyon renounced the theory of evolution and began teaching creationism. In an interview the professor said: "In the relatively recent past ... the entire cosmos was brought into existence out of nothing at all, by supernatural creation." Kenyon also argues ... that the "evolutionary theory is too full of 'holes'" [and] "The better scientific model is the creationist one.."." Though

---

345 Pearcey, 1989, p. 2.
346 Pearcey, 1989, p. 3.

some of Kenyon's colleagues are highly upset by his teaching, others are rather supportive. For example, physicist and astronomer Charles Hagar noted: "All too often evolution has been presented as fact, and it's kind of interesting to see that challenged by alternative theories. If they're wrong let the scientists knock them down."[347]

The administration claims that Kenyon's problem at San Francisco State came to a head in the fall of 1992, when three students filed a complaint regarding the way Kenyon presented biological origins in his introductory biology course. The concerns of his opponents arose not only because he critically assessed evolution, but also because he presented information that lends credence to the "Intelligent Design" view—i.e., that an Intelligent Designer exists.[348] The chair of the biology department, Dr. John Hafernik, viewed Kenyon's critiquing evolution and covering the philosophical implications of the complexity exhibited in nature as synonymous with teaching creationism (a term that he never defined). This is another example of the common tendency to view *any* theistic position, as well as evidence against Darwinism, as creationism and, consequently, declaring it banned in all public-school forums.

Specifically, Hafernik told Kenyon: "I order you not to discuss creationism in your class. You can regard that as a direct order! I have the support of the Dean. I have consulted with [Dean] Jim Kelley and we agree on this."[349] Still not sure exactly what Kelley meant by the very general label creationism, Kenyon wrote to the dean to ask him to delineate specifically what he was not allowed to discuss, and Kelley replied that Kenyon was to teach only "'the dominant scientific view,' not the religious view."[350]

Kenyon replied that he *did* teach the dominant scientific view, and merely briefly added information that some biologists see as evidence for Intelligent Design such as the difficulty of understanding how an irreducibly complex structure such as ATP syntase could evolve in view of the fact that it must function well enough to charge ADP for life to be possible. Hafernik responded that this was not allowed—*only* non-theistic (atheistic) evolution could be taught.

---

347   *Los Angeles Herald Examiner*, December 21, 1980, p. A14, quoted in Wayne Jackson, 1981, p. 4.
348   Holden, 1993. pp. 1976-1977.
349   Meyer, 1993b, pp. 1-2.
350   Meyer, 1993a, p. A14.

Consequently, Kenyon was removed from teaching the introductory biology course and reassigned to teaching primarily labs (a task often assigned to graduate students).

Admittedly, concerns about Dr. Kenyon's religion also surfaced—he is a Roman Catholic—but it's important to note that Kenyon arrived at his new conclusions honestly from a scientific perspective, and not a religious one. And, evidently he made some comments that could be seen as critical of abortion in a biology class.[351] Hafernik evidently felt that only pro-abortion beliefs are permitted in academia. In the scores of documents that I reviewed about this case originating from within Kenyon's biology department, absolutely no consideration was given to Dr. Kenyon's academic freedom. Furthermore, most of Kenyon's colleagues were so involved in their individual research and teaching that they were only vaguely familiar with the creation-evolution arguments.[352]

The extensive literature in the cell biology field documents the fact that thousands of scientists have concluded outside intelligent intervention is necessary to account for life on Earth.[353] Researchers of the stature of Nobel laureate Francis Crick and Sir Fred Hoyle have both concluded that life could not have evolved from non-life, but that life must have somehow come from outside of the Earth.[354] Even though this view is widely acknowledged as tenable in the scientific world, Kenyon found himself in the position of being forbidden to "report the negative results of research or give students his candid assessment of it."[355] The debate did not revolve around teaching religion, but the requirement that he teach *only* atheistic evolution or, what is often referred to as naturalism. As Kenyon explained to his supervisors, his view

> hardly qualifies as unscientific biblicism, let alone religious advocacy... As Kenyon's personal history suggests, his present view has resulted from long years of experimentation and study, not a prior religious commitment... Why must theistic professors refrain from discussing evidence that seems to lend credibility to their philosophical predilections? If universities no longer

---

351 Letter from Dean Kenyon to Jim Foley, dated February 6, 1996.
352 Interview of Dean Kenyon by Jerry Bergman, 1993.
353 Robert Shapiro, 1986.
354 Robert Shapiro, 1986, pp 11-313 Crick, 1981 pp. 13-166; Hoyle, 1983, pp 1-150.
355 Meyer, 1993a, p. A14.

are a free market place for ideas, on what basis do they command pride-of-place in public financing?[356]

The Kenyon case unequivocally underscores the point that, among the set of beliefs required to pass the political-correctness censors in academia—violation of which can result in loss of one's job, occupation, or worse—is belief in atheistic Darwinism. The reason for this is that critiquing orthodox Darwinism in science courses raises the possibility of intelligent origins which, according to many Darwinists, is one of the worst sins possible.[357] In the words of former UC Berkeley Professor Thomas Jukes: "The arguments for 'Intelligent Design' presuppose the existence of a Creator and are therefore religiously biased" and for this reason cannot be presented in a state university.[358]

The concerns raised in the Kenyon case are not isolated pronouncements made by extremists. Fortunately, the *San Francisco State University's Academic Freedom Committee* (AFC) recognized this and ruled decisively in Kenyon's favor, arguing that the university *cannot* require professors to teach some in-vogue political/religious orthodoxy, but rather "should permit and encourage vigorous dialogue, even controversy." The committee ruled that, although "mandated teaching of creationism in the K-12 schools has been forcefully rejected by the courts," Dr. Kenyon's teaching of Intelligent Design does not violate the separation of church and state principle because his teaching does not constitute endorsement by the university of a specific religious view: "AFC's support of Dr. Kenyon's right to teach his ideas does not ... constitute endorsement by AFC or the university of any religious viewpoint."[359] This remarkable pronouncement is a rarity in cases like Kenyon's, as universities often claim that they own the right to determine any material or information presented by a professor because it is widely alleged in these cases that whatever a professor says reflects an endorsement by the university itself.

AFC's extensive investigation of the case concluded that Kenyon's academic freedom was abridged by the process that led to his reassignment from Biology 100 (which is the same course that I regularly teach without problems, and I am

---

356   Meyer, 1993b, p. 3.
357   Hearn, 1993; Sykes, 1988.
358   Jukes, 1993, p. A17.
359   Gregory, 1993, p. 12.

far less qualified than Dr. Kenyon). Not unexpectedly, Kenyon's opponents refused to honor the Academic Freedom Committee report. In a letter to Kenyon, Hafernik stated:

> Your letter regarding the staffing of biology 100/101 distresses me. In it, you say that I have "indicated willingness to abide by the decision of the Academic Freedom Committee" regarding your complaint of January 1993—that is, we had a deal. This is a bold misrepresentation of fact. **There was no deal**... I respect their effort and the congenial spirit in which the recommendations are offered; however ... I am unable to meet your request to teach biology 100 this summer... Course assignments have also been made for next fall and I see no basis for changing them at this time.[360]

Thus, in spite of the extensive well-documented, sixteen-page report strongly in favor of Dr. Kenyon, signed by five fellow professors at his university, the biology chair refused to assign Kenyon the basic biology course often taken by non-majors to fulfill their basic science requirement.

Although on occasion successfully challenged, often only atheistic views can be presented in a state university, a situation that hardly results in religious neutrality as the American constitution requires. Those who do not "toe the line" may well face the same problems that Kenyon has experienced. As Johnson argues, many science educators, including Kenyon's detractors, openly claim that "academic freedom does not extend to those who would question the philosophical materialism that rules evolutionary biology."[361] Johnson concludes by asking: "Is a scientist allowed to criticize the reigning materialist theories of chemical and biological evolution, even to the point of suggesting that something other than purposeless material processes may have been at work?"[362] In many universities across America today, the answer is a resounding "no way."

Among the developments in this case was the publication of a *Wall Street Journal* Op-Ed piece that Stephen Meyer wrote about the case arguing strongly in favor of Kenyon's academic freedom, the validity of the Intelligent Design critiques of neo-Darwinism, and condemning the university's actions. The article was published on Monday, December 6, 1993, and on the following day the

---

360 Letter from John Hafernik to Dean Kenyon, 1993, p.1, emphasis in original.
361 Johnson, 1993, p. A15.
362 Johnson, 1993, p. A15.

university faculty senate met to discuss Kenyon's censorship case. The article was discussed and likely influenced the committee. Although one faculty member at the meeting compared teaching the problems of evolution to teaching that the Holocaust never occurred, numerous other faculty members spoke out in Kenyon's defense against such ridiculous and slanderous charges.

In the end, the faculty senate vote was twenty-five *in favor* of Dr. Kenyon, eight opposed, and three abstentions.[363] Furthermore, even the *American Association of University Professors* openly came out in support of Professor Kenyon! The intolerance of Kenyon's detractors was so obvious, blatant, and open that even moderates now clearly discerned who was the actual enemy of academic freedom. Only then did the biology chair budge, but he almost immediately put the issue to Dr. Kenyon's biology colleagues. They voted twenty-seven to five with two abstentions to go on record as opposing the presentation of both critiques of naturalism and evidence of Intelligent Design. In the words of Mims:

> Dr. Kenyon's case raises the troubling secondary issue of institutionalized pathological science practiced by scientists whose faith in what they have failed to prove is as dogmatic as that of the staunchest religious fundamentalist.... Although his views are at least as philosophically tenable as those of the Darwinists, to the Darwinists Dr. Kenyon is a threat. Irrational howls of protest appear any time a suggestion is made that views like those held by Kenyon be included in a school textbook. Any so-called scientific institution or publication that reassigns a distinguished professor or fires a columnist .solely because of a scientific view that leaves room for God is neither scientific nor American. Tolerating such religious discrimination or soft-pedaling it as "political correctness" erodes the cause of science and blocks one of the most fundamental of human rights.[364]

Summary Remarks on the Kenyon Case

Dr. Kenyon's situation was important for one key reason: "[He] was forbidden to teach his course not because he taught evolutionary theory (which he did), but because he offered a critical assessment of it."[365] At issue in situa-

---

363   Johnson, 1993, p. A15.
364   Mims, 1993, p. A15.
365   Meyer, 1993a, p. A14.

tions like that of Kenyon is not just the question of whether Intelligent Design and creationism can be discussed in the classroom. The major concern among many university officials is their suspicion that students are being *influenced in a direction away from Darwinism*. The consequences for professors perceived as endorsing such a view are often similar to what happened to Kenyon. This is hardly academic freedom—the only way that the origins controversy will be resolved is for open debate to occur.[366] Presently students are commonly being indoctrinated in dogmatic Darwinism.[367]

The fact is that Kenyon was vindicated by his university colleagues, but his fellow department members were ideologues and seemed to behave like staunch materialists, raising the question: "why were the biologists in this case, more than the other professors involved, so dogmatically materialist?" One reason is simply because teaching naturalism against the design view dominates American education. Most biology textbooks constantly argue against *any* form of Intelligent Design—or even theistic evolution. In reviewing scores of textbooks in the process of selecting one for a college-level biology class, I have never become aware of *any* recent textbook that argues for, or even favorably presents, theistic evolution. All of them, without exception, argue openly for evolutionary naturalism. Typical is the following from an introductory biology textbook:

> Darwin compiled enough support for his theory of descent with modification to convince most of the scientists of his day that organisms evolve *without supernatural intervention*. Subsequent discoveries, including recent ones from molecular biology, further support this great principle—one that connects an otherwise bewildering chaos of facts about organisms.[368]

Furthermore, not only is atheism implied, but in many texts used in colleges and universities the philosophical implications of this world view are implicitly taught, such as the following:

> All appearances to the contrary, *the only watchmaker in nature is the blind forces of physics...* A true watchmaker has foresight: he designs his cogs and

---

366 Meyer, 1994. pp. 26-28.
367 Wiester, 1990 and 1991 p. 12
368 Campbell, Mitchell, and Reece, 1994, p. 258, emphasis added.

springs, and plans their interconnections, with future purpose in his mind's eye. Natural selection, the blind, unconscious, automatic process which Darwin discovered, and which we now know is the explanation for the existence and apparently *purposeful form of all life, has no purpose in mind. It has no mind and no mind's eye.* It does not plan for the future. It has no vision, no foresight, no sight at all. If it can be said to play the role of watchmaker in nature, it is the *blind* watchmaker.[369]

Summary

Both of these cases illustrate the fact that the material covered in a class or seminar was less an issue than the Darwinist's assumption about what was being taught. Very little or no documentation existed in both cases to determine what was taught in class was in violation of school policy or state law, and no supervisors were in their classrooms to document what was said, nor do we have documented evidence from students. What we *do* have is some irresponsible rhetoric from those who have no first-hand knowledge about the case, such as a response to the Meyer's *Wall Street Journal* article cited above.

Mr. Meyer has the Kenyon affair all mixed up. As a teacher of the history of science he should know that "Intelligent Design" of organisms stopped being a tenable hypothesis early in the 19th century.[370]

---

369   Dawkins, 1986, p. 5, emphasis added.
370   Thwaites, 1993, p. A17.

Chapter 6: The Ray Webster Case

A Court Bans Darwinian Criticism in a Social Studies Class

This chapter reviews one case in detail—that of twenty-year veteran public school social science teacher Ray Webster—which illustrates how these cases are almost always dealt with by the courts. This case epitomizes how the lives of those involved are affected when only naturalism is allowed in the schools. Mr. Webster's situation shows not only the problems that critics of Darwinism experience, but also that the courts (and the schools) attempt to totally censor ideas and facts commonly critical of Darwinism.

Those who oppose the creation world view commonly claim that they are not opposed to teaching creation in the public schools, but are opposed only to teaching it *in science classes*. They argue that only non-theistic Darwinian views can be taught in science classes. Yet, Ray Webster *was a social studies teacher*, and endeavored to present alternative viewpoints in his *social studies classes*. Those opposed to teaching creation repeatedly stress that social studies classes are the appropriate forum for discussing this viewpoint. For example, the California board of education officially encourages limiting "discussion of creationism to social science and literature classes."[371] Don Chernow, chair of California's Curriculum Commission, said that "creation theory should be discussed along with other religious issues, either in the history and social science curriculum or the English and language arts curriculum."[372]

Many others openly encourage creationism to be taught, but not in science classrooms. Niles Eldredge, curator of the American Museum of Natural History, forcefully argued that creationism should be taught "either in an entirely separate course or as a segment of the social studies curriculum" in a section that is "part of a discussion of different notions of origins." He even states that "it would *always* be proper for a science teacher to acknowledge that creationism exists at the onset of the evolution part of a biology course..."[373] Although Eldredge

---

371 Jay Mathews, 1989, p. A7.
372 Don Chernow, quoted in Buderi, 1989, p. 219.
373 Eldredge, 1982, p. 148 (emphasis added)

makes it clear that he firmly holds the evolutionary view, and does not in any way support the creationist world view, his position was banned in the Webster case by Judge George M. Marovich of the United States District Court for the Northern District of Illinois, Eastern Division.

Background of the Webster Case

The case occurred in New Lenox, Illinois, a small, middle-class town near Chicago. In the spring of 1987, a student in Webster's Oster-Oakview Junior High School social studies class alleged that Webster violated the separation of church and state.[374] On July 31, 1987, the school board, through its superintendent, advised Webster by letter to refrain from critiquing Darwinism in his classroom. In October of 1987, Webster was then informed, in a letter written by Superintendent Alex M. Martino, that he was to teach *only information in favor of evolution.*

The letter from Martino openly rejected Webster's contention that he had an obligation to teach both sides of controversial issues. Realizing the injustice of this directive, which was contrary to the Supreme Court ruling that teachers have the freedom to teach all of the scientific evidence on the question of origins, Webster and one of his students, Matthew Dunne, looked to the courts for support. They were sorely disappointed—on May 25, 1989, a court ruled against them.

The court ruled that the school's order to Mr. Webster—to cease presenting information that supports a "non-evolutionary origin of life"—did not violate his constitutional right, or case law on academic freedom.

The positions on origins can be dichotomized into two views—namely, life was ultimately created by an entity or outside intelligence, or life as we know it was created as a result of time, chance, and natural law.[375] The former view is often termed Intelligent Design, while the latter view is known as Darwinism or naturalism. The judge ruled that evidence for the former view, which he called creationism, must not be taught, and that if anything is taught about origins, only information supporting the latter view, non-theistic evolution, is permis-

374   Bergman, 1990.
375   Westacott and Ashton, 2005.

sible. Webster, understandably chagrined at this decision, sought relief from the Court of Appeals, which also ruled against him.

When his case went to court, Webster was a sixty-year-old social studies teacher who had taught in this particular school for fifteen years. He had "an excellent employment record in the district." Unlike some educators caught in the middle of such cases, Ray Webster was acknowledged as an excellent teacher by both sides.

The roots of the controversy began in the spring of 1987, when one lone student alleged that Mr. Webster violated the principles of separation of church and state in his social studies classroom by discussing both sides of the creation and evolution controversy. The student contacted both the *American Civil Liberties Union* and *Americans United for Separation of Church and State.*[376] As a result, the school district and the school superintendent advised Mr. Webster, by a letter dated July 31, 1987, that he was to cease teaching both sides of evolution. According to the plaintiff's brief which Webster was later to file in court, the aforementioned letter.

> failed to identify any specific incidence in Mr. Webster's classroom instruction which would even remotely indicate that he had violated the constitution or laws. Furthermore, said letter was vague and conclusionary, and did not provide for any specific detail or guidance as to how Mr. Webster might discuss topics relevant to his social studies classes and issues of common interest to all students without violating the principle of separation of church and state.[377]

Mr. Webster responded to the school district's correspondence in a letter dated September 4, 1987, explaining that he usually would note in class that although the majority of scientists accept the evolutionary viewpoint, many scientists did not. He added that after he mentioned this, typically a discussion of the various possible viewpoints would occur. He went on to describe his pedagogical motive:

---

376   Cain, 1988. p. 4
377   Plaintiff's brief, *Webster v. New Lenox School District #122*, 917 F. 2d 1004 1989. pp. 3–4.

My goal in class is not to necessarily persuade the young people of a particular viewpoint, but rather to open their minds to the fact that numerous viewpoints exist and advise the students of the merits or demerits of each viewpoint.[378]

In response, the district superintendent stated in a letter dated October 13, 1987, that Mr. Webster was "forbidden from engaging in the instruction" as outlined in his letter, and was therefore in effect forbidden to cover the material on origins according to his professional judgment as a trained, certified teacher. Webster's court brief noted that it was Mr. Webster's understanding that he was "forbidden from engaging in any instruction in the classroom relative to the scientific theory of creation ... from mentioning that many people accept such theories or reject evolution, and from mentioning that evolution is not a fact, but is only theory." Websters brief states in part: "as a result of said acts of the defendant, Mr. Webster fears that he will suffer reprisal and discipline should he teach in such a fashion consistent with his constitutional rights and those principles outlined in his letter dated September 4, 1987."

The brief also noted that "Mr. Webster believes, in the exercise of his professional judgment as a professional teacher, that he should teach consistent with his constitutional rights and said principles in order to present his social studies curriculum competently and to encourage the students to think analytically." Co-plaintiff Dunne's concern was that "he will not hear alternate non-religious points of view that Mr. Webster seeks to teach, and that he will be indoctrinated in state-approved orthodoxy while censorship occurs of alternate views." Plaintiff argued that this creates a

chilling effect on the social studies classroom in that the defendants have not provided plaintiff with adequate guidelines or procedures for determining the appropriateness of discussing religious or religiously consistent issues of national importance in the social studies classroom. Rather, the defendants have chosen to implement an absolute prohibition and ban against Mr. Webster from even mentioning certain topics in the classroom, contrary to his professional judgment and academic freedom. Said restriction con-

---

378   Plaintiff's brief, , 1989. pp. 3–4.

stitutes a prior restraint in violation of the first amendment of the United States Constitution.[379]

In the school board's letter, dated July 31, 1987, even though the issue was creation/evolution, the superintendent also pressured Webster *not* to bring up "Christian viewpoints" on *any* social issues. Nor was he to use any materials that "advocated Christian interpretation of world events, history, government and science" because such "is not permissible." He further was under order to "refrain from utilizing or displaying any such materials" in his classroom. The superintendent warned him that, for violating this directive, he would be "subject to disciplinary action by the school district, including issuance of a letter of remediation and/or dismissal." The Board claimed that they wanted a "neutral" viewpoint expressed, which Webster concluded amounted to saying that he was to argue *only* for non-Christian views, which many argue was actually anti-Christian, or atheistic viewpoints, in his classroom.

In his response, Mr. Webster on September 4, 1987, indicated his belief that the poor academic results of the complaining student lay behind the charges against him:

> The genesis of this entire matter involves a student who was unable to perform satisfactorily in my class. It is my belief that the allegations by the student and her mother relative to my violation of the principles of separation of church and state serve only to detract from the real issue, which involved the student's ability to apply herself and learn the material.[380]

He added that he had never been told that he lacked competency in the classroom; rather, his evaluations "reflect a high degree of concern for young people and an above-average ability to communicate with and teach students." He also stated his belief about the meaning of the First Amendment:

> Society should value the free flow and exchange of numerous ideas. I find it quite disturbing that those ideas which may be religious in nature are somehow treated by different standards and are subject to much more intense scrutiny as to their acceptability. I am very much aware of the principle of

---

379   Plaintiff's brief, pp. 5–6.
380   Plaintiff's brief, 1989. pp. 5–6

separation of church and state, but I have never recognized the principle to mean that a frank discussion of matters which might involve religious issues is intolerable.[381]

He then related examples of how he approached these issues in his social studies class. One example is the historically well-documented fact that Columbus's motivations (which led to the discovery of America) stemmed primarily from his desire to do the will of God. Webster added that God was so important to Columbus that he was considered by some a religious fanatic, and this fanaticism led to his monumental discovery.[382] This historical fact is information that, according to the Judge, Webster's students are not allowed to learn.

No charge was made in any of the documents I have seen that Mr. Webster was abusing his privilege as a teacher by inappropriately pressuring students to make a religious commitment or accept a religious view. From interviews that I completed with those involved, as well as a review of the court documents, it is clear that Webster was simply endeavoring to teach the controversy in a way that he felt was both neutral and reasonable.[383] There was no allegation he was teaching that Darwinism was not true, or even presenting a theological view that a Creator exists; rather, he was presenting the middle view, actually the agnostic position, by objectively evaluating both sides. He was advocating *neither* the theistic nor the atheistic position, and for this the school found him at fault.

Although claiming that they had no objection to his personal religious beliefs, school officials in fact objected to a truly neutral classroom presentation, in effect insisting that *only* the naturalistic world view could be presented. They did not even acknowledge his right to mention the theological viewpoint only as part of the *historical* development of our country, much as Professor John Moore advocates in his book *How to Teach Origins (Without ACLU Interference).*[384] According to Cindy Cain, "Webster maintains that the main battle is [over] freedom of speech, stating: 'Even though I disagree with the philosophy [of evolution], I'd fight for your right to teach it'."[385]

---

381   Plaintiff's brief, 1989, pp. 5–6
382   Ferris, 1988, p. 54.
383   Feldman, 1988, p. 17.
384   Moore, 1983,
385   Cain, 1988, p. 4.

Webster concluded that "the district's efforts to restrain me from frank and open discussion in the classroom on religious issues is exactly the type of close-minded thinking that I would hope my students disdain." Lastly, he requested to be advised if any of the examples he gave in his letter represented improper instruction. The October 13, 1987, response from principal Alex Martino was open and blunt, ignoring his questions and instructing him not to do something that he was not doing: "The school district neither condones nor will it tolerate 'thought-provoking discussions in the classroom setting' on religious topics," adding that Webster is not to "advocate a particular religious point of view," specifically stressing that he is "not to teach creationist science as the Federal Courts have held that this is a religious advocacy." As I noted, according to my interviews with both Webster and several of his students, he was not "teaching" creation science, but merely objectively teaching Darwinism. Second, the Supreme Court has not held that evidence against evolution cannot be taught. In *Edwards v. Aguillard*, 1987, the Supreme Court actually ruled that teachers *have the right* to teach non-evolutionary theories of life:

> It is equally clear that requiring schools to teach creation science with evolution does not advance academic freedom. The Act does not grant teachers a flexibility that they did not already possess to supplant the present science curriculum with the presentation of theories, besides evolution, about the origin of life. Indeed, the court of Appeals found that no law prohibited Louisiana public schoolteachers from teaching any scientific theory. 765F. 2d, at 1257. As the president of the Louisiana Science Teachers Association testified, "[a]ny scientific concept that's based on established fact can be included in our curriculum already, and no legislation allowing this is necessary." 2 App. E616. The Act provides Louisiana schoolteachers with no new authority.[386]

This misunderstanding has become an axe in the hands of school administrators and others who want to purge their schools of any and all information that discredits Darwinism. The court in *Edwards* even ruled that

> A decision respecting the subject matter to be taught in public schools does not violate the Establishment Clause simply because the material to be taught "happens to coincide or harmonize with the tenets of some or all religions."[387]

---

386 Edwards v. Aguillard, 482 U.S. 578 (1987), p. 8.
387 Edwards v. Aguillard, 482 U.S. 578 (1987), p. 9.

Analysis of the Court's Ruling

The district court in their ruling against Webster cited the Supreme Court ruling in *Edwards v. Aguillard*, that "the theory of creation science includes a belief in the existence of a supernatural Creator... As such, the requirement that creation science be taught violated the establishment clause and was unconstitutional." Of course, the Webster case was in fact not about requiring the teaching of creation science. The issue was the freedom to critique Darwinism, which is quite another matter.

The district court responded to this by concluding that "if a teacher in a public school uses religion and teaches religious beliefs or espouses theories clearly based on religious underpinnings, the principles of the separation of church and state are violated as clearly as if a statute ordered the teacher to teach religious theories such as the statutes in Edwards did." As noted above, the claim that the freedom to critique Darwinism does not exist was contradicted by the Supreme Court in the *Aguillard v. Edwards* case. Furthermore, nowhere did either the Supreme Court or the District Court attempt to define religion; so one hardly knows exactly what was banned.

The court noted that Webster denied he had been teaching religion, and endeavored only to teach *both* sides of controversial subjects. The court concluded relative to this issue that "as previously discussed, the term 'creation science' presupposes the existence of a Creator and [teaching such] is impermissible religious advocacy that would violate the first amendment." Obviously, so is saying "under God" in the pledge of allegiance, which the Supreme Court has ruled is constitutional. Ruling that advocating "the existence of a Creator" is impermissible in a classroom opens the door to arguing for the impermissability of exclusively advocating for the non-existence of a Creator.

The Ruling Regarding Co-Plaintiff Matthew Dunne

A student in Webster's class, Matthew Dunne, by and through his parents, Philip and Helen Dunne, "argued that he had a right to hear the social studies curriculum that has been censored and banned, and that Mr. Webster believed he should teach in his professional judgment."[388] The court ruled on Matthew Dunne's claims as follows:

> Plaintiff Dunne's claims, if not moot, are without merit. Dunne has not been denied the right to hear about or discuss any information or theory including information as to creation science. He is merely limited to receiving information as to creation science to those locations and settings where dissemination does not violate the first amendment. Dunne's desires to obtain this information in schools are outweighed by defendant's compelling interest to avoid the establishment clause violations and in protecting the first amendment rights of other students.

The court ruled that students *have no right to hear both sides of this controversial issue in the classroom* because creationism implies the existence of a Creator, and it is "unconstitutional" to imply His existence. Therefore, *only* views that do not require or imply a Creator (thus excluding even theistic evolution) can be taught in the classroom. This "proper" state-approved view is the non-theistic world view often understood as atheism. The court made no reference to either theistic or atheistic evolution, and did not even define creationism, noting only that creationism implied the existence of a Creator, and that teaching a view that had this implication could not be permitted.

Analysis and Criticism of the Webster Decision

The district court concluded that the New Lenox schools have *"the responsibility of monitoring the content of its teachers' curricula* to ensure that the establishment clause is not violated." One might wonder how the school system plans to carry out what the judge concluded was its "responsibility" to monitor its teachers' curricula "to ensure that the establishment clause is not violated." One way would be to tape record all of their teachers' lectures to insure that values and beliefs that are not clearly secular (and may support a religious interpretation) are not presented in any class. Most teachers would be strenuously opposed to this approach and it would seem very unjust to apply it only to Webster or

---

388   Plaintiff's brief, 1989, pp. 2–3.

targeted teachers on the suspicion that they may cross some vague line between church and state.

Furthermore, according to the school board's letter, a teacher is prohibited from presenting a Christian view *in any field being taught* in the public school. Obviously, this is difficult, since our society is based upon the Christian ethic and world view—and it is so much a part of it that many of us often view other societies without this ethic as strange, barbarous, and even cruel. Since our entire society and its laws and morality are based on religion, to be consistent none of the moral principles based on Christianity should be taught, including the immorality of incest, polygamy, child sacrifices, or cannibalism—all of which have been practiced in other societies, and all of which were originally condemned on the basis of religion.

The Double Standard: Rights of Anti-Christian Teachers Upheld in Court

By contrast, there are rulings from the courts that appear to clearly support the very same issues that many Darwin Doubter teachers are fighting for. Some of these rulings uphold the academic freedom and freedom of speech rights of educators who openly speak out against religious views, or share their personal religious beliefs with students. In *Moore v. Gaston County Board of Education*[389] a federal district court case in Gaston County, North Carolina, the right of Mr. Moore, a high school science teacher who endeavored to teach his atheistic viewpoint, was openly upheld by the district court. In this case, the court persuasively argued that students had a *right* to be exposed to *all points of view*, and that the academic freedom for educators to do so is an important constitutional right. The court ruled that discharging a teacher, any teacher, for teaching his personal religious views including questioning the validity of the Bible in class did *not* violate the establishment clause. When the students asked Mr. Moore if he believed that humans descended from monkeys, he responded that Darwin's theory is true and that the story of Adam and Eve was false. He also told the class that he did not attend church, did not believe in life after death, or in heaven or hell.

---

389   357 F. Supp. 1037 (W.D.N.C. 1973).

He further undertook to discuss his view of how the ancient belief in numerous tribal gods "evolved" into a belief in the Christian God. In one incident, several students found this anti-Christian teaching objectionable, and one or two students attempted to leave the classroom and were ordered to sit down.[390] The entire class was so upset that the class was dismissed early. The students then went to their homeroom and told their homeroom teacher about their experience. That evening, the superintendent of schools, Mr. William H. Brown, received several phone calls from irate parents. A meeting was held the next day, during which Moore was asked if he in fact had stated "that he did not believe in God, nor in life after death." He described his belief that death was only "ashes to ashes, dust to dust," and further stated that he could neither prove nor disprove the existence of a Supreme Being. Because of this, Moore was terminated from his position at the school and brought suit.

The District Court ruled that Moore had a *right to advocate his particular religious* views in the classroom, in this case an anti-Christian view. The court concluded that "teachers are entitled to first amendment freedoms," quoting *Tinker vs. Demoine Independent Community School District,*[391] because "it can hardly be argued that either students or teachers shed their constitutional rights to freedom of speech or expression at the school house gate." Iowa state law also declares that these constitutional protections are unaffected by the presence or absence of tenure.

However, the ruling in Moore is also a double-edged sword, and provides strong support for educators who are improperly mistreated by misinformed university administrators and attorneys. Part of the Moore ruling includes this instructive language:

> To discharge a teacher without warning because his answers to scientific and theological questions do not fit the notions of the local parents and teachers is a violation of the Establishment clause of the First Amendment. It is "an establishment of religion," the official approval of local orthodoxy, and a violation of the Constitution. Most people do not attend college. Many do not finish high school. To forbid discussions of scientific subjects like Darwin's theory of evolution on "religious" grounds is simply to postpone the

---

390   Moore v. Gaston County Board of Education, 357 F. Supp. 1037 (W.D.N.C. 1973),
391   *Tinker v. Demoine Independent Community School District*, 393 US 503,506,89 S.CT.733, 73621 L.ED.2D.731 (1969),

education of those children until after they get out of school. If a teacher has to answer searching, honest questions only in terms of the lowest common denominator of the professed beliefs of those parents who complain the loudest, this means that the state through the public schools is impressing the particular religious orthodoxy of those parents upon the religious and scientific education of the children by force of law. The prohibition against the establishment of religion must not be thus distorted and thwarted.[392]

The Moore ruling also stated that "although academic freedom is not one of the enumerated rights of the first amendment, the Supreme Court has on numerous occasions emphasized that the right to teach, to inquire, to evaluate and to study is fundamental to a democratic society" and that "the safeguards of the first amendment will quickly be brought into play to protect the right of academic freedom because any unwarranted invasion of this right will tend to have a chilling effect on the exercise of the right by other teachers."[393]

The Supreme Court has elsewhere concluded that "this court cannot ... find any substantial interest of the schools will be served by giving defendants unfettered discretion to decide how the first amendment rights of teachers are to be exercised." Furthermore, it is "well settled that even non-tenured public school teachers do not shed first amendment protection in speaking on matters of public concern."[394] In the Webster case the court ruled exactly the opposite of these precedents, demonstrating that the courts are inconsistent: They ruled in the Moore and other cases that a teacher can openly discuss science and theology questions in class, but ruled that Webster could not.

The federal district court argued in the Moore case that the importance of open discussion of religious issues in the classroom is imperative, noting that the effect that this suppression of scientific thought and discussion had "upon the technological and scientific development of Italy and Spain is well-known."[395]

The Moore decision, written in support of a secular teacher, *clearly demonstrates that the same rights the court ruled in support of for Moore were denied*

---

392   *Moore v. Gaston County Board of Education*, 357 F. Supp. 1037, 1043 (W.D.N.C. 1973)
393   *Moore v. Gaston County Board of Education*, 357 F. Supp. 1037, 1043 (W.D.N.C. 1973)
394   *Timothy Kirkland, v. Northside Independent School District*, Defendant-Appellant. No. 88-5640. 890 F.2d 794 58 USLW 2412, 57 Ed. Law Rep. 396 United States Court of Appeals. Also see Mt. Healthy, 429 U.S. at 283-84, 97 S.Ct. at 574-75; Pickering, 391 U.S. at 574, 88 S.Ct. at 1737; Givhan, 439 U.S. at 415-16, 99 S.Ct. at 696-97; Hillis v. Stephen F. Austin State Univ., 665 F.2d 547, 549 (5th Cir.), cert. denied, 457 U.S. 1106, 102 S.Ct. 2906, 73 L.Ed.2d 1315 (1982).
395   *Moore v. Gaston County Board of Education*, 357 F. Supp. 1037, 1043 (W.D.N.C. 1973)

to Webster. In fact, since 1926, *with only two exceptions*, the courts have ruled against creationists of all stripes.[396] The most well known case in American history is the Scopes trial, which has been touted as the case that Darwinists lost in the courts, but won in the press and our colleges.

Another case involved the West Allis public library in Wisconsin, which refused creationists the right to use the library facilities. The court ruled that the library could not discriminate against creationist beliefs. Christopher A. Pfeifer had sought the use of a room to make a presentation and U.S. District Judge Lynn Adelman ruled April 11, 2000 that while the library may seek "to avoid controversy" through "the exclusion of partisan political meetings and religious services or instruction," such a motive is not a valid ground for restricting speech about creationism in a public forum.[397] Pfeifer's attorney, Erik Stanley of the Orlando, Florida-based Liberty Counsel, said in the *Milwaukee Journal Sentinel* that the decision "ensured that freedom of speech applies to all citizens."

The double standard vividly demonstrated between the Moore and Webster cases also exists in many other rulings handed down throughout the court system. Without a standard of accountability for judges, the court system cannot, and will not, rule fairly or consistently in matters of academic freedom and freedom of speech cases for educators.[398] Unfortunately, the bias of judges is very common and often very evident, making a neutral court unlikely in these kinds of cases. Until and unless a genuine respect for neutrality is required of judges, conflicts and contradictory rulings in the area of academic freedom will continue. The Supreme Court in *Edwards v. Aguillard*, in a dissenting opinion written by Justice Antonin Scalia and joined by Justice William Rehnquist, acknowledged this concern, but the majority on the court chose to ignore it:

> The Louisiana legislators had been told repeatedly that creation scientists were scorned by most educators and scientists, who themselves had an almost religious faith in evolution. It is hardly surprising, then, that in seeking to achieve a balanced, "nonindoctrinating" curriculum, the legislators protected from discrimination only those teachers whom they thought were

---

396   Bergman, 2006b.
397   Christopher A. Pfeifer, Plaintiff, v. City of West Allis, Defendant. No. 99-C-0653. United States District Court, E.D. Wisconsin. April 10, 2000. see http://www.lc.org/misc/pfeifer.htm
398   Bergman, 1989. p. 13.

suffering from discrimination. (Also, the legislators were undoubtedly aware of *Epperson v. Arkansas*, 393 U.S. 97 (1968), and thus could quite reasonably have concluded that discrimination against evolutionists was already prohibited.) The two provisions respecting the development of curriculum guides are also consistent with "academic freedom" as the Louisiana Legislature understood the term. Witnesses had informed the legislators that, because of the hostility of most scientists and educators to creation science, the topic had been censored from or badly misrepresented in elementary and secondary school texts.[399]

What These Cases Mean for Educators

The Supreme Court in *Edwards v. Aguillard*, in its definition of the term "creationism" took a balanced approach—the very approach the district court in the Webster case later ruled unconstitutional.[400] The minority opinion noted:

> Appellants insist that it [creationism] is a collection of educationally valuable scientific data that has been censored from classrooms by an embarrassed scientific establishment. Appellees insist it is not science at all but thinly veiled religious doctrine. Both interpretations of the intended meaning of that phrase find considerable support in the legislative history.[401]

To achieve the legal mandate of neutrality and avoid indoctrination, both sides of this and other controversial issues should not be censored in public classrooms but should be fairly presented. Contrary to the objections of many Darwinians, this can be accomplished without promoting Biblical texts. Challenging students to consider objections to evolution raised by qualified scientists who have published in reputable peer-reviewed science journals can hardly be legitimately described as an effort to promote religion, yet this is precisely the argument offered to rebuff many educators. If Mr. Webster were presenting only material that argued for one side, and censored or ridiculed the other side, he would be in violation of court rulings.

---

399   *Edwards v. Aguillard*, 482 U.S. 578 (1987), dissent, pp. 21–22.
400   *Edwards v. Aguillard*, 482 U.S. 578 (1987). p. 8
401   *Edwards v. Aguillard*, 482 U.S. 578 (1987), dissent, p. 2.

Academic freedom in public schools does not presume the right to indoctrinate, but rather to educate, which requires a fair presentation of both sides of controversial issues. The courts in the Webster case not only failed to make the vital distinction between education and indoctrination, but the ruling actually *requires* indoctrination of an anti-Christian viewpoint as the official state-approved educational approach, and ruled that deviations from this approach are illegal. This is only one of many court rulings where reinforcement of the pervasive movement toward forced secularization of American society has occurred. The erosion from, at first, support, then accommodation, and now hostility toward the theistic world view has been slow but steady.

Chapter 7: Peloza, Bishop and Johnson

As a result of attempts by Darwin skeptics to secure a place at both the table of scientific discussion and in the classroom, the federal courts have put evolution "virtually beyond criticism."[402] Yet, according to evolutionist Eugenie Scott, theists "claim" truth as conscientiously as Darwinists do, and, she admits, "there is truth on both sides."[403] This fact, however, cannot be legally admitted in the public schools, and Darwin skeptics have lost every single court case that attempted to convey "there is truth on both sides" since 1925, with the exception of the Scopes trial. Court rulings in cases involving those who are open critics of Darwinism have been blatantly discriminatory, dishonest, and unconstitutional. Indications now exist that the Supreme Court is aware of this and may try to correct this problem in future rulings.

In past cases involving Darwin skeptics, my research of over 300 cases over the past 30 years indicates that schools typically presented trumped-up and often obviously bogus reasons for dismissal or denial of tenure such as incompetence, erroneous claims that a faculty member falsified documents, or other allegations that were clearly proposed to cover up the real reason—religious discrimination. Several more recent cases have been increasingly open about the rationale for termination; consequently, in these cases it is easier to litigate the actual issues in court. Thus, several cases have been fought openly on freedom of speech and First Amendment grounds. For example, in referring to the Bishop case, *University of Chicago* law professor Mike McConnell stated: "This is principally a free speech case. It was litigated as a free speech case; it was decided as a free speech case."[404]

A major problem is that many of these court decisions were based on stereotypes and common beliefs. Professor Ronald Numbers vividly demonstrates that many common beliefs about both creationists and the history of creationism are wrong. In reference to the thesis set forth in Andrew Dickson White's 1896 classic, *A History of the Warfare of Science with Theology in Christendom*, he successfully argues that "creationist conflicts rarely conformed to the battle lines

402 Witham, 2002, p. 7.
403 Witham, 2002, p. 270.
404 Quoted in John Myers, 1992a.

drawn by White."[405] Yet the courts are still likely to be influenced by the portrait of religion sketched by authors like White.

In order to explain the background of the three major cases—Peloza, Bishop, and Johnson—which are reviewed in this chapter, it is necessary to backtrack a bit, and review the prior history of cases involving evolution in the American courts.

Attempts to Legislate Balance in the Teaching of Evolution

One of the activities supported by a number of creationists in the 1980's was legislation requiring some type of "balance," or at least an approach they felt was less biased about the evidence for the divine origin of the universe, life, and humans. Although many prominent creationists of all types oppose this approach because they believe that the state should not regulate specific science content, most agree that science is being inaccurately presented in the classroom, where evolutionary naturalism is usually taught as the only explanation for how life began and developed. They believe that a sizable amount of scientific evidence exists that contradicts evolution and supports the concept of a creator or designer of the universe.[406]

One group involved in this effort was the *Citizens for Fairness in Education* (CFE) headed by Roman Catholic Paul Ellwanger. The two-model bill passed by the state of Arkansas in March (and by Louisiana in July) of 1980, and soon introduced in nineteen other states as well, was essentially the bill that CFE developed.[407] Ellwanger concluded that the idea of "balanced treatment" (presenting both evolution and creation) in public schools "is considered by legal and scientific professionals as the only constitutional way to achieve a fair hearing of the powerful scientific case for creation in our pluralistic society," and added that:

> This balanced treatment on origins can be attained by only two methods—
> the voluntary (by resolution) route or the mandatory (by legislation) route.
> CFE is in favor of both but we accentuate the latter method for reaching the
> most schools in America in the shortest possible time... Our balanced treat-
> ment bill leaves the religious aspects on origins for the homes, synagogues,
> temples, churches, and philosophy courses.... CFE is not a creationist or

---

405 Numbers, 1992, p. xiv.
406 Phillip Johnson, 1991, pp. 15–110.
407 Larson, 1985, pp. 1–14.

religious group [and is] ... in favor of academic freedom and opposed to the suppression of scientific information on the subject of origins, whether that information happens to contradict either evolution or creation.[408]

The Arkansas bill was ruled unconstitutional by the courts because of separation of church and state concerns. The act, as summarized by the Supreme Court, is as follows:

> The Creationism Act forbids the teaching of the theory of evolution in public schools unless accompanied by instruction in "creation science." No school is required to teach evolution or creation science. If either is taught, however, the other must also be taught. The theories of evolution and creation science are statutorily defined as "the scientific evidences for [creation or evolution] and inferences from those scientific evidences."[409]

A similar bill, passed in Louisiana was later overturned by the Supreme Court in 1987.

One of the main allegations of Darwinists that the courts agreed with in the aforementioned cases was the claim that creationists were attempting to inject what many Darwinists viewed as religious dogma into science education. Most leading creationist and Intelligent Design groups staunchly denied this claim, however. Concern about such religious or ideological control over teaching is legitimate, but the question that needs to be asked by the courts is whether the mere presentation (as opposed to teacher endorsement) of non-Darwinian viewpoints in a classroom amounts to an imposition of religion by the state. We believe under the umbrella of academic freedom, an educator should be allowed, at the very least, to present his students with criticism of any aspect of Darwinism or evolution that has previously been published in reputable peer-reviewed science journals.

The Current Trend

Since the 1987 Supreme Court ruling on creationism in *Edwards*, courts have resoundingly ruled against creationists of all types in all of the important

---

408   Ellwanger, 1984, pp. 1–4.
409   *Edwards v. Aguillard*, 482 U.S. 578 (1987).

cases, including those of Webster, Peloza, Johnson, and Bishop discussed in some detail later in this chapter. A review of these cases involving educators who have been terminated (or censored) due to their objections to naturalistic Darwinism, illustrates a trend in the courts to rule against educators who are labeled not only creationists, but who are also Christians. In all of the cases, the problem teachers encountered that caused then to end up in court, or which caused them to lose their position, occurred due to who the Darwin skeptic was, or the beliefs they held, not what they *did*. These are all well-documented religious discrimination cases where the courts, in essence, have ruled against the civil rights of creationist and ID professors, teachers, and science professionals, thus guaranteeing that only the Darwinian position on origins can legally be presented in public schools.

Peloza v. Capistrano Unified School District

Our first example is the case of a Mission Valley, California biology teacher, John E. Peloza. The court case began on September 30, 1991, when Peloza filed a lawsuit in the U.S. District Court against the San Juan Capistrano Unified School District and its administrators for alleged violations of his civil rights. Peloza claimed that the school district was in violation of the establishment clause by requiring him to teach atheistic evolution as fact thereby unlawfully establishing the "religion of secular humanism and atheistic naturalism."[410] Peloza also asked the court to declare that "he had the right to discuss his personal beliefs, including those touching on religious matters, with students during non-instructional time at the high school, such as during lunch, class-breaks, and before and after school hours."[411]

On January 16, 1992, in the United States District Court, Central District of California, Judge David W. Williams handed down a ruling which forbade Peloza from discussing his personal beliefs *anytime, anywhere*, on school property, and concluded that the school acted properly in requiring Peloza to teach only naturalistic evolution and not present the arguments for design in nature. Since much of human communication, including that in the schools, is colored by "personal beliefs," the only way Peloza could

---

410   Zal, 1992, p. 1.
411   Zal, 1992, p. 1.

comply with this was to not talk to anybody about anything that could be seen as reflecting his personal beliefs—a difficult judgment.

The record and my interviews with those involved in the case confirms that Peloza was not teaching, or even arguing for the right to teach any form of creationism, but rather was only endeavoring to help students think critically about Darwinism and this topic in general.[412] His complaint argued only that it is improper for the school district to *require* him to teach evolutionary naturalism *as fact*, and his request was merely to be allowed to critique evolution as a teacher would any other theory. As a result of this request, he was removed from the biology classroom and forced to teach physical education where the subject of biological origins would be less likely to surface.[413] The school district ordered him, in writing, to refrain from

> initiating conversations about your religious beliefs during instructional time, which ... includes any time students are required to be on campus as well as the time students immediately arrive for the purposes of attending school for instruction, lunch time, and the time immediately prior to students' departure after the instructional day.[414]

No evidence exists that Peloza was trying to convert students to any religion but rather he was only helping them to understand both sides of the origins controversy. Secondly, no other teachers were similarly restricted—Darwinist teachers were free to indoctrinate students in their views. Yale law professor Stephen Carter, who studied this case in detail, concluded that Peloza "was not telling his students about creationism in the sense that the term is usually meant." Carter's account continues as follows:

> "I never quote Genesis in my classroom," [Peloza] told an interviewer. "I have taken God out of this." Still, Peloza must have had in mind something like the classic creationist position: "When I give my presentation," he said, "I give two sides, one that we are here by chance and the other that we are here by design." *Here by design*: in other words, created by a designer—which is probably why an attorney for the school district shot back, "Creationism

---

412   Zal, 1992; Peloza, 1991, p. 2.
413   Nahigian, 1992; Rutan et al., 1991.
414   *Peloza v. Capistrano*, 1994, No. 8171.

is not a scientific theory, it is a religious belief. It is inappropriate to teach religion in a science class."[415]

District Judge David W. Williams concluded, *without* even bothering to give a hearing to both sides, ruled that to "teach" creationism (a term he never defined) is "illegal," relying on the Supreme Court case, *Edwards vs. Aguillard* constitutionality of teaching creationism in public classrooms case, which in fact stated *exactly the opposite*, namely that teaching creationism and alternate theories to Darwinism such as Directed Panspermia, are perfectly legal:

> It is equally clear that requiring schools to teach creation science with evo-lution does not advance academic freedom. The Act does not grant teach-ers a *flexibility that they did not already possess to supplant the present science curriculum* with the presentation of theories, besides evolution, about the origin of life... The Act provides Louisiana school teachers with no new authority.[416]

Judge Williams concluded that Peloza had no basis for claiming that the school officials violated his rights by ordering him to follow their interpretation of the state-mandated science curriculum.[417] His decision could be interpreted as giving free rein to California public schools to force teachers to teach Darwin-ism as a fact, and that no higher intelligence was involved in the process. The decision also precludes theistic evolution, and is one more indication that the United States has "officially embraced atheism as the state religion."[418]

The media commonly characterized Peloza as endeavoring to "teach" cre-ationism.[419] This ploy has been very successful in stifling the religious and aca-demic freedom of many teachers, such as those who were terminated (on suspi-cion alone or an erroneous understanding of terms, such as "Intelligent Design") because they "might have discussed" creation in the classroom—something now commonly deemed such a serious "crime" in America that mere suspicion has been enough to terminate a career. The media also widely repeated the Judge's

---

415   Carter, 1993, p. 158.
416   *Edwards v. Aguillard*, 482 U.S. 578 (1987), p. 578, emphasis added.
417   Wood, 1992, p. 658.
418   Zal, 1992, p. 2.
419   See, e.g., Wood, 1992, p. 658, and Scott and Cole, 1992, p. 1.

claim that Peloza was a "loose cannon," implying that he was a contemptible person.[420] The judge's irresponsible comment hardly describes someone who simply wanted to teach evolution as science and talk about his personal beliefs during free time with students—a right that atheistic and agnostic instructors have. Furthermore, Peloza was not quibbling with the requirement that he teach evolution, *but rather* teaching "evolution as fact."[421]

After Peloza lost at the district court, the school district filed a motion requesting reimbursement for "attorney's fees," a motion granted by Judge Williams on April 14 for the whopping amount of $32,633.49. Peloza's attorney eloquently argued that this award could only be interpreted as punishment against Peloza for endeavoring to defend his right to discuss his conclusions with students. The U.S. Court of Appeals (9th circuit) agreed with Peloza, and on July 25 and October 4, 1994, reversed this ruling. Judge Williams ruled as to Peloza's other claims:

> While at the high school, whether he is in the classroom or outside of it during contract time, Peloza is not just any ordinary citizen. He is a teacher. He is one of those especially respected persons chosen to teach in the high school's classroom. He is clothed with the mantle of one who imparts knowledge and wisdom. His expressions of opinion are all the more believable because he is a teacher. The likelihood of high school students equating his views with those of the school is substantial. To permit him to discuss his religious beliefs with students during school time on school grounds would violate the Establishment Clause of the First Amendment. Such speech would not have a secular purpose, but would have the primary effect of advancing religion, and would entangle the school with religion. In sum, it would flunk all three parts of the test articulated in *Lemon v. Kurtzman*.[422]

The difficulty with this argument is obvious. If consistently applied, it actually would rule out the discussion of any arguments that have a religious base or foundation. For many people, abortion, polygamy, pedophilia, adultery, and incest all are wrong, and the basis for their position on these issues is ultimately re-

---

420   For example, see Ohio National Education Newsletter February 1992 page 1 sent to all NEA members in Ohio

421   Zal, 1992, p. 1.

422   *Peloza v. Capistrano School District,* No. 12057; *Lemon v. Kurtzman,* 403 U.S. 602 (1971). *See Roberts v. Madigan,* 921 F.2d 1047, 1056-58 (10th Cir. 1990) , *cert. denied,* 112 S. Ct. 3025 (1992).

ligious. All of these behaviors have been widely practiced by some societies without problems, and the original sources of their condemnation were Judeo-Christian ethics. To be consistent, an argument against all of these behaviors would "have the primary effect of advancing religion, and would entangle the school with religion," thus, would be forbidden. Consequently, only one side of these issues could be presented. In addition, the position in favor of marital fidelity and against same-sex marriages, plus numerous other topics that have a religious basis, could not be discussed except in cases where one side only is advocated. Of course, some could argue that condemning these behaviors has a valid secular purpose, but so does teaching the controversy for all of these topics.

The court did not address the difference between a teacher initiating a religious discussion (in or out of class) and merely *answering questions* raised spontaneously by students about religious beliefs outside of class time. It is also absurd to argue that high school students equate a teacher's obviously personal views with those of the school—most all junior high and high school students know full well that the teacher's views on politics, religion, sports, and most other topics covered in class are not the state's views. It is far more beneficial to the students' education if teachers are allowed to express and discuss a wide variety of views. It is hard to imagine a more repressive ruling—one that would have been unusual even in the Soviet Union during the heyday of communism.

Ironically, even though Peloza evidently was required to teach evolution as fact, The Science Framework for California Public Schools *prohibits* teaching evolution as a fact: "science is limited by its tools—observable facts and testable hypotheses ... nothing in science or in any other field of knowledge shall be taught dogmatically. A dogma is a system of beliefs that is not subject to scientific tests and refutation." The policy also proclaims that "science is never dogmatic; it is pragmatic—always subject to adjustment in the light of solid new observations like those of Joule, or new, strong explanations of nature like those of Einstein and Darwin"[423] Thus, it could be argued that Peloza, in expressing doubts about the factuality of Darwinism, was acting, not out of religious motivation, but out of a secular purpose dictated by the State of California.

---

423 *The Science Framework for California Public Schools* adopted by the State Board of Education on November 9, 1989, p. 18

One problem in understanding the court decisions is the fact that key terms such as "creation" and "evolution" are rarely defined; thus, one does not know for certain what the court briefs and judgments are permitting or forbidding, and the observer has to infer all this from reviewing the entire case. Evolution, for example, can be defined simply as any biological change, such as the process of breeding the over 300 modern dog types from a mongrel. On the other hand, evolution is often more commonly defined as a naturalistic process in which life forms slowly change by processes of natural law into different life forms that are better adapted to their environments. What is often insisted on in the California Framework is not simply evolution, but naturalism or atheistic evolution (as discussed by Provine—see below). Thus, the framework sometimes appears to be religiously biased in favor of atheism. Likewise, the term "creation" is a term which can be defined to mean only that an intelligence is responsible for what we see in the natural world—and does not need to carry any Christian or religious connotations.

The Bishop Case

Dr. Philip Bishop, an honor graduate of the U.S. military academy at Annapolis, *James Madison University*, and the *University of Georgia*, is now a tenured professor of exercise physiology at the *University of Alabama*, director of the university's human performance laboratory, and an expert in exercise physiology. His *curriculum vitae* listing his many publications, honors and awards is over 45 pages long, and includes over 300 articles in peer reviewed publications and conference publications. He has published more extensively than most professors at his university. His record was so outstanding that he was recommended for early tenure by his department chair.[424] It was also "undisputed that [Bishop] covered the course material fully and that he was a well-regarded and successful teacher."[425]

The focus of the Bishop case was the university's claim that it had the absolute right to restrict all "occasional in-class comments" and any "optional out-of-class lecture" that mentioned "the professor's personal views on the subject of his academic expertise." Bishop admitted that his "personal religious bias" colored

---

424 Wagner, 2000. p. 131.
425 Bishop supreme court brief, *Bishop v. Delchamps*, p. 15.Note: Bishop won his case at the lower court level but lost on the University of Alabama appeal

his teaching perspective of his subject matter, human physiology, to the following extent: he had begun each semester's classes with a two-minute discussion and his conclusions from his study of physiology only, that his field provided abundant evidence for Intelligent Design, and not evolutionary naturalism.[426] At other times he also may occasionally mention his doubts about Darwinism's ability to create the living world, spending no more than 5 out of the 2,250 minutes of class time, which is about the typical time other professors spend relating their personal beliefs.[427] When the university learned what he was doing, they totally forbade him from even mentioning his *"religious" beliefs in class* (they never defined religion, so, again, one cannot be certain what was being censored). To defend his academic freedom Professor Bishop took the university to court. The U. S. District Court for the Northern District of Alabama in a summary judgment ruled against the university on most every count on the basis of academic freedom, noting that faculty members are free to divulge their personal views in the classroom as long as they are not disruptive.[428] The university appealed this decision to the court of appeals for the eleventh Circuit court,[429] which agreed with the trial courts statement of facts but the three judge panel reversed the decision "thereby reinstating the censorship of professor Bishop."[430] The court added that "restricting Bishop's speech was a part of" the university's authority to control the content of its curriculum.[431] They added that any lecture where he mentioned his doubts about Darwinism must be clearly separated from his classes, and the time and place both must be approved by the university prior to the lecture. Dr. Bishop also included an optional lecture titled "Evidence of God in Human Physiology," taught on his own time, which the district court "ordered him to stop."[432]

Although Bishop's "comments were nondisruptive, noncoercive, and clearly identified as 'personal bias,'" the university argued that allowing professors to present their own views in class implies that the university endorses them. In other words, the university argued that it endorses "everything it does not censor."[433] Bishop argued that occasional expressions of personal belief at a public

---

426   McFarland, 1992, p. 2; Wolf, 1991.
427   Wagner, 2000. p. 132-133.
428   Wagner, 2000. p. 133.
429   *Bishop v. Aronov*, 926 F.2d 1066 (11th Cir. 1991)
430   Wagner, 2000. p. 133.
431   Wagner, 2000. p. 133
432   Jaschik, 1991, p. A23; Hartwig, 1991, p. 55, McConkey, 2000, pp. 131-140
433   Bishop supreme court brief, *Bishop v. Delchamps*, p. 10.

university "cannot be construed as bearing the university's imprimatur, and thus are protected under the First Amendment when they are non-disruptive and non-coercive."[434]

The University endeavored to stop Bishop and *only* Bishop from mentioning, even briefly, his personal world view in the classroom, which he voiced to "help students in understanding and evaluating" his classroom presentations.[435] His brief argued that suppressing only one philosophical perspective, as the university had done, would be intellectually dishonest. Bishop's attorneys also argued that if only those with an atheistic or agnostic world view could freely express their views, students might come to the erroneous conclusion that all professors shared the same world view. McFarland characterized the case as follows:

> The university administration ordered Dr. Bishop to discontinue his classroom speech as well as his optional on-campus-talk. No other faculty and no other topic have been similarly curtailed. Dr. Bishop obtained a federal court order protecting his free speech and academic freedom, but it was overruled in a disastrous opinion by the U.S. Court of Appeals... The Court held that public university professors have no constitutional right of academic freedom and that their right of free speech in the lecture hall is subject to absolute control (censorship) by the University administration.[436]

Bishop makes a valid point. Nearly everyone who has studied sociology in some depth has had an instructor who has openly argued for Marxism in class, but it is a rare student who infers from this that the university officially endorses Marxism. Why is there such a high degree of sensitivity when a Christian point of view, or even simply a design theory point of view, is expressed even only in passing in a class, but not when a professor systematically preaches Marxism, radical feminism, atheism, or other views of the world which are broadly just as "religious" in character? Wagner concluded the court ruled that the University in this case had the absolute right to censor Bishop in clear violation of his academic freedom because the issue involved a professor critiquing Darwinism.[437]

---

434 Bishop supreme court brief, *Bishop v. Delchamps* p. 9.
435 Bishop supreme court brief, *Bishop v. Delchamps* p. 7.
436 McFarland, 1992, p. 2.
437 Wagner, 2000, p. 135-137.

Labeling Used to Marginalize Bishop's Views

Another concern in this case was the university's attempt to apply derogatory labels to Bishop's view of origins, referring to them as "Bible belt" and therefore "inappropriate" at a university.[438] Professor Carl Westerfield (the head of Bishop's academic unit) even claimed that Bishop's beliefs "hurt the reputation" of the university![439] Bishop's brief argued that the school officials "proceeded on the mistaken assumption that religious discussion must be 'kept out of the classroom' entirely, on account of the establishment clause," and that the establishment clause forbids not only open government endorsement of religion—but also forbids government employees to act as individuals (as Bishop did).

The Amicus Curiae and the brief prepared by Bishop's attorneys to appeal the case to the U.S. Supreme Court documented the fact that the type of censorship Bishop suffered is "reoccurring on campuses throughout the nation":

> "We are shocked at the breadth of speech rendered vulnerable by the court of appeals' decision... the decision ... [gives] universities broad power to censor any comments that might "produce more apprehension than comfort in students" (Pet. App. A10). This view is completely antithetical to the premise underlying higher education—that students grow intellectually from confronting new or disturbing ideas, not from avoiding them.... [and the] petitioner was reprimanded for his expressions solely because of the religious viewpoint presented in it ... [and that the university] ... routinely permits faculty to present non-religious perspectives in the classroom in their area of expertise. Amici's experience shows that such discrimination is, unfortunately, typical. Religiously committed academics in public universities across the country face resistance when they attempt, however briefly, to discuss or even disclose their ideological perspective in the course of their teaching or scholarship.[440]

Valid concerns in this case include the court of appeals limiting the petitioner's classroom speech goes far beyond both the petitioner and the classroom because the court's rationale authorizes limitations on other forms of faculty expression:

---

438   McConkey, 2000, p. 132
439   Myers, 1992a, p. 2.
440   Bishop supreme court brief, *Bishop v. Delchamps,*91-286 pp. 5–6.

If a professor's in-class speech can be attributed to the university merely because he is employed there, so can his comments in the media or statements in his scholarly work. Surely, some students taking a professor's classes might feel discomfort or anger at his extra-curricular speech or scholarship. A major concern in this case is that the university imposed restrictions on Bishop's speech that it did not apply to any other professor and specifically singled out religious speech—specifically Bishop's religious speech—for censorship but did not attempt to censor the religious speech of any other professor.[441]

Bishop's acircuit court appeal argued that the university restricted Dr. Bishop's speech "solely because of its religious content," and argued that "speech presenting a religious perspective is entitled to the same non-discriminatory treatment as other forms of speech."[442] Contrary to extensive case law and the Constitution, the court of appeals' decision authorized "virtually limitless censorship of in-class or classroom-related speech by professors" if it can be construed as "religious" or "religiously motivated" even "if the views expressed are clearly identified as personal."[443] Strictly applied, it would be inappropriate for a professor to state that he is Jewish or Muslim, goes to church, celebrates Christmas, or believes in God.[444] Yet the same professor is allowed to state that he does *not* believe in God or does *not* believe in a religious world view. In short, he can lecture *against* whatever the state defines as "religious" values or beliefs, but not *for* them.[445] As pointed out by attorney and law professor Phillip Johnson, the decision in this case reflects an obvious contempt for those who have serious questions about Darwinism. Johnson concluded the following about the appellate court's opinion:

A subtext of contempt appeared when [Judge] Gibson explained why a professor of physiology was not allowed to tell his class about his doubts concerning the orthodox theory of human evolution... If Bishop really had opinions about evolution that qualified as rational (let alone authoritative!), they would be welcome in classroom discussion. Of course the university could not, and would not, prevent a professional from saying (to whoever

441   Bishop supreme court brief, *Bishop v. Delchamps* 91-286 p. 15.
442   Bishop supreme court brief, *Bishop v. Delchamps* 91-286 p. 13.
443   Bishop supreme court brief, *Bishop v. Delchamps* 91-286 p. 9.
444   Robinson, 1991
445   Wood, 1992; McFarland, 1991; Larson, 1985

would listen) that he had been held captive on a flying saucer or that he thought the Holocaust never happened—although the university would certainly regard such a professor as an embarrassment and would try to keep the damage to a minimum. The court even tried to imply that Bishop was somehow guilty of dishonesty—by discussing his religious beliefs "under the guise of University courses."[446]

The appeals court held that the university could suppress religious speech merely to avoid a "potential establishment conflict"[447] and even argued that the "expression of a religious position in a secular subject, no matter how carefully presented, creates the appearance of endorsement of that position by the university and engenders anxiety in students who may feel compelled to feign a similar belief and, worse still, deny their own beliefs."[448] The U.S. Supreme Court rejected the petition for *Writ of certiorari*, and thus the case ended.[449]

Negative Implications of the Bishop Case for Academic Freedom

To suppress speech on these grounds is ludicrous—it would be close to impossible for instructors to teach courses that range from the behavioral sciences to political science to philosophy (and even physics and chemistry classes) if this rule were consistently applied. As Bishop's attorney argued, "discomfort, anger, anxiety on the part of a student or two cannot authorize suppression of a viewpoint."[450] The whole point of free-speech laws is to protect speech *specifically* in cases where it might engender disputes, disagreements, discomfort, anger or anxiety. Speech that does not generate these emotions is never suppressed, and thus its protection is of little concern.[451] Certainly, *anti-Christian speech* in universities "engenders anxiety" in Christian students and others, but efforts to suppress *that* type of speech have consistently failed.

Furthermore, if strictly applied this would require courses in the history of western civilization (and every other civilization) to expunge all discussion of the significant contributions that religion and religious beliefs have made to civiliza-

---

446   Johnson, 1995a, p. 181.
447   Pet. App. A21,
448   Pet. App. A22
449   Petition for Writ of Certiorari. (the document a losing party files with the Supreme Court asking the Supreme Court to review the lower court decision. Rejecting it means that they refused to hear the case).
450   Bishop Supreme Court brief, *Bishop v. Delchamps*. p. 15
451   Hudson, 1992

tion in history, and that no college or university could offer *any* general course on philosophy or the history of philosophy and even the history of science.

Yet, the court of appeals ruled that the university *can* "restrict speech"— even that which "falls short of an establishment violation."[452] In other words, this court ruled in this case that it can convict one of a First Amendment establishment clause violation even if it rules that the person's actions fell short of committing the violation! This position is totally irreconcilable with the long history of freedom-of-speech rulings in America. Although the courts have held that schools may restrict student or teacher speech that "substantially interferes" or clearly impinges upon "the rights of others,"[453] the courts' past rulings have required *overwhelming evidence* that such major effects have occurred, and not merely indications that such *might* have occurred, as the ruling in this case indicates. This decision signifies a new trend: for statements that can be interpreted as an endorsement of theism, all other considerations (including the First Amendment) must be suppressed.

The Bishop case is critically important because, as Berkeley emeritus law professor Phillip Johnson explains, the judge's opinion is a prime example of what he calls the "sham neutrality" of liberal Rationalism:

> What gives anyone, even a federal judge, the right to say how things really are?... Nonetheless liberal rationalists, like other people, do make metaphysical judgments... When metaphysical statements cannot be made honestly, they have to be stated in code and enforced with power. Thus ... toleration (which may include the right to censor the "insensitive" speech of others) is extended to the morally worthy and denied to the unworthy without any explanation of the difference.[454]

The blatant bias shown in this case was so extreme that even many secular organizations were appalled. *Americans United for Separation of Church and State* are well-known for their opposition to presenting theism in a positive light in public schools, and generally advocate the presentation of only non-theistic world views. Robert Boston, a spokesman for *Americans United*, noted that he believed this was the first time "a Federal Court had applied the secondary-

---

452   Pet. App. A22
453   Tinker, Supra 393 U.S. At. 509
454   Johnson, 1995a, pp. 181-182

school ruling to a public university," and that courts in the past have viewed college students as "more mature and better able to judge" if a professor's statements amount to institutional endorsement of religion.[455]

General counsel for the *American Association of University Professors*, Robert M. O'Neil stated that, while the court might have been correct to affirm the university's right to prevent Bishop "from mentioning his personal religious beliefs on campus," the judges had given university administrators far too much discretion, and the decision's wording was "dangerous and very sweeping," and "could represent an invitation for intrusion into the core of academic freedom—what goes on in the classroom."[456] J. Scott Houser, executive director of the *Southern Center for Law and Ethics*, concluded that this appellate court decision should concern all faculty: "In effect, it reduces the professor to a puppet of the university. The court held that the institution retains academic freedom, but professors do not."[457]

Even the *University of Alabama* counsel, Kenneth R. Goodwin, stated that he was surprised by the court's broad ruling, giving his university "unprecedented authority" to manage course content and professors' speech. Mr. O'Neal added, "I think there is general agreement within the academic community that faculty ought not to intrude their own religious views into the teaching of secular material."[458] Of course, faculty commonly (and often blatantly) inject their personal religious views in class—and this has been almost universally accepted by academia as appropriate, as long as the professor's views are close to agnosticism or atheism.[459] Such views, however, normally are not circumscribed, and if an attempt was made to do so, a howl of protest from the academic community likely would result. Furthermore, the courts have consistently ruled in favor of faculty who endeavor to inject anti-religious, atheistic, or agnostic material into their classes.[460] Attorney and emeritus law professor Phillip Johnson said of this case:

> The opinion by Judge Floyd Gibson for the federal court of appeals said that the relevant principle was not freedom of speech but the right of educational

---

455 Jaschik, 1991, p. A23.
456 Jaschik, 1991, p. A23
457 quoted in Jaschik, 1991, p. A23.
458 quoted in Jaschik, 1991, p. A23
459 Smith, 1990; Fairhurst, 1923
460 Bergman, 1984a.

administrators to control what is said in the classroom. The judiciary should not interfere with such internal university matters, said Gibson, because "federal judges should not be *ersatz* deans or educators." If Bishop and other professors were dissatisfied with the restrictions placed on them by their academic superiors, their remedy was not to go to federal court but to seek employment at a different university that was more tolerant. As the court stated in this *reductio ad absurdum* of free-market ideology, "University officials are undoubtedly aware that quality faculty members will be hard to attract and retain if they are to be shackled in much of what they do."[461]

From Johnson's point of view Judge Gibson's avoidance of the freedom of speech issue is completely unacceptable. Wagner concluded that "viewed in the light of our tradition of academic freedom the *University of Alabama* failed in its responsibility to defend Professor Bishop...all of us who teach in public colleges and universities ... are left to contend with one of the worst judicial opinions on higher education in recent memory."[462]

One of the most extensive studies on academic freedom was completed by an academic study committee at *Columbia University* in 1955. On the important question "Does academic freedom mean the freedom of the academy or the freedom of the scholar in the academy?" the committee ruled that

> Have we academic freedom when the academy runs its own affairs without outside interference? ...Obviously that would be a violation of what is always meant by academic freedom. True, it means the freedom of the academy, but it refers to the intellectual life of the academy. For that is what gives it its character, its being. This intellectual life consists in the activities of a faculty, including in the first place their relation to the students. It is an educational freedom that is at issue. *The academy is free when the scholars who make it are free, as scholars.* And the academy is free when its governing board is free to protect and to advance this freedom.[463]

One would hope this sentiment still finds broad support within academia. The court in the Bishop case clearly violated this widely accepted standard. The academy is not free when the educators who are in it are not free.

---

461   Johnson, 1995a, p. 176.
462   Wagner, 2000. p. 139.
463   MacIver, 1955, p. 3-4, emphasis added.

The Byron Johnson Case

Byron R. Johnson was an assistant professor of criminology at *Memphis State University* from 1986 until 1991, when his contract was terminated one semester before he would have been eligible for tenure.[464] The reason given was that "he did not fit in" because of his religion. The university further told him that he "should consider teaching at some smaller religious affiliated school." His problems began when he formed the Christian Faculty/Staff Fellowship.[465] His department chair, Jerry Sparger, was evidently his major critic. The background of the case is as follows:

> Beginning in 1987, Dr. Johnson was instrumental in organizing a Christian Faculty/Staff Fellowship at Memphis State. He did not, however, discuss his religious beliefs in class. Although Dr. Johnson published more and received higher teaching evaluations than any other assistant professor in his department, he received substantially smaller salary increases from 1988 through 1990 than other department members, and was eventually terminated. During discussions with Dr. Johnson, university officials told him he "did not fit in" and that "given his philosophical leanings, he should consider teaching at some smaller religious affiliated school." Dr. Johnson has sued the university in Federal District Court under Federal Civil rights laws ... and that lawsuit is now in pretrial discovery.[466]

This is one of the very few Darwin Doubter cases that I have researched where the victim was able to survive in academia in spite of his problems. Dr. Johnson was, against all odds, able to obtain another position at *Morehead State University* in Kentucky before his case reached the final stages in the court of appeals. Amazingly, his new employer did not even inquire about his past position! This case eventually was settled out of court in Johnson's favor under terms that both parties agreed not to make public (Johnson, 1995a). This outcome indicates that Johnson's claims of illegal discrimination were either valid or the defendants agreed that the court would find in Johnson's favor. Johnson is now the director of the Criminal Justice Research Center at Lamar University in Beaumont, Texas.

---

464 *Johnson v. Carpenter et al.*, No. 91-2075, at 4-8, W.D. Tenn. Jan. 25, 1991
465 see *Action*, March, 1991, p. 6
466 *Bishop v. Delchamps*, 1991, p. 4.

Common Elements in All Three Cases

In all of these cases, I found no evidence that the teachers were "teaching creationism," as opposed to merely criticizing Darwinism. Furthermore, in none of these cases was it alleged that the teacher was anything less than fully competent. Peloza in fact was acknowledged as an excellent teacher, and was a runner-up for biology teacher of the year.[467] As for Bishop's opening statements of belief, which never exceeded a few minutes each semester, he clearly labeled them as his personal bias, and no one has alleged that he engaged in prayer or Bible reading, or lectured on religious topics in class.[468] According to Bishop, "the university had to scratch around to find two students who complained," and "one of those later called me up and said ... 'I'll testify on your side.'"[469] In the Bishop case, Ray Mellichamp, a tenured faculty member at the University of Alabama for twenty-three years, concluded from his work with Bishop that Bishop is a

> good teacher, doing a good job of research, and he makes one comment in class, that a student complains about, and the university goes into orbit. It has been a complete puzzle to me ... why they ever appealed the decision from the district court—it just doesn't make sense.[470]

Many schools are no longer afraid to press the issue of censoring their instructor's who have personal theistic religious beliefs that cause concern that the professor may influence students toward accepting, or evaluating positively, those beliefs. Conversely, no corresponding concern seems exist in the case of individuals who have expressed atheistic or Marxist ideas, and the courts consistently have defended the professor's academic freedom to make statements about their notions in this area. Only the cases of theists creationists have not prevailed in the courts. My search of published academic freedom cases has found no exceptions to this generalization.

---

467 Larsen, et al., 1992.
468 Bishop, 1991 p1-2.
469 Myers, 1992a, p. 2
470 Myers, 1992a, p. 4

Teaching Atheism

In both the Bishop and Johnson cases the university alleged that expressing what it judged as religious (anti-Darwin) views—no matter how carefully done—might cause students to accept similar views, and the courts agreed. Yet in these cases it seems likely that the court's actual concern was over the direction in which the students' beliefs might change, i.e., away from Darwinism and possibly towards theism. In reference to past court cases in this area, in general, if the change in students' beliefs is in the direction of religious disbelief and atheism, the professor typically has been firmly supported by the courts.[471] A good example of this situation is revealed in a study by the *Cornell University* Professor of the History of Biology in the Department of Ecology and Evolutionary Biology, Charles A. Alexander Professor of Biological Sciences Will Provine.[472]

Provine first presents his students with the theistic side of the origins debate, then for the rest of the quarter endeavors to demolish the arguments for theism by teaching Darwinism. He noted that at the beginning of his course, about 75% of his students were either creationists, or at least believed there was a "purpose in evolution," (i.e., were theists and believed that God directed evolution). Provine proudly notes that the percentage of theists dropped to 50% by the end of the course—this compares to about 95% in society as a whole.[473] He obviously is enormously successful in influencing his students to move toward the atheistic world view, and is very open about his success. Yet the university and courts have not interfered, even though he not only has openly "expressed his religious viewpoint" (which the court ruled Bishop could not do), but furthermore, has *deliberately tried to indoctrinate students in atheism*. Although Cornell is a private University, it does receive enormous amount of public funds in research grants, student loans, and grants. Consequently, the Bishop case does influence their policies because private universities that receive public monies are under obligation to obey most court rulings, even if they originally were applied to state supported institutions.

Another case of a professor who deliberately indoctrinates students in Darwinism is biology Professor Tom Langen of *Clarkson University* in Potsdam, New York, who openly *admitted* that he spends much time in his introductory

---

471 Myers, 1992a. p. 4
472 http://www.eeb.cornell.edu/provine/provineworks.html
473 Provine, 1993, p. 63

biology course focusing on Darwin, the history of life on Earth and even the "antievolutionary alternatives to the standard scientific account":

> I provide an overview of the basic claims of young earth creationism and Intelligent Design theory, and then have students evaluate them in relation to the foundational assumptions and ethical ideals of science. I provide my opinion about why these antievolutionary theories are merely pseudoscientific alternatives to the standard scientific account, followed by a discussion among the students on whether these popular antievolutionary alternatives can be categorized as science.[474]

Essentially, he is teaching about a 'religious' view which educators who are skeptical of Darwinism have been reprimanded for by their university and the courts. He feels the educational system, both public and private *must* teach against creationism and ID because to "ignore antievolutionary theories in the science classroom because they are not accepted science" ignores the question of what is "accepted science":

> Examining antievolutionary theories in relation to the assumptions and ideals of standard accepted science can help to clarify on what ethical and epistemological grounds most scientists come to vehemently reject antievolutionary claims as coequal rivals to the standard evolutionary account.[475]

Scott and Branch, who actively oppose "teaching creationism" because it is (in their view) religion, wrote that Langen's approach is commendable.[476] This shows that they *do* support teaching creationism (which the courts have ruled is a religious view), *as long as the teaching opposes it*. Many additional cases could be cited to show teaching creationism or ID is permissible, as long as you teach *against* it.

Keith M. Parsons, a paleontologist at the *University of Houston*, Clear Lake, is even more hostile against creation in his teaching than the professors cited above. He writes:

---

474   Langen, 2004, p. 114
475   Langen, 2004, p. 114
476   Langen, 2004, p. 116

When lecturing to my students about any subject dealing with the history of life, I am quickly made aware of the pervasive influence of creationist propaganda in insulating my students' minds against knowledge of evolution. I consider creationism in all of its guises—whether "young earth" fundamentalism or the allegedly more sophisticated "Intelligent Design" variety—to be pernicious nonsense. I find that before I can instruct my students on evolution, I have to disabuse them of large amounts of misinformation and disinformation spread by creationists. Therefore, I have included a second appendix explaining what evolution is, how it is known to be true, and why the arguments against it are empty.[477]

Can Darwin Doubting Educators Who Are Religious Prevail in Court?

The cases cited above are instructive as to what the future may hold. The courts consistently have ruled that all attempts to challenge or present the "other side" of Darwinism in the classroom constitutes "teaching religion," yet opponents of creation or ID are free to discuss and attack those same views in their classrooms. The result is that our schools now indoctrinate, not educate. Today it is very difficult to teach science objectively and still survive, if one's colleagues and students perceive that one holds a Christian or a "religious" world view. Good education requires teachers to present several viewpoints in their classroom, but not coercively, thus allowing students to form their own conclusions. If it is perceived that the instructor is functioning as an advocate for theism, and not objectively teaching science, the likelihood of prevailing in court is less likely. Yet another problem, according to former Senator Rick Santorum, is the fact that many judges are "hostile to religion in any form."[478] Thus, even when educators who are Darwin Doubters present only scientific and philosophical considerations to their students, the perception that disagreement with Darwinism implies "creationism" or "religion" will continue to prejudice all cases of discrimination against Darwin Doubters that reach the courts.

---

477 Parsons, 2004, p. ix.
478 Santorum, 2004, p. 61

Conclusion

This chapter documents the fact that those who question the Darwinian world view and are challenged, could end up in court and, in all of the cases I have researched, the victims have lost. The courts have not upheld their academic freedom if they were accused of supporting the anti-Darwinian view but their academic freedom was upheld if they supported the opposing worldview. Furthermore, very rarely are those who challenge Darwin skeptics in the classroom required to account for their actions. I am aware of only two cases in this category, both discussed in some detail elsewhere in this book,[479] that made it to court in the last half century, and in both of these cases the court ruled that the instructor has a right to teach against not only creationism, but against the religious beliefs of their students as a matter of academic freedom, a freedom denied to Darwin skeptic educators.

---

479   *Moore v. Gaston County Board of Education*, 357 F. Supp. 1037, 1043 (W.D.N.C. 1973

Chapter 8: Rodney LeVake and Larry Booher

The majority of cases reviewed in this book indicates a pattern worth noting -- that fault was found with *who these people are* (or who they were perceived to be), not what *they did* in the classroom. Many of the cases also reveal a misinformed, hypersensitive reaction to what an educator is permitted to present to students and how it can be presented (see the conclusion at the end of this chapter). This chapter presents two more examples of just how far college administrators fail to understand the latitude and freedom educators should be given according to standard academic freedom policies. The first is Faribault, Minnesota science teacher Rodney (Rod) LeVake and the second is Larry Booher. Both a biology teachers are no longer allowed to teach biology because they are not true believers in Darwinism. Rodney LeVake was blocked by his high school (and the judicial system) in his attempt to expose his students to some of the problems with Darwinism. In July 2001, a circuit court judge ruled that the school district had the right to remove Mr. LeVake from his high school biology class because of his views critical of Darwinism. Typically, the media incorrectly highlighted the controversy as a "teaching creation" case.[480] In the first part of this chapter, we will consider LeVake's case in detail.

Introduction to Rodney LeVake's Doubts about Darwin

Rod, his wife Chris, and their four children have lived near Faribault for 25 years. He trained in evolutionary biology, and it was only after he graduated from college with a degree in biology that he and his wife became Christians. Forced to deal with contradictions between his faith and Darwinism, he studied the subject in detail, reading extensively on the topic. Among the many books he read that he was impressed include *Evolution: A Theory in Crisis* by microbiologist Michael Denton. Eventually, Rod concluded that Darwinism was not wholly supported by the empirical facts of science.

---

480   Anonymous 1999; Anonymous 2002b; Anonymous 2005.

Highlights of Rodney LeVake's Brief Career Teaching Biology

LeVake had been teaching biology in a public school for only a year when, in 1998, he told a fellow high school teacher, during a casual conversation, that he had doubts about Darwin's theory, and planned to inform his students about his conclusions, such as the problems with Haeckel's embryos.[481] As James Kilpatrick observed in his *Augusta Chronicle* column, "this was a grave mistake."[482] He was within a few weeks confronted by the school's administration about his beliefs, not because of state requirements—in Minnesota "how schools teach evolution is a local issue for communities to decide"—but because the administration objected to LeVake's world view.[483] He "repeatedly" assured school officials that "he could and would teach the theory of evolution."[484] After being questioned by the administration about *how* he intended to teach Darwinism, he was eventually required to write "a position paper" (something no other teacher had been asked to do) on his views. The position paper was Rodney LeVake's synopsis of how he intended to handle evolution.[485] He stated in this paper that he had concluded from his research that "life's complexity and the fossil record do not support the theory of macroevolution or biochemical evolution," and that he would accompany his discussion of evolution "with an honest look at the difficulties and inconsistencies of the theory without turning my class into a religious one." He also stressed that, as a biology teacher, his fundamental responsibility is "to kindle in my students an appreciation for the complexities and subtleties of various forms of life and their systems":

> I don't believe an unquestioning faith in the theory of evolution is foundational to the goals I have stated in teaching my students about themselves, their responsibilities, and gaining a sense of awe for what they see around them.[486]

The superintendent of the school did not like what he read and responded to LeVake's paper as follows:

---

481   Cushman, 2001, p. 18.
482   Kilpatrick, 2001, p. A4.
483   Welsh, 2003, p. 1.
484   Foster, 2000d, p. 1.
485   Beckwith, 2002.p. 1312
486   Rodney LeVake, quoted in Kilpatrick, 2001, p. A4.

You asserted to me that you believe that you can teach the prescribed curriculum. However, in your explanation, you continue to justify why it is appropriate not to follow the curriculum by pointing out the discrepancies that you believe exist [between evolutionary theory and the scientific evidence]... You ... have made it clear that you cannot teach the curriculum.[487]

The superintendent evidently believed that students should have an "unquestioning faith in the theory of evolution" and did not want it challenged in class. Yet, as Frank York says, "What LeVake wanted to do is common practice across the country: In most classrooms, teachers aren't confined to the words of the text; they're allowed to depart from the text and recommend supplemental readings."[488] Of course, part of the problem is that LeVake was well-known among his faculty as a conservative Christian. Although he rarely discussed his faith with fellow faculty, he would occasionally speak up on issues such as abortion. He also led football award banquet prayers when the head coach neglected to invite a clergy for the task.[489]

At one meeting, an administrator asked LeVake if his students knew that he was a Christian. LeVake knew that this was one question that he could not answer without some thought. He recounts how he answered:

"I would like to have said, 'Yes, they do know, just because of the way I act.' But I didn't want to say it that way because she would probably think that I was proselytizing in my classroom. So I said, 'I would hope so because I don't curse, and I don't do things that would make people think I'm not a Christian'."[490]

Although surprised by these inappropriate (and illegal) questions, LeVake said, "It gave me some light on where they were coming from. Those questions betrayed what they were thinking." What they were thinking became blatantly obvious on April 7, 1998 when LeVake was summoned to a meeting with both the principal and members of the science department. The following passage

---

487   Quoted in York, 2000, p. 5.
488   York, 2000, p. 7.
489   York, 2000, p. 5.
490   Rodney LeVake, quoted in York, 2000, p. 5.

gives an indication of the tone and contents of the meeting. One of LeVake's fellow science teachers intimated at the meeting that

> if LeVake didn't accept evolution as fact, he probably also believed that the world was flat. Another made it clear he thought LeVake was crazy for questioning evolution. LeVake was up against a widespread stereotype that portrays [Darwin] dissenters as religious fanatics: "They thought that the only way you can question evolution is from a religious standpoint, when there's just volumes of evidence [against evolution] from a scientific stand-point, from a purely secular standpoint."[491]

After this meeting it was clear to LeVake that he was not in trouble because of what he *did*, but because of perceptions about who he *was*. LeVake knew that this line of questioning clearly raised legal problems. At this point, LeVake knew he needed to consult with an attorney. As his attorney concluded, "School officials may not pry into an employee's religious beliefs and then discriminate against him because of what officials think about those beliefs."[492] On May 24, 1999, Le-Vake filed a lawsuit against respondents Independent School District #656, Keith Dixon, Dave Johnson, and Cheryl Freund (respondents), but it was

> ...dismissed in June of 1999 by judge Judge Bernard Borene of the Rice County District Court, who granted a motion for summary judgment by the school district and dismissed the suit saying that LeVake had no right of academic freedom and could be prevented from presenting criticisms of evolution even "though they may be scientifically meritorious."[493]

On June 1, 1999 *The American Center for Law and Justice* (ACLJ) took on his appeal because they "believed LeVake had solid grounds for a lawsuit... LeVake has never refused to teach evolution, nor has he insisted on teaching creationism." The suit stated in part that

> LeVake has told his superiors that he is not interested in teaching creation-ism in biology class, but simply wants his students to be aware that not all

---

491   Quoted in York, 2000, p. 6.
492   York, 2000, p. 7.
493   Business Wire, July 24, 2000. http://findarticles.com/p/articles/mi_m0EIN/is_2000_July_24/ai_63633530

scientists accept evolution as an unquestionable fact and wants to present "an honest look at some of the scientific weaknesses of Darwin's theory of evolution."[494]

LeVake's ACLJ attorney Frank Manion said, "As opposed to other cases we're all familiar with, you don't have a teacher who wants to teach creationism." Rather this case involved "a teacher who says, 'I don't believe in the theory of evolution, but I'm willing to teach it.'"[495] An ACLJ news release quoted Manion, who concluded that this case is about "academic freedom and a desire to present information about the origins of life":

Teachers must be able to tell students information they need to make up their minds about issues such as evolution. In this case, our client wants to be able to look closely at the theory of evolution and point out flaws concerning Darwin's evolutionary theory—flaws that are often articulated by other evolutionists. Unfortunately, it appears the school district is determined to censor this teacher because they do not agree with his message.[496]

LeVake was not terminated, but was assigned to teach chemistry even though he was the only teacher in the department with a master's degree in biology.[497] As a result of this reassignment, LeVake brought suit against his school, noting that "The ironic thing about this whole situation was that I was reassigned, not for what I had actually said in class, but for what I thought about evolution."[498] LeVake's opponents openly argued that he *should* be fired for having "doubts about Darwin." Biology teacher Rodney Sheffer stated that evolution (a term he never defined) is a *fact* like gravity, and a teacher who questions Darwinism is blatantly incompetent and *should* be fired.[499] Conversely, judging from his mail, LeVake commented "I think that there is a lot more people out there who think like me [than I expected]." The fact is no evidence has ever been presented that he taught creation in his classes.

---

494   Business Wire, July 24, 2000. http://findarticles.com/p/articles/mi_m0EIN/is_2000_July_24/ai_
63633530
495   Frank Manion, quoted in York, 2000, p. 6.
496   Frank Manion, quoted in ACLJ news release, 2000, p. 1.
497   Tevlin, 2000. p. 3
498   LeVake, 1999.
499   Olson, 2001, p. 1.

The Court Ruling

On June 23, 2000, the school's decision removing LaVake from the biology classroom was allowed to stand uncontested by Judge Bernard Borene of the Rice County District Court—without even bothering to have a trial. The court ignored the religious inquisition that LeVake was forced to endure, and wrote that LeVake "has no constitutional right to teach his proposed criticisms of evolutionary theory, though they may be scientifically meritorious."[500] Tyrangiel quotes Manion as saying "This is a landmark case ... we have a teacher who is not asking to teach creationism. He simply wants to teach science the way he thinks—and the way a lot of people think—it should be taught, in a more balanced way."[501] LeVake concluded the court condoned teaching evolution as dogma and prohibited all criticism of Darwinism.

On July 24, 2000,[502] LeVake filed with the Minnesota Court of Appeals to be reinstated to teach biology classes. Until his appeal was decided, he was reassigned by the school to teach general science and chemistry, where Darwinism did not come up much, if at all.

ACLJ attorney in this case, Wayne B. Holstad, wrote in court briefs he filed that "This case presents the court with an opportunity to reaffirm that public high school teachers are not First Amendment orphans." Kay Nord Hunt wrote in the court filings for the school district that "This court has never held that under the First Amendment, schools are the mere instruments of the advancement of the individual agendas of its teachers." On May 8, 2001, his appeal was rejected by the Minnesota Court of Appeals. The court wrote that "... the established curriculum and LeVake's responsibility as a public school teacher to teach evolution in the manner prescribed by the curriculum, overrides his First Amendment rights as a private citizen."[503] The court concluded that LeVake's free speech rights were not abridged by preventing him from teaching "criticisms of evolution." The appeals court noted the established curriculum requires that:

---

500   *Rodney LeVake v. Independent School District* No. 656, 01-665 Court file CX - 99 - 793.
501   Tyrangiel, 2000, p. 10.
502   http://findarticles.com/p/articles/mi_m0EIN/is_2000_July_24/ai_63633530 (as of 05/28/08)
503   Minnesota Court of Appeals: Rodney LeVake ISD #656, Case file C8-00-1613. See the decision at http://caselaw.lp.findlaw.com/scripts/getcase.pl?court=mn&vol=apppub%5C0105%5Cc8001613&invol=1

students will be able to understand that evolution involves natural selection and mutations, which constantly cause changes in living things. In the required course book for the biology class, three chapters dealt with evolution but only one was required as part of the curriculum. None of the chapters addressed alternative theories to, or criticisms of, evolution. The syllabus provided examples of topics that should be covered in class, which included evolution. Minnesota's high school graduation standards do not specifically refer to evolution; rather, the standards provide that a student must demonstrate an understanding of biological change over time.

In the court's words, the curriculum "dictated that evolution should be taught as the *accepted* theory for how life has changed over time," yet the court never defined evolution or explained what "changed over time" means. One could also ask what "accepted" means—accepted by whom? Did the court intend to imply that Darwinism is accepted by everybody? What about the tens of thousands of scientists who do not fully accept all tenets of evolution? Is it wrong for students to know that evolution and Darwinism are *not* fully accepted by all scientists? The court also claimed that the school's position on this matter was religiously neutral, that the classroom is a "marketplace of ideas," and that "academic freedom should be safeguarded."[504] Yet the court then contradicted the ruling, forbidding "LeVake, in his role as a public school teacher ... to discuss the criticisms of evolution."

How, in this case, did the court uphold the "marketplace of ideas" requirement by preventing LeVake from discussing "criticisms of evolution"? If LeVake were a committed Darwinist, would he have a problem discussing criticisms of evolution? He certainly would not have a problem discussing "criticisms of creationism" as many teachers do all the time in science classes without problems.

In its ruling the court addressed LeVake's due process, freedom of speech, and freedom of religion. If the Court had determined LeVake's rights were violated in just *one* of these areas, he would have prevailed. The one area where he clearly *should* have prevailed was with respect to his freedom of religion claim. It is clear that LeVake's *perceived* personal beliefs were the deciding factor in this case, *rather than his teaching ability*. The court openly admitted his doubts about Darwin the:

---

504   citing *Keyishian v. Board of Regents*, 385 U.S. 589, 603, 87 S. Ct. 675, 683 (1967)

respondents' concern about his inability to teach the prescribed curriculum was well-founded. Thus, the district court did not err in granting respondents' motion for summary judgment because LeVake did not demonstrate a genuine issue of material fact regarding his claim that respondents violated his right to free speech (emphasis added).

But the Court *did* err, and egregiously, on this point. In fact, the inability of the court to see the folly of its argument is staggering. The school district's concern was *not* well founded, and for at least one very obvious reason that all of us recognize: an educator need not be required to be an advocate for any particular point of view before he can be considered competent to teach about it. For example, must a teacher believe in Marxism before being allowed to discuss it with his students? The Court's conclusion that LeVake should not be allowed to teach "evolution" because he did not personally accept Darwinism, is both irresponsible and inconsistent, given that teachers are (typically) freely allowed to discuss why dissenting views are valid or not. LeVake's beliefs about evolution had absolutely no bearing on whether he was competent to teach the subject. Many, if not most, professors of history do not accept biblical Christianity as a personal faith—many history professors are agnostics, atheists, Jews, Muslims, or of another faith—yet they teach Christianity in their Western Civilization classes, and I doubt if anyone has been removed from teaching about Christianity because they are not believing Christians. It is impossible to teach a survey of religions course and, at the same time, be a true believer of *all* the religions presented. The court is not basing LeVake's removal on what he *did*, but what some individuals thought he *might* do in class, and what they thought he believed. No school (or court) has the right to *require* an educator to *believe* in evolution before he can teach the subject. Many who have examined this case agree, including legal scholar Francis Beckwith:

> The Court's free exercise analysis is terribly confusing, for it seems to use the terms of *belief* and *practice* interchangeably when in fact the Supreme Court has recognized a clear distinction between the two. State action that discriminates against someone because of his or her religious beliefs is de facto unconstitutional, whereas a state action that discriminates against a citizen because of his or her religious practice is prima facie constitutional if it is the result of a generally applicable law. Thus, since the court concedes that Mr. LeVake's reassignment was based on his beliefs, an act that is de-

facto unconstitutional, therefore, the Court should have ruled in his favor on those grounds.[505]

The Court also ruled that LeVake must teach what was in the text *only*. The fact is most schools do not prohibit a teacher from covering a relevant class topic if the text does not cover it. ***If this were the case, teachers could not teach about most current events!*** It is also significant that the court ruled against LeVake not on the basis of what he did—or did not do—but rather based on his *beliefs* (and the assumption that his beliefs would render him unable to teach the prescribed curriculum).

On January 7, 2002, the U.S. Supreme Court refused to hear the case, ending Mr. LeVake's quest to criticize Darwinism.[506] For an incisive review of the LeVake case, see Francis Beckwith's analysis.[507]

Media Misrepresentations

The LeVake case received national media attention. Even the global news weekly, *Time*, covered the story but, as is true of this issue in general, the magazine seemingly could not objectively report on issues relating to science or Christianity, and indirectly mocked LeVake's beliefs. For example, in its July 10, 2000 report on Rodney LeVake, *Time* portrayed creation-believing scientists as an almost non-existent minority, claiming "reputable scientists who agree with LeVake can be counted on one hand," a claim which is patently false. In fact, many thousands of reputable Darwin skeptics with graduate degrees in science are educators and/or are actively involved in scientific research in America alone. Time went so far as to portray Mr. LeVake (in a full-page article) as a hillbilly, and some readers would not unreasonably conclude that *Time* was mocking his language (Mr. LeVake was quoted as using "kinda" and "golly," for example).

In related stories, *Time* has repeatedly misrepresented the events in other evolution education cases. For example, in the state of Kansas, when the state school board voted in August 1999 to de-emphasize evolution in its public schools, *Time* incorrectly claimed that evolution had been *removed* from the sci-

---

505 Beckwith, 2003, pp. 71-72 (emphasis in original).
506 LeVake interview with Jerry Bergman. 2002.
507 Beckwith, 2002.

ence standards (or guidelines). Outsiders have contacted *Time* magazine on at least three separate occasions to correct their misreporting, but *Time* refused to print a retraction.

Evaluation of the LeVake Case

The Court evidently agreed with the notion that someone can be fired for what he or she personally believes. According to an Associated Press report, LeVake's attorney (Wayne Holstad) said LeVake "was silenced, not for anything he said in the classroom," but merely for personally holding a contrary viewpoint and expressing a desire to discuss honestly ideas "that the school district deemed out of step with its officially imposed orthodoxy." This has been true in almost every case examined in this book. There was no credible evidence that LeVake was teaching creationism, and LeVake has made it clear that he has never felt it was appropriate to teach creation science to his public school students because he did not believe, and still does not believe, that imposing his beliefs about origins on his students "was in their best collective interest." He explains:

> If I were to teach creation science correctly, after all, I would need to use a Bible... A student's education about God and His creation are best handled by his or her family along with their place of worship. Instead, in Biology class, I concentrated on highlighting the extraordinary complexity of life to my students. These amazing stories about mysterious creatures turned out to be favorites in class.[508]

In Foster's words, an "Evolution Critic [was] Censored" and a teacher was "Punished for Pointing Out Flaws in Darwin's Theory."[509] In short, Darwinism must not, by law, be questioned! As a result of this and many other cases, Darwinism now has become state-supported orthodoxy. LeVake was branded guilty of "heresy."[510]

Fortunately, not all the press was negative. A well-written and balanced update on Mr. LeVake's struggle for academic freedom was published in the Min-

---

508 LeVake, 1999 (and in an interview with *Creation Digest*, 2004).
509 Foster, 2000d, p. 1.
510 Kilpatrick, 2001, p. A4.

neapolis paper, *The Star Tribune*.[511] The article illustrated how America's court system and public schools are increasingly intolerant of anything that may even hint of criticizing Darwinism.

Dream Ended

Mr. LeVake's life-long dream was to teach biology at the high school level. In spite of what happened, he very much wants to return to teaching biology classes, where he is most qualified as an instructor. His master's degree is in biology and this is the field that he enjoys teaching over all other areas. It now looks like his dream has been shattered forever. He firmly believed that he had the academic freedom to offer the evidence both for and against Darwinism, but as LeVake and so many other educators have discovered, to their chagrin and amazement, they are typically not supported in that endeavor by their colleagues, their school district, support organizations, the courts, and the media.

The Case of Larry Booher

Another example where the media attacked a biology teacher, producing world-wide publicity, was the case of Larry Booher. The Booher incident turned out very differently than the LeVake case, largely due to the support of Booher's fellow science teachers. Mr. Booher teaches basic and advanced biology at John S. Battle High School in Washington County, Virginia. During his teaching career, Booher had collected a set of articles written by scientists and scholars critical of Darwinism. He then copied the set at his own expense, assembled it in a three-ring binder, and gave a copy to each of his students "as a voluntary, extra-credit option."[512] A past student loaned a copy of the collection to a friend, and it ended up in the hands of a newspaper reporter. The reporter anonymously contacted the school, and the school investigated. In the words of a *Bristol Herald Courier* report, "a freelance reporter from another part of this state called to inquire about the home-made text." At that point the story hit the media—and the rest, as they say, is history.

---

511   Tevlin, 2000.pp. 1-3.
512   Associated Press,"Teacher Told to Revise Creationism Lesson Plan" June 10, 2005. http://www.msnbc.msn.com/id/8169240/ (as of 05/24/08)

Almost immediately the American Civil Liberties Union and other opponents of Darwin skeptics entered the fray. The reason they gave for intervening was, in the words of Kent Willis, executive director of the ACLU of Virginia, "Creationism is not biology and has no place in a biology class." Booher was not "teaching creationism" in his biology class, according to all of the reports and interviews that I completed—he was only giving students a voluntary extra-credit option that they could take advantage of on their own time if they elected to. Furthermore, the material was not on "biblical creationism" but was merely writings by recognized scientists critical of orthodox Darwinism.

During his twenty-five-year teaching career, the forty-eight-year-old Booher has never had a single complaint concerning his use of this extra-class material. In fact, many students came out of the closet strongly in support of him following this incident. Only a handful of students have ever expressed any concerns in class, which Booher reportedly responded to appropriately and professionally. His students have consistently stated that he is an excellent teacher, and some students felt so strongly about Booher that a number of them placed statements on the internet in support of him. For example, note the following testimony:

> Mr. Larry Booher (LD to all of us at John S. Battle HS) was my Biology I teacher in my sophomore year of high school. He is perhaps the smartest science teacher I've ever encountered, and I look up to him as an example of what teachers should be... [T]his morning ... I noted a front-page story about Mr. Booher, that stated an "anonymous" tip [claimed] that Booher was teaching creationism in his Biology II class and was ordered by the superintendent to stop. A 500-page folder he made and paid for himself was passed out to students that disproved evolution. He taught us small bits and pieces of it in my Biology I class, and I'm glad that he did. Every student at Battle clamored to be in his class.[513]

Another former student said that Mr. Booher is the "most brilliant science teacher to ever grace the halls of John S. Battle" yet, the student added, some woman in California had the audacity to criticize his curriculum!

---

513   Quoted in Neal, 2005.p. 1

In the words of Allen Lee, Superintendent of Washington County schools, Booher is "one of the finest science teachers I have ever been around."[514] Interestingly, *all* of the science teachers at his school support the creationist world view. Some of the teachers in non-science departments, though, are outspoken Darwinists.

A more important concern is that critics have roundly condemned Booher for "breaking the law" with statements such as the false claim that Booher believed that "it was okay to break a law because no one was complaining."[515] Rasmussen quotes the words of one of Booher's defenders as evidence that America is "heading in the direction of theocracy." He adds that Booher "has been teaching the non-scientific, religious creation story from the Christian religion to the public high school students in a biology class ... and teaching it well. So well, that one of his young students defends the illegal nature of the teacher's fifteen-year-long criminal career." *No law was cited because no law exists prohibiting educators from presenting the scientific evidence challenging neo-Darwinism.*

Commentators repeatedly stated that it is "against the law" to discuss Creationism or the "biblical account of creation" in a biology class (terms that were never defined in *any* of the articles that took this view). For example, an editorial in the *Bristol Herald Courier* stated:

> a high school biology classroom is not the proper place to talk about the Biblical account of the earth's creation. That has been the law of the land for more than fifteen years and public school teachers are obligated to follow it, no matter their personal religious beliefs. If their faith won't allow them to follow the law, they can always teach at a private school or teach a different subject. School administrators have a duty, too. They must make sure that teachers adhere to the rules and that the curriculum complies with the law."[516]

Booher did not teach about the Earth's creation, but used habdouts that documented the scientific problems with the Darwinian creation of life view. A definition of the "Biblical account of the Earth's creation" was never given in the editorial (and the only statement that the Bible makes about the Earth's creation

---

514   Associated Press,"Teacher Told to Revise Creationism Lesson Plan" June 10, 2005.
515   Rasmussen, 2005, p. 1.
516   Editorial in *Bristol Herald Courier*, June 12, 2005, p. 1.

was that God created the Heavens and the Earth). The comments were way off point – the problem is not the Earth's creation, but whether criticism of neo-Darwinism should be allowed.

The media also condemned the school for "winking and nodding" at "Booher's unauthorized lesson plans."[517] Of course, no unauthorized lesson plans existed—only an extra-credit handout. The Courier editorial then incorrectly stated that the "literal interpretation" of the Bible (creationism) and "the theory of Intelligent Design" are both "the Biblical account of creation," and a faith position. This type of inaccuracy and uninformed bias is typical of many media reports and editorials in these cases.

Fortunately, although the Darwinists tried very hard to get Booher fired (or worse), the only change in his teaching is he is no longer able to use the extra-credit handout that he provided at his own expense. Of course, *since he never formally taught religion, or religious ideas, there was no need to make changes in his teaching or in his lesson plans.* The allegations made by Darwin fundamentalists did not stick because he was a twenty-five-year teaching veteran in a close-knit high school, his colleagues and administrators were well aware that he was effectively teaching empirical science and aiding students to understand controversial issues by helping them learn the process of experimentation, research, and reasoning, and by encouraging them in the healthy habit of asking good questions.

Conclusion

Both of these cases are typical of many I have reviewed. The problem is that educators presenting material in favor of creationism, Intelligent Design or critical of evolution are finding that when challenged for doing this, the courts have consistently ruled against them. Conversely, educators who present material (not part of the 'standard' and sanctioned curriculum) opposing creationism or Intelligent Design are rarely challenged and when they are, typically nothing is done. The result is creationism and Intelligent Design are commonly taught as long as the material opposes these worldviews. This conclusion is discussed in more detail in other chapters of this book.

---

517   Editorial in *Bristol Herald Courier*, June 12, 2005.

The courts have made it clear that although public schools may not indoctrinate in a religion (or anti-religion), they *can* teach *about* religion. A well worded document titled "Secretary's Statement on Religious Expression" by Richard Riley, U.S. Secretary of Education (1993-2001), contains a statement written to clarify court rulings:

> Public schools can neither foster religion nor preclude it. Our public schools must treat religion with fairness and respect and vigorously protect religious expression as well as the freedom of conscience of all other students. In so doing our public schools reaffirm the First Amendment and enrich the lives of their students.[518]

Under the subheading, "Teaching about religion," Riley wrote that public schools may not engage in religious advocacy, but can

> teach *about* religion, including the Bible or other scripture: the history of religion, comparative religion, the Bible (or other scripture)-as-literature, and the role of religion in the history of the United States and other countries all are permissible public school subjects. Similarly, it is permissible to consider religious influences on art, music, literature, and social studies.[519]

Finally, the secretary, under the subheading "student assignments" concluded that students are allowed to

> express their beliefs about religion in the form of homework, artwork, and other written and oral assignments free of discrimination based on the religious content of their submissions. Such home and classroom work should be judged by ordinary academic standards of substance and relevance, and against other legitimate pedagogical concerns identified by the school.

Consequently even if both LeVake and Booher discussed religion in their class, a problem would exist only if they indoctrinated students in one religious view, something that neither man was ever accused of doing. Another document worth reading (although it has not been updated since 1995) is a joint state-

---

518   Riley, revised in 1998. http://www.ed.gov/Speeches/08-1995/religion.html (as of 05/20/08)
519   Riley, 1998, p. 7.

ment produced and endorsed by several leading religious and other interested groups titled "Religion in the Public Schools – A Joint Statement of Current Law."[520] This document, archived at the US Department of Education web site, is instructive in gaining a better understanding of what is and is not permissible in the way of religious expression by educators and students. Altgough very useful, this document needs to be updated to reflect current law.

---

520   http://www.ed.gov/Speeches/04-1995/prayer.html

Chapter 9: The Nancy Bryson Case

Nancy Bryson's entire working life has been devoted to science teaching—now over twenty years at various American universities. After she completed a B.S. in biology from Mississippi University for Women (MUW) and a M.A.T. from Mississippi State University, she earned her Ph.D. in chemistry from the University of South Carolina. Early in 2003, the story surfaced that the university administration had demoted her for "teaching the controversy" about Darwinism in a public lecture held at MUW. At that time she was an associate professor of chemistry and head of MUW science department.[521]

Her problems began in October, 2002, when the director of the MUW Honors Program invited the faculty to give presentations to the Honors Forum held during the spring semester. Dr. Bryson had just returned from Atlanta, where she had read about the controversy in Cobb County surrounding the school board's vote to allow teaching "disputed views" on the origin of life in the county schools. In the 1990's, she had studied the writings by Darwinism critics, including Phillip Johnson, Michael Behe, and others, and became persuaded that the case for Darwinism was far from proven.

Dr. Bryson shared with her supervisor, Vice-President of Academic Affairs Dr. Vagn Hansen, a major article in the December, 2001 *Chronicle of Higher Education* that covered the Intelligent Design movement. Because Dr. Hansen wanted MUW to become involved in the distance-learning market, Bryson then suggested developing a distance-learning course that covered some of the flaws in the Neo-Darwinian synthesis and discussed ID as an alternative view. Dr. Hansen was unreceptive (actually somewhat dismissive) of her suggestion.

Anxious for an avenue to discuss with others the results of her study and interest in this area, in October of 2002 she volunteered to present an Honors Forum talk at the college. The talk was given on Thursday, February 20, 2003. She told the audience of around 50 that one of her objectives was to introduce them to some "contrarian" thinking about evolution by highly credentialed academicians. She discussed the nonexistence of evidence for chemical (prebiotic) evolution, the "Haeckel's embryos fraud," the evolution-disconfirming evidence

---

521   Interview of Nancy Bryson by Jerry Bergman, 2003.

from the field of paleontology, and the subjectivity of paleoanthropology and its interpretation about where the thus-far-discovered human-like fossil skulls fit in the "human evolution" family tree. She also noted that the general biology text used at MUW greatly misleads students by not only ignoring all of the disconfirming evidence, but also by presenting false "evidence" for Darwinism.

She then introduced the ID topic by reading a discourteous, not to mention ignorant, quotation about this developing area from a recent issue of *Scientific American*. She continued with a description of the ID movement from one of its most prominent proponents, William Dembski. After noting that the Intelligent Design worldview had great scientific currency throughout history up until the rise of uniformitarianism (Lyell and Darwin) in the mid-nineteenth century, she concluded with quotations from contemporary philosophers of science who implied that restricting science to methodological naturalism actually *limits* its truth-finding mission.

At the conclusion of her talk, a professor of biology, Dr. William Parker, rose and read a 4-to-5 minute *prepared* diatribe against Dr. Bryson as a person, and against her talk. He said Dr. Bryson was "unqualified" to speak on the subject of evolution, and that her presentation was "religion masquerading as science." Although Parker teaches the evolution course at the college, none of the life sciences faculty, including Parker, have academic or publication credentials as evolutionary biologists. When Dr. Bryson asked Parker to identify one incorrect statement she made, he could not. Parker's protégé, an assistant professor of biology, although unable to find any errors in Dr. Bryson's presentation, made a similar protest.

In contrast, the students were uniformly supportive and enthusiastic about the talk, and at least a dozen students came up after the talk to thank her. In written evaluations of her talk requested by the Honors Forum director, all responding students (over 20) said they enjoyed the talk and expressed clear disapproval of Parker's unprofessional behavior.

The next morning, a congratulatory e-mail from a biology major had been sent to Dr. Bryson and copied to others on the science/math student LISTSERV. It was followed by a rude e-mail that Dr. Parker sent out on the LISTSERV with a copy to the vice-president. Bryson claimed that his e-mail contained "untruths" that she believed were legally "actionable."

Around 5:15 that afternoon, Dr. Hansen went to Dr. Bryson's office to pressured her to resign as department head. Dr. Bryson asked Dr. Hansen for reasons, which he refused to provide, so she refused the request. She describes the rest of the interview as follows:

> This cycle of his asking and my refusing continued for about 5 minutes. (It should be emphasized that he was most anxious for my *voluntary* resignation, insisting that such would be better for me. It is wonderful to have such an altruistic boss.) He finally gave up and said he would prepare a non-renewal notice on Monday morning. I did indeed receive written notice on Monday.[522]

No one at the administration gave her *any* indication before this that she was going to be demoted. Dr. Bryson added that she did *not* teach Intelligent Design (ID) in her presentation, but only critiqued Darwinism, although she felt ID would be acceptable content for a forum lecture. As Bryson noted, a forum "is a medium of open discussion or voicing of ideas."[523]

At this meeting Dr. Hansen also queried her in detail about her religion and church affiliation (of course, this line of inquiry is illegal). Bryson answered that she had been living in Columbus, Mississippi, for only about 22 months and had not yet found a church. She added that she "would not consider regular fellowship with a church that subscribes to Darwinism or, for that matter, 'theistic evolution.'" The issue is important to Dr. Bryson. Convinced of evolution as an undergraduate, she became an atheist until her in-depth study of Darwinism convinced her that the Darwinists' philosophy was bankrupt.

Controversy over the Talk

The specific issues raised in her talk that upset the Administration included questioning the belief that "evolution is a fact" and the issue of Intelligent Design. Yet the Administration has steadfastly denied that the talk and her non-renewal decision were in *any way* related. The rationale for her demotion given in the non-renewal letter (copies of all other written correspondence between the University and Bryson are now in the hands of her attorney) included vague claims about

---

522 Interview of Nancy Bryson by Jerry Bergman, 2003.
523 Interview of Nancy Bryson by Jerry Bergman, 2003.

dissatisfaction with her performance. These claims appear implausible, since those I interviewed stated that Dr. Bryson was a very competent administrator, nor does there seem to be any other reasonable grounds to terminate Bryson except because of her talk. Not one student openly objected to the presentation, nor did *any* members of the science faculty, aside from the two aforementioned biology teachers. Thus, the Administration's denial compounds its error: *No one* familiar with this incident doubts that the talk precipitated her demotion.

It is not known if the actions of the administration had the formal support of the faculty or the board of trustees. Regarding the faculty, Dr. Bryson was told that a "self-described atheistic mathematician who was in attendance at the talk, and has bragged that she can 'get rid of anyone,' visited the VPAA the morning after the talk, urging my dismissal." Bryson said that she would be "very greatly surprised" if the morning after her lecture one or even several life sciences faculty hadn't "visited the VPAA" to protest her lecture. University-wide, a few faculty had been very supportive, and a few others critical, but most were noncommittal.

In contrast, students and the public alike were uniformly supportive of Bryson's right to present the case against Darwinism, and the college received a total of almost 1,000 e-mails and phone calls in her support; Bryson had time to respond to only about 200. She notes that "the most encouraging reaction" she received was from students, who were "enthusiastically supportive" of her.[524] The students I interviewed uniformly said that Dr. Bryson is an excellent teacher—hard and demanding, but patient and willing to go the extra mile to help them learn.

Bryson's observation is that some of her students believe in evolution because they were taught it as "fact" by teachers that they trusted from an early age, but that "I am reasonably certain that the *majority* of MUW students are evolution-disbelievers. So far as I can determine, *all* students ... supported my right to present contradictory evidence." She also concluded that "Darwinism has significant flaws" and that to conceal this evidence from students, who in her experience "often uncritically accept what they are told by authority figures," would be dishonest.[525]

After the community and other support for Bryson surfaced, the university backtracked and decided not to demote her.[526] In the words of *Science* maga-

---

524   Brown and Vitagliano, 2003, p. 1.

525   Keller, 2003, p. 27.

526   Kanengiser, 2003.

zine, "they reinstated her after a Christian radio station broadcast her story."[527] Dr. Hansen claimed the school reinstated her "to clear up the perception of academic censorship."[528] It is widely speculated that the board of trustees directed the MUW Administration not to demote her. Dr. Bryson has learned from trustworthy sources that two or three persons in the upper echelons of the MUW administration were officially reprimanded for their foolish and outrageous actions against her. Dr. Bryson's response to this turn of events was:

> I do not report that vindictively or gleefully; I report it in hopes that others like me will enjoy the freedom to criticize a dubious scientific "theory," which is really nothing more than a set of questionable hypotheses. The incident was a public relations fiasco for the University. I believe that close to 1000 E-mails flooded the BOT and the MUW administration on my behalf. I thank God for the Christians and other truth-seekers who bombarded the University and the Board with protests.[529]

If the MUW had the documentation proving that other issues precipitated their action, they would not have caved in so quickly either to public pressure or impending legal action. Every employer knows (or should know) that concerns about employees should be *thoroughly* documented so that, if court action is ever taken, the employee cannot try to blame it on something else (such as sex, age, race, religion, etc.).

In a letter to two concerned citizens, Mr. and Mrs. Trainon, dated March 12, 2003, Dr. Hansen said "MUW values freedom of thought and expression. Dr. Bryson's rights will be defended, as will the rights of others. This university is a place where debate about issues can take place freely." One must ask *how* Dr. Bryson's rights were defended, and *by whom*. Why would her rights even need to be defended if MUW is a place "where debate about issues can take place freely"? The nature of the conversations that the professors who attended the talk had with Hansen, and the decision to not renew her position as division head clearly indicates a lack of concern with academic freedom.

Dr. Bryson's unfortunate experience shows that universities all too often, despite their common claim to the contrary, engage in viewpoint discrimina-

---

527   Bhattacharjee, 2003, p. 247.
528   Bhattacharjee, 2003, p. 247.
529   Interview of Nancy Bryson by Jerry Bergman, 2003.

tion. What was said by the various professors to Dr. Hansen, and their differing stories of what they recollect, needs to be evaluated.

The threat of legal action no doubt also motivated the administration to reverse its position and restore Bryson to department head, or they may have recognized the many academic freedom concerns that their actions raised. Bryson believes that the administration never recognized the academic freedom issue, and the actual thinking of the board of trustees remains unknown. Ideally, the directive that the non-renewal decision be reversed should have been given out of *principle* rather than to forestall litigation.

Bryson stated that she is aware of the fact that first-amendment case law encourages "teaching the controversy" in public education by presenting students with alternative views as long as "religion" is not taught. She intends to follow this legal guideline in future presentations to her students. She added that the MUW Administration made her uncomfortable because of its

> refusal to acknowledge that my academic freedom was violated and its eagerness to comply with the demands of a couple of vicious, anti-intellectual faculty members indicates not only a lack of judgment but also a chilling lack of commitment to ethics. Whatever the law may be, crafty people can often get around it. In my case, all that would have been necessary to get rid of me would have been to wait a couple months after the talk and then trump up some spurious charge... [M]y case got national coverage. It would have gotten zero coverage if I had just succumbed to the VPAA's request for my resignation, and zero coverage if my supervisor had been more sensitive to the timing. Jerry Bergman has ... documented many cases such as mine... There continues to be some viciousness here, and nothing would surprise me as to my future on this campus.[530]

The Biology Faculty Unite Against Bryson

In the meantime, the university's biology professors "launched a classroom effort to repair the damage Bryson's lecture ha[d] done to student understanding of evolution."[531] No doubt the students will now be hearing much more about

---

530   Interview of Nancy Bryson by Jerry Bergman, 2003.
531   Bhattacharjee, 2003, p. 247.

evolution in the near future then they did in the past, and all of it would be in favor of Darwinism (and nothing contrary to Darwinism will be allowed). The pressure was on, and the administration, for the second time, removed her from the chair position. This time they attempted to justify her dismissal on the basis of "poor job performance," obviously a ploy to cover the real reason. Dr. Bryson's account of her new situation was as follows:

> On the morning of May 1 VPAA Vagn Hansen called my office and asked that I report. When I arrived at his office, the HR Director was there. Dr. Hansen then gave me an envelope containing a written copy of his evaluation of my performance plus evaluations of me by the faculty in my division. He said that I could read it right then, but I didn't want to read through so much material there in his office. He then said that because of my poor job performance, I would not be renewed as division head at the end of my contract, but could stay as a faculty member. He said I should consider resigning (so as not to have a dismissal on my record). There was some additional tense but calm exchange between us, and I left.[532]

In answer to Dr. Hansen's claims, Bryson humbly admitted that she had not been a perfect division head (no one can claim that they have been), but added that she was amazed that she had survived in the fractious science division. Dr. Hansen admitted that she had the most difficult division head position on campus, yet refused to give Bryson a full-time secretary (she had a half-time secretary) even though she had one of the larger academic divisions and all other units had full-time office support. Dr. Hansen's written evaluation of Bryson mentioned dropping enrollments in her unit, insinuating that she was at fault. (In my judgment, from interviews with her students, her high standards may have something to do with this. Her classes were some of the most difficult and demanding in the college).

He also wrote that Bryson did not publish during her last evaluation period, yet none of the MUW chemists have published recently, partly due to the heavy MUW teaching load. If this was a concern, she would never have been hired. He wrote that she had written four grant proposals and that only one was funded, yet for anyone at MUW to be awarded an external grant is unusual and

---

commendable. Furthermore, to have one out of four grants funded is a very good record. Bryson added that Dr. Hansen had never supported Bryson with grant-matching money, though he gave matching money to others in her unit. Bryson added that in her first year at MUW she wrote exhaustive (and generous) evaluations of all her faculty but, in contrast, Dr. Hansen did not complete the required evaluations of his subordinates,

> which got the school in trouble during our March SACS reaffirmation visit. Additionally, he states in my evaluation that I have been involved in "limited teaching" while here. Actually, I took the most menial assignments on purpose, because I didn't want to take the best courses from the other faculty, and because I thought I could make a big contribution in our rather weak lab program.

In his letter Dr. Hansen stated that, in spite of excellent reviews from students on her service as division head, Bryson failed to form peer

> relationships of "mutual respect." That he would say this having in-hand a probably libelous e-mail about me sent around on the student listserve [sic] by biologist Bill Parker (copies available) is reprehensible. I wonder if Parker was disciplined for his vicious written and verbal attacks on me... Perhaps four faculty in this division are truly vicious. Around half are atheists. A few claim to be Christians, but will not take a stand that would cost them anything. In 1999 a woman came here to head the division and ... was disliked and "run off" after one year. The next division head was in the job for two years and has told me that his difficulties in the job were largely due to problems that led him into a forced resignation from MUW in December 2002.[533]

The evolution issue clearly was central to Bryson's demotion and dismissal. Bryson wrote that she is now

> certain that being an evolution-disbelieving Christian has actually cost me my position. My first Fall here, I gave a *Spectator* (campus newspaper) interview in which I listed Christian apologetics as an interest. I was featured on a bulletin board in Martin Hall with my favorite quote (from the book of Job)... And then there was the evolution talk and the angry backlash... I

---

533   Interview of Nancy Bryson by Jerry Bergman, 2003.

think I was a little too "out" as a Christian to suit folks here. And my talk absolutely enraged the biologists.

I would no longer advise a student to study biology here. None of the biology professors know (or will admit) to having knowledge about the rapidly mounting evidence that disconfirms evolution and points to a Designer. Although students here were at first strongly and vocally supportive of me, I have seen that fade. I believe that they saw that I had become a virtual outcast, realized what open friendliness to me might cost, and backed away. Or perhaps some believed Bill Parker's e-mail. Then my General Chemistry 2 students, who were very weak coming into the class, struggled with the work that I required. They then exploited the fact that I was under attack from the faculty and my boss, and used that as a springboard to complain about my teaching. Previously to this I had received great student evaluations.[534]

Bryson wrote that, although she was not only upset but overwhelmed by what had happened to her, the only thing she would change is that she "would now give a much stronger talk revealing the many flaws in Darwinian theory." She also still wants to be able to discuss her concerns

about evolution without fear of retaliation, though that might not be possible even in most "Christian" colleges. At the risk of sounding vindictive, I would like the world to know how badly MUW has acted. Mostly I want the world to know how much it can cost an academic person to challenge Darwinism.

Finally, the reason I believe that MUW backtracked on its decision to retain me is due to poor follow-through on the part of my lawyer. After public opinion seemed to turn the tide in my favor, he just completely dropped the ball. The administration saw that and went after me. In part, I was the victim of the usual sort of politics that goes on in academia. But there is no doubt that my Christian stance hurt me, the final straw being the evolution talk.[535]

Bryson determined that the embarrassing publicity her case generated for the University made them very angry. Ray Bolan, commenting on this case, noted that almost every outspoken Darwin Doubter today has had his or her

---

534 Interview of Nancy Bryson by Jerry Bergman, 2003.
535 Interview of Nancy Bryson by Jerry Bergman, 2003.

work hindered, has "been labeled 'crack-pot' to some degree, and has been ostracized and isolated from science and academia." One reason for this is that when a person challenges someone's cherished ideas, they put themselves in a position to be attacked. This is especially true because the academic community is now more aware of the creationism controversy than they have been in decades. Bryson attended the evolution meetings several years ago at the University of Colorado, and noted that "at that time there was no indication or awareness that creationists even existed. You may have heard a smattering of discussions if somebody had seen a debate." Several years later, she attended the meetings again, and noted: "When I was there recently, this last summer, there was a very dramatic change. Almost everywhere you went in private discussions there was talk about creationism and what they can do to stop it."[536] She added that several sessions discussing anti-Darwin arguments and how they can be combated were on the program. The Society for the Study of Evolution even organized a special committee to attempt to answer anti-Darwinists' arguments.

Forced to Leave Mississippi University for Women

After the 2003-2004 school year ended, the situation became intolerable and Dr. Bryson felt that she has no choice but to leave Mississippi University for Women. She was previously told she could stay on as a professor, but they reneged on this promise and she could no longer take the harassment and ugly behavior of the Darwinists there. She was fortunate to land a faculty chemistry position at Kennesaw State University in Kennesaw, Georgia. She was hired by Dr. Leon Combs, chair of the Kennesaw department of chemistry, who has also come to doubt Darwinism and is now supportive of Intelligent Design. Dr. Combs is a physical chemist with over 80 publications to his credit.

Thus, the career of a talented and gifted professor ended at MUW, all because of one volunteer lecture she gave critiquing Darwinism! Such is the intolerance of Darwinists. They will allow no one to systematically point out potential flaws in their theory.

---

536   Interview of Nancy Bryson by Jerry Bergman, 2003.

Chapter 10: Caroline Crocker: Expelled Twice

Dr. Caroline Crocker did not intend to "start a controversy when she mentioned Intelligent Design while teaching her second-year cell-biology course at *George Mason University* in Fairfax, Virginia."[537] But her colleagues claimed that "the soft-spoken molecular biologist" had "gone too far,"[538] and she was terminated. This was the beginning of the end of her secular scientific career. Crocker came to doubt Darwinism not because of religion, but because of the immunology research she was doing for her Ph.D."[539]

Dr. Crocker's Background

Dr. Crocker graduated from high school at age 16 and soon thereafter received an associate's degree from *Des Moines Area Community College* in Iowa. She then earned her Bachelors of Science degree in microbiology and virology from *Warwick University*, a Masters of Science in medical microbiology from *Birmingham University*, United Kingdom, and a Ph.D. in immunopharmacology from *Southampton University* in the U.K. She also did post-doctoral studies in the area of fluorescence resonance energy transfer analysis of interactions between proteins involved in the T-cell receptor/NF-KB signal transduction pathway at Uniformed Service University. Dr. Crocker also had a research associate scientist position at *Creighton University*, Omaha, Nebraska. At Creighton she brought in numerous grants, conducted basic immunology research, and published extensively. Dr. Crocker was at this time deeply involved in a very promising career—that is until her doubts about Darwin surfaced.[540]

Problems Begin

Dr. Crocker had taught biology for five years at *George Mason University* (GMU) without problems. At GMU she received commendations for her high student ratings and was awarded three grants, including one from the prestigious

---

537 Brumfiel, 2005a, p. 1064.
538 Brumfiel, 2005a, p. 1064.
539 Vedantam, 2006.
540 Brumfiel, 2005a, p. 1064.

Center for Teaching Excellence. She also authored a cell biology workbook. In her study she began to doubt orthodox Darwinism due to her study of the cell, specifically the immune system, which was the topic of her Ph.D. dissertation.[541] She then began to mention some of the results of her research in her classes.

Trouble began in 2004 when she was called on the carpet for a single lecture she presented on the problems of Darwinism to her second-year cell biology class.[542] Evidently a single student complained to her supervisor, falsely claiming that she was "teaching creationism" (she is not a creationist). As a result, her supervisor told her that, as a disciplinary measure, she would no longer be teaching the cell biology class.

Although recognized by most as an excellent teacher, in response to the single student's accusation of "teaching creationism," numerous students, including an attorney headed for medical school, wrote letters in her defense, noting in their letters that she never "taught creationism," but only discussed her doubts about Darwin. Nor did she ever mention religion in her classes: students did not even know what religion she was or where she personally stood on the Darwin/ID issue.

As the result of her "sin," Dr. Crocker was "barred by her department from teaching both evolution and Intelligent Design, an "infringement of academic freedom," she says." Brumfiel adds:

> Sitting in an empty teaching lab, Crocker tells how she has barred her department from teaching both evolution and Intelligent Design. "It's an infringement of academic freedom," she says. She is appealing the case to a grievance committee.[543]

Because she did not prevail in her grievance, she was eventually dismissed.

Her lectures "drew criticism from some and praise from others—notably, she says, her Muslim students" appreciated her lectures. She concluded that her critiques of Darwinism help students to "think independently about ideas such as evolution" and Intelligent Design.[544] The former scientist, who has 29 major

---

541 Vedantam, 2006, p. 9.
542 Brumfiel, 2005a, p. 1064.
543 Brumfiel, 2005a, p. 1064.
544 Brumfiel, 2005a, p. 1064.

refereed scientific publications, explains that her goal is to teach students to think for themselves. Many of her students were openly very supportive of her teaching but it is noteworthy that many of Dr. Crocker's students did not want their names used in the media for fear of retaliation due to their sympathy of ID.[545] Accordingly, the dean of the College of Arts and Sciences at George Mason University, Daniele Struppa, stated, "The university doesn't have a policy or a rule on whether certain topics should be discussed" but

> he questions whether a concept with theological underpinnings really belongs in a science course... Darwinists are divided over whether Intelligent Design deserves a classroom airing. Forrest says that she believes... "This is not a question of academic freedom, this is a question of professional competence," ... But Eugenie Scott, director of the National Center for Science Education in Oakland, California, which vehemently opposes teaching Intelligent Design in high schools, takes a different view. She thinks such discussions are more acceptable in a college environment, but believes it must be made clear to students that Intelligent Design is theology, not science...[546]

Dr. Crocker is now working on her first non-academic book, *Science Censored*, which recounts her experiences as a university lecturer who strove to present Darwinian evolution from an intellectually honest viewpoint. In a recent National Public Radio interview with Barbara Hagerty on her case, Dr. Crocker said:

> ... is it OK to question evolution? Well, let me tell you from personal experience, people lose their jobs for doing it. So ... is it OK? Yes. Is it safe? No.

> **Hagerty:** Crocker believes she's living proof. About a year ago she was teaching her cell biology class when she arrived at the section on evolution.

> **Dr. Crocker:** I gave one lecture on the evidence for and against evolution, and at the end of the lecture I said to the students, "Well, you need to make up your own mind. Think about it for yourself."

> **Hagerty:** A student complained to her supervisor that Crocker was teaching creationism. Her supervisor, she says, told her she would not be teaching

---

545 Vedantam, 2006.
546 Brumfiel, 2005a, p. 1064.

the cell biology class in the spring as a disciplinary measure. Her supervisor declined to comment. Later, Crocker learned that her contract was not renewed. She believes it was because of that class. A spokesman for George Mason would not comment on the circumstance surrounding Crocker's departure because it's a personnel issue, but, he said, it's not unusual for a contract to lapse.

After one of Dr. Crocker's talks, "students told similar stories of ridicule by their peers and even teachers when they expressed doubts about Darwinian evolution." Jessica Young, a senior at George Mason University majoring in biology, said

> It does get overwhelming having it crammed down your throat every day in biology classes... my animal biology professor said the same thing: "This is not a theory; this is a fact... evolution is a fact." You know, it's comforting to know that there are other people who question evolution.[547]

Typical of Dr. Crocker's positive student feedback is the follows (due to fear of retaliation the student requested anonymity):

> I was wondering if you might ever teach microbiology or genetics?? I am not the only one wondering this. Several classmates were wondering if you teach other classes. We learned a lot from your class and are worried about having an unorganized, unclear teacher for a really challenging class, such as microbiology.

Another note from one of her students, who also requested anonymity, is as follows:

> I had the honor of being in two of Dr. Crocker's classes (Biology 101 and Cell Biology). I value Dr. Crocker as one of the most outstanding professors I've had throughout my undergraduate career. Most students find cell Biology a very difficult and challenging course, but Dr. Crocker's lectures were always excellent and very clear. I found myself liking this course. She was always willing to help us with questions, and how she explained the material was one of the reasons why I enjoyed being part of her class. She is a very responsible professor, very helpful, and very encouraging. The exams were

---

547   Vedantam, 2006, p. 10.

always fair and any student who is puts forth the effort and is attends all of her lectures could earn a perfect grade.

Another one of Crocker's former students, Irene Kamel, noted that "she heard exasperated sighs from professors" about Crocker's teaching, but in private "many students said they agreed with her."[548] Kamel added that she "would be surprised to find another teacher talk about ID in class, unless they have tenure."[549] In fact, most of her students found her lectures very "convincing," and, as a result, "the university administration quickly sent Caroline Crocker the pink sheet,"[550] Günther concluded that "one cannot simply shrug her off as crazy, one must take her seriously, one must hear her out, one must think things through with her."[551] George Mason University was unwilling to do any of this, so sent her packing.

While teaching at George Mason she was moonlighting at *Northern Virginia Community College*, a position which she also soon lost. The publicized reason she lost this position was, as a "highly trained biologist," she wanted her students to know what she herself had come to believe as a result of her research and studies, namely that the "scientific establishment was perpetrating fraud, hunting down critics of evolution to ruin them and disguising an atheistic view of life in the garb of science."[552] Her immediate supervisor argued in her favor, noting her high student ratings and clear evidence of classroom effectiveness, even though she was a very demanding professor. Unfortunately, one particular administrator was determined to get rid of her. Criticizing Darwin cost her career at George Mason and Northern Virginia Community College, and so far she has not been able to find another teaching position. According to several persons that I interviewed, she has been blacklisted.

The Opposition

As soon as her story surfaced in the media, the "dogmatic Darwin fundamentalist" websites railed against her, leveling all kinds of false and irrespon-

---

548   Vedantam, 2006, p. 10.
549   Vedantam, 2006, p. 10.
550   Günther, 2006.
551   Günther, 2006.
552   Vedantam, 2006, p. 1.

sible charges against her. P.Z. Myers proclaimed, without knowing anything about her or her teaching except that she had problems with orthodox Darwinism, that she "should have been fired" because of "educational malpractice" for doubting Darwinism.[553] An example he gave that supports her firing (in his view) is the following:

> She told the students there were two kinds of evolution: microevolution and macroevolution. Microevolution is easily seen in any microbiology lab. ...While such small changes are well established, Crocker said, they are quite different from macroevolution.[554]

Myers wrote that this statement, and others like it, proves that Dr. Crocker is "peddling ignorant garbage in her classes, making this less an issue of academic freedom and more one of basic scientific competence."[555] Before the ID controversy erupted, her students wrote numerous laudatory comments about her teaching, among which included the following, corrected for spelling and grammar:

> 1. Awesome teacher; helpful website. Strongly recommend her for medical students. If you do all the assignments you will pass!!!!!!

> 2. Exams are VERY HARD... A LOT OF LAB write-ups; if you not a biologist, you're in big trouble. She gives too much information in her lectures; she doesn't consider that it's only General Biology. If you don't want to spend all your time on biology, stay away, but I've to admit, she is proficient in her field. VERY SMART.

> 3. She is a nice person, but her class is pretty difficult. It's supposed to be GENERAL Biology, but it's extremely in-depth! I managed to get an A but only because I studied my butt off and did all the extra credit.

> 4. As long as you do what you need to, you'll pass ... also she gives a lot of extra credit.[556]

---

553   P.Z. Myers, 2006 p. 1.
554   Vedantam, 2006, p.1.
555   P. Z. Myers, 2006, p.1.
556   Taken from student evaluations from a source that asked not to be identified.

Marianna Lowe said Dr. Crocker has "expressed what others didn't dare say, but what I always thought" about the problems with Darwinism.[557] Günther concluded that her former students are very "thankful to their fired professor" for her instruction.

After the ID controversy, some of her students allegedly wrote, and some posted on the Internet, inaccurate and demeaning comments about her teaching, such as the following selection:[558]

1. Crazy religious nutter teaching Intelligent Design, not evolution.

2. Just another Bible-whacking lunatic ... do we really need wingnuts like this in a public college?

3. I wish I could give a lower clarity rating. Considering that she is lying through her teeth, a 1 seems a bit high. Professor Crocker is an ID proponent who consistently lies and misrepresents the facts. I'm not sure if she is incompetent and doesn't understand what she is saying, or if she is simply incredibly dishonest. Either way, avoid her.

4. Interesting class, but she teaches ID and uses a bunch of inaccurate propaganda to do it. ... You'll still get credit, but just keep in mind she's teaching a bunch of BS.

5. Horrible teacher! She only lectures and then leaves. She is unwilling to help you outside of class. She doesn't explain assignments and then marks off for everything. This is the second institution that has fired her. If you see her at another institution, don't take her.

6. Another moron ID freak with no publications, stuck teaching at a community college with a chip on her shoulder.[559]

Many of these comments are not only incorrect but irresponsible, such as the claim that she has no publications. Before making this comment, the "student" (if he or she actually was a student), should have checked with Professor Crocker or the college. Furthermore, these "students" are only reflecting P.Z.

---

557   Günther, 2006.
558   I could not verify that these comments were actually made by her students, but have no evidence that they were not
559   Taken from student evaluations provided to me from a source that elected not to be identified.

Myers's demand for "the public firing and humiliation" of any scientist and professor that criticizes Darwin. In Myers's own words:

> the "civilized academic debate" was settled about a century ago ... Unfortunately, while we have been doing everything in the proper civilized way, the forces of ignorance have not; they have lied their way into considerable power. Here I am, a biologist living in the 21st century in one of the richest countries in the world, and one of the two biology teachers in my kids' high school is a creationist. Last year, the education commissioner in my state tried to subvert the recommendations for the state science standards by packing a hand-picked 'minority report' committee to push for required instruction in Intelligent Design creationism in our schools. All across the country, we have these lunatics trying to stuff pseudoscientific religious garbage into our schools and museums and zoos. This is insane ... Our only problem is that we aren't martial enough, or vigorous enough, or loud enough, or angry enough. The only appropriate responses should involve some form of righteous fury, much butt-kicking, and the public firing and humiliation of ... [Darwin skeptic] teachers, many schoolboard [sic] members, and vast numbers of sleazy far-right politicians.[560]

A common claim by others was that she was not a scientist, yet as late as 2006 she had a position at Uniformed Services in Bethesda, Maryland, working on T-cell transduction research and training scientists in molecular biology techniques.

Dr. Crocker, her scientific career over, has recently been appointed executive director of the IDEA center.[561] She now has her own story to tell about what happens when one's doubts about Darwin ruin a scientific career and is writing a book that carefully documents her experience.[562] Look for her book, "*Expelled: How I Was Shut Down for Opening Minds*,"[563] currently scheduled to be published sometime in 2008. Dr. Crocker also has a web site at www.intellectualhonesty.info where you can learn more about her and her current activities.

---

560 P.Z. Myers, 2005c, p. 2.
561 www.ideacenter.org
562 Günther, 2006.
563 http://www.intellectualhonesty.info/index_files/Mybook.htm

Chapter 11: The Case of Biology Professor Dan Scott

Many acts of discrimination against Darwin Doubters are open and blatant. One of many examples is the case of an adjunct biology professor, Daniel R. (Dan) Scott, at *Wright State* in Dayton, Ohio. Scott, an *Ohio State University* graduate in biology, completed his Ph.D. from Ohio State. After joining Wright State in 1994, he was terminated later that same year after he assigned a paper on the creation-evolution controversy and evidently presented some criticism of Darwinism in his introductory biology class.

His Termination

Ironically, Professor Scott obtained permission *in writing* from his department chairwoman, Barbara Hull, to cover both sides of the evolution controversy before he started teaching. On the first day of his class he assigned a paper on the controversy and stressed that students were "to use science to back up their arguments."[564] This piqued the interest of students and, after class, one asked him for his personal thoughts about the ultimate source of matter. Scott, answered that, in his view, the ultimate source of all reality is God.

Not having heard this thought before, the student sometime later relayed these comments to the department chair—who immediately set in motion steps to terminate Professor Scott. (His chair thought he was going to lecture *against* creationism and for this reason gave him permission to discuss the topic). Professor Scott was allowed to teach only one more class, and then was unceremoniously dismissed. He was not trying to "sneak creationism" into the class, as some of his critics accused him of doing, but worked closely with the administration. For example, a memo from the Department of Biological Sciences to Professor Scott reads:

> I would like to stress the importance of covering the evolution part of the BIO 115 syllabus... While I respect your religious beliefs and certainly do not object to your presenting the Creationist perspective, it is essential that

---

564   Fisher, 1994b, p. 1B.

you also present the material on evolution and allow the students to draw their own conclusions.[565]

This response relates exactly what Scott wanted to do in his class: achieve a balanced presentation so as to allow students to draw their own conclusions. He was adamant that he never "taught creationism," and objectively taught evolution.[566] He did, though, honestly answer students' questions about his beliefs after class.[567] This was his only crime. Scott responded to the March 29, 1994, memo attaching his syllabus, which showed that he would be spending a full three weeks on evolution:

> I don't know what you heard, but I do intend to present a balanced view. In fact, the paper they will write addresses the question of which way the student leans. The paper will be graded on reasoning and not theology or dogma. I hope this meets with your approval.

A follow-up memo from the Department of Biological Sciences to Mr. Scott, dated April 7, 1994, said in part:

> I have received a great deal of feedback from students and faculty in the department who feel that you have been teaching religion rather than science. I am asking you to complete the sequence of lectures for the first unit test and to give that test on April 21. I have assigned other Biology faculty to give the lectures of BIO 115, effective April 21.

To assess this "great deal of feedback" claim, Scott's student Jim Simonson passed out two statements and asked his fellow students to respond to them. Their responses, which are reproduced at the end of this chapter, show that the department chair's claim was false. Some students chose not to become involved in the controversy, but of those that spoke out (most all of the class), every student signed the first statement. Not one student signed the second one, proving the university's claim about negative student feedback inaccurate. The statements were:

---

565   Memo from Barbara Hall, Wright State Dept. of Biological Sciences to Dan Scott dated March 29, 1994.
566   Gomez, 1994.
567   Woods, 1994.

1. I believe that the lectures given by Mr. Dan Scott have been within the course guidelines of Biology 115 and that no attempt to disprove or disqualify Evolution has been made within the scope of the lectures. I also believe there have been no attempts to teach religion. Finally, I do not see the subject of the term paper "Creationism and Evolution: Are they antithetical?" as an attempt to direct the focus of the course from evolution to creation.

2. I believe that the lectures given by Mr. Dan Scott have gone beyond the course guidelines of Biology 115 and attempts have been made to disprove and disqualify Evolution within the scope of the lectures. I also believe there have been attempts to teach religion. Finally, I see the subject of the term paper "Creationism and Evolutionism: Are they antithetical?" as an attempt to direct the focus of the course from evolution to creation.

All of the student feedback is reproduced at the end of this chapter, which also shows that the claim of indoctrination is false—the problem was not with the students, but with the biology faculty. The one student who, according to the chair, complained was never identified and did not comment in the survey taken. Mr. Scott's response, dated April 7, 1994 to the department of biological science memo said in part:

> Apparently, some in class felt I had overstepped some imaginary bounds last week. I'm sorry you felt that way. It's sad that academic freedom does not allow the airing of all viewpoints without repercussion.

Scott felt that the department believed that, as a Christian, he could not be objective about Darwinism, and therefore should not teach biology. The antagonism of the chairwoman was reflected in her comment, "This is not a religion department."[568] On April 17, 1994, Scott wrote the following memo to the department chair, which clearly illustrates the hypocrisy that pervades academia today:

> No one questions the objectivity of the agnostic to teach religion... [I]f there are agnostics teaching religion, then obviously their institutions do not pre-

---

568   Quoted in Fisher, 1994b, p. 1B.

suppose that their agnosticism clouds their judgment or undermines their credibility to teach Christianity in their classrooms.

WSU spokeswoman Lynnette Heard even claimed that Scott's "credibility as a scientist was undermined because of his creationist perspective."[569] How it was undermined, she never said. Based on the above evidence, one must ask if the Department of Biological Sciences at *Wright State* truly strives to meet the following stated teaching policy:

> At Wright State, good teaching is more than just helping students pass a test. As faculty, we're intent on inspiring the critical thinking that will carry our students into successful careers and lives.[570]

On April 23, 1994 the *Dayton Daily News* headline, "Creationism Classroom Invasion Causes a Pseudo-Science Controversy"[571] stirred up the issue, and evidently most professors at Wright State strongly supported the university's actions. Yet Scott was not arguing in favor of any particular view, but only endeavoring to explore the question with his students. He had no qualms about teaching Darwinism—and one of his supervisors at *Wright State*, Dr. Dan Krane, who was asked by the department chair to audit the second half of one biology 115 lecture to determine if Scott should be terminated, stated he did an excellent job teaching the material. Dr. Krane noted that Scott was "a very engaging teacher, he had the students very interested, and he has a wonderful rapport with the students. He was very effective at communicating with the students, and maintaining their interest."[572] Dr. Krane also said that it was his impression, based on his class visit and interviews with students, that there existed "strong support for Dan Scott" and that his students

> really enjoyed his style of lecturing, that he is very effective and I think that they probably would like to see him carry on for the remainder of the quarter ... they got quite a great bargain in the course... I think though that they really did get interested in what Dan Scott had to say and he was a very

---

569   Quoted in Fisher, 1994b, p. 1B.
570   Wright State University Catalogue 1994 edition, page 4
571   Wheeler, 1994.
572   Interview of Dan Krane by Jerry Bergman, 1994.

effective instructor for that course. There was no doubt about that. I also think that they are concerned that they are going to get some real snoozer to take his place... their concern is somebody that will see we had a great class, we had a good professor here, now they are going to put in some [loser] ...

Dr. Krane added that what really surprised him was that Scott did not fit the stereotype of a creationist. For example,

at one point he said something like, the predominant life on earth two or three hundred million years ago was such and such, and ... as of the last million years conifers are starting to take over again, and I think, wait a minute here, this isn't a fundamentalist, this isn't somebody who is relying on [an] interpretation of the Bible after all.[573]

Dr. Krane added that Scott "never mentioned God in the course of the lectures, as far as I can tell, and I have talked to students [and] that seems to be the case..." What upset the faculty was that Scott told a student that atoms are held together by God, and the faculty felt that this statement is "dangerous" because it "could cause them some real difficulties" in their school career in the future (and indeed, as the case studies I present in this book indicate, it certainly could if they ever repeated such a claim). Even though Scott did not teach creationism, or anything close to it, Dr. Krane added that he perceived the students were seeing the world from Dan Scott's perspective, and this bothered him:

I do not think that the students really can appreciate that they were being pulled by creationism ... the real issue is, can they get a good foundation in evolution thinking and ... the students really aren't in a perspective to gauge that, so while they may not feel it was a problem, I don't know that they are the best people ... to know if they were or not.

The real concern, as expressed in this quotation and my conversions with Dr. Krane, was that Scott did not enthusiastically present Darwinism as fact and his demeanor might permit some of his students to believe that there was some merit to the alternative world view. The administrators could not allow this, so dismissed him. The university also decided in this case that students were

---

573   Interview of Dan Krane by Jerry Bergman, 1994.

not allowed to write a paper on the creation-evolution controversy. Dr. Krane added the reason provided for Dan's dismissal was that he was not going to give a "solid enough background in ... the scientific basis of evolution."[574] If this was true, why not just ask Professor Scott to cover this material more completely? *Wouldn't that be easier?*

The Media Response and an Evaluation

After the story broke in the media, one reporter write "Dan Scott's class made it clear what they thought of their embattled *Wright State University* instructor Thursday night when they greeted him with an enthusiastic—and sustained—round of applause.[575] Scott also made it clear he was only trying to get his students to think for themselves but learned that academia does not allow professors to question Darwinism.[576]

The evaluations from the entire class for the controversial course, including the few negative ones, are provided below. The evaluations are extremely instructive, and provide much insight into the controversy. It is clear from these evaluations that the University was not interested in quality instruction, but only in indoctrinating students in a worldview accepted by only 10% of the U.S. population. As students Daniel and Brenda Francis stated, *Wright State University*

> is not a "university"—one institution in which a diversity of ideas are explored and appreciated. It's just another intolerant, liberal bastion of political correctness. WSU will never see another dime of our politically incorrect money.[577]

Community leader Harmon Meldrim adroitly opined:

> Whatever happened to academic freedom? When a university professor is not allowed to express his opinions or beliefs, we all lose. When only politically correct opinions are authorized, how can we expect new ideas to be developed?[578]

---

574   Interview of Dan Krane by Jerry Bergman, 1994, p. 3.
575   Fisher, 1994b, p. 1B.
576   McWhirter, 1994.
577   Francis, 1994, p. 15A.
578   Meldrim, 1994, p. 15A.

One of the best reviews of the case was an editorial in the *Dayton Daily News.* Under the headline "WSU's Reasons for Firing Have Had Odd Evolution" the editor correctly concluded that:

> Wright State University has not handled its evolution-creationism contro-versy well. When it relieved biology instructor Dan Scott of his teaching duties, it gave him no written reason other than some unspecified number of people had complained about his alleged practice of pushing his creation-ist views on students. That is certainly not enough. Now some students— apparently a larger number—have made clear that they support him... After Mr. Scott was relieved, the university floundered for an explanation. On the day after the dismissal became public, the department head who took the action was refusing calls from the press. And the university's public in-formation office was looking into the situation. By the end of the day, that office was offering a somewhat different explanation for the department's action than had originally been given. Originally the complaint was that Mr. Scott was pushing his views too aggressively. Later, the explanation was that students were arriving at lab sessions unprepared, because Mr. Scott's lectures had focused too much on the evolution-creationism debate.[579]

Spin doctoring an incident like this is a typical outcome in discrimination cases, and consistency of reasoning of the media is often muddled. The editorial concluded that about "the only thing that's undisputed in this case" is that Scott told the class that he was a creationist. The editor added that this is not a valid reason to fire someone because there are clear advantages for a teacher to explain his position to the class in order to allow them "to be alert for any signs of bias as the term proceeds":

> Many professors in controversy-laden subjects—such as political science— do this regularly. However, the teacher should take pains to assure the stu-dents that they are not required to agree. Merely being a creationist should not disqualify Mr. Scott from teaching biology. The issue is whether he understands evolutionary theory and is eager to help students understand it. In a sensitive case like this, a university must proceed in a way that fosters confidence that it has all the facts when it acts and that it is bending over backward to foster academic freedom. WSU hasn't done that.[580]

---

579 Cawood, 1994, p. 10A.
580 Cawood, 1994, p. 10A.

The evaluations of his course are noteworthy because they completely contradict the undocumented and wholly irresponsible claims made by both the university and many reports in the media. For example, the Fort Wayne, Indiana, *Journal Gazette* claimed that "one third of the 50-student freshman biology class complained about Scott's teaching because they were concerned about not being ready to advance."[581] This claim is clearly contradicted by the evidence—at least 72 percent of his students signed a petition *in favor* of his teaching. The number likely would have been higher, but several students preferred not to get involved in the controversy, and we cannot assume that this group was uniformly unhappy with Scott's teaching.[582] In fact, several students who did not become involved informed me that they were only trying to avoid jeopardizing their own academic careers. It is clear that Scott had a high level of support for his teaching.[583] Dayton News writer Mark Fisher actually claimed Scott was "relieved of his teaching duties" in part because he focused more on creation than evolution.[584] Spin doctoring an incident like this is a typical outcome in discrimination cases, and consistency of reasoning of the media is often muddled. For example *The Fort Wayne Journal Gazette* "jeered" Scott, claiming that he was fired

> for teaching creationism in a biology class. He says he was teaching both sides of the issue; the university says he favored creationism. The debate belongs in a philosophy class. This is not a case of academic freedom; it is simply fraudulent or incompetent to present creationism as a science. The university properly removed Scott from his duties.[585]

Such erroneous claims were common in this, and most other cases involving the firing of Darwin skeptics that I investigated. Scott's "religious" teaching basically amounted to telling his students that he was a creationist, and only when asked![586] This admission was "offensive to some students."[587] Chris Hondros wrote that "to have a creationist teach biology is as obscene as having a Holocaust-denier

---

581 Anonymous, 1994b.
582 Gomez, 1994.
583 Fisher 1994b, 1994c, 1994d.
584 Fisher, 1994a, p. 1A.
585 Klugman, 1994, p. 4.
586 Rutledge, 1994, p. 4.
587 Hannah, 1994a, p. 3.

teach Jewish history."[588] According to this logic, around one-third of all science teachers should be fired immediately. Reporter Arthur Wheeler wrote that it is sad "that creationism could invade science classrooms to undermine learning that would end that controversy."[589] He concluded that

> The only justification for raising the subject of creationism in a science classroom is to expose the fallacy of its scientific pretensions—an impossibility for a creationist. That Mr. Scott deemed creationism appropriate for discussion in his classroom is, in itself, telling evidence of his unsuitability for teaching biology. His presentation of creationism as a scientific alternative to evolution makes his unsuitability incontestable.[590]

Obviously, Wheeler would not allow a debate about this issue in his class, but instead would declare by fiat that the class should accept his view or fail. Wheeler also would judge students by who they are, not by what they do. Although most editorials did not support Scott,[591] several letters were printed that did support Scott, such as Lottie Pozarzycki's "Teacher's Censure Perplexing."[592] Another letter writer said that "as a scientist ... I fully understand that neither creationism nor evolution is provable; consequently neither meets the criteria of pure science... I hope WSU will change its one-sided approach and allow a free examination of all plausible scientific evidence."[593] Other sympathetic letters, all published in 1994, include those of Etz, Frair, Hemmerich, Hensley, Klopfenstein, Meldrim, Minch, Reke, and Strong.

The few editorials that supported Scott stressed academic freedom issues.[594] One Wright State faculty member, John Cole, called the Scott event a dark chapter for academic freedom in the history of Wright State.[595] No doubt many more supportive letters were sent, but most probably were not published. (I knew of several that were sent in support of Scott, none of which were published.) As admitted by Wheeler,[596] Scott was let go not because of what he did, but because of what he believed.

---

588   Hondros, 1994, p. 4.
589   Wheeler, 1994, p. 4.
590   Wheeler, 1994, p. 4.
591   See, e.g., Anonymous 1994a, 1994b, 1994c.
592   Pozarzycki, 1994, p. 8.
593   Cowherd, 1994, p. 15A.
594   See Jennings, 1994.
595   John Cole, 1994.
596   Wheeler, 1994.

Addendum

Course Evaluations of Professor Dan Scott, Wright State University, Administered on his Third Class

(All comments are verbatim, except minor corrections for spelling and grammar, by Cathy Hern, who notarized this transcription on May 5, 1994. All respondents to these questions were informed in advance that their responses would likely be published).

The answers given below were responses given by Scott's students to the following three questions (some students included their names, which are also noted):

1. **What are your thoughts concerning the paper on Creation-Evolution? Is this a good idea? A waste of time? A challenge to be met?**

2. **What did you think of Dan as a teacher? As a scientist?**

3. **Would you take another class from Dan?**

(Notes: (1) WSU = Wright State University; (2) the comments about Clark State are in reference to the fact that professor Scott also taught at Clark State)

Not signed:

1. The subject of the paper seemed to be very interesting and it would definitely be a challenging paper to write, but the amount of time it would have taken would have been very difficult to research and write an effective paper along with three tests and quizzes every lab during the quarter.

2. I think Dan did a great job as a teacher. He made me think about the application of science, not just memorize it. His enthusiasm was contagious and made class very enjoyable. It is unfortunate that the university is not open-minded enough to look past some differences in opinions (creation-

ism vs. evolution) to allow a good teacher to have educational freedom to express his opinion.

3. I would definitely take another class from Dan

Fred Klaber:

1. A good idea, it's important to think and question differing ideas; that is how one learns and is a challenge to be met.

2. Very good. I wish he would continue to be our teacher. I felt comfortable in asking questions and I learned. Excellent scientist--he seems open minded, knowledgeable and can teach it to others.

3. Yes, in a heartbeat!!

Not signed:

1. I would have done the paper as required. Inspires students to think independently.

2. Very dynamic presentation. Cannot fully evaluate his ability as a scientist. He completed undergraduate and graduate level course work, so he is obviously knowledgeable in his field, able to meet educational requirements for scientists.

3. Yes. Although it would probably be very difficult, his style encourages thought. He seems available and willing to assist students, appears to enjoy his chosen career in education.

Crystal Patherick:

1. The paper, I think, was an excellent idea just because it got college students to explore both sides even if you are biased. This is a controversial subject, but it still needs to be addressed. I personally am for creation—I believe in God wholeheartedly. There are some days when I can't imagine why anyone doesn't, but that's just my opinion. I think it was a very good idea, though, we are students, and I think it would have benefited us to do it. And, if WSU wants to take someone's job away simply for stating a belief, I think it's silly!

2. Dan as a teacher was great--he taught great. He knew what he was here for. This tests were also very fair, more than any other class, because he mentioned everything in class and what he didn't he told us the pages to read. As a scientist--he knew his stuff! Especially about agriculture and plants! He was a very good professor! WSU doesn't know what they're missing!

3. Yes, I most certainly would!!

Not signed:

1. I thought the paper was a good idea, it would make a person recollect their thoughts. I thought it would be very interesting to see what I would come up with.

2. Dan as a teacher was very interesting. He added interesting facts, that helped keep the students interested. As a scientist, he knows what he's talking about.

3. Yes, I would, even if it was something that wasn't required.   N o t signed:

1. I think it would have been a challenge to be met. I think it's good that maybe a student should stop and think about what he is learning instead of eating information and spitting it out!

2. I think he's an excellent teacher. Made me stop and think about what he was teaching me. As a scientist, I think he knows his material and a lot about plants—plants are good!

3. Yes, I would!

Not signed:

1. At first I was apathetic about it, but after thinking more on what it can be for me as in terms of a better learning experience, I thought of it as a very good idea!

2. I thought he was a very good teacher and he stimulated a lot of interest in the natural forms. This is important for a 2.5 hour lecture.

3. I sure would!

Not signed:

1. A challenge to be met.

2. He is one of the most thought provoking teachers I've ever had and feel he's an excellent teacher.

3. Definitely.

Not signed:

1. I believe that the paper is a big part of biology. The creation of life and its evolution is the backbone of biology, and therefore *very* relevant. It would have been challenging. It would also have made students study in depth the two theories. The students could have then made their own choice.

2. Dan is one of the best teachers I've ever had. He doesn't just lecture, but instead adds meaning to everything, making it easier to understand. He does this by making the students feel at ease and most importantly by telling his stories. He made us think about the material and understand it, while at the same time kept us entertained so we didn't lose interest.

    As a scientist he is fantastic. He knows more about biology and especially plants than any other professor I think I've ever known. He loves the subject and his passion is reflected in his teaching.

    In doing what Wright State did they showed very poor judgment. Little investigation was done before the decision to let him go was made. Dan should be commended for this great teaching ability instead of punished by a group of misinformed hypocrites!!

3. YES!! (I've even thought of going to Clark State just to take his classes.) Dan, keep up the good work!!

Not signed:

1. The reason for education is to learn new ideas and to express your opinion. If you can learn from it, it's a good idea.

2. He was one of the best biology teachers I've had. Anyone who can keep an entry level class that alert for 3 hours has to be good. Dan knows and loves science. It shows in his teaching.

3. Hell yes. I want to take this class from Dan.

Jim Simonson:

1. The paper, specifically its subject matter, I felt was designed to be a philosophical discussion of views and ideas that center on the subject matter that was to be discussed in *this* class, i.e., Biology 115. An attempt to promote creative thought rather than merely "rambling facts" would be a useful addition to this particular curriculum.

2. Mr. Scott's lecturing technique promoted a relaxed learning environment while covering necessary material. His organizational skills were excellent and his ability to relate course topics to everyday knowledge aided in the comprehension of the subject. I have always found that learning concepts and how to apply them rather than rote memorization gives me a better understanding of material. Mr. Scott addressed this goal well. Scientifically, his knowledge of plants and cell/molecular biology was excellent.

3. Yes, I would be interested in taking this class with him again in a different setting. His philosophy and understanding of ecosystems and diversity seems exemplary! Also, any advanced course on botany or specific plant biology.

J. Miller:

1. I thought the paper was a good idea. It was concerning questions and topics that I have always wanted to investigate and compare. I was looking forward to the challenge of deciphering such a controversial topic.

2. I thought Dan, as a teacher and scientist, was very qualified to teach it. Moreover, he brought such enthusiasm to the class because of how much he enjoyed the subject, that I was eager to go to lecture. *Rarely* do you find an instructor so enthusiastic about the material. Even more inspiring was the fact that he *challenged* us to investigate, find new answers, be

our own scientists, and don't settle for decisions made by other scientists. Constantly challenge, question, and made new discoveries.

3. YES!

Not signed:

1. I thought the paper was a challenge to be met. I looked forward to doing it, because it was on a topic that I am very interested in and it is a topic relevant to scientific thought today. I work full time, so I didn't know about having time.

2. I think Dan is a very talented teacher and the best one I have had at Wright State.

3. DEFINITELY!

Not signed:

1. I personally don't like to write papers on anything, but I think the paper was a good idea. This *is* a college level course. I had started reading material on the paper and was really getting interested in it.

2. I think Dan is a very dynamic teacher. I was looking forward to really learning this quarter instead of absorbing and regurgitating. Dan is great at stimulating thought and discussion. I think Dan knows his subject well and has one of the most important characteristics of a scientist—an open questioning mind. Dan is the best professor we've had all year. It is also obvious that he really cares about his students.

3. Definitely.

Not signed:

1. A fantastic idea! I'm sorry we didn't get to meet his challenge! Not many classes allow a student to think own thoughts and write about it! As the same time, it would have shown us a lot of diversity in theories regarding evolution and even creationism!

2. Terrific and *very* educated in his field. His teaching method is very charismatic and he can keep your attention for 2.5 hours without a problem!

3. I'd love to cross-register and take a course at Clark State!

Not signed:

1. I thought the paper was an excellent idea. It would definitely have been a challenge, but it would not have been impossible since each student was allowed to present their own view.

2. I believe Dan was an excellent teacher and scientist. I personally am not a creationist, but I was not offended by his views. Like he said, he is a creationist who believes in the big bang, etc...

3. YES!

Not signed:

1. The topic was interesting and certainly appropriate in a biology class. I don't think everyone was prepared to deal with the subject as a freshman class. It is never a waste of time to explore possibilities and formulate hypothesis. It would have been a challenge because it is a topic constantly skirted in other biology classes.

2. Honest, humorous, interesting, challenging. I believe you have done your "time" and are qualified even though I had little time to observe you as a scientist.

3. Yes.

Not signed:

1. I was actually looking forward to doing the paper. I would have learned a lot about myself and whether or not there is a link between creation and evolution.

2. Dan is obviously an extremely intelligent, thoroughly knowledgeable scientist. His lively, engaging, dynamic and thought-provoking lecture style was thoroughly enjoyable and greatly enhanced the learning environment.

He was one of the best college instructors I've ever had. Students can learn so much from him. It is extremely unfortunate that he was not given the chance to enhance other students' academic endeavors. He will be *greatly missed* by the majority of this class.

3. ABSOLUTELY!!

Tim Hilty:

1. Initial thought. OH NO! I don't like writing papers anymore than the next person. It does make you evaluate where you stand when it comes to science. Certainly not a waste of time. I'm going to write it anyway and use it for an English class. A challenge for those who haven't given it any thought!

2. Interesting, knowledgeable, and entertaining. All three necessary to be effective as a teacher. As a scientist, not narrow-minded in willing to entertain options that modern science refuses to acknowledge.

3. Certainly!

Not signed:

1. The paper would have been a good way to get us to think about the different hypotheses and reflect our views on them.

2. Great in both aspects. It's no wonder there is not school spirit at W.S.U. They get rid of the good ones and keep the old boring ones.

3. Yes.

Not signed:

1. An excellent idea! Writing is one of the most important events that goes on in science—and in life also—I would have loved to have written an essay on creationism vs. evolution, but because of the stupid church vs. state law—or whatever it is—we can't have an essay or Dan.

2. He is a wonderful teacher. What happened to him was a real shame. Personally, I think a lot of the same thoughts that Dan did. I think if "cre-

ationism" (which I still don't really even know the meaning of. Does anyone?) and religion should be taught; maybe society wouldn't have so many problems that are going on in the world today (e.g., violence, prejudice, and drive-by shooting). Dan is an excellent teacher and I wish him the best throughout his life and I wish there would have been more I could have done in order to stop this mess. Damn the science department for letting this happen!

3. Yes, certainly. Good luck and God bless. Brian M. Smith.

Not signed:

1. A challenge to be met.—glad I don't have to do it, but would have been interesting to see what viewpoint I held.

2. Dan was probably one of the most lively and interesting professors I've ever had. He should teach the morning biology class—the kids would actually stay awake to listen to lecture. Has the administration been smoking too much weed to have let go such a great teacher? WSU loss and Clark's gain.

3. YES!

Eve Heinricks:

1. A challenge to be met—exactly! I felt challenged, which is all too rare in these freshman survey courses. Too often, people's "opinions" are not given the rigorous test of reason, but are merely knee-jerk reaction. We all benefit by considering diverging viewpoints, intelligently made.

2. As a teacher, interesting and thought provoking. I felt prepared for labs—I had a syllabus of the lab schedule, a lab book and what we mentioned in lecture. I have had many courses—notably chem 121-123 where lab material often predated the lecture topics, which was not a problem. As a scientist, I have no objections to Dr. Scott. The purpose of the scientific method is to preclude personal opinions from "creeping unaware" into research. Personal beliefs thus have little effect on the integrity of well-de-

signed research, and Dr. Scott gave no indication of having an "agenda," merely of presenting his personal opinion.

3. Certainly, if given the opportunity... Incidentally, I do not consider myself a creationist, but I am interested in any major area of human thought, religion not excluded.

Not signed:

1. Not a good idea for me. My objective in taking courses at WSU (currently) is to get information to pass the MCAT exam. I work full time, and am taking this course along with organic chemistry (2 courses & 2 labs). I'm glad I don't have to worry about the paper too.

2. Overall, very good. Knows the material, and very dynamic as an instructor. Made very boring material seem interesting.

3. Yes, no problem.

Not signed:

1. I thought the paper was a good idea because it stimulates students to think about both sides of an issue and arrive at their own ideas as to how they believe, rather than a spoon-fed version of how their parents believed. Definitely not a waste of time and would have been a <u>challenge to be met</u>—isn't that what college and a broad education is for?

2. I think he is one of the best teachers which are very few and far between in this research centered approach to college teaching. Half of them have not taught or taken a class on how to educate. He was a natural!! As a scientist—great: he was not so biased or close minded. He admitted his belief of evolution too!

3. YES!

Not signed:

1. I thought the paper was a good idea even though I don't enjoy actually writing a paper I also learn a lot from doing one. Plus I thought the topic would be interesting.

2. I completely enjoyed having Dan as my teacher and I wish he were to be here to finish the quarter. It's hard to go to class at 7:00 after working all day and then to pay attention to a professor., but with Dan I actually enjoyed and got something out of class even during the last 1/2 hour. I think he's a fine scientist. Having certain belief is nothing that would cause someone to be a bad scientist. If one thing you taught us to take everything with a grain of salt and to come to your own conclusions.

3. Yes, Definitely! I think it's just awful what WSU did to you. They are losing probably one of the best biology teachers around!

Not signed:

1. I wanted to do it. It's a topic I've always wanted to research anyway.

2. Very dynamic lecturer. I dreaded this class until I met the teacher. I really don't know him as a scientist, but I'm sure he qualifies as much as anyone at Wright State (at least that I've had).

3. I'd drive to Clark Sate to take a biology course from Dan before I'd ever take another one here. Dan is the only instructor I've had that showed any interest, enthusiasm.

Not signed:

1. I thought that the paper was a wonderful idea, by having to support our finding with science, the view point of the student was restricted by science. Yet, it makes a student realize there are other theories, I found that evolution is a much younger theory than creationism. And that, before Darwin, creationism was the main theory. It's a shame some don't see the ability for both to coexist.

2. Dan, was the best Biology professor I have had at Wright State. As a teacher, and a scientist, he encourages free thinking. Where would we be without freethinkers.

3. IN A HEARTBEAT AND I HATE BIOLOGY.

Not signed:

1. The paper is a good idea. It would of been a way to consider other means of development rather than only evolution. (We are in college, I know the liberal university is only out to protect us but let me make up my own mind.) Homophobia is condemned, but God-phobia is alright?

2. Maybe I'll go to Clark State.

3. Most Definitely.

Not signed:

1. At first I thought the paper was a waste of time. After thinking about it for a while I was actually looking forward to doing the research in order to learn more about both the creation and evolution theories and where they diverge and converge. So, although I hate to write papers I think it would have been a good learning experience.

2. Dan was an enthusiastic and energetic teacher. He presented the material in a way that made learning easy. Dan was very knowledgeable in all of the material he taught.

3. YES!

Not signed:

1. I think that the paper is a very good idea and a challenge to be met. It teaches students to think and analyze facts vs. theory. That is the whole point in paying this much money to go to college. We want to learn to think and form educated ideas and opinions.

2. A scientist seeks the truth and is not a tool in politics. Unfortunately, at this university politics is more important than a well-rounded education. Dan is a true scientist who will state his opinion and the facts. He is a very good teacher who gives his class a sense of motivation. He conveys an excitement for science to his students and makes them think. This university has disgusted me so much that I am attending OSU where my education will not be censored, and my money will be well spent.

3. <u>YES</u>, but it would have to be at a different university. I refuse to attend WSU next quarter.

Not signed:

1. Would be interesting to research. But, not interesting enough to be done w/o a course forcing me to do it. I did not feel that a paper written from the evolutionist point of view would have been graded negatively.

2. Was able to take an absolutely boring topic and make it palatable. No question about his knowledge of subject.

3. Yes, but I dislike learning about plants.

Not signed:

1. A good idea, and a challenge to be met. It would have been difficult but interesting. I would have like to see how I could have done on it.

2. I thought he was a very good teacher. Interesting, and he kept the class interested in him. I thought he knew what he was talking about and he should not have been dismissed for his belief.

3. YES.

Not signed:

1. Paper—definitely a challenge—perhaps one the scientific community is not yet prepared to meet—obviously fears.

2. <u>Outstanding</u> teacher. As a scientist he presents material as all scientists should—view data—w/some doubt & and clear comprehension of theory holes & limitations. His inclusion of student knowledge, comments, & discussion was thought provoking & inspirational. His humor was refreshing & kept people in tune & aware of their surroundings. Truly, WSU's loss—and ours.

3. Yes, in a heartbeat.

Not signed:

1. It was a paper to make you think. If all of the professors were as concerned about making us think, then maybe we would learn something.

2. As a teacher he was challenging and never just "gave you the answers." He made us think. As a scientist he has a right to form his own opinions.

3. If I knew he was teaching another class I would specifically ask for him.

Chris Reuter:

1. I was looking forward to writing the paper because I still am not sure which theory I believe. I think the research that I would have put into the paper would have helped me form my opinions.

2. I thought Dan was a very interesting and exciting teacher to be around. I thought his classes were always enjoyable and thought provoking. I have no idea as for his ability as a scientist.

3. <u>Yes</u>.

Not signed:

1. Good idea—Gets you to think about stuff that you shouldn't in a science class.

2. Scientist—someone who dares to question science.

3. A cosponsored religion-science class, yes.

Not signed:

1. The paper and the controversy made me read books on both sides of the issue. I wouldn't have done so before. I think it was a challenge, I know more about the sides & of creationists & evolutionists.

2. As a teacher I found him very engaging and he kept my interest. I don't agree with some of his theories on debunking evolution. Since he bases his beliefs on unscientific theories I don't think he is much of a scientist, though I am sure he knows a lot.

3. If it had nothing to do with biology I would.

Not signed:

1. I feel that creationism is very undefined. It seems that there would exist a wide range of brands of creationism. It's even possible to define creationism in a way so as to make it completely harmonious with evolution. Creationism is a fuzzy term. Does it mean that the earth was created 6,000 years ago?, 200 million years ago?, or 4.5 billion years? Was the universe created 10 billion years ago or 20 billion years ago? Were the processes that allowed the "Big Bang" to occur created? Have other universes been created before our universe existed?

2. The 1st lecture was extremely one-sided and biased in favor of creationism. Dan unleashed an attack on evolution by expressing opinions, personal conclusion, and scientifically erroneous arguments (thermodynamics). Dan needs a course in thermodynamics. I really liked the test. I think it will show how much each person learned.

3. No.

Chapter 12: Raymond Damadian: Inventor of the MRI

Was the Inventor of the MRI System Denied the Nobel Prize
Due to His Creationist Beliefs?

Can a person's beliefs about the role of an intelligent creator prevent an otherwise deserving scientist from being awarded a Nobel Prize? One of the most blatant cases of discrimination against a scientist, the awarding of the 2003 Nobel Prize in Medicine for the discovery of magnetic resonance imaging, suggests this may be true. Instead of awarding the prize to the actual inventor, Dr. Raymond Damadian, the Nobel committee gave it to two persons, Paul C. Lauterbur of the University of Illinois, and Sir Peter Mansfield of the University of Nottingham, England, who improved on Dr. Damadian's original idea and invention.[597]

The invention of MRI was no small achievement. MRI technology is now over a five-billion-dollar-per-year industry, and is the premiere medical diagnostic imaging method in use today. It is, in general, able to image diseased tissue more accurately, more safely, and more efficiently than any other medical imaging technique. Over a half-billion MRI scans have now been completed since its invention. MRI is widely recognized as "one of the great medical breakthroughs of the 20th century" that has saved and enhanced "countless lives."[598]

Raymond Damadian was, according to the U.S. Supreme Court, the National Inventors Hall of Fame of the U.S. Patent Office, the Smithsonian Institution, the Franklin Institute, and numerous other organizations, the undisputed inventor of MRI technology. MRI technology simply would not exist had it not been for Dr. Damadian. This chapter explores why Damadian was not awarded the Nobel Prize and strongly suggests that the likely reason was Damadian's deeply held religious beliefs, specifically his creationist beliefs. He is an "active creationist" and is on the boards of several creationist organizations.

---

597 Schwarzschild, 2003; Weed, 2003.
598 Evans, 2004, p. 442.

The Inventor and His Invention

Raymond Damadian was born in Manhattan on March 16, 1936. When he was ten years old, his grandmother died of breast cancer. Her great pain made a lasting impression on young Raymond, especially because he was very close to his grandmother.[599] This event set young Damadian on a course to find a way to help diagnose and treat cancer.

When Damadian was studying violin at the world famous Juilliard School of Music, he triumphed over nearly 100,000 other applicants, and was awarded a Ford Foundation Scholarship at age fifteen. This enabled him to attend the University of Wisconsin to complete a degree in math, and he then completed his MD at the Albert Einstein School of Medicine. He later finished graduate work in biophysics at Harvard University. His interest was not in clinical practice, but in research and development.

He first got the idea for MRI while working with nuclear magnetic resonance (NMR), scanning some Dead Sea bacteria called halophiles that had twenty times the potassium level of most other bacteria.[600] The research with the bacteria went so well that Damadian recognized it might be possible to discriminate a mortal disease like cancer from healthy tissue by its MR signal. As chronicled in *A Machine Called Indomitable*, Damadian spent most of the rest of his career (and lifetime) developing the new type of medical body scanner, now known as MRI, to achieve this goal.

In 1969, he was the first to propose the use of magnetic resonance to scan human bodies for signs of disease. In his 1969 grant proposal to the Health Research Council of the City of New York, he requested funds to research the "instrumentation and probes that can be used to scan the human body externally for early signs of malignancy." His body scanner proposal stated his purpose was the "detection of internal tumors during the earliest stages of their genesis" when treatment is normally highly successful.[601] In 1970, he found a major difference in the MR signals between cancer and normal tissue,

---

599   Mattson and Simon, 1996, p. 615.
600   Damadian, 1994a, p. 55.
601   Mattson and Simon, 1996, Appendix and Chapter 8.

as well as major differences among normal tissue types, a critical discovery that made MRI scans possible.[602]

These newly discovered signal differences would eventually enable development of a technology to overcome medicine's age-old deficiency of visualizing the body's critical soft tissues (e.g., brain, heart, liver, kidneys, and pancreas). The very large MR relaxation differences in the soft tissue organs that Damadian discovered provided the contrast that conventional x-ray images had been unable to generate for more than a century.[603] The maximum difference in brightness (contrast) that x-rays can generate among the image pixels of soft tissue structures is four percent.[604] When the relaxation differences discovered by Damadian were exploited to maximize pixel contrast of MR images, differences of up to 130 percent in healthy tissues and 180 percent in cancers were achieved to visualize details in vital organs. The new clarity achieved by these scans enabled MRI technology to be used for numerous practical medical applications.[605]

In March of 1971, his results were published in the journal *Science*. A review of Damadian's MRI case in *Science* concluded, "Damadian published the first paper that used [what is now called] MRI to distinguish between healthy and cancerous tissue."[606] Damadian's research also was becoming widely known, and as early as 1973 articles were appearing in popular magazines about his work.[607] Then, in the spring of 1971, he proposed the MR voxel (volume element) scanning method for carrying out MR scans of a living human body.[608] His method took advantage of the fact that MR magnets used at the time to analyze test-tube samples had a "sweet spot" (volume element or voxel) that was sufficiently homogeneous to generate an MR signal, whereas off-center, less homogeneous regions lacked sufficient homogeneity to generate usable signals. He now is acknowledged as the first person to recognize that normal and pathological tissue can be differentiated by MRI.[609]

---

602   Damadian, 1971; 1988; Damadian, Goldsmith and Minkoff, 1977.
603   McRobbie et al., 2003, p. 2.
604   Phelps, Hoffman, and Ter-Pogossian, 1975.
605   Kevles, 1997, pp. 173-200.
606   Vogel, 2003, p. 382.
607   Edelson, 1973, p. 99.
608   Johnson, Jeannette, 1971.
609   Wehrli, 1992, p. 38.

In March of 1972, Damadian filed for a patent for his MR scanner based on both his *time 1* (T1) and *time 2* (T2) discovery and his voxel body scanning method. T1 refers to the time required for realignment of nuclear spins with the magnet field and T2 is the transverse relaxation time, a small but critical difference that enables MRI to function. The patent involved the magnet sweet spot, further trimmed by shaping the magnetic component of the radiofrequency (rf) field. The MR's radiofrequency (rf) magnetic field induces the MR signal, and also enables its detection. It can be spatially shaped in the same manner as any magnetic field, permitting use of the rf magnetic field to trim and shape the spatial dimensions of the signal-producing voxel of the MR magnet. Damadian's 1972 patent makes use of both the static DC magnetic field and rf magnetic field to control the aperture (volume) of the mapping voxel in order to achieve the spatial localization required to accomplish spatial mapping by MR.

In 1977, Damadian and his graduate students, Michael Goldsmith and Larry Minkoff, built the first MR scanner, which they named Indomitable. On July 3 of the same year, they produced the first MRI scan by using his patented voxel scanning method. The scan was achieved by moving the subject, Larry Minkoff, stepwise across Indomitable's magnetically trimmed sweet spot (voxel) at the magnet's center, thereby accomplishing the world's first ever MR scan of a live human body.[610] In 1980, Damadian introduced the first commercial MRI scanner, which was built by Fonar Corporation of New York, a company Damadian founded.[611] It utilized the voxel scanning method covered by Damadian's 1972 patent. Four of these QED 80 scanners were sold to users in Mexico, Japan, Italy, and Cleveland. In 1983, Damadian introduced the Beta 3000, a machine that "created quite a stir," and produced excellent reviews from doctors who examined the images it produced.[612]

Soon, several other companies also began building MRI scanners, forcing Damadian to appeal to the courts to protect his patents. In spite of his incontestable patents, Damadian faced a long struggle to vindicate his patent claims. A 1982 jury trial found Damadian's MRI patent valid and infringed upon by his competitors. Yet, six weeks after the trial, the judge voided the jury's verdict and

---

610 McRobbie et al., 2003, p. 2.
611 Damadian, 1994a.
612 Kleinfield, 1985, p. 217.

substituted his own verdict, even though Damadian's company had spent 2.2 million dollars in legal fees during the lawsuit. Damadian went to Court a second time; this time against GE, Siemens, Hitachi, Toshiba, Philips, and Shimadzu, and eventually, in October 1997, prevailed when in 1977 the U.S. Supreme Court enforced Damadian's 1972 patent by allowing the lower court decisions to stand, affirming his priority over Lauterbur, and asserting that all MRI scanners that use Damadian's T1 and T2 method to create MRI images are infringing on Damadian's rights. His lawsuits had taken a full fifteen years to resolve, the first lawsuit having been filed in 1982 against Johnson and Johnson.[613]

The 1997 damage award from General Electric alone was 128.7 million dollars (Siemens, Hitachi, Philips, Shimadzu, and Toshiba all settled out of court for undisclosed amounts). Damadian used none of these financial awards for himself, nor asked the Board to pay him royalties for his invention. He invested all of this money back into research and development in order to further improve MRI technology. By this means his company pioneered oblique imaging technology that had not been possible in other modalities as CT, and also introduced the world's first "Open" MRI in the 1990's.

Damadian's concern about how easily someone's patent rights can be infringed upon (and the harm this problem causes America and our economy) was detailed in a *Saturday Evening Post* article that he wrote.[614]

The Open MRI technology which Damadian and his company pioneered, and obtained the first patents on, does not require the patient to lie in a small confining tube, but rather on a large open platform. His latest development is the innovative Stand-Up MRI that allows much more detailed imaging of dynamic-kinetic maneuvers of body joints than were previously possible.[615] Fonar's Stand-Up unit is the only open MRI on the market today that allows imaging while the patient is in an upright position. This unit enables for the first time imaging of all parts of the human body in their normal physiologic upright position.

Upright imaging makes possible the evaluation of orthopedic structures (especially the spine, hips, and knees) under a full weight load, and also produces images of blood flow in cardiovascular structures such as the heart, arteries, and veins in their upright position. In addition, the funds from the patent litigation

---

613   Damadian, 1994b.
614   Damadian, 1994b, pp. 58ff.
615   Jinkins et al., 2003.

were also used to develop the Fonar 360, a new scanner to be used by surgeons and radiologists to enable use of the MRI image to guide intraoperative and interventional procedures.

The invention of MRI was more difficult than had been anticipated at first because many of the experts firmly believed that building a magnet large and homogeneous enough to scan a human body was not possible. Moreover, constructing rf antennas that could be externally mounted on the body that would have enough sensitivity to detect nuclear signals from deep within the human anatomy was believed to be beyond the reach of available technology.[616] Mansfield did not achieve a scan of the human body until a year after Damadian's first scan, producing a scan of the human abdomen in which, unlike Damadian's first image, the internal organs were not discernible.

Another product development concern was the health of patients who were being scanned. Scanners today use magnetic fields as much as 60,000 times stronger than the Earth's background magnetic field. A common concern by researchers at the time was that the MRI magnetic field could adversely affect magnetizable molecules within the body, such as the iron in hemoglobin. Extensive research has proven this fear unfounded.

Some specific landmark steps in MRI technology made by Damadian include:

1. scientific research and theory of the cell and cell water that led him to propose water molecule scanning by NMR (MR) as a method for detecting cancer;
2. discovery of the cancer MR scanning signal in animal tissue together with his demonstration of the pronounced diversity of MR relaxation times among healthy tissues;
3. building of a superconducting magnet (his competition were all then experimenting with commercially available electromagnets);
4. filing of the original (and the foremost) patent on MR scanning;
5. achievement of the first whole-body MR scan of a human and the resultant image;
6. development of the world's first commercial MR scanner.[617]

---

616   Kevles, 1997, p. 178.
617   Mattson and Simon, 1996, p. 613.

Recognition of Damadian's Achievements

In 1988, President Ronald Reagan awarded the National Medal of Technology jointly to Damadian and Lauterbur for their magnetic resonance technology contributions. In 1989, Damadian was inducted into the National Inventors Hall of Fame of the U.S. Patent Office, joining other distinguished inventors including Edison, Alexander Bell, Morse, and the Wright Brothers. The first MRI scanner ever built—Damadian's—was placed in the Smithsonian Institution in the same year. Damadian was also awarded the seventh annual Lemelson-MIT Lifetime Achievement Award on April 25, 2002 for pioneering magnetic resonance scanning technology. In March of 2004, he was awarded the Franklin Institute Medal "for his development and commercialization of magnetic resonance imaging ... which has transformed the diagnosis and treatment of disease."

The record of Damadian's achievements in developing MRI, and his priority, are both well documented and supported by these awards, plus his many patents and dated, refereed publications.[618] Damadian clearly originated the MRI concept, and Lauterbur even cited Damadian's 1971 *Science* paper in his notebook, although he did not cite Damadian in his March 1973 *Nature* paper, claiming lack of room. The work of Mansfield and his co-authors, which further improved on Damadian's and Lauterbur's work, was not published until 1974.

Furthermore, Damadian's contributions in the commercial development of the MRI machine are also widely recognized. Kean and Smith, in their standard textbook on the history of MRI, note that the two factors primarily responsible for the decision of various research centers and commercial investments to investigate developing a technique of NMR imaging in vivo were, first, the work of Damadian and, second, the impact of CT on medical imaging.[619] Lauterbur is mentioned later, and only then as the originator of the term "zeugmatography" for MRI (a term that never caught on). Mattson and Simon, in the definitive history of MRI, note that when GE television ads claim, "We bring good things to life," and show a patient being scanned with MRI, some viewers will assume that "magnetic resonance scanning was invented and brought to

---

618   McCool, 2003.
619   Kean and Smith, 1986, p. 1.

market through the efforts of a large team of corporate scientists"; to counter this mistaken assumption, they offer this corrective:

> In reality, MR scanning was invented, patented, and brought to market largely through the efforts of one man, a medical doctor, Raymond V. Damadian, who was assisted along the way by others who believed in him and his dream. Instead of a deep-pocketed corporate R&D budget, he had only his salary as a professor and just enough funding scrounged up from here and there to pay the salaries of his two graduate assistants and to buy the second-hand components and the liquid helium used for constructing and cooling his first scanner.[620]

Damadian Slighted for Nobel Prize

As previously noted, the 2003 Nobel Prize in Medicine for the discovery of magnetic resonance imaging was given to Paul C. Lauterbur and Sir Peter Mansfield, both of whom improved on Dr. Damadian's original idea and invention. Many scientists who had worked with Damadian were upset at the Nobel committee's slight. One, Dr. Eugene Feigelson, Dean of the College of Medicine at the *State University of New York* (SUNY) Medical Center in Brooklyn, where Damadian was on the staff, stated that "all of MRI rests on the fundamental work of Dr. Damadian."[621] Dr. Feigelson added, "we are perplexed, disappointed and angry about the incomprehensible exclusion" of Dr. Damadian from the Nobel.[622] Kevles, in a study of MRI, concluded:

> in the summer of 1977—in the footsteps of Edison rather than Roentgen—Damadian preempted his scientific competitors. He called a press conference to introduce and demonstrate a whole-body NMR imaging machine which he called the "Indomitable." Whether or not there really were contenders for this particular prize at this particular time is open to discussion. What is not debated is the fact that Damadian, with his vision of a body-size NMR machine, leaped from using magnets only large enough to examine tissue specimens in test tubes to building his own superconducting magnet with a bore (or opening) large enough to encircle a grown human being. No one

---

620 Mattson and Simon, 1996, p. 611.
621 Quoted in McCool, 2003.
622 Montgomery, David, 2003, p. C1.

else had the imagination, or hubris, to skip the in-between steps undertaken by others—examining first small mammals and then parts of the human body—and jump to the construction of a whole-body machine.[623]

Florida State University professor and well-known philosopher of science, Michael Ruse, conceded that Damadian first conceived and invented the MRI machine, yet notes that the Nobel award "went to two other and somewhat subsequent scientists, Paul Lauterbur and Peter Mansfield." Ruse's comment on this was: "Notoriously, the Nobel committees never reveal their deliberations (until everyone is long dead) and never change their minds."[624]

The Claims

Why was Damadian excluded from the Nobel for his many critical contributions to MRI technology? A common claim by the researchers in this area is that Damadian's technique by itself was not feasible to produce viable, commercial, economical scanners. It is correctly noted that Damadian's first scan took four hours and forty-five minutes to complete 106 data points, and its resolution was not the quality of today's machines (although, as Damadian realized, one did *not* need pictures to diagnose disease, only data points). History shows that all firsts only establish the proof of a principle, i.e., that the goal is achievable, even if the demonstration is fragile. The Wright brothers' first flight was aloft for only 12 seconds, and is a long way from the performance of today's F-16s. The Wright plane turned by twisting its wings, a far cry from today's ailerons. Further, Lauterbur did not even attempt a human scan, and Mansfield made a scan about a year after Damadian.

Lauterbur, after seeing Damadian's original T1 and T2 differences in cancer and normal tissues, came up with the idea of combining Professor Herman Carr's gradient techniques for achieving spatial mapping with the backprojection technique of the CT to reconstruct a picture from a set of projections. Lauterbur eventually submitted his idea to *Nature*, which rejected the paper because the editors could not see a practical use for his scanning procedure.[625] It

---

623 Kevles, 1997, p. 179.
624 Ruse, 2004, p. 4.
625 Kevles, 1997, p. 181.

was accepted in 1973 after he revised the manuscript, and showed MRI could be used to scan and detect cancers (which was Damadian's original claim). In the same year Peter Mansfield published a paper in which he used a gradient to detect the faces of a crystal. It did not, however, describe a method for *mapping* the atoms of a sample as is required to achieve a scan. Nor did the paper mention *scanning* anything. In addition, evaluation of crystal faces, the subject matter of the 1973 paper by Mansfield, is not directly relevant to human imaging.

Nor was the use of a linear magnetic gradient for spatial delineation of atoms a new concept. The mathematics was published in the 1950s by Professor Roger Gabillard. Furthermore, Professor Herman Carr demonstrated the first-ever spatial map of atoms using the magnetic gradient in his 1952 Harvard Ph.D. thesis.[626] Carr's linear gradient method for achieving spatial maps of atoms provided a far more efficient scanning method than Damadian's voxel by voxel data acquisition method. Nonetheless, Damadian's method, like the Wright Brothers' (whose wing-twisting method was soon surpassed by Curtiss's ailerons), was the first method that achieved results—the first scan of a live human body, proving the feasibility of MR body scanning. Damadian's achievement of the first scan of a live human body was made in 1976 and published in 1977 using the "focused field" imaging technique. This achievement launched the possibility of whole-body MR scanning, and was the published purpose of his original discovery.[627] Later, in 1978, Mansfield produced the first MRI image of a live human body using Lauterbur's technique. These facts are not questioned.

Many of Damadian's supporters are not arguing that Mansfield and, especially, Lauterbur did not deserve recognition, but that Damadian did the pioneering work and made many of the critical initial discoveries. Lauterbur and Mansfield only improved upon his discoveries. Specifically, Lauterbur discovered how radiation in an applied magnetic field could be used to produce two-dimensional images by combining Carr's gradient method and the back-projection of CT. Garroway, Grannel and Mansfield showed how the magnetic gradients could be used in sequence to improve both the speed and efficiency of the image generation process, allowing the unit to be even more practicable. An excellent summary of the invention by Harold Evans concluded that

---

626   Carr, 1993.
627   Macchia, et al., 2003, p. 784-785.

Damadian's technique was indeed much inferior to Lauterbur's—as Lauterbur's was to be somewhat inferior to Mansfield's, as both were to Ernst's, which was improved by researchers at the University of Aberdeen. But Damadian did it first, with no help and no funding. He had to publicize himself á la Edison because no one else would. No one else took him seriously. Donald Hollis said of the first image: "It was nothing but a publicity stunt. It's not good enough to even be sure it's human..." Any medical resident, however, can identify the image as a human chest cavity. Minkoff tested this. So did we. Hollis was plain wrong. Not long afterward, he gave up science to raise chickens and sheep.[628]

Today more than ninety-five percent of all MRI scans use T1 and T2 measurements that Damadian first conceived.[629] Furthermore, the will of Alfred Nobel states that the prize in medicine is to be awarded to the person that has "made the most important discovery within the realm of physiology or medicine," not the person who has devised techniques or inventions that exploit that discovery, as Lauterbur and Mansfield did.[630] Some even feel that the question

is not whether Damadian should be included in the Nobel Prize to Lauterbur and Mansfield, but whether they should have been included in the Nobel Prize that Damadian deserves. The contribution of Lauterbur and Mansfield is mainly that of the multiplex advantage, but Damadian was able to make the initial discovery in an environment which was hostile from the outset.[631]

Comparisons with the Wright Brothers

Parallels with the invention of the airplane are critical to illustrate Damadian's case. The Wright brothers achieved the specific discoveries that made the first heavier-than-air manned flight possible, but their crude, rickety contraption clearly was impractical. The Wright brothers' first successful plane flight on December 17, 1903 required the pilot to recline on a wood frame covered with paper and cloth, and used skis to land. The craft flew only 852 feet, and was in

---

628   Evans, 2004, p. 451.
629   Stracher, 2002, p. 2.
630   Fant, 1993, p. 329.
631   Letter from Peter Lassen to Jerry Bergman, 2005, p. 1.

the air for only twelve seconds. More importantly, the Wright brothers' plane was turned in flight by an elaborate network of crisscrossing wires that twisted the plane's entire double wing. The wing twisting controls were rigged to their hips.[632] Furthermore, numerous other aspects of the Wright brothers' design had to be modified. For example, the tail had to be moved to the rear rather than the front before manned flight was practical.[633]

Many important improvements were made by others, such as Glenn Curtiss, who invented the hinged aileron (a development that even the Wright brothers' planes later used).[634] Nonetheless, no one today claims that Curtiss invented the airplane, even though the aileron invention is the basis of modern aviation; credit is rightfully given to the Wright brothers, because they were first to make the critical inventions that made flight possible—especially the wing design that created lift—and they were the first humans to fly in a heavier-than-air craft.[635]

Damadian's first MRI machine used a point-by-point analysis, a very impractical approach for scanning. Nonetheless, as noted above, his T1 and T2 observation "was a Eureka moment for Paul Lauterbur. After seeing Dr. Damadian's experiment repeated by a graduate student, Lauterbur … realized he could subject the nuclei to a second magnetic field that varied in strength in a precise way."[636] Lauterbur employed the gradient spatial mapping technique invented by Carr. Lauterbur realized he could use Carr's technique for the same purpose Carr invented it for spatial mapping of hydrogen in a sample. He recorded Carr's gradient mapping idea in a notebook and had it witnessed the next day.

As Stracher notes, "Over the years, Mr. Lauterbur has been less than forthcoming about giving Dr. Damadian credit." Although Lauterbur acknowledged Dr. Damadian's 1971 paper in his notebook, his subsequent articles neglected to mention it. As noted above, Lauterbur claims that by the time he published his first paper, another group had made measurements on a tumor in a mouse's tail and he "needed to keep the list of references to very few, so I used 'the later one.'"[637] Regarding the introduction of the magnetic gradient for mapping, Lauterbur was

632 Schneider, 2003, p. 502.
633 Jakob, 1990.
634 Combs and Caidin, 1979.
635 Jakob, 1990.
636 Stracher, 2002, p. 2.
637 Lauterbur, quoted in Stracher, 2002, p. 2.

also less than forthcoming. It was invented by both Gabillard and Carr before him, whom he also did not cite, even though this was pointedly called to his attention in print at the Royal Society Meeting in London, March 14-15, 1979, (which he attended) and on numerous other occasions.

The failure to cite has had a predictable outcome. Lauterbur is credited for the invention of the gradient mapping technique that was invented by others before him.[638] Others have observed that Lauterbur's achievement, in essence, involved taking the signals and drawing them on a piece of paper rapidly and efficiently—clearly a major improvement, but hardly equivalent to making the initial discovery.

The documented evidence is clear: Damadian is the pioneer of MRI, has the first patents, and built the first MRI scanner; conversely, Lauterbur augmented Damadian's accomplished work by utilizing the Carr and Gabillard gradient spatial mapping technique to provide a more efficient spatial mapping method and representing the acquired data as pixel intensities (an image) instead of as numbers. Damadian focused on normal versus cancer tissue, but Lauterbur on signal variations from all tissue.[639] Although Lauterbur, by introducing the Carr and Gabillard gradient mapping technique, succeeded in proposing a better method than others for producing an MRI image, Damadian built the first workable unit that could achieve a scan of a live human body, which Lauterbur himself attempted but did not achieve.

The Nobel decision in this instance is like crediting Curtiss for inventing the airplane, and snubbing the Wright brothers. Although Lauterbur's use of the Carr gradient mapping technique is today used with Damadian's equipment, just as all modern planes use Curtiss' improvements, this should not detract from the Wrights', nor Damadian's, original developments. Similar examples occurred in the history of television: flying spot (mechanical scanning) predated the cathode ray tube. Donald Vickers concluded that

> Damadian made four pivotal contributions that preceded Lauterbur's insight: (1) he was the first person to think of using NMR medically to differentiate healthy and cancerous tissue; (2) he was the first to prove this hypothesis in his experiments at NMR Specialties; (3) he was first to think

---

638   Andrew, 1980, and Carr, 1993, 2004.
639   Evans, 2004, p. 445.

of building a full-body NMR scanner capable of diagnosing disease; (4) he was the first to invent a method for spatially localizing an NMR signal to make a point-by-point scan (which he used six years later to make the first MRI scan of a human body).[640]

Philip Yam noted that controversies about Nobel Prize awards are not uncommon, but in Dmadians case the "Nobel committee's decision ... seemed to be an intentional slap in Damadian's face. Award rules permit up to three winners in each category; *so the committee could have included Damadian.* Curiously, the Nobel's press release describing the winners typically acknowledged other contributors, but failed to mention Damadian."[641] Most articles about the award totally ignored Damadian's involvement with inventing and developing MRI technology.[642]

The Patents

In a review of the MRI patents, I found Lauterbur had only four relating to MRI; Peter Mansfield had a total of seventeen; Damadian, a total of sixty— including many of the most important patents. No MRI unit can be manufactured today without reference to Damadian's patents. The discovery that allowed NMR to be used for imaging was the use of a gradient magnetic field (superimposed on a volume of uniform magnetic field) together with the FFT (Fast Fourier Transform) to convert the radio frequency spectrum into useful spatial information. This basic concept allowed the formation of proton density images in a feasible time to achieve a practical scan. The patent shows this method was first described by Garroway, Grannell and Mansfield, filed in September 1975 and issued in March 1977.[643] Elemental (in this case, proton) density imaging is now the fundamental mode used for MRI imaging.

Conversely, Dr. Damadian was the first one to identify the use of the T1 and T2 information for abnormal tissue detection. (His US3,789,832 U.S. Patent on this was filed in 1972 and issued in 1974). T1 and T2 produce secondary

---

640   Donald Vickers, quoted in Evans, 2004, p. 446.

641   Yam, 2003, p. 42 (emphasis added)

642   See, e.g., Fort Wayne Newspapers, 2003, p. A3.

643   Mansfield and Grannell, 1973.

information that can also be extracted with additional imaging pulse sequences. The method of "focusing" a magnetic field could not be used as a practical method for imaging for several reasons, including the fact that it took hours to obtain a usable image. However, once the gradient field and FFT method was invented, T1/T2 imaging became a source of important clinical information, and all MRI machines are now capable of obtaining these images.

Since Damadian was the inventor of the T1/T2 information system (his '832 patent), whoever used those signals (no matter how they were obtained) for clinical diagnostic information would have infringed on his patent. The court agreed with this, and as a result, many companies had to pay him royalties. Dr. Damadian's contribution was, therefore, clearly significant, even though the basic enabling technology used today is contained in the Garroway et al. patent. Although it is difficult to judge the Nobel Committee on this and to conclude conclusively that they were biased because of Dr. Damadian's faith, clearly a three way recipient award was more than warranted.

Damadian's Religious Beliefs Central to the Case

Damadian became a born-again Christian in 1957 at a Billy Graham Crusade in Madison Square Garden, New York.[644] Extensive reading and study on science and theology since then has put his faith on firm footing, especially on the creation/evolution question. Furthermore, he has been active in this controversy.[645]

Numerous articles have suggested that Damadian's religious beliefs were central to the denial of the Nobel award. For example, a *Christianity Today* article suggested that the reason for the Nobel Prize Committee's snubbing Damadian was that he was a devout Christian and a creationist.[646] In an excellent article about the Nobel Prize and Damadian in *Scientific American*, Yam asked: "... did his creationist viewpoint play a role? He is on the technical advisory board of the Institute for Creation Research."[647] Damadian is also on the reference board for the *Answers in Genesis Creation Museum*. Farrar wrote: "Some suspect that Dr. Damadian's creationist views, which include opposition to the theory of evo-

---

644 Chuvala, 1996.
645 Hiebert, 1996, pp. 30–31.
646 Olsen, 2003.
647 Yam, 2003, p. 42.

lution… influenced the committee."[648] And Professor Steve Jones editorialized that "Raymond Damadian, like Newton … is a fundamentalist Christian (and some blame his Nobel rejection on that fact). He denies Darwinism: life, he says, began with a miracle…."[649] Jones argues that the belief life began with a miracle is unacceptable.

Furthermore, Damadian is "identified by many web sites as a prominent creation scientist" and, according to Olsen, "most scientists are not creationists and [they] tend to look askance at scientists who believe that way."[650] *Vision* magazine's Ronald Bailey added that the Nobel committee could have been "swayed by the fact that Damadian, although a brilliant inventor, is apparently a creation science nut. In … contrast, Lauterbur's current research is on the chemical origins of life."[651]

His colleagues mentioned to Damadian many years ago that his stand on creationism might create problems for him in earning a Nobel Prize because of the scientific establishment's clear bias against this world view.[652] When I was a graduate student studying MRI in the early 1990's, several University of Michigan professors I worked with berated Damadian for his beliefs. Eminent philosopher Michael Ruse concluded that perhaps Dr. Damadian does have good reasons to believe that he was passed over because of his beliefs. Ruse wrote that Damadian is a "very prominent Christian" and a

> Creation Scientist—one of those people who believes that the Bible, especially including Genesis, is absolutely literally true—six days of creation, Adam and Eve the first humans, universal flood, and all of the rest. It is at least as likely a hypothesis that Damadian was ignored by the Nobel committee because they did not want to award a Prize to an American fundamentalist Christian as that they did not think his work merited the fullest accolade. In the eyes of rational Europeans—and Swedes are nothing if not rational Europeans—it is bad enough that such people exist, let alone give them added status and a pedestal from which to preach their silly ideas. Especially a scientific pedestal from which to preach their silly anti-science ideas. Is this unfair? One certainly feels a certain sympathy for the Nobel committee. Creation science is wrong and (if taught to

---

648   Farrar, 2003. p. 1
649   Jones, 2003, p. 18
650   Olsen, 2003.
651   Ronald Bailey, quoted in Ted Olsen, 2003.
652   Letter from Roger Richards to Jerry Bergman, dated October 22, 2003, p. 1.

young people as the truth) dangerous. It does represent everything against which good science stands.[653]

Weiss adds that an explanation that must be considered for Damadian's rejection is that the Nobel committee scientists or other persons of influence could not deal with "Damadian's staunch support for creationist science." He writes that:

Damadian has served as a technical adviser to the Institute for Creation Research, which rejects the standard model of evolution. "The non-biblical account would have us believe that all life originated from a single common ancestor—a slime mold—and give or take a billion years, we're expected to believe that the descendants of this slime mold climbed out of the ocean and stood up and started giving lectures," Damadian says. "Do the math on that. The sheer statistics of that violate any sense of reality."[654]

Weiss notes that various creationist Web sites have for years proudly "touted Damadian as a respectable scientist supporting their cause" and suggests:

It is tempting to speculate that some assembly members might have weighed the additional legitimacy a Nobel imprimatur would have conferred upon groups whose views are so diametrically opposed to so much of the modern science.[655]

Wieland adds that "the exclusion of Dr. Damadian as the third co-recipient of the Nobel" is so surprising "that even some of the secular media have talked of the possibility of a link between Dr. Damadian's exclusion and his creationism."[656]

Ruse stressed that Damadian's case should be looked at from a historical perspective. Even the most well-respected scientists have believed in "very strange things," says Ruse, but:

if we start judging one area of their work in terms of other beliefs that they have, we could well do more harm than good. Isaac Newton, the great-

---

653 Ruse, 2004, p. 1.
654 Weiss, 2003, p. 38.
655 Weiss, 2003, p. 38.
656 Wieland, 2003, p. 40.

est scientist of them all, had some very strange views ... that make today's Creation Scientists seem comparatively mild. More recently, Alfred Russel Wallace, the co-discoverer of natural selection along with Charles Darwin, became an enthusiast for spiritualism, believing that there are hidden forces controlling every aspect of life. People knew this and were embarrassed by it, but it did not stop them from celebrating and praising Wallace's great scientific work. He was made a Fellow of the Royal Society, and given Britain's greatest award for achievement, the Order of Merit.[657]

Ruse's conclusions are not those of a creationist sympathizer; rather, he has argued forcefully in favor of evolution over any form of creationism or ID. Yet he writes:

> But as one who loves science above all and thinks it the greatest triumph of the human spirit—as one who has no religious beliefs whatsoever—I cringe at the thought that Raymond Damadian was refused his just honor because of his religious beliefs. Having silly ideas in one field is no good reason to deny merit for great ideas in another field. Apart from the fact that this time the Creation Scientists will think that there is good reason to think that they are the objects of unfair treatment at the hands of the scientific community.[658]

The Nobel Prize committee may have felt that awarding Damadian the Nobel Prize would legitimize his creationist views. It was for the same reason that award-winning science writer Forrest Mims was fired from *Scientific American*. They told him that, as a writer for one of America's top science magazines, he would give credibility to creationism, and for this reason only was he terminated.[659]

A. E. Wilder-Smith documented another case similar to Damadian's:

> the situation is such today that any scientist expressing doubts about evolutionary theory is rapidly silenced. Sir Fred Hoyle, the famous astronomer, was well on his way to being nominated for the Nobel Prize. However, after the appearance of his books expressing mathematically based doubts as to Darwinism, he was rapidly eliminated. His books were negatively reviewed and no more was heard about his Nobel Prize.[660]

---

657   Ruse, 2004, p. 1.
658   Ruse, 2004, p. 1.
659   Bergman, 1993a, p. 38.
660   Wilder-Smith, 1987, p. iii.

Interestingly, the Nobel committee in the past used the phrase "without prejudice" to describe the selection process. The secretary of the Nobel committee on physiology and medicine, *Karolinska Institute* professor Hans Jornvall, wrote that the last will and testament of Nobel requires that the prize shall be awarded to the most important research finding, without reference to other criteria. He claimed that he has

> never, ever, heard that there has been any other concerns [sic] other than those in the last will and testament and ... I have never heard anything about creationism in any prize discussions. Before I received your e-mail, I did not even know that anybody believed that this had been discussed or investigated... I am convinced that creationism has not influenced the prize in physiology and medicine. Be totally satisfied on this point![661]

It is well-known that Damadian and Lauterbur have been at odds for years. Damadian believes that the Nobel decision was no mere oversight but that "an intense lobbying campaign, conducted by the winners and their supporters, resulted in Damadian's exclusion."[662] Several others that I interviewed confirmed this conclusion. An anonymous reviewer of this chapter wrote: "It may very well be that the ... Nobel committee (or some ... powerful members) indeed did not want to give a prize that is assumed by the general public to be an indication of 'genius' to somebody who would clearly use the authority of the prize to advance creationism."[663] It is charged by some that the Nobel committee, since its beginnings, has been very influenced by inappropriate criteria, including nationality and politics.[664]

The Case against Damadian

Some people argue that Damadian was not awarded the prize because he chose to leave academia and pursue research at his own company. This reasoning is hardly valid, because many researchers have left academia to continue their work elsewhere. Some, such as William Shockley (the inventor of the transistor),

661 Hans Jornvall, quoted in Molén, 2004, pp. 10–11.
662 Weiss, 2003, p. 38.
663 Letter from Bernard Lightman to Jerry Bergman, dated April 6, 2007, p. 1.
664 Crawford, 1984.

and the Wright brothers, even founded companies that allowed them to profit from their discoveries.

Others claim that Damadian's denial was due to resentment, because he defended his patent rights in court. Damadian is often characterized as rash and litigious for pursuing the court cases to defend his company.[665] Although a number of individuals in the MRI community have criticized him for doing this, Damadian had no choice, because fighting for his patent rights was a matter of his company's survival. It is very common for inventors to be forced to defend their patents in court—Edison, Bell, Marconi, and Philo Farnsworth, the inventor of the television, all had to fight for their patent rights.

Likewise, the Wright brothers had no choice but to defend their patents and spent many years in court, including five years in litigation with the Herring-Curtiss Company. The court also eventually vindicated the Wrights, and ruled as they did in Damadian's cases, that the Wrights held the "pioneer patent" on manned flight.[666] The Wrights engaged in a dozen lawsuits in three nations. Of those cases that went to court, the Wrights won every single one.[667] One interesting difference between the Wrights' and Damadian's case is that the Smithsonian spent four decades trying to discredit the Wright brothers, but from the beginning formally acknowledged Damadian as the inventor of MRI.

Some have also claimed that the prize is to be awarded only for a scientific development, not an invention. Judson notes that, in fact, the Nobel Prize is frequently awarded to inventors of new technologies. He cites several cases, including that of Svedberg, who was given the chemistry prize for the ultra centrifuge, and of Frederick Sanger, who was given the award for inventing a method of sequencing amino acid chains. Among the many other examples include the inventors of electrophoresis and chromatography.[668]

Yet another specious reason is jealousy. Kenneth Olson, director of the diagnostic branch of the National Cancer Institute, even claimed that the reason was that "Damadian was a physician, and he came in and discovered it [MRI]. The physicists missed the boat. Nobody likes to miss the boat." [669] Jealousy is

665   Stracher, 2002, p. 2.
666   Combs and Caidin, 1979, p. 357.
667   Combs and Caidin, 1979, p. 357.
668   Judson, 2004, p. 289.
669   Kenneth Olson, quoted in Evans, 2004, p. 447.

probably involved in most great inventions; but this is also not a valid reason to deny the award. Furthermore, many M.D.'s have been awarded the prize.

Many competitors have unscrupulously attacked Damadian's personality, implying or claiming that his "egotism" and "megalomania" were the issue.[670] Sir Harold Evans noted that even Nobel committee members "admit that Damadian's personality worked against him."[671] It is not rare to accuse potential Nobel laureates of this fault. Evans, who spent five years researching the Damadian and similar cases, concluded that Damadian's character defects are "similar to those of many other" great inventors who made America what it is today.[672] Traits that Evans mentioned include excitable zeal unmitigated by doubt, and some paranoid feelings (often justified by history, as the many patent wars demonstrate). These very traits no doubt allowed Damadian to succeed against almost overwhelming odds. This may be one reason why Evans concluded that he has "a great deal of sympathy with" Damadian.[673]

Even if Damadian was egotistical and had some personality quirks, as Evans notes, these are not valid reasons to deny him the Nobel. Kary Mullis, the inventor of PCR, was given the award inspite of major personality issues.[674] Dwyer opines:

> Mullis is not likely to fit most people's profile of a serious scientist. He is a man who quit the lab to work in a restaurant, a man who had a midnight brawl on a beach with a fellow researcher, a man who elicits both giggles and awe from other scientists. Yet Mullis, 48 ... is responsible for what many consider the most important advance in genetic research since the discovery of DNA's double helix ... his invention—the polymerase chain reaction, or PCR—has revolutionized microbiology, medical diagnostics, criminal investigation, even evolution.[675]

If Mullis could be awarded a Nobel Prize in spite of his personality shortcomings, then claims of similar impropriety are not a valid reason to deny the same prize to Damadian.

---

670   Hollis, 1987, pp. 104-105, 171-182.
671   Evans, 2004, p. 442.
672   Sir Harold Evans, quoted in Frederick Allen, 2005, p. 35.
673   Sir Harold Evans, quoted in Frederick Allen, 2005, p. 35.
674   Mullis, 1998, pp. 18-25..
675   Dwyer, 1993, p. 8.

Conclusions

A very strong case can be made that Damadian's beliefs about origins were a major part of the reason for his not receiving the Nobel Prize. He is the undisputed inventor of MRI, and it appears that all of the reasons so far provided to justify denying him the award are clearly specious.[676] In the United States, because a smoking gun is rare discrimination is proved by comparative data. Those who discriminate almost never admit to it. It is evident that no valid reasons exist for the Nobel committee's failure to award the prize for the invention of MRI to its actual inventor, based on what was clearly his primary role in its development.[677] Peter Lassen concluded that, although Damadian is a "controversial creationist," he should have at least been included in the 2003 medicine Nobel Prize.[678]

Acknowledgments: I would like to thank Raymond Damadian, M.D., Clifford Lillo, M.A., Bert Thompson, Ph.D., Michael Dennis, Ph.D., Peter Lassen, M.Sc.E., Shelley Hausch, and Ellen Yeske for their critical review of an earlier version of this manuscript.

---

676   Macchia et. al., 2007, p. 785.
677   Kjelle, 2003; Simmons, J. 2002; Prasad, Amit. 2007.
678   Lassen, 2003, pp. 15, 20.

Chapter 13: Guillermo Gonzalez and the Privileged Planet

After a favorable initial internal review, the Smithsonian announced it would provide a private screening of a movie featuring the work of Guillermo Gonzalez titled *The Privileged Planet* in Baird Auditorium at the Natural Museum of History in Washington, D.C. in June of 2005.[679] This simple event would resonate throughout the world, shattering of the promising career of Dr. Gonzalez. When the movie announcement was first made, protests from the media, including *The New York Times* and *The Washington Post*, were strident and immediate. The media, as usual in stories about Intelligent Design (ID), were often inaccurate as they covered this story. For example, *The New York Times* incorrectly claimed that the film was "intended to undercut evolution."[680]

The Darwinist community was first alerted to the film's showing when invitations that included the Discovery Institute's name (the film's original sponsor) were sent out which indicated that the event was "co-sponsored" by the Museum's director. This "shocked" Darwinists because " ...it looked as though the Smithsonian was supporting Intelligent Design."[681]

Nguyen noted that once the news was out about the Smithsonian's plan to show the film, it spread across the internet like wildfire, especially among those opposed to ID.[682] Pro-evolution, atheist, humanist and other websites organized a campaign to send e-mails and letters and make phone calls protesting the film's showing.[683] In addition, one opposition group was willing to pay several thousands of dollars to ensure that the film was *not* shown.[684] The next step was to pressure the academic community to boycott the film. For example, an archeology doctoral student reported that an e-mail was sent to the *entire* department of anthropology at *George Washington University*, "warning" everyone there not to watch the movie.[685]

---

679   Stokes, 2005.
680   Schwartz, 2005, p. A8.
681   Brumfiel, 2005b.
682   Nguyen, 2005, p. C1.
683   For example, see Gilberti, 2005.
684   P.Z. Myers, 2005a.
685   Steiner, 2005.

As I will document, the response by Darwinists to the film illustrates their absolute intolerance of a worldview with which they disagree—a view that implies the universe exists for a purpose, and that our Earth is a "privileged planet." This perspective hardly seems threatening to the vast majority of Americans. Clearly, only those with a desire to ensure that their own philosophical views are perceived as the only acceptable ones, and who wish to force their own agenda on the public, objected to the film.

Professor Laurence Krauss, who seems to spend much of his time fighting any attempt to support theism with scientific fact, stated that "the Smithsonian was duped." The common claim is that the Smithsonian was duped because the Discovery Institute did not follow the proper protocol. Jay Richards of the Discovery Institute responded by noting that they had carefully "followed the invitation template that the Smithsonian provided."[686] The film says nothing about religion, evolution, Darwin, or even Intelligent Design. Nonetheless, "within only a week, the Smithsonian had yielded to pressure from Darwinists to censor the film: it canceled its 'co-sponsorship' of the event and returned Discovery's 16,000 dollar contribution" to the Museum.[687] Although the film was not produced by religious fundamentalists and is not about religion, the mainline media claimed that the Smithsonian was "caving into" religious fundamentalists. The film simply argues that the conditions on our planet (and in our solar system) are rare in the universe, and that the earth lies in one of the few potentially inhabitable locations in the galaxy. As Gonzalez noted, the film does not try to prove the existence of God, but merely shows "some purpose to the universe."[688]

The storm of protest caused the Smithsonian Museum's director, Christian Samper, to announce that "the content of the film is not consistent with the mission of the Smithsonian Institution's scientific research."[689] The Smithsonian claimed that presenting information supporting Intelligent Design—and they have never argued that the information in the film is incorrect—"violates the museum's scientific and educational missions."[690] Even though it would require breaking its contract, "…some Museum scientists wanted the event canceled"

686   Brumfiel, 2005b, p. 725; see also Richards, 2005.
687   Tucker, 2005a, p. 1.
688   Quoted in DuCharme, 2004, p. 2.
689   Bhattacharjee, 2005b, p. 1526.
690   Bhattacharjee, 2005b, p. 1526.

anyway.[691] Nonetheless, because they had signed an "iron clad contract" to show the film and breaking the contract could have resulted in costly litigation, in the end they elected to carry out their legal obligation.[692] On Thursday, June 23, 2005 at 6:00 p.m. the movie was shown as planned at the Smithsonian.

The Film

The film is based on a book co-authored by Professor Guillermo Gonzalez, a highly-credentialed, well-published astronomer then at Iowa State University. The book argues that there may be many billions of stars, and even possibly many millions of planets, but that many conditions must be met before a planet is able to host life. For example, the planet must be in a temperate orbit (the temperature range must be approximately between 0°F and 100°F), and must also have a liquid ocean. These requirements are not met on any other known planet. In fact, most planets are infernos, unable to support any form of life. The film showcases information such as the uniqueness of the Earth's atmosphere and its orbital position to affirmatively answer the philosophical question if life on earth was part of a grand design and not the result of time, chance, and chemistry as taught by Darwinists.

Interestingly, Professor Peter Ward coauthored a book titled *Rare Earth* that advocates almost the same idea.[693] This best seller received rave reviews and, as far as I am aware, virtually no criticism. Ward was a colleague of Gonzalez when he wrote his book. As of April, 2008 *The Privileged Planet* DVD had 92 reviews, an unusually high number, on Amazon.com. Over 70 reviewers gave it the highest rating (five stars) 7 gave it four stars, 3 three stars, 4 rated two stars and only 6 gave it only one star.

The Claim of Purpose

Why was the film so controversial? Tucker concluded that it was because the empirical evidence presented in the film leads to one conclusion—our planet is not only designed for life, but it is also designed with a "purpose," namely to

---

691   Bhattacharjee, 2005b, p. 1526.
692   O'Leary, 2005b.
693   Ward and Brownlee, 2000.

support a species like humans.[694] The idea that there is purpose behind the universe is what causes so many prominent scientists to go ballistic—and it is this idea that the Smithsonian found so unacceptable. Most leading scientists teach that life has no purpose or meaning except that which we ourselves give to it. We are simply living on an ordinary planet, one of many that exist in an average galaxy, which is just one of many millions of galaxies in the known universe.

Orthodox science also teaches that life ultimately evolved here because of time, natural law, mutations and chance, and will soon disappear. William Tucker, an opponent of *The Privileged Planet's* implication of purpose, maintained that "instead of arguing that everything on earth has been 'designed for some mysterious purpose,' I think it is much more instructive to look at some of God's little errors."[695] One of those "little errors" noted by Tucker is the fact that ice floats—for which "there doesn't seem to be any real explanation." In fact, it is well-known why ice floats—a subject typically covered in introductory chemistry classes. In short, lower heat energy allows more hydrogen bonds to form as water cools, producing a honeycomb lattice that expands the structure and reduces its density as a solid, thus ice floats on liquid water.

The film, at best, only "makes a subtle argument for Intelligent Design," however the Museum, "after heavy criticisms from its scientists and outsiders... promises it won't happen again."[696] Museum spokesman Randall Kremer admitted that the "major problem with the film is the wrap-up" because it "takes a philosophical bent."[697]

The objectionable "philosophical bent" of purpose for planet earth, the view "that the suitability of Earth as a habitat for scientific observation is evidence that the universe was designed for human beings..."[698] The Museum apparently has no qualms about presenting other films that have other clear philosophical bents, such as the late Carl Sagan's film that concluded the "Cosmos is all that is, or ever was, or ever will be"; i.e., that only matter exists—and nothing else.[699] In 1997 the Smithsonian even featured a "Cosmos Revisited" show in memory of Carl Sagan. DuCharme noted that the controversial film (*The Privileged Planet*)

---

694   Tucker, 2005a, p. 2.
695   Tucker, 2005a, p. 2.
696   Bhattacharjee, 2005b, p. 1526.
697   Bhattacharjee, 2005b, p. 1526.
698   Bhattacharjee, 2005b, p. 1526.
699   Gonzalez, 2005.

is "a rebuttal of astronomer Carl Sagan's principle of mediocrity" which states that the earth's small size and its unimportant position proves "our planet is insignificant in the universe."[700] Interestingly, while *The Privileged Planet* supports its view with empirical facts, Sagan did not support his faith statement with any evidence. In fact, his oft-repeated claim about the cosmos cannot be tested scientifically.

Thus, the Smithsonian has not only without apology presented Sagan's materialistic philosophy, but has blocked the presentation of any scientific arguments suggesting a contrary conclusion. For this reason, Sheppard called the Smithsonian "one of the greatest Evolutionary propaganda machines in the world."[701] Jewish mathematician David Berlinski said he thought the "uproar was indecent," and that he was "appalled but not surprised by the willingness of academics to give up every principle of free speech and honest debate whenever they think they can do so without paying a price."[702]

Why the Museum Changed Its Mind

Following an initial screening by Hans Dieter-Sues, the Museum's associate director for research and collections, the film was approved for showing. After the media storm, the Museum did a second review which, according to anthropologist Richard Potts, determined that the "film fell within the Museum's guidelines for such events."[703]

But "after dozens of calls and e-mails from researchers and the public," the Museum decided to "issue a statement disavowing the event."[704] After the storm of protest, the Museum argued that the film was "trying to insinuate science within the wider realm of belief," concluding that the film is "metaphysical and religiously based." As noted, Carl Sagan's conclusion was clearly metaphysical and religiously based—yet no storm of protest ensued (and if there had been, the protesters would have been roundly condemned by the media and the science establishment).

---

700   DuCharme, 2004, p. 1.
701   Sheppard, 2005, p. 1.
702   Quoted in O'Leary, 2005b, p. 22.
703   Bhattacharjee, 2005b, p. 1526.
704   Brumfiel, 2005b, p. 725.

The Museum also reevaluated its policy and broadened its definition of religious content—now *any* evidence that supports design, purpose or theism will be banned. Of course, in a state institution such as the Smithsonian, this approach is clearly state-sanctioned unconstitutional hostility towards theism (not to mention the intentional refusal to look at explanations of where the scientific evidence leads).

The Opposition

Evaluation of the film's opposition is especially informative about the nature of the objections to it. Jerry Coyne, who also spends much of his time ensuring that criticism of Darwinism, and especially criticism of Darwinism philosophy, is supressed, was also active in motivating his followers on the website "evoldir" to oppose the film's showing. He wrote to thank those who had e-mailed the Museum's director. The director e-mailed back to those persons that the Smithsonian was taking steps to make sure this would never happen again. Coyne commented that "it looks as if we have won a small skirmish in the continuing battle against ID."[705]

Among those who felt the Museum should not show the film were many leading Darwinists such as the Director of Outreach for the *American Geophysical Union* Pete Folger.[706] In contrast, the *University of Toronto* showed *The Privileged Planet* without controversy, allowing people to make up their own minds about the film.[707]

Leading professional paranormal "debunker," James Randi, (popularly known as The Amazing Randi) after posting an article about the film, stated that "the volume of mail I received on this matter has been staggering."[708] He actually offered the Smithsonian $20,000 to *not* show the film. The reason he gave for wanting the film banned was because the Smithsonian is "dedicated to promoting science, and not supporting religious claims." He did not object if the Smithsonian showed a film that supported *his* religious claims—it is only the claims of *others* to which he objects. His "bribe," he admitted, "looked like

---

705   Coyne, 2005.
706   Brumfiel, 2005b, p. 725.
707   O'Leary, 2005a.
708   In P.Z. Myers, 2005a, p. 1.

an attempt to suppress free expression of an opinion." However, to defend himself, Randi stated that the Smithsonian should come up with an alternative presentation—one that would "demonstrate their dedication to the support of legitimate science," by which he meant support for Darwinism and the idea that our earth is *not* a privileged planet.

Randi repeatedly implied that the notion of life in the universe is the result of the outworking of natural law, chance, time, and other factors is "science," but the idea that the universe is the result of purpose and design is "superstition." He equated evidence for the role of intelligence in shaping the design of the physical universe with mythology, and neo-Darwinism with science and rationality. Randi concluded that "we should be fighting back by using every means at hand short of making the ID people into martyrs, which suppressing this film just might have done."[709]

Evaluation of the Film

It is clear that Randi and others want to censor ideas with which they disagree, that they want to control information presented to others, and do not want to give others the privilege of viewing the film and forming their own opinions. Randi even argued that the public is not intellectually able to make their own judgments in this area—suggesting that he and his cohorts must make these judgments for them.[710]

Especially telling were the comments on the various internet talk groups. For example, on Pharyngula.org, Professor P.Z. Myers stated that, by showing the film, the Discovery institute is trying to fool the whole National Museum of Natural History by putting on a white lab coat and that they look "ridiculous in it...Keep laughing at these frauds, everyone."[711] A University of Cambridge student remarked that, "the Smithsonian has gone absolutely insane...I have just sent the following e-mail to the dear people at the Smithsonian. I intend upon being a major pain until they give up this nonsense."[712] In her e-mailed letter, she stated that the Smithsonian was short sighted, and asked if they realized that they have

---

709 In P.Z. Myers, 2005a, p. 1.
710 In P.Z. Myers, 2005a, p. 1.
711 P.Z. Myers, 2005a, p. 1.
712 Gregory, 2005, p. 1.

"done a major disservice to the parents, educators, and scientists who have fought tirelessly against this nonsense." She ignorantly concluded, "do you not realize that if ID had anything scientific to say they would publish their findings in peer reviewed journals?"[713]

In fact, Gregory had not seen the film, had not read the book, and was not aware of the published literature in this area, including publications by those who teach at the University of Cambridge where she hails from. Nor is she evidently aware that Gonzalez has published numerous major articles in peer reviewed publications.

Nguyen called the film—which largely summarizes astronomical data and at best implies a conclusion based on these data—"creationism in disguise."[714] This is a common ploy to censor any science-based evidence that could be interpreted in a manner that does not align with the naturalistic, Darwinist, evolutionary worldview (and is therefore judged by many as off limits in public places such as museums).

Hector Avalos, associate professor of religious studies at Iowa State University and a self-described former fundamentalist who is now an evangelical atheist, stated that the film should not be shown because "Intelligent Design is a religious concept cloaked in the language of science."[715] In the same report, Avalos described the film as "'pseudoscience,'" but he failed to provide any evidence for this conclusion (as was also true of all of the other critics that I reviewed). In a letter to the campus newspaper, he condemned the film because it is the "old teleological argument...Design implies a Designer" and Christians believe this designer is God.[716]

Gonzalez noted that Intelligent Design is simply a "systematic way of detecting design in nature," a modest proposal that generates an enormous amount of hostility.[717] This idea, concluded John Patterson, professor emeritus of engineering at Iowa State University, has "no place in science because history has proven these explanations 'pathetic.'"[718] Interestingly, even outspoken atheist John Patterson admitted that Gonzalez's book *The Privileged Planet* is "rich with good science in

---

713 Gregory, 2005, p. 1.
714 Nguyen, 2005, p. C1.
715 Oltman, 2005, p. 2.
716 Avalos, 2004, p. 1.
717 Quoted in Grundmeier, 2004a.
718 Grundmeier, 2004a.

it" but hastened to add that it is nonetheless a "religious apologetic disguised as science."[719]

Fortunately, the irrational criticism against *The Privileged Planet* has been noted by other scientists. For example, Tom Ingebritsen, associate professor of genetics, development, and cell biology att ISU, thought that Patterson's response reflected "a confounding bias against the supernatural," and that Patterson's "'worldview is coloring his [perception] of whether Intelligent Design could be legitimate in science.'"[720]

As Scott Rank noted, the reaction to the film's showing has been anything but rational. In his words, "[p]rominent researchers are scrambling to write articles against it, universities are firing staff members who are publicly advocating it, and *Wired Magazine* even devoted a cover article to it, affectionately titled 'The Crusade Against Evolution.'"[721] He added that Professor Avalos, Iowa State's most beloved atheist who is neither a scientist nor a philosopher argued against ID from a philosophical perspective.[722] Rank added that most ISU students know that Avalos will throw mud at theism whenever possible. So much for the claims of rationality and impartial objectivity among scientists.

Problems Begin

As noted above in 2004, Dr. Gonzalez co-authored the book *The Privileged Planet: How Our Place in the Cosmos is Designed for Discovery*, which presents empirical evidence for the hypothesis that the universe is the product of Intelligent Design and that the Earth is in a priviledged place in the galaxy for scientific discovery.[723] It was this book, and the film made from the book, that got him into trouble and ended his promising career at *Iowa State University* (ISU). The book critiques the "Copernican principle," the idea that "everything we see around us is commonplace in the universe, that we are average beings in a run-of-the-mill planetary system in an average galaxy populated by scores of

---

719   Grundmeier, 2004b, p. 2.
720   Grundmeier, 2004b, p. 2.
721   Rank, 2004. p. 1; see WIRED magazine article: http://www.wired.com/wired/archive/12.10/evolution.html
722   Rank, 2004, p. 1.
723   Gonzalez and Richards, 2004.

other mediocrities."[724] Esteemed Harvard astronomy professor Owen Gingerich wrote that critics of the film based on Gonzalez's book

> raised the alarm that the showing of the film *The Privileged Planet* at the Smithsonian Museum would somehow constitute an endorsement of Intelligent Design. I suppose that few of the critics actually saw the film, for it contains no explicit mention of Intelligent Design. It did, however, contain implicit criticism of the Copernican principle, for the film argued that the earth is indeed a very special place, something that we would all intuitively agree with, since it is, after all, our home. But the film carried its assertions to a cosmic level, in proclaiming how very special, how unique, in fact, our planet's location and circumstances are. The implicit message of the film was that ... *Homo sapiens*, have been endowed with a highly unusual environment, not only conducive to our existence here, but also remarkably well suited as a vantage point from which to investigate the cosmos itself. Who can fail to be thrilled by the idea that we have inherited a place uniquely situated for surveying the universe?[725]

Gonzalez is described as an easygoing intellectual who is well liked by students and faculty alike. His student ratings were excellent—he was consistently described as smart but hard, yet his classes were "lots of fun" and that he "has a nice structure to everything and is very organized." He uses PowerPoint presentations which students describe as "awesome" and add "I enjoyed his class and loved going to it. I learned a lot, I think he's great!" The most common complaint is his course is "a little tough for some" and "the material was a little more scientific than it should've been," some "stuff went over my head" and "much was expected from us, for a 100 level class." In other words, he was demanding and his class was not easy. A colleague of Dr. Gonzalez at ISU, Dr. John Hauptman, wrote that Professor Gonzalez is

> very creative, intelligent and knowledgeable, highly productive scientifically and an excellent teacher. Students in my Newspaper Physics class like to interview him. I have always been fascinated by his ideas, for example, that the first few millimeters of moon dust contain pieces of ancient Earth, the circling moon acting as a vacuum cleaner scooping up impact debris, or

---

724 Gingerich, 2006, pp. 13–14.
725 Gingerich, 2006, p. 16.

that numerous but precise and delicate conditions allow life on our Earth. Where else is life allowed? These are great questions.[726]

Several of his colleagues have admitted that Gonzalez was denied tenure at ISU as a result of his support for Intelligent Design. Tenure denial often means the kiss of death in academia, making it very difficult to find an academic position elsewhere. Although the story of his tenure denial was first broken publicly in the Iowa paper, *Ames Tribune*, on May 12, 2007, the actual decision to deny him tenure took place earlier in the spring.[727] Dr. Gonzalez had just bought a house, married a local woman, and wanted to start his family and continue his career as an astronomer at ISU. He tends to keep to himself, focusing on his highly productive research program, which would continue if he were allowed to stay at the university. His supporters have argued that this is what ISU does not want because of his alleged scientific heresy.

According to ISU's Department of Physics and Astronomy, as outlined on page 4 of its Procedures and Promotion and Tenure Policy and Procedure, the tenure process requires "excellence sufficient to lead to a national or international reputation ... [that] would ordinarily be shown by the publication of approximately fifteen papers of good quality in refereed journals." Having produced 68 refereed scientific papers, Dr. Gonzalez has exceeded his own department's standard for "excellence" requirement for tenure by more than 350 percent. ISU considered 66 faculty for tenure during the past academic year, and only Gonzalez and two others were denied.[728]

Besides being the author of many peer-reviewed scientific papers, Gonzalez is also the co-author of a major peer-reviewed college-level astronomy book, *Observational Astronomy*, published by Cambridge University Press (now in its second edition).[729] Publication of a major academic book is typically considered by many universities to be sufficient to merit promotion to a full professor.[730] Clearly, his research had caught the attention of a receptive audience within the scientific community and was making inroads into publicly accessible made-for-TV and

---

726 Hauptman, 2007.
727 Dillon, 2007.
728 Dillon, 2007.
729 Birney, Gonzalez, and Oesper, 2006.
730 Bardwell Smith, 1973.

popular science journal outlets. Gonzalez's research on stars was highlighted on the National Geographic Channel. He also co-authored a cover story about the Galactic Habitable Zone in *Scientific American*.[731]

His work has also been cited in *Science*, *Nature*, and many other leading scientific journals.[732] A citation search of the author's name located 1,638 unique citations in peer-reviewed science journals as of July 2007. This is an astounding number of citations for an untenured junior faculty and more than most of the faculty in his department. It is true that he published fewer articles toward the end of his career at ISU, but during this time he published two books, thus would have less time to produce new papers for journals publication. Also, the research for many of his articles was completed when he was a post-doc and his only responsibility was research and publication. As a faculty his responsibilities include teaching, new class preparation, grading papers, developing tests and power points, faculty committee work, working with graduate studets, office hours, community service and course development, so we would expect his publication level to drop at least until he was more established. Even so, Guillermo published more than most other faculty members in his department during his time at Iowa State.

His research led to the discovery of two new planets, and he is now developing new techniques to discover even more extrasolar planets. Gonzalez also served on the NASA Astrobiology Institute Review Panel, the National Science Foundation Advanced Technologies and Instruments review panel, and is or was a referee for *Astronomical Journal, Astronomy & Astrophysics, Astrophysical Journal (and Letters), Icarus, Monthly Notices of the Royal Astronomical Society, Nature, Naturwissenschaften, Publications of the Astronomical Society of Japan, Publications of the Astronomical Society of the Pacific, Origins of Life, Evolution, Biospheres* and *Science*.

---

731 Gonzalez et. al., 2001, pp. 60–67.
732 For example see Murray, 1998. A few more examples include Nuno C. Santos, Willy Benz, and Michel Mayor, "Extrasolar Planets: Constraints for Planet Formation Models," *Science*, 310:251-255 (Oct. 14, 2005); Charles H. Lineweaver, Yeshe Fenner, and Brad K. Gibson, "The Galactic Habitable Zone and the Age Distribution of Complex Life in the Milky Way," *Science*, 303:59-62 (January 2, 2004); N. Murray, B. Hansen, M. Holman, and S. Tremaine, "Migrating Planets," *Science*, 279:69-72 (January 2, 1998); and Raul Jimenez, Chris Flynn, James MacDonald, and Brad K. Gibson, "The Cosmic Production of Helium," *Science*, 299:1552-1555 (March 7, 2003).

His Background

Born in Havana, he and his family fled from Cuba to the United States in 1967. In 1970 Gonzalez received his first telescope. After graduating from high school in 1983, he studied astronomy at the University of Arizona on a full-tuition scholarship. At age 19 Gonzalez was featured in the *Miami Herald* as one of five south Florida finalists in the national Westinghouse science competition for building a device that measured changes in the conductivity of water as it moves from its solid to its liquid states. In 1987 he graduated from the *University of Arizona* with high honors, and in the same year his first refereed paper was published in *Solar Physics*. In 1993 he received his Ph.D. in astronomy from the *University of Washington*, and two years latter he conducted postdoctoral research on solar eclipses at the Indian Institute of Astrophysics in Bangalore. This experience motivated him to formulate what would later become the Privileged Planet hypothesis. Gonzalez also did a postdoc at the University of Texas. The director there, David Lambert, said: "He proved himself very quickly" and was "one of the best postdocs I have had."[733]

In 1999 he was appointed research assistant professor at the University of Washington. I was told by one of his supportive colleagues at the University of Washington that they would not grant him tenure due to his views on Intelligent Design so he left in 2001 to become Assistant Professor of Astronomy at ISU. In 2001 Gonzalez also co-authored the cover story in *Scientific American*,[734] and in 2002 a feature story on his research was published in *Nature*.[735]

About this same time he began constructing his new telescope attachment to discover extrasolar planets. In 2004 a feature story on Gonzalez's research was published in *Science*.[736] Soon after *The Privileged Planet* was published in late 2004, Dr. Gonzalez began working on a series of projects examining stars with planets to determine their properties. So far he has published twelve articles in peer-reviewed science journals on this topic alone, and continues to research new planets and planet systems.

---

733 Quoted in Brumfiel, 2007, p. 364.
734 Gonzalez et al., 2001, pp. 60–67.
735 C. Chapman, 2002.
736 Irion, 2004.

Dr. Gonzalez's research led him and his associate researchers to discover what is known as the Galactic Habitable Zone, a term Dr. Gonzalez coined.[737] He concluded from his research that our sun, because of its composition and its orbit around the galactic center, is one of the few stars in the Milky Way Galaxy capable of supporting complex life. Our solar system is also far enough away from the galactic center to protect life from disruptive levels of gravitational forces and from the high levels of radiation existing at the galactic core. All of these and many other factors exist together as a set to create a Galactic Habitable Zone. Dr. Gonzalez concluded that every form of life on our planet owes its existence to the balance of these unique conditions.

Dr. Gonzalez has also made novel contributions from his discovery that the moon functions as "Earth's lunar attic," by serving as a repository for meteorites that originally came from nearby planets. For this reason our moon serves as a museum for our solar system's history, and he believes that its further exploration could yield much insight into our planet's own history.

Attacking Gonzalez's Work

The attacks were very open even before Gonzalez's book came out. Soon after it was released, the university and the ISU Atheist and Agnostic Society cosponsored a campus forum that openly attacked *The Privileged Planet* in spite of the fact that Gonzalez's book is clearly based on science, a fact that even his critics, such as ISU emeritus professor John Patterson, acknowledged.[738]

The event featured ISU religious studies professor Hector Avalos, characterized by some as a militant atheist and faculty advisor to campus Atheist and Agnostic Society, who launched a campaign attacking Dr. Gonzalez's work. Although Dr. Gonzalez never introduced Intelligent Design in his classes, Avalos helped to spearhead a faculty petition urging all ISU faculty to "uphold the integrity of our university" by rejecting all efforts to portray Intelligent Design as science. Avalos, a religion professor, later conceded to a local newspaper that the motive for his petition was to attack Gonzalez.[739] The petition, signed by 120 faculty, stated that claims for Intelligent Design

---

737 Irion, 2004.
738 Grundmeier, 2004a.
739 http://www.evolutionnews.org/2007/05/biosketch_of_dr_guillermo_gonz.html

are premised on (1) the arbitrary selection of features claimed to be engi-
neered by a designer; (2) unverifiable conclusions about the wishes and de-
sires of that designer; and (3) an abandonment by science of methodological naturalism. Whether ones believes in a creator or not, views regarding
a supernatural creator are, by their very nature, claims of religious faith,
and so not within the scope or abilities of science. We, therefore, urge all
faculty members to uphold the integrity of our university of 'science and
technology,' convey to students and the general public the importance of
methodological naturalism in science, and reject efforts to portray Intelligent Design as science.[740]

The philosophical absurdity of the Avalos petition was recognized by
some colleagues in several departments, but none of them wanted to challenge
Avalos's tactics.

Avalos, in a widely cited article posted on the anti-ID web site *Talk Reason*,
concluded that the privileged planet "is a religious concept cloaked in the language
of science."[741] He could find no fault with the science, but rather labeled it religious and philosophical, and on this basis condemned it. For example, he wrote

> Dr. Gonzalez concludes that the earth was positioned for his convenience
> (in order to make scientific measurements of the universe). He begins Chap-
> ter 1 ... with a story about how the observation of a solar eclipse led him
> eventually to posit the idea that Earth was positioned so that he could make
> such observations. This rationale is analogous to a plumber arguing that if
> our planet had not been positioned precisely where it is, then he might not
> be able to do his work as a plumber. Lead pipes might melt if the Sun were
> much closer. And, if our planet were any farther from the Sun, it might be
> so frozen that plumbers might not exist at all. Therefore, plumbing must
> have been the reason that our planet was located where it is.[742]

It is clear from this statement that Dr. Gonzalez's beliefs, *and not the actual
content of the book or film*, were central to the antagonism that he faced. The
logical conclusion from this campaign against Dr. Gonzalez came in the spring
of 2007 when he was fired. By this time Gonzalez had published almost 70 peer-
reviewed scientific papers—more peer reviewed articles than all but one faculty

---

740   http://www.wnd.com/news/article.asp?ARTICLE_ID=55667
741   Avalos, quoted in Oltman, 2005, p. 1.
742   Avalos, 2008, pp. 3–4.

member granted tenure that year, not just in his department but across the *entire university*.[743] He had also earned a research grant from the Templeton Foundation for his book, which was administered by ISU.

The book earned praise from eminent scientists including David Hughes, vice president of the Royal Astronomical Society, Harvard astrophysicist Owen Gingerich, and Cambridge paleobiologist Simon Conway Morris. *The Privileged Planet* was developed into a documentary, was screened at the Smithsonian Institute and began airing on PBS stations around the nation. As of March 2007, the book had the unusually high number of 63 customer reviews on Amazon. com, most very positive, 41 giving it five stars, the highest rating possible.

The misleading claim that Gonzalez did not have many graduate students, and those he had never completed their degrees, was first promulgated by an anti-ID group in Iowa. The claim is misleading because non-tenured faculty typically do not supervise many graduate students for the reason that they are required to focus on teaching and their other responsibilities such as research. Nevertheless, in 2001, shortly before Gonzalez left the University of Washington (UW) to join the ISU faculty, he served as the primary advisor to UW astronomy doctoral student Chris Laws over the course of his entire doctoral thesis. Laws successfully graduated with a Ph.D. in astronomy in December of 2004. Gonzalez also served on the committee of UW Ph.D. student at Rory Barnes, who also successfully graduated in 2004. Secondly, non-tenured faculty usually do not normally have many graduate students, a role usually reserved for more senior faculty with long publication records and established research programs. The younger faculty are often responsible for heavy teaching loads, often the introductory classes as was the case with Gonzalez.

Dr. Gonzalez appealed his tenure on the basis that his beliefs, not the quality of his work, were the reason for his tenure denial.[744] The specific grounds of his appeal were that (1) he met the university's standards for receiving tenure, and (2) the university discriminated against him based upon his views about Intelligent Design. In the spring of 2007 Iowa State University (ISU) President Gregory Geoffroy denied Dr. Guillermo Gonzalez's application for tenure,

---

743   http://www.discovery.org/scripts/viewDB/filesDB-download.php?command=download&id=1362
744   Brumfiel, 2007.

which means he was terminated. Gonzalez's only option left was to appeal to the Board of Regents.

Given what can only be described as the vociferous antagonism toward Intelligent Design on ISU's campus, his only hope for a successful appeal was if enough people raised concerns that Gonzalez's denial of tenure would harm the university's public reputation and thus impact its fundraising efforts. Only then would the Board of Regents be willing to go against the university faculty and render a different decision. This did not happen. Although it is clear that Gonzalez has not only met, but has far exceeded ISU tenure requirements, in February of 2007 the Board ruled against him 7 to 1. They openly refused to even examine the incriminating documents in his case. This denial is directly a result of the opposition on ISU campus to his support for Intelligent Design.

The attitude expressed toward Intelligent Design by many ISU faculty alone document that Gonzalez was evaluated unfairly. The evidence frames an inaccurate comment made by the department chair Eli Rosenberg that "the decision had nothing to do with Gonzalez's support of Intelligent Design."[745] Rosenberg himself said in Gonzalez's tenure dossier that the problem with Gonzalez is "Intelligent Design is not a scientific theory" and the "fact that Dr. Gonzalez does not understand what constitutes both science and a scientific theory disqualifies him from serving as a science educator."[746] Green adds:

> Gonzales said he never taught Intelligent Design (ID) in his classes. "The recent controversy surrounding me is strictly about the research I have done on ID," he said. "My ID research [published in *The Privileged Planet*] was funded in part by a grant from the Templeton Foundation, which ISU administered."[747]

Since all of Guillermo's activities in support of Intelligent Design took place off campus in his capacity as a private citizen, both academic freedom and First-Amendment free-speech issues are involved. John G. West, associate director of the Center for Science and Culture, concluded that this case involves clear-cut "'ideological discrimination,'" and that "the statement against Intelligent Design

---

745 Green, 2007, p. 15.
746 Quoted in Green, 2007, p. 15.
747 Green, 2007, p. 15.

drafted at ISU played a large part in the denial of Gonzalez's tenure."[748] West asked, 'What happens to the lone faculty member who doesn't agree and happens to be untenured. That is practically, with a wink and a nod, a call to deny him tenure."[749] This conclusion is based on the statements of those persons who voted to deny Gonzalez tenure. One of Gonzalez's opponents at ISU, Dr. John Hauptman after first listing some of the many conditions that allow the possibility of life, admitted the reason was Guillermo's views on Intelligent Design:

> The Earth is the right distance from the sun to maintain its temperature midway between the freezing and boiling points of water. The Earth has a magnetic field, an atmosphere and salt-water oceans. It spins not too fast and not too slow. The sun is a normal star and is positioned in our Milky Way Galaxy far enough from the active center. The moon is just the right size to allow a total solar eclipse on the surface of the Earth, etc. Why are these conditions so "perfect" for us, allowing humans to exist, and above all, to ask these questions? Intelligent design is the notion that a supreme being arranged it for us.[750]

It was this idea that Gonzalez's colleagues vociferously opposed. Hauptman argued that

> The Greeks thought in a similar way. Grains grew, so there had to be a god Ceres who managed this. ... We are past this way of thinking about nature. ... Intelligent design is not even a theory. It has not made its first prediction, nor suffered its first test by measurement. Its proponents can call it anything they like, but it is not science. ...this tenure decision ... is purely a question of what is science and what is not, and a physics department is not obligated to support notions that do not even begin to meet scientific standards.[751]

Hauptman wrote about Gonzalez that "religious nutcases should be challenged at every opportunity, but in ways that do not hand them more free publicity."[752] Another colleague of Gonzalez, Dr. Curtis Struck, a professor at ISU for 24 years, opined that he was not surprised by ISU's decision to deny tenure, add-

---

748   Dillon, 2007, p. 1.
749   Quoted in Dillon, 2007, p. 1.
750   Hauptman, 2007.
751   Hauptman, 2007.
752   Hauptman, e-mail, June 5, 2007.

ing that: "Some of Guillermo's papers on astronomy he would be proud to have written. Some others that is not the case ... [because he took] a coincidence too far."[753] Specifically, the chair of the ISU Department of Physics and Astronomy, Eli Rosenberg, admitted that the book, *The Privileged Planet*, played heavily into the decision-making process. Two of the five active tenured astronomy professors in the department are connected to the widely publicized statement that denounces Intelligent Design as "creationist pseudoscience" noted above.[754]

Professor Steven Kawaler, the program coordinator for astronomy in the Department of Physics and Astronomy at ISU, even provides a link to both the anti-Gonzalez statement and an article about it on his website. University Professor Lee Anne Willson is married to ISU mathematics professor Stephen J. Willson, who also signed the anti-ID statement. The statement, created by the anti-Intelligent Design, and The National Center for Science Education, declares that "it is scientifically inappropriate and pedagogically irresponsible for creationist pseudoscience, including ... 'Intelligent Design,' to be introduced into the science curricula of our nation's public schools."[755]

This fact is important because Dr. Gonzalez's tenure application was first rejected at the department level, and the tenured faculty members in one's academic area typically have the most weight in tenure recommendations.[756] The denial of tenure for Gonzalez was clearly related to his views on Intelligent Design. It is critical to note that the ISU faculty handbook specifically states that the department's standards "must not impinge upon the academic freedom of the probationary faculty."[757]

Not unexpectedly, some of Gonzalez's many supporters have feared that speaking out in his favor could hurt their own careers. One astronomer, who concluded, "It looks to me like discrimination ... They can't say that he doesn't have a decent publication record, because he absolutely does," did not want to be named, fearing that openly speaking up in favor of an "intelligent-design proponent" would damage his career.[758] Based on the research I have done on this issue, it probably would have.

---

753   Quoted in Bergin, 2007, p. 24.
754   West, 2007.
755   Anonymous, 2003.
756   West, 2007.
757   Anonymous, no date [c].
758   Monastersky, 2007, p. A10.

The most common bogus claim offered as to why Gonzalez was denied tenure, was his failure to acquire a sufficient number of grants.[759] To put this claim in perspective, observational astronomers are often not very dependent on grants to support their research. They require primarily telescope time, transportation to and from the facility, and computer time to analyze their data. Furthermore, securing external funding was not listed as a tenure qualification in his ISU department guidelines. It is typically not easy for an untenured professor to obtain grant money on his own. Funding is usually a group effort that involves senior professors cooperating with younger professors.

Gonzalez's Supporters Condemned

Gonzalez's supporters have also faced persecution. Frederick N. Skiff, Professor of Physics at the University of Iowa, agreed to participate in a forum on ID only on the condition that it was not a debate, but a panel discussion where the emphasis was on hearing different perspectives on ID and responding to audience questions. What happened was very different from what he was told to expect. Dr. Skiff commented that he had never, ever, faced such blatant hostility at the hands of colleagues.

He was not only personally ridiculed and insulted but, in contrast to the supposed plan, the two fundamentalist Darwinists dominated the forum with ridicule and a slide purporting to show how the fossil record and a modified "ontogeny recapitulates phylogeny" akin to Haeckel's embryos are unassailable proof of Darwinism. A large segment of the biology faculty were in the "freethinker" audience. The dean of the college, an evolutionary biologist, is doing what he can to move the biology department in that direction.

Ever since he spoke up in defense of Dr. Gonzales, Dr. Skiff has experienced conflict with Hector Avalos. Several "freethinkers" e-mailed Dr. Skiff after the event and commented that the behavior of their colleagues, in contrast as to the way he responded, made them ashamed to be atheists.

---

759   http://www.expelledexposed.com/index.php/the-truth/gonzalez and http://www.pandasthumb.org/archives/2007/12/the-disco-insti.html

Commentary by Others

Commentary by others about the Gonzalez case was often verbally abusive, and is especially revealing. *Nature* magazine's web editor Adam Rutherford,[760] brazenly wrote, "Farewell, I hope, to the scientific career of Guillermo Gonzalez" because as a

> vocal supporter of the demonstrably unscientific guff that is Intelligent Design, Gonzalez displays ignorance of the scientific process, and appears to willfully defy it. And for that reason, he neither deserves the use of the facilities of a university to conduct scientific research, nor the privilege of teaching the next generation of scientists.[761]

Rutherford adds the notion that "13 billion years ago ... God made it" is unfalsifiable, and therefore not science. Therefore "were I in a position to offer Guillermo Gonzalez tenure, I would deny it for the precise reason that his, yes, religious *views about purpose in the universe* explicitly mean he is a crap scientist, regardless of his ability to generate valid data" (emphasis added).[762]

Of interest is the fact that when researching this case in detail I have not come across anything, anywhere, about Gonzalez's religion except that no one seems to know what it is, or even what his religious beliefs are except that he believes in God. He never discusses this issue with his peers, although speculation abounds about whether he is Catholic or Protestant. Nor has Gonzalez claimed his religion was the reason for his tenure denial, although irresponsible claims, such as the following, have often been made:

> The case of Guillermo Gonzalez being denied tenure at Iowa State University should figure prominently in court next time there is an attempt to introduce Intelligent Design into the school science curriculum. According to your News story (*Nature* 447, 364; 2007), Gonzalez, as a proponent of Intelligent Design is appealing against the decision on the grounds that his application was rejected because of his religious beliefs, rather than his science. Is there any better evidence that Intelligent Design, by the admis-

---

760 See https://ideotrope.org/index.pl?node_id=23525
761 Rutherford, 2007, p. 2.
762 Rutherford, 2007, p. 2.

sion of its own supporters (when convenient), belongs in classes teaching religion, not science?[763]

Conclusions

Believing that "God made it," which is a tenet of many religions (Judaism, Christianity, Islam and their offshoots), has now become a justifiable reason to terminate a professor from his university and, unfortunately, reflects the current widespread situation across nearly all of academia in the U.S. Not unexpectedly, this case has generated international publicity. Senator Sam Brownback expressed concern in the U. S. Senate, stating that "such an assault on academic freedom does not bode well for advancement of 'true science.'"[764] Very true.

---

763 Lessios, 2007, p. 22.
764 Combs, 2007, p. 5.

ADDENDUM

E-mails Show ID was at the Center of the Gonzalez Termination

scanned copies of the original emails can be found at
www.slaughterofthedissidents.com/cases/gonzalez/emails.zip

The president of Iowa State, Gregory Geoffroy, claimed that Gonzalez was not denied tenure due to his research into the view that the earth holds a very special place in the universe, as suggested in The Privileged Planet.[765] A review of the e-mails from Gonzalez's department colleagues, however, indicates otherwise. The attitude expressed toward Intelligent Design by many ISU faculty eloquently documents that Gonzalez appears to have been evaluated unfairly on illegal criteria.

The evidence also reveals Gonzalez's department chair Eli Rosenberg's claim that "the decision had nothing to do with Gonzalez's support of Intelligent Design" was misleading, at best.[766] Rosenberg himself said in Gonzalez's tenure dossier that Gonzalez's problem is "Intelligent Design is not a scientific theory" and the "fact that Dr. Gonzalez does not understand what constitutes both science and a scientific theory disqualifies him from serving as a science educator."[767]

Below I have reproduced a set of e-mails, mostly from Guillermo's ISU colleagues, that eloquently document the fact that he was let go because of his support for the view that the earth exists for a purpose, a notion held by over 90 percent of the American population. All information in brackets was added as was the bold for emphasis. One of the first persons to object to Gonzalez's research interest was Professor Wilson, who wrote she was very concerned about Gonzalez's support for the "Earth's privileged place in the universe and Intelligent Design" view:

---

765   http://www.weeklystandard.com/Content/Public/Articles/000/000/013/733rlosv.asp
766   Green, 2007, p. 15.
767   Quoted in Green, 2007, p. 15.

Guillermo has a book coming out in April on ... Earth's privileged place in the universe and Intelligent Design. **Steve K. is very upset about possible impacts**. ... I'm rather sad that he wants to be so very public about something that **I see as intellectually vacuous, though it may be spiritually satisfying**. I think I will talk to him about it at some point.[768]

It is irresponsible to claim that the conclusion that the earth has a privileged place in the solar system is "intellectually vacuous." It is, rather, a well-documented fact. Lee Anne Wilson wrote in reply to Curtis Struck that it is clear Gonzalez's support of this view would jeopardize his tenure and that he is clearly qualified:

I am aware of this and not exactly thrilled. **I talked with him last year about perhaps waiting with the public bit until he gets past the tenure review**, but I gather he feels strongly enough to be willing to take the risk. **George Wallerstein calls him "the best post-doc I ever had"** and it took me 24 hours to realize that the special look he gave along with that statement could be interpreted "including present company." Who knows how this will go. At least it will get full daylight at the 3yr review, not hit folks as a surprise at the final tenure decision. **Actually, I think it is more than just vacuous; he is supporting a movement that is endangering science.**

Wilson then claims that the organization(s) that sponsor this work are also busy in the courts challenging evolution. I do not know of one single example where the Discovery Institute has challenged evolution in the courts.[769] Bruce Harmon wrote:

Under medication I decided to watch "The Privileged Planet" last night. Wow. Really glossy, professional filming, with a nice British accent to add authority. It saved the message until the last minute, when **the argument became "all this neat stuff just could not happen by accident ... there must be an Intelligent Designer; now we can rejoice that there is a meaning to everything." I suspect that is how primitive humans explained things, and then rejoiced.** It is a long way from science, although the package is disguised to copy a Disney approach to dispensing science to the public. Gonzalez is right up front, nearly holding hands with the

---

768   E-mail from Lee Anne Wilson to Curtis Struck, dated February 17, 2004 (emphasis added).
769   E-mail from Lee Anne Wilson to Curtis Struck, dated February 17, 2004 (emphasis added).

Discovery Institute guru. This one could approach a supernova during and particularly after the tenure meetings. I bet ISU even makes the international press (how many days?). Maybe we should help Eli gird his loins before he loses them.[770]

My response is 90 percent of Americans believe in the existence of an Intelligent Designer, and it appears that the only view Dr. Harmon will accept is dogmatic atheism. He later wrote that he knows full well what he and his peers are doing is illegal:

> I was very pleased to see you, "produced the best letter to the editor on Intelligent Design." It is a topic that is simmering in my blood .... I am uncertain of how best to react. He will be up for tenure next year, and if he keeps up, it might be a hard sell to the department (but maybe not so difficult for his lawyers, who will certainly be retained by the Discovery Institute).[771]

Dr. Harmon then quoted an announcement about Gonzalez' presentation, which is reprinted below:

> INTELLIGENT DESIGN SPEAKER: The UNI Chapter of Sigma Xi, the Research Honor Society, presents Guillermo Gonzalez, Senior Fellow of the Discovery Institute and assistant professor of Astronomy at Iowa State University, speaking on Intelligent Design (ID). He will review the leading ideas proposed by ID theorists and explain why they believe ID is properly a branch of science. He will end with a brief description of the evidence for design which he presented in his book, "The Privileged Planet." Wednesday, September 28, 7 p.m. in MSH Lantz Auditorium.

Harmon wrote that Gonzalez's support of ID will surely cause him to be denied tenure:

> Gonzalez has given permission to tape the talk, so I guess we will see. ... I don't have trouble voting for tenure based on his astronomy (I don't yet know the quality), but here he is claiming **ID is a proper branch of science**, and so I think he opens it up in his tenure consideration. **I would**

---

770   E-mail from Bruce Harmon to Paul Canfield, dated July 20, 2004 (emphasis added).
771   E-mail from Bruce Harmon to Fritz Franzen, dated September 23, 2005 (emphasis added).

have thought an intelligent person would have at least kept quiet until after tenure. Then you can advocate blowing up the moon.[772]

Harmon also noted that he was concerned, allowing someone to question the view that no purpose exists behind the universe could alienate potential students who presumably cannot deal with this view:

> There have been a **number of potential candidates for our CMP and Bio positions who have called asking about the climate in the department relative to ID. Who knows how many simply decided not to apply** or to inquire? And what about prospective graduate students?[773]

In other words, because *Iowa State University* has an ID friendly professor, some students will not want to study at this school. The same problem existed not too many years ago—if blacks can join a club, some whites would not join. This is classic bigotry that any university should oppose.

> In **response to Behe's testimony**, colleagues at Leigh were quick with a **statement in an attempt at damage control**. I'm afraid we have not been quick enough to avoid damage, but I'm afraid further delay will lead to much more. If we have to take on the Discovery Institute, let's do it before we have an incoming class of ID students. The issue is not going away, and it may get worse. A few of us over the weekend crafted a statement which we would like you to see before we send it on to the higher administration, and probably the local press.[774]

> *This is like saying we do not admit blacks, but one got in by mistake, and we cannot do anything about it now, but will ensure it does not occur in the future*
> *-- JB*

Steve Kawaler's response also shows that he knows full well that what they are doing is illegal:

---

772 E-mail from Bruce Harmon to Fritz Franzen, dated September 23, 2005 (emphasis added).
773 E-mail from Bruce Harmon to Eli Rosenberg, dated November 21, 2005 (emphasis added).
774 E-mail from Bruce Harmon to Eli Rosenberg, dated November 21, 2005 (emphasis added).

I think it is a big mistake for anyone in our department to go on the record on this issue, given the upcoming (next year) up-or-out decision regarding our most vocal advocate for the use of ID to guide scientific inquiry. We will at that time (next fall) be taking on not only that faculty member, but advocates for his position with deep pockets and significant influence.

The statement is clear: we cannot support ID, nor can we accept anyone who does support ID -- JB

Yes, it will get worse before it gets better. But circulating such a statement could accelerate the process and could easily play into the hands of your perceived adversaries. For example, it could be used to justify a legal claim of a 'hostile work environment' that could be ammunition in any appeal of a tenure decision.

This is exactly what they have produced, and it is clear that they were fully aware of this fact -- JB

Damage has been done, and more will happen—we need to minimize that damage. Pushing ahead with this statement will serve no purpose but to increase the damage, I feel. Simply put, next year's tenure review will be very closely scrutinized by the public and the press-and we must do whatever we can to make it a fair process. An unprecedented step such as a statement, signed by members of the department doing the tenure review that the science being done by the candidate is no good, works directly against our need to ensure, and a fair tenure review. If you think things are tough for us now, imagine what things will be like under those circumstances. I would be happy to talk with you and the others about this-you'll probably find **Eli feels even more strongly about this** but that he and I have different perspectives.

I fully understand your collective frustration over this-and share it. Behe has tenure, so Bucknell's [sic] bio folks **have freedom to express their opposition without worry**. Isn't tenure a wonderful thing?

He seems to be saying that the tenure process allows for the expression of bigotry and intolerance without worry -- JB.[775]

---

775   E-mail from Steve Kawaler to Bruce Harmon, dated November 21, 2005 (emphasis added).

Behe is not at Bucknell, but Leigh University. Bruce Harmon then responded to the problem of "how do we let someone go on illegal grounds who is clearly qualified?" by stating:

> I don't see how waiting until a year from now for a tenure decision is going to make things easier. Do we do everything at **secret meetings** and then hope the Discovery Institute Lawyer's don't subpoena our records? If I were Gonzalez, I would prefer my colleagues were honest and forthright in their opinions, as he seems to be with his. Anyway, I've not talked with Eli or had a response from him yet. I will test a few more waters...it will help to have as many signatures as possible.[776]

> *The fact is, it is clear that the petition was directed at Gonzalez in spite of their denials – It is clear that his colleagues were not honest with him -- JB*

Marshal Luban then wrote that ID needs to be clear—people who doubt that evolution can explain all of life are not welcome here and will be censored:

> ...I believe that it is time for the department to take a stand, HOWEVER I think that it would be best to LIMIT public statements pertaining to our department and ID, rather than jump to endorse a host of organizational proclamations of a broad nature...unless people VERY carefully go through and carefully consider the details of these grandiose proclamations, and then debate in the dept. Whether we as a dept. NEED to be so specific, that ID is not "science." Instead I would suggest that our department go officially on record with a very simple and clear declaration, such as: We do not offer, nor will we offer any course on ID, nor will we sponsor or advocate any lecture or debate or public forum on the subject of ID.

> *i.e. freedom of speech does not exist here at the university -- JB.[777]*

Bruce Harmon then responded that the department should be less blunt:

> I don't think the department should take a stand. This was an effort to release the enormous frustration that a number of us are feeling as individuals to the onslaught of national publicity. I think **phone calls from prospec-**

---

776   E-mail from Bruce Harmon to Marshall Luban, dated November 22, 2005 (emphasis added).
777   E-mail from Marshal Luban to Bruce Harmon, dated November 22, 2005.

tive candidates and the Wall Street Journal article last Monday were the final straws. We will think some more about it before proceeding.[778]

We cannot allow Darwin Doubters any of their rights -- JB

Vladimir Kogan wrote that the department needs to openly and aggressively attack those who challenge Darwinism, and that those who doubt Darwin are not welcome at ISU:

Any simple idea can be turned around by a shrewd enough lawyer. In my view the best publicity ISU can dream about is a direct and open confrontation with Discovery Institute and alike, even in the worst situation of the court turning against the Dept. On the other hand, **our open statement signed and put in a visible place, will show to GG that this is not a friendly place for him to develop further his ideas.** He may look for a better place as a result. Also, I agree with Bruce: it is not nice to discuss all this behind his back, after all he probably honestly believes in what he is doing and he is certainly a courageous man. An open statement will clear up the air.[779]

Here they are open about their intolerance -- JB

Bruce Harmon then wrote:

He has crossed the line in a few places where he has admitted that he uses ID to do "science." I think he is sincere, so perhaps he would not mind talking and discussing it so that he could learn where the faculty stood.[780]

Is this a crime? Is it Illegal? -- JB

Steve Kawaler acknowledged that they knew full well that what they were doing was illegal:

---

778   E-mail from Bruce Harmon to Marshall Luban, dated November 22, 2005 (emphasis added).
779   E-mail from Vladimir Kogan to Bruce Harmon, dated November 22, 2005 (emphasis added).
780   E-mail from Bruce Harmon to Steve Kawaler, dated November 22, 2005 (emphasis added).

We should expect that the DI (or whoever comes to Guillermo's aid) will be subpoenaing our records and anything else they can get (including copies of the e-mails that are being exchanged between all of us). So with that in mind, keeping the process as fair as possible should be utmost.

i.e. we need to cover our tracks better, and practice more subterfuge -- JB

Before doing anything further on this, you should get some sort of advice from Tanaka's office [their lawyer]—see my previous note, which reflected discussions I have already had with the former employment lawyer that I sleep with each night.

And remember that every member of the tenured faculty votes on tenure decisions for assistant professors, so unless the signatories on any statement are ALL retired faculty, the issues I raised earlier will be up front.[781]

John R. Clem then wrote that it looks like ISU has clearly produced a hostile work environment:

I had a discussion yesterday evening with my son Paul, who has had management training at Sandia. I told him about the current situation and the concerns about "hostile work environments." His opinion was that indeed **lawyers might well be successful in convincing a jury of average Americans that publication of our statement was responsible for creating a hostile work environment.** He even thought that **if Eli got a written opinion from the university attorney, this might be offered as further evidence of collusion to create a hostile work environment.** (Paul thought that the farthest he would go is to have Eli ask the university attorney off the record for what courts have considered as hostile work environments.)

As strong as my feelings are on this matter, I have come around to Steve Kawaler's point of view. I now feel that **publication of such a statement might become the most important piece of evidence in a successful court case to guarantee tenure to the person whose scientific credibility we would be attempting to discredit...** I fear that a published statement from a group of scientists closely connected to the department, might put the whole situation in jeopardy. I therefore wish to withdraw my name from any public statement from a group of scientists closely connected to the department.

781 E-mail from Steve Kawaler to Bruce Harmon, dated November 22, 2005.

As for candidates for faculty positions, I think it is best to simply reassure them on a one-one basis that the highly publicized views of one untenured faculty member are not at all typical, and that, to the contrary, **no other faculty members in our department inject their religious views into their scientific research in this way.**

How does he happen to know this? – JB

As for the unfortunate publicity we are receiving and the embarrassment we feel as a department, I think the best policy is just to grin and bear it for the next couple of years.[782]

Joerg Schmalian wrote in response that, even if their actions make it clear that we are creating a hostile work environment, we should not let this stop us from doing so:

As much as I understand and respect John's point of view, I think we should nevertheless proceed. What we plan to do is to endorse a statement made by the [American Physical Society] APS,[783] explaining clearly that we strongly support each person's right to express their points of view. This isn't hostile as far as I am concerned.

I honestly hope Gonzalez' promotion will be **based on his abundant measurements of metallicity in planet carrying stars.** As I pointed out earlier, **our statement may well convince him to base his case just on this. He may well have a solid tenure case then.** If he will be promoted based on this, fine. I only want people to know that I disagree with him on other issues, something that does not exclude to work in the same building and to deal with respect with each other.

Let me turn it around. If it becomes clear that there were efforts to write such a statement and that the statement was not made only to avoid the impression of a hostile environment, isn't this strong evidence for secrecy in the department? It may be argued that this proves that **we wanted to have him out all along, and only kept it quiet to make a false impression.** Maybe this is constructed, but I am sure good lawyers can make this one work as well as any other option. Thus, I prefer to be more naive, go ahead

---

782   E-mail from John R. Clem to Bruce Harmon, dated November 27, 2005 (emphasis added).
783   American Physical Society.

with this or a modified statement and see whether there actually is support in the faculty.[784]

John Hauptman then wrote:

However, and this is critical, the basic principle is that during this period **there must be no persecutions or even reprimands that would tend to diminish freedom of inquiry to any degree. This principle has been violated massively** in the physics department [Which is where Gonzalez taught] and, concerning my use of the word reprehensible, was violated by your petition.

Ah, the truth comes out! -- JB

Denial of tenure in this case is not a penalty, but a judgment. This is the ideal, although **I suspect many voted for other reasons,** and I suspect the Discovery Institute will drag these people out in court. **Your petition was more than "merely saying ID is not science." It did not spontaneously arise from your outrage over ID,** although the coincidence with Bush's speech supporting ID was helpful. **It had to do with Guillermo.**

There are thousands of outrages (I have a long list) **and ID is one of them, but a university is still a place for free inquiry no matter how unpopular or even wrong some ideas may be.** Likewise, we have an obligation to criticize and, for example, I criticize what I think is garbage physics in my department, and in the public arena **I criticize those who support fascist policies.**

What would you call the treatment Gonzalez received at ISU? -- JB

I believe the **religious nutcases should be challenged at every opportunity,** but in ways that do not hand them more free publicity. I copied [for] you … an email [I sent] to Hector Avalos which may relate to your comments, in particular the question of "aimed at Gonzalez." I am not a lawyer, but be prepared for the Discovery Institutes' lawyers to hone in on this one.

No one even knew what Guillermo's religion was, so they had no basis to criticize his religion. They just knew that he was religious -JB

---

784   E-mail from Joerg Schmalian to John R. Clem, dated November 27, 2005.

In my letter I wrote that the petition, primarily its timing and in my mind its intent, was reprehensible. You are quite right to be sensitive to the issues of ID among your students, but you needn't be reminded that these are "teaching moments" and you have the upper hand holding vastly more knowledge and information. If you handle this well, you win by a large margin.

If you start talking about "methodological naturalism," you lose by a large margin. You say that your "job [is] made more difficult" by these ID notions, but I would say it makes your job more important and more interesting. **I also face students in my Newspaper Physics class who espouse ID and creationist notions,** and I handle them like a scientist. It doesn't take much.[785]

Jim Colbert then wrote:

I won't comment further on being called "reprehensible" in the Des Moines Register other than to affirm that you have the right to hold that belief if you wish. I feel, however, that your comment "obviously aimed at Gonzalez" requires a response. As you can see in the letter (below) we did not:

1. Mention Dr. Gonzalez by name.

2. Make any comments regarding tenure decisions for assistant professors in natural science departments at ISU, or elsewhere, who choose to espouse "Intelligent Design" ideas as science.

3. Restrict our objections regarding "Intelligent Design" to the astronomical arguments advanced by Dr. Gonzalez (and others), but also included the much more common and widespread "Intelligent Design" claims made about the complexity of the biological organisms present on Earth.

Are you saying biological organs are not complex? -- JB

On a personal note, at the time we wrote this statement (August 2005) I was aware of Dr. Gonzalez in only a very vague way and had never looked at "The Privileged Planet." As a biological scientist I was, however, very aware that about two weeks prior President G.W. Bush had been quoted by the national media as saying we should teach both evolution and "Intelligent Design" as science in public schools.... After 20 years (in 2005) of being

---

785   E-mail from John Hauptman to Jim Colbert, dated June 5, 2007 (emphasis added).

a college biology professor and **having my job made more difficult by many students under the misimpression that there is a substantial (or any) body of scientific evidence supporting the idea that a supernatural being must be responsible for the origin and diversity of life on Earth,** but a conspiracy of "secular scientists" represses this evidence, I am very sensitive to these issues.[786]

Conclusions

I can think of no other description that applies to this situation except that the ISU administrators and faculty openly lied in claiming that the ID issue or Gonzalez's (unknown) religious beleifs had nothing to do with the reason why he was fired from ISU. Martha Stewart and many other persons have been convicted of perjury and yet what clearly appears to be lying in this case has been ignored. Universities must be held accountable for their illegal and immoral conduct, and it is about time the public (who pays their bills) demand they be held accountable.

---

786   E-mail from Jim Colbert to Dr. Hauptman, dated June 5, 2007.

Chapter 14: Survivors Von Braun, Adler and Chain

This book has focused on the problems Darwin Doubters have experienced primarily in academia and in the science sector. While the discrimination against them is widespread and ubiquitous, some do manage to survive (and a few even prosper). For example, the University of South Carolina hosted a book signing for astronomy professor Danny Faulkner's new book titled *Universe by Design*. As far as I am aware, this was the first time that a creationist book was honored with such a signing on a state university campus. The Dean even offered some very kind words when he introduced Dr. Faulkner. As a philosopher, the Dean is very interested in the questions the book deals with. At the well-attended event—probably about 130 people—all 40 books on hand were sold, and many more were ordered. Professor Faulkner concluded that this was probably the most successful book signing ever held on his campus.

This chapter reviews in some depth how some students managed to survive discrimination and also how three well-known luminaries managed to avoid most of the problems documented in this book.

How Some Students Survived

Despite a widespread effort by Darwinists to deny degrees to Darwin Doubters, many students do survive and some even earn doctorates. In rare cases, they obtain doctorates with no serious obstacles. However, the rarity of such exceptions is informative, as the case of Arthur J. Jones illustrates. Jones earned two degrees from the *University of Birmingham* (a degree in comparative physiology and a Ph.D. in zoology). Yet, according to Numbers, Jones "occasionally found himself the object of warnings and innuendoes" and was

> repeatedly pressured by his professors to abandon his creationist views... At the completion of his studies he ignored well-meaning advice not to risk his degree by revealing his colors in his thesis, but he suffered no ill effects for doing so. The external examiner from the British Museum did not even seem upset. Nevertheless, Jones remained convinced that his positive experience was "almost unique" in the annals of British creationism.[787]

---

787 Numbers, 2006, p. 300.

A parallel American case would be that of Dr. Walter Lammerts. Lammerts earned his doctorate in cytogenetics at the *University of California at Berkeley*, and, although he engaged in many arguments "with fellow graduate students over the issue of evolution, he never experienced any discrimination because of his particular views."[788]

For every creationist student such as Jones and Lammerts, however, there are many more who have to develop strategies to enable them to get through the system against the threat of real opposition and failed. One strategy, illustrated in the following case, is to conceal their creationist sympathies.

When Paul E. Kohli was a university undergraduate, one of his geology professors saw to it that he did not make the dean's list because Kohli refused to respond to test questions involving creation and evolution the way his professor expected them to be answered. His mineral and rock identifications were more than 95 percent correct during the two semesters in his classes, all to no avail. Kohli adds that when completing his doctoral degree two of his

> pre-dissertation, dissertation and post-dissertation committee members—professors of philosophy and psychology—openly suggested that a professing Christian and a believer in creation likely would not be a candidate for an earned doctorate in my field of study. Fortunately for me, the others on my committee supported my dissertation and my beliefs, and I was granted the degree.[789]

The Case of Stephen Austin

Among the Christian students who have survived Ph.D. programs in science, one of the most well known is young-earth creationist Stephen A. Austin. Austin earned his Ph.D. in geology—with his faith intact—from *Pennsylvania State University*. How he achieved this feat is very instructive. Ron Numbers wrote that Austin had come to the CRS's attention in 1970 after he had submitted a paper to the CRSQ, under the pen name Stuart C. Nevins,

---

788   Numbers, 2006, p. 240.
789   Kohli, 2002. p. 6.

hoping thereby to protect himself from a fate like Burdick's. Leaders of the CRS found Austin's work so impressive they commissioned him to study the origin of fossil reefs, which presented flood geologists with a problem because of the length of time they required for growth.[790]

When he first contacted CRS, Austin had only a BA in geology from the *University of Washington*, but soon completed an M.S. from *San Jose State University* with a thesis critical of uniformitarianism. He survived by concealing his biblical views and, in 1975, enrolled in the geology Ph.D. program at *Penn State University*. To do research related to creationism, which he felt would not be supported by departmental funding, he applied to the CRS Research Committee to cover his tuition and living expenses, but "begged them" to be "discreet in announcing his award, suggesting that they say only that Stuart Nevins had received support for work on coal." Although Austin felt that the faculty at Penn State

were sympathetic to his catastrophic point of view, he did not want his professors to discover his biblical beliefs regarding earth history. He was sure that if they learned the truth, they would deny him his degree. Morris hailed Austin's dissertation on the formation of coal bed in western Kentucky— written without CRS support—as ... a giant step toward the development of the first-ever theory capable of predicting the location and quality of coal. But most important of all, Austin's graduation from Penn State signaled the beginning of a new era in the history of scientific creationism, when at least some flood geologists could claim to speak as real geologists.[791]

The Case of Kurt Wise

Kurt P. Wise, who completed his palaeontology Ph.D. at Harvard in 1989 under the well-known evolutionist Stephen J. Gould, is a prime example of survivorship. Although he received much ribbing from his professors and fellow students, he did manage to earn his degree.

Begley notes that creationist Kurt Wise's beliefs didn't handicap his doctoral research at Harvard, and was able to land a position teaching geology at Bryan College. Though he survived, Wise did encounter challenges along the way:

---

790   Numbers, 2006, p. 309.
791   Numbers, 2006, p. 309-310.

When Kurt Wise arrived at Harvard University as a graduate student in paleontology, he was bright and intellectually ambitious, just like everyone else in the department. But unlike everyone else, he was, and is, a creationist. He believes . . . that every plant and animal species, from Arabian steeds to maple trees to humans, was created by the hand of God, rather than evolving . . . At Harvard, such views are heretical. When Wise met evolutionary theorist Stephen Jay Gould, "he bawled me out," says Wise.[792]

Gould at times mockingly read letters in class, mostly from allegedly uneducated but committed "creationists" who condemned him to a fiery hell. Numbers noted that the Kurt Wise case is of particular interest because Wise was a

protégé of the arch critic of creation science, Stephen Jay Gould. ... In 1981 he graduated from the University of Chicago with honors in the geophysical sciences and immediately headed east to work with Gould at Harvard. Fellow graduate students sometimes taunted their creationist colleague, but the bemused Gould always treated him with respect. Proud creationists speculated that God had planted Wise "right in the middle of S. J. Gould's paleontology program as a testimony to a man who otherwise might not have been reached."[793]

Numbers adds that, although Wise believed that most pre-Cenozoic fossils were buried during Noah's flood and that the entire universe was about six thousand years old, "he insisted on honestly looking at the scientific evidence." Wise also had doubts about some commonly held creationist ideas, such as Gentry's polonium halo research and "other popular weapons in the creationists' arsenal."[794] As a result, some creationists did not appreciate Wise's iconoclasm: "After he curtly dismissed the arguments of a senior creationist regarding rapid cave formation, the offended man retaliated by accusing his 'arrogant' Ivy League critic of 'warmed-over uniformitarianism.'"[795] How Wise survived as an out-of-the-closet creationist is hinted at by Hitt, and illustrates the importance in understanding human nature. Jack Hitt, after noting Wise's humor, said that unlike "many of his colleagues, who look out into the world to see a horizon darkened by pagans and pederasts," Wise

---

792 Begley, 1996, p. 82.
793 Numbers, 2006, p. 310.
794 Numbers, 2006, p. 310.
795 Numbers, 2006, p. 310-311.

is unafraid of Harvard and Chicago and science's reductionist establishment. He has matriculated through the most prestigious quarters of that
world and emerged with his faith unscathed. He quite intends to return—
not as a peer but as a conquering hero. ... Wise believes that science can
lift that weight and heal a fallen world. He is a modern Adam who quite
literally plans to rename all creatures great and small ... [and] restore them
to their place in the original Grand Unified Theory...[796]

After completing his Ph.D., Wise became an assistant professor of science
and director of the new *Origins Research and Resource Center* at *Bryan College* in
Dayton, Tennessee, the location of the 1925 Scopes trial. There he hoped "to
formulate a model of earth history which is consistent with both the Scriptures
and the physical data—constructed according to a code of excellence and integrity in ethics and practice." Numbers adds that Wise "forswore the evolution-
bashing characteristic of early scientific creationism and pledged to shrink from
no evidence, however distasteful."[797] Along with geologists Andrew Snelling and
Steve Austin, Kurt P. Wise dreamed of completing an

updated edition of *The Genesis Flood* that would present a "new creationism"
for the twenty-first century. Critics of creation science found his candor
both amazing and refreshing. He is, wrote one, "the closest thing to an ally
that science has in the creationist movement."[798]

Matthew Chapman, a relative of Darwin, wrote a book on the Scopes trial.
A significant part of his book recounts his visit to *Bryan College* to interview
Kurt Wise, who, he stated, is "one of the leading creationists in the country"
and is probably "smarter than most of his critics."[799] He also concluded, like "everyone else, scientists crave the recognition of their peers," but, as a creationist,
when "Kurt goes to a scientific meeting, his fellow scientists often clamber across
chairs to avoid walking down the same aisle as him."[800] He adds that by coming
out of the closet as a creationist, Kurt Wise "committed academic suicide."[801]

796   Hitt, 1996, p. 59.
797   Numbers, 2006, p. 311.
798   Numbers, 2006, p. 311.
799   Chapman, 2000, p. 124.
800   Chapman, 2000, p. 146.
801   Chapman, 2000, p. 219.

He noted that Kurt entered into a Harvard Ph.D. program only because Gould accepted him without knowing he was a creationist

> and didn't find out until it was too late.... The issue of creation didn't come up for another two years. One day Gould stopped and asked him, "Do you still believe the same way?" "Well, I'm still a creationist, if that's what you mean." "Oh, okay" replied Gould. Another couple of years later, it came up again when Kurt was sitting in his office chatting. Again Kurt reaffirmed his position. Since then they have spoken of it calmly and seemingly without tension. Unfortunately, it is not this easy with everyone. One graduate student declared war on Kurt. "I am going to do everything in my power," he told him, "to make your life hell while you're at Harvard."[802]

Chapman thought he would dislike Wise because for his entire adult life he "despised religion, in particular its resistance to scientific progress. Galileo is a greater hero to me than any saint." Chapman admitted that professor Wise is "one of the most influential creationists in the world—and a religious nut by all previous standards—and I like him and feel sympathy for him."[803] Interestingly, Chapman says that his trip to Bryan College to visit real creationists caused his intellectual views to remain the same, but his *feelings* changed: "faith in God or any of the fairy tales that surround Him may be absurd, but the *need* for faith is anything but. When you encounter someone like Kurt, you realize that faith is sometimes an absolute necessity."[804] Hitt adds that Wise's goal is nothing less than to

> undo the Great Divorce—that time after Galileo when theology and science went their separate ways. . . . My idea is not to attack evolution," he said. "My goal is to develop a theory that explains the data of the universe better than conventional theory but is consistent with Scripture." His major beef with other creationists, he explained, is that they only take pleasure in picking at the weakness of evolution. . . by the time I finished at Harvard, I realized I could destroy macroevolutionary theory at will. I don't want to *challenge* evolution . . . I intend to replace it."[805]

---

802   Chapman, 2000, pp. 149–150.
803   Chapman, 2000, p. 152.
804   Chapman, 2000, p. 152.
805   Hitt, 1996, p. 57.

Choosing a "Safe" Research Topic

Numbers cites the case of creationist Richard M. Ritland, who, after receiving a master's at *Oregon State* in vertebrate zoology, completed a doctorate at *Harvard University* under the eminent vertebrate paleontologist Alfred S. Romer. Ritland was successful, partly because he wrote "a philosophically safe dissertation in comparative morphology and vertebrate paleontology, for which he received his Ph.D. degree in 1954."[806] A safe topic would one that deals with areas in which Darwinism is largely irrelevant, such as techniques used to locate or study minerals. Ritland has since published a number of articles and books supporting creation.

Finding Open-Minded Supervisors, Even among Darwinists

On the other hand, some studies indicate that there may be more openness toward the unorthodox (such as creationists) at schools such as Harvard and Yale. Stephen J. Gould himself was rather heterodox in some of his evolutionary views. After all, he was among the first respectable scientists to propose the radical notion of *punctuated equilibrium.* Thus, a minority himself, he may have been more tolerant of other minorities. Vehement anti-creationist rhetoric, such as that produced by Gould, is likely motivated by a number of factors, one of which is probably part of an effort to appear kosher in science in spite of his eccentricities. When actually responding to a living, breathing, educated creationist before him, his demeanor expressed more tolerance than was reflected in his writing. As Ruse once remarked, it is harder to hate creationists in person than in print. Wise said of his experience with Gould at Harvard:

> Steve knew my views from the beginning and we spoke about it from time to time. Steve was what I called a heart libertarian—he believed that everyone has the right to believe whatever they want. Therefore he not only believed I had a right to believe anything I wanted about origins, but he even defended my right to be a creationist. His response to my position was usually to say something like, "Of course you know I think you are wrong." Steve always

---

seemed to see me as an intriguing curiosity—probably wishing (as most of my professors did) that I was an evolutionist and not a creationist.[807]

Survival is Sometimes Possible Outside of the U.S.A.

Professor A.E. Wilder-Smith noted that students who do not conform to Darwinism will face problems, and he knew professors in both the United States and in Europe "who will tell that student that he will not get a Ph.D. if he doesn't [accept Darwinism], because every educated person does believe it." Yet, he continues to say: "... on the other hand, people like Jehovah's Witnesses have got Ph.D.'s in Europe and have found supervisors to do their Ph.D.'s to show that evolution is chemically and physically outside the pale of reason. And they got through and got good grades..."[808]

Survival Is Facilitated When the Candidate Is Intellectually Respected

Some out-of-the-closet creationists, such as Paul Nelson, seem to have relatively few problems. On December 19, 1997 Nelson "successfully defended his doctoral thesis before a faculty committee of the University of Chicago, and was duly awarded the degree from the Department of Philosophy." Brock Eide, M.D., an assistant professor in the department of neurology at the University of Chicago, sat in on Paul's defense. Professor Eide reported that the atmosphere was "surprisingly cordial," and went on to say:

> Paul's thesis was limited to a consideration of the plausibility of universal common descent as a scientific theory, and as such did not directly challenge the naturalistic metaphysics underlying much of evolutionary theory ... Yet it was obvious from the nature of the exchange that his metaphysical and religious views were known by all. It was also obvious, both from the tone and the content of the questions asked, that their many years of contact with Paul had given them a deep respect for his intellectual abilities. The more philosophical attendees seemed to place less emotional stake in protecting the notion of universal common descent than ... most biologists.[809]

---

807 Quoted in O'Leary, 2004, p. 138.
808 Interview of A.E. Wilder-Smith by Jerry Bergman, October 1986.
809 Reported in The Newsletter of the ASA and CSA, April, 1998, 40(2):3–4.

Yet the Closet Is Still Often the Safest Place

The education experience for Darwin skeptics typically does not go as well as it did for Nelson and Wise. Many students survive only by staying in the closet. However, this creates a major dilemma, says one graduate student studying cell biology at a major research university who dreams of having a career as a research scientist. He explains the negative effects of having to hide his views:

> For example, when the Miller-Urey experiment comes up in class, part of me wants to offer some slight criticisms such as, "however, this experiment produces only a racemic mixture (both left and right-handed molecules) and because we know that only left-handed molecules are important biologically, this causes some to question its contribution to origin of life question." But another part of me quickly puts on the brakes and doesn't say anything. Is there some small amount of "stirring the pot" that would be safe for me at this point or am I right to just say nothing? Or should I appear as one who is knowledgeable of ID but not necessarily supportive? I want to do what's best and right now so that I can be useful in the future, and I am willing to bide my time. However, if there are small opportunities for me to contribute to the discussion now, I don't want to miss them due to unwarranted fear. Because many folks in ID came to this position in mid-career, I often feel that I'm traveling in uncharted waters.[810]

It is easy to understand the cautious attitude of this student when one looks at some of the hard-line positions taken by instructors. A case in point is to be found in the syllabus, dated January 21, 2003, for Geology 3332, offered at the University of Texas at Dallas. In the syllabus, Dr. Homer Montgomery tells his students "[never to] cite a religious science source such as ICR, Answers in Genesis, or anything else like that." He goes on to characterize the critical positions of various Darwin Doubters in this way:

> It is easy to recognize these groups. They are virulently anti-evolution. This caution also extends to the new ID (Intelligent Design) movement—another anti-evolutionary charade. These are 95% wrong. As for the other 5%, no answer is known so they make up things that are not supported by experimentation. More than 100 years of rigorous investigations in fields

---

810   letter from Anonymous to Jerry Bergman, dated Feb. 1, 2004. The author does not want his identity revealed to protect his career.

from biology to geology have proven evolution as a fact... You will be penalized for citing anti-evolutionary material. It is not science. If the thesis of your paper is anti-evolutionary (akin to arguing against the germ theory of disease or against the atomic theory of matter) you will receive a failing grade. Scientific journals do not publish papers with creationist and ID themes. I will certainly not accept them.[811]

A similar position is taken by Donald Tosaw, the author of the "evolution happens" web site, who reasons as follows:

Should a geology professor pass students who submit papers suggesting that the earth is flat? Should a chemistry professor pass students who submit papers that suggest that matter is not made up of atoms? Of course not. That's because astronomers figured out that the Earth is a sphere many centuries ago... These things are no longer in question. The only reason that some people refuse to accept the evidence supporting evolution, is that evolution is inconsistent with Genesis or some other mythological creation story they subscribe to. It is that simple...[812]

Statements like these can have no other effect than to drive Darwin Doubters into the closet.

Another way to survive is to retire. Distinguished Service Professor at the Johns Hopkins School of Medicine, Dr. John McHugh, has recently written several excellent articles in support of Intelligent Design. When asked why he chose to speak out now, he stated that he is now retired and in his 70's, and thus feels he can finally reveal his thoughts without fear of retaliation (except hate mail, of which he has received plenty).

Do Racial Minorities Have Fewer Problems?

Some evidence exists that certain minority statuses can protect creationists. African-American Alton Williams earned his Ph.D. in theoretical nuclear physics from the University of Massachusetts in 1978. He then became a physics professor at Alabama A & M University in Huntsville in 1978 without

---

811   Homer Montgomery, 2003, p. 4.
812   Letter from Donald Tosaw to Jerry Bergman, dated January 18, 2003.

problems.[813] He later worked at NASA in Huntsville, analyzing x-rays emitted from various stars and galaxies, and has published widely in the scientific literature. He claims he has had no problems due to his religious beliefs, and, as of 2004, is still at Alabama A&M.[814]

Three Science Superstars Who Survived

In the first case, the life and work of Wernher von Braun, the father of modern space flight, will be reviewed, focusing on his achievements and his creationist world view. A staunch supporter of creationism, he has openly publicized his views that the universe was designed by a Creator.

The second case reviewed is that of Dr. Mortimer Adler's conversion from an evolutionist to a creationist and, eventually, to Christianity. A critical factor in his acceptance of Christianity was his life-long investigation of evolution, which eventually resulted in his rejection of Darwinism.

The third case reviewed is that of Nobel laureate Ernest Chain. An active opponent of Darwinism and evolution, he nonetheless revolutionized medicine by his work as one of the principle founders of the antibiotics revolution. The reasons for his views will be summarized briefly, relying heavily upon Dr. Chain's own statements, speeches, and publications.

The lives of these three intellectuals belie many of the negative allegations against Darwin Doubters. From my own limited contacts, I have compiled a list of almost 3,000 professors and scientists, mostly Ph.D.'s and several Nobel laureates, who are out-of-the-closet Darwin Doubters.[815]

Wernher Von Braun: The Father of Modern Space Flight

In 1934, a twenty-two-year-old student by the name of Wernher Von Braun (March 23, 1912 – June 16, 1977) who would change the world of science forever received his Ph.D. in physics from the University of Berlin.[816] For security reasons, his dissertation bore the nondescript title "About Combustion

---

813   Alton Williams, 2004, pp. 20–21.
814   Alton Williams, 2004, p. 24.
815   http://www.rae.org/darwinskeptics.html
816   Ward, 2005, p. 19.

Tests." His theoretical discussion and experimental investigation of the injection, combustion, equilibrium, and expansion phenomena involved in liquid-fuel rocket engines was, even then, recognized as critical for the future technological development of Germany. Called *the father of modern space flight*, von Braun, probably more than any other single scientist, brought about the space age.[817]

An account of von Braun's career reads like a history of the American space program.[818] His accomplishments are legendary. He was the recipient of the Certificate of Merit, National Health Agency; the State of Alabama Academy of Honor; the Order for the Merit of Research and Inventions of Paris, France; American Society of Mechanical Engineers' Man of the Year Award; Associated Press Man of the Year in Science Award; Smithsonian Institution Langley Medal; and the 1972 Federal Cross of Merit medal from the Republic of West Germany, which are only a few of his many prestigious honors.[819] His scores of honorary academic degrees included doctorates from Notre Dame University, Emory University in Atlanta, and the University of Pittsburgh.

His Scientific Work

One of the first men to describe in detail the principle of a two-stage liquid-fuel rocket was German physicist Hermann Oberth. In 1930, Oberth tested a small liquid-fuel rocket engine—and one of his assistants was eighteen-year-old engineering student Wernher von Braun. The son of a baron, von Braun was educated in Zürich, Switzerland and Berlin, Germany.[820] As an adolescent, von Braun was fascinated with rocketry and in 1930, at age seventeen, he joined a group of Germans involved in a rocket club. Included in this club were Willy Ley and other now-prominent rocket scientists.[821] By the time Hitler came to power in 1933, von Braun's rocket work accomplishments were widely recognized.[822] Von Braun soon had eighty scientists and technicians working for him at Peenemünde in northwest Germany and, by 1938, a rocket with an eleven-mile range had been developed.[823] Under his leadership, the first true rocket—a

---

817 Bergaust, 1976.
818 Von Braun, 1971.
819 Ward, 2005.
820 Greene, 1966.
821 Asimov, 1972, p. 736.
822 Asimov, 1972, p. 736.
823 Lamont, 1994.

missile that carried both its own fuel and oxidant—was successfully launched in 1942. This rocket is now known as the V-2, meaning the second model of the *vergeltung* (German for vengeance). The V-2 was the world's first operational guided ballistic missile—a technical coup achieved under von Braun's able direction. To achieve this, his team had to make significant progress in understanding aerodynamics, rocket propulsion, and guidance systems.

Although von Braun at first supported the German war effort, he soon became disenchanted with Hitler's policies and war aims. As a Christian and a creationist, he could not accept Hitler's racial theories, and soon began to voice opposition against his policies, especially the war. Even before this, Hitler's suspicions of von Braun, and the German government's interference with his programs, delayed the development of the V-2.

Eventually Heinrich Himmler tried to take over the program, widening the gap between von Braun and the German government even further. When, beginning in September 1944, thousands of V-2 rockets were launched in attacks on the civilian populations of London, Paris, and elsewhere, von Braun objected. As a result, he and his top aides were jailed. Just before the war ended, he was released because Hitler realized that without him, the program could not progress. However, von Braun soon fled Peenemünde with his entire team and their families—some 5,000 people—and surrendered to the Americans in the spring of 1945. He became one of the 118 "paper clip scientists" and the more than 4,500 German army technicians who were brought to the United States between 1945 and 1946. Approximately ninety men, "about the entire German staff at the rocket-weapon base," were transferred in September of 1945 alone.[824] The story of his well-known escape to America began in the spring of 1945 when the war was ending. A German had

> walked up to an American soldier in Bavaria and announced: "We are a group of rocket specialists... We want to see your commander and surrender to the Americans." The soldier was startled, but brought the man to see his commander. By September, the German scientists were on their way to the United States. Among them was an imaginative young visionary who wanted to fly to the moon—Werner von Braun. He had been largely re-

---

824   *New York Times*, Nov. 18, 1945.

sponsible for the development of the world's most successful rocket up to that time—the German V-2.[825]

The American space program was thus largely a transplant of the German program. When von Braun arrived in America in 1945, he and his German associates continued their research using captured German V-2 rockets, first at Fort Bliss, Texas, and then at White Sands, New Mexico. Once in the United States, he gained the trust and respect of his fellow scientists and his new boss, the American government, winning numerous loyalty and patriotic awards for his service to his new country.[826]

He soon became the leader of scientists based in Huntsville, Alabama who placed America's first satellite—Explorer I—into orbit on January 31, 1958.[827] Asimov states that von Braun "might have preceded Sputnik if he had been given the go-ahead, but he was as hindered by the American policy under Eisenhower as he had been hampered by German policy under Hitler."[828] Von Braun's problems in the United States were caused by different reasons than in Germany, and included lack of support for his space program. The Soviets' coup in achieving the first successful satellite, an enormous embarrassment to Americans, did much to encourage the development of von Braun's goals for the American space science program. After this, von Braun's success became nothing short of phenomenal.

Also critical to von Braun's success was his enormous dedication. Holmes[829] concluded that von Braun "must certainly rank among the most single-minded men in recorded history." With great devotion, for thirty-five years he pursued the idea of building rockets for space travel. Although early in his career he built weapons rockets, he did so only because he realized this was the only way that he could obtain the support required to develop the technology and hardware for his dream—a space-exploration program.[830] It was only in America that he was able to fulfill his dream to use rockets for the good of humanity in space exploration and by putting up satellites. The incredible importance of satellites for our

---

825   Gourlay, 1962, p. 48.
826   Holmes, 1962,
827   Greene, 1966,
828   Asimov, 1972, p. 736.
829   Holmes, 1962, p. 107.
830   Gourlay, 1962.

modern way of life is demonstrated by their use in communications, weather, scientific research, and the military.

Between 1950 and 1955, von Braun directed the development of the Redstone, the first American operational ballistic missile. A modified Redstone served as the first stage of the rocket that launched America's first artificial satellite, Explorer I, into space. In 1959, von Braun and his team also launched Pioneer IV, the USA's first interplanetary probe, which traveled around the Sun. In 1960, he supervised the development of the Saturn liquid-fuel rocket that eventually provided the basis for manned space flight—taking Neil Armstrong and his crew to the Moon. Project Apollo was probably the peak of the American space program—and Wernher von Braun was at the center of it all.

The Scientist as Creationist

Dr. von Braun, a Lutheran and an active creationist, wrote "a good deal about his Christian faith," and gave "a number of speeches on the subject."[831] An open supporter of creationism, he concluded that this a view was "a viable scientific theory for the origin of the universe, life and man." [832] In a letter he wrote in support of the two-model approach, which was read to the California State Board of Education by Dr. John Ford on September 14, 1972, Dr. von Braun stated:

> For me, the idea of a creation is not conceivable without invoking the necessity of design. One cannot be exposed to the law and order of the universe without concluding that there must be design and purpose behind it all. In the world around us, we can behold the obvious manifestations of an ordered, structured plan or design. We can see the will of the species to live and propagate. And we are humbled by the powerful forces at work on a galactic scale, and the purposeful orderliness of nature that endows a tiny and ungainly seed with the ability to develop into a beautiful flower. The better we understand the intricacies of the universe and all it harbors, the more reason we have found to marvel at the inherent design upon which it is based.

> While the admission of a design for the universe ultimately raises the question of a Designer (a subject outside of science), the scientific method does

---

831   Bergaust, 1976, p. 109.
832   Quoted in Seagraves, 1973, p. 7.

not allow us to exclude data which lead to the conclusion that the universe, life and man are based on design. To be forced to believe only one conclusion—that everything in the universe happened by chance—would violate the very objectivity of science itself. Certainly there are those who argue that the universe evolved out of a random process, but what random process could produce the brain of a man or the system of the human eye?[833]

He added those who argue that science has been unable to prove the existence of a designer are forced to admit the

miracles in the world around us are hard to understand, and they do not deny that the universe, as modern science sees it, is indeed a far more wondrous thing than the creation medieval man could perceive. But they still maintain that since science has provided us with so many answers, the day will soon arrive when we will be able to understand even the creation of the fundamental laws of nature with a Divine Intent. They challenge science to prove the existence of God. But, must we really light a candle to see the Sun?[834]

His beliefs regarding the importance of studying God's creation—to learn more about God the Creator—are vividly expressed in the following words:

The more we learn about God's creation, the more I am impressed with the orderliness and unerring perfection of the natural laws that govern it. In this perfection, man—the scientist—catches a glimpse of the Creator and his design for nature. The man-to-God relationship is deepened in the devout scientist as his knowledge of the natural laws grows.[835]

Relative to the modern church-state conflict in America, von Braun openly stated that God had "the same position in our modern world that He held before the natural sciences began to pierce through the wall of dogma erected by the Church."[836] He was especially impressed by Paley's watch hypothesis, and von Braun's own words reveal how important he felt the design argument was:

---

833   Quoted in Seagraves, 1973, pp. 7–8.
834   Quoted in Seagraves, 1973, pp. 7–8.
835   Bergaust, 1976, p. 113.
836   Bergaust, 1976, p. 112.

I have discussed the aspect of a Designer at some length because it might be that the primary resistance to acknowledging the "Case for Design" as a viable scientific alternative to the current "Case for Chance" lies in the inconceivability, in some scientists' minds, of a Designer. The inconceivability of some ultimate issue (which will always lie outside scientific resolution) should not be allowed to rule out any theory that explains the interrelationship of observed data and is useful for prediction.

Many men who are intelligent and of good faith say they cannot visualize a Designer. Well, can a physicist visualize an electron? The electron is materially inconceivable and yet, it is so perfectly known through its effects that we use it to illuminate our cities, guide our airliners, ... and take the most accurate measurements. What strange rationale makes some physicists accept the inconceivable electron as real while refusing to accept the reality of a Designer on the ground that they cannot conceive Him? I am afraid that, although they really do not understand the electron either, they are ready to accept it because they managed to produce a rather clumsy mechanical model of it borrowed from rather limited experience in other fields...[837]

Von Braun also stressed that he hoped that more scientists would

publicly say what I am saying here ... with all the modern means at our disposal, with schools, churches, educational institutions, press, radio, and television, they should tell the world that religion and science are not incompatible; that, to the contrary, they belong together.[838]

He believed that the two-model approach should be presented in the schools, and his own words vividly reveal the depth of his conviction. Dr. von Braun also stated that NASA scientists are often asked the reason

for the amazing string of successes we had with our Apollo flights to the Moon. I think the only honest answer we could give was that we tried to never overlook anything. It is in that same sense of scientific honesty that I endorse the presentation of alternative theories for the origin of the universe, life and man in the science classroom. It would be an error to

837   Seagraves, 1973, pp. 8–9.
838   Bergaust, 1976, p. 112.

overlook the possibility that the universe was planned rather than happening by chance.[839]

Von Braun added that the two major realities of human existence are

the laws of creation and the divine intentions underlying the creation. Through science man attempts to understand the laws of creation; through religious activities he attempts to understand the intentions of the Creator. Each approach is a search for ultimate truth.[840]

He did not argue, as many do today, that science and religion should be separate and not mixed, but on the contrary, he concluded that science,

in its drive to understand the creation, and religion in its drive to understand the Creator, have many common objectives. Nevertheless, there have been conflicts in the relationship between science and religion. ... Personally, I find this state of affairs unsatisfactory, for I wish to regard the Creator and His creation as an entity... science and religion are like two windows in a house through which we look at the reality of the Creator and the laws manifested in His creation. As long as we see two different images through these two windows and cannot reconcile them, we must keep trying to obtain a more complete and better integrated total picture of the ultimate reality by properly tying together our scientific and religious concepts.[841]

His Religious Views

In the authoritative and definitive biography of von Braun, Erik Bergaust recorded a conversation he had with von Braun in which the rocket scientist openly stated:

More than ever, our survival depends upon adherence to some basic ethical principles... It seems to me that two stimuli are necessary to make man endeavor to conform to the accepted ethical standards. One is the belief in a last judgment, where every one of us has to account for what we did with

---

839   Quoted in Seagraves, 1973, pp. 8–9.
840   Bergaust, 1976, p. 112.
841   Bergaust, 1976, p. 114.

God's precious gift of life on Earth. The other is the belief [that we] ... can cherish the reward or suffer the penalty decreed in the Last Judgment.[842]

When Bergaust asked him about religion and science, specifically if "technological methods and religious beliefs are really compatible," von Braun answered:

While technology controls the forces of nature around us, ethics try to control the forces of nature within us. ... I think it is a fair assumption that the Ten Commandments are entirely adequate—without amendments—to cope with all the problems the technological revolution not only has brought up, but will bring up in the future. The real problem is not a lack of ethical legislation, but a lack in day-to-day guidance and control... When science freed itself from the bonds of religious dogma, thus opening the way for the technological revolution, the Church also lost much of its influence on the ethical conduct of man.[843]

The father of the American space program believed the Bible was the "most effective bulwark ever built against the erosive effects of time. ... The Bible is ... the revelation of God's nature and love."[844] Prayer, too, was critically important to von Braun. Asked when his need to pray was particularly strong, he stated that he prayed a lot before and during the crucial Apollo flights, and also during

the last days in Germany—when things collapsed all around me. Indeed, during those hours of decision, when we decided to surrender to the Americans, my anxiety was at the bursting point. I prayed then that our surrender would be accepted in good faith.[845]

In summary, as Morris notes, von Braun believed that manned space flight is

an amazing achievement, but it has opened for mankind thus far only a tiny door for viewing the awesome reaches of space. An outlook through this peephole at the vast mysteries of the universe should only confirm our belief in the certainty of its Creator. I find it as difficult to understand a scientist

---

842   Bergaust, 1976, p. 110.
843   Quoted in Bergaust, 1976, p. 111.
844   Bergaust, 1976, pp. 115–116.
845   Bergaust, 1976, p. 117.

who does not acknowledge the presence of a superior rationality behind the existence of the universe as it is to comprehend a theologian who would deny the advances of science.[846]

Von Braun died in Alexandria, Virginia, on June 16, 1977, leaving the world a radically different place than existed when he was born in Wirsitz, Germany on March 23, 1912.

Summary Remarks on von Braun

A study of the history of Western science has revealed that religion was the major motivation for many of the world's greatest scientists. A few examples are Newton, Copernicus, Galileo, Kepler, and George Washington Carver. They concluded that God reveals Himself both in the Scriptures and in His creation and, to get closer to God, it is incumbent upon the believer to study His creation. This is clear from the writings of the aforementioned (and many other) scientists. That this motivation is also important today for some scientists is also illustrated by the case of Wernher von Braun.

Although he is by no means a rare example, he was more open about his religious beliefs than many eminent scientists. Dr. von Braun knew the consequences of speaking out publicly for what he believed—and was willing to pay the price, both in Nazi Germany and in America as well.

Mortimer Adler's Life-Long "Crusade Against Evolution"

Mortimer Adler (December 28, 1902 – June 28, 2001) was considered by many leading intellectuals to be one of the greatest thinkers of all time and, according to a 1987 *Time* magazine article, he was also the "last great Aristotelian." Adler wrote or co-authored over 45 books (all of them very successful) and 200 articles. He was also chairman of the board of editors of *Encyclopaedia Britannica* for many years. His 54-volume *Great Books of the Western World* has sold over a quarter of a million copies since 1952.[847]

---

846   Henry M. Morris, 1982, p. 110.
847   Bowen, 1987.

Dr. Adler did his undergraduate work at Columbia University, where he finished a four-year program in three years, was ranked highest in his class, and was ranked first on the Phi Beta Kappa list.[848] He completed his Ph.D. in psychology at Columbia, and then served as a professor at the University of Chicago for twelve years, becoming a full professor before he became involved with *Encyclopaedia Britannica*. His work is of such stature that a national center based on his educational concepts was established in Chapel Hill, North Carolina.

An Outspoken Opponent of Darwinism

Dr. Adler also was an active and outspoken opponent of Darwinism for almost a half-century.[849] In 1985, *Time* magazine noted that Adler "dismasts Darwin" because, among many other reasons, Darwinism categorizes humans "as simply an animal with higher sensory perceptions."[850] Martin Gardner even remarked that Adler "has for some time been carrying on a one-man crusade against evolution." As a result of Adler's life-long interest in Darwinism, he eventually wrote two books on the topic. In one, titled *What Man Has Made of Man*, Adler branded evolution a 'popular myth,' and insisted that it was not an established fact.[851]

Adler used the word "myth" to express his belief that Darwinist conclusions "*vastly exceed the scientific evidence... This myth is the story of evolution which is told to school children and which they can almost visualize as if it were a moving picture.*"[852] Specifically, Adler concluded that the theory of evolution "is not a theory in the sense of a systematic organization of scientific facts and laws, in the sense in which Newton's *Principia* is a theory," but is an attempt to explain certain facts in biology by proposing *hypotheses* that are "not propositions to be proved, but are merely imaginative guesses about unobservable processes or events." This is the sort of hypothesis that Newton said no scientist should make.[853] Adler adds that evolution as a theory is "wild speculation," and that "Darwin himself is partly responsible for much of this speculation":

---

848   Rothe and Lohr, 1952, p. 377-378.
849   Gardner, 1957.
850   Bowen, 1985, p. 68.
851   Gardner, 1957, p. 135.
852   Gardner, 1957, pp. 135–136, emphasis added.
853   Adler, 1957, p. 115, (emphasis in original).

The Origin of Species is full of guesses which are clearly unsupported by the evidence. (To the extent that *The Origin of Species* contains scientifically established facts, these facts are not organized into any coherent system.) Furthermore, these guesses, which constitute the theory of evolution, are not in the field of scientific knowledge anyway. They are historical. This conjectural history, begun by Darwin, was even more fancifully elaborated by the 19th century evolutionary "philosophers."[854]

He added that the "post-Darwinian 'scientific cosmologies'"—Spencer, Haeckel, and the post-Darwinian 'evolutionary philosophies' such as that of Bergson—also consisted of wild speculations. Adler affirmed that evolution "is not a scientific fact, but at best a probable history, a history for which the evidence is insufficient and conflicting." The fields of embryology, genetics, palaeontology, and comparative anatomy

establish only one historical probability; that types of animals which once existed no longer exist, and that types of animals now existing at one time did not exist. They do not establish the elaborate story in which is the myth of evolution; nor do they establish any of the aetiological guesses about the way in which species originated or became extinct, such as natural selection, adaptation to environment, struggle for existence, transmission of acquired characteristics, etc.[855]

He also concluded:

If the grand myth of evolution, as a history of the development of the forms of life, and the grand theory of evolution, as an explanation of how it all happened, are not scientific knowledge, how much less are they philosophical knowledge. (This type of speculation, peculiar to the 19th century, did much to bring discredit upon the name of philosophy which it so wrongly arrogated to itself.) For the most part, the wild speculations of Spencer, Haeckel, Schopenhauer and Bergson are now generally discredited both by scientists and philosophers.[856]

---

854 Adler, 1957, pp. 115–116.
855 Adler, 1957, pp. 116–117.
856 Adler, 1957, p. 117.

While still just a young man, Adler had read a collection of articles by different authors in a 1924 book by Ernest Haeckel and others titled *Evolution in Modern Thought*. Afterwards he said this book caused him to be "puzzled" by the "conflicting points of view" on evolution expressed by the different authors.

> Try as I might, I simply could not figure out how evolution was supposed to work. I spent hours writing notes to myself and making diagrams in an effort to put down the steps by which a new species came into being.[857]

He added that this puzzlement remained with him for years, and only when he read Darwin's *Origin of Species* for the third time did he believe that he finally understood Darwinism. However, when he finally understood evolution, he found much with which he disagreed. Gardner concluded that one of the things Adler objected to was the view that life lies "on a continuum in which one species fades into another by imperceptible changes. The evidence indicates, he argues, that 'species' differ not in degree but in kind, with a radical 'discontinuity' separating them."[858]

The Radical Discontinuity between Humans and Animals

Adler devoted an entire book to the "radical discontinuity" that exists between humans and animals. In this 1967 book, *The Difference of Man and the Difference It Makes*, he argued that the difference is both major and critical. In his autobiography, Adler stressed that the theme of this entire book is that humans and animals differ not just in *degree* (quantity), but in *kind* (quality) as well. He later added that "since *The Difference of Man and The Difference It Makes* was published, scientific investigations have turned up additional evidence ... [and thus, my conclusion] that man, with the powers of syntactical speech and conceptual thought, differs in kind from all nonlinguistic animals remains as clear and certain as before."[859] This view is reflected in many of Adler's other writings.[860]

---

857   Adler, 1977, p. 13.
858   Adler, 1957, p. 136.
859   Adler, 1977, p. 300.
860   Holley, 1992.

As do all creationists, Adler recognized that variation within the "Genesis kinds" is valid, and wrote in detail about this problem in his 1940 book, *Problems for Thomists*. (A Thomist—a follower of St. Thomas Aquinas—champions the view that there exists a "self-existent Prime Mover," an uncaused first cause, i.e., a creator and Intelligent Designer). In this book, Adler examined in great detail the question of how many "species" exist so he could determine how many creative acts of God were required "to explain the evolutionary jumps." He suspected that each "species" was created in several different types, e.g., flowering and non-flowering plants.[861] Modern creationists now recognize that the created kinds do not correspond to the "species" concept (which is now recognized to be very problematic).

Adler was an active anti-evolutionist for decades. The conference on *Science, Philosophy and Religion* was held in New York City and other large cities each year from 1940 to 1968 and drew many top scientists and philosophers, including Dr. Adler.[862] At these meetings, Adler, who once said Darwinism is "full of guesses which are clearly unsupported by the evidence," expressed concern about "materialist ideology" and "scientism which dominates every aspect of our modern culture."[863] Gardner recalls that one of many examples of what he calls Adler's "blasts" against evolution was expounded in a lecture presented at the University of Chicago, in 1951:

> Men and apes, he declared, are as different "as a square and a triangle. There can be no intermediate—no three and one-half-sided figure." Most of Adler's arguments were straight out of the arsenal of Bible Belt evangelism... If a scientist would only produce an ape that could speak "in simple declarative sentences," Adler said, he would admit a close bond between man and monkey... Only two explanations will fit all the facts, Adler concluded his speech. Either man "emerged" from the brute by a sudden evolutionary leap, or he was created directly by God.[864]

Adler once said that "scientists...are theologically naive. But that doesn't seem to stop them from talking about beginnings and endings. The beginning

---

861   Gardner, 1957, p. 136.
862   Witham, 2002, p. 28.
863   Witham, 2002, p. 28.
864   Gardner, 1957, p. 137.

wasn't a Big Bang and the end won't be a final freeze. But don't try telling a scientist that."[865]

Mortimer Adler was one of millions of Americans (including around
10,000 active scientists in various fields in America) who do not accept Darwinism.[866] Fortunately, Dr. Adler was willing to speak out about his doubts about
Darwinism in his lectures, articles, and books. As a result, he articulated many
major concerns that have not been satisfactorily addressed by evolutionists, even
today. And as expected, Dr. Adler endured his share of attacks by Darwinists,
especially from those in the atheistic community.[867]

Born of Jewish parents, as a young man he "fell away from religious observance" to the point of becoming a "religious scoffer."[868] Only in 1984, when he
was 82, did he become a professing Christian.[869] After that, until his death he
remained active in writing and speaking about his faith. He became a Christian
because his life-long research proved to him that "Christianity is the only logical,
consistent faith in the world."[870]

Summary Remarks on Adler

Until he died, Dr. Adler was deeply committed to demonstrating God's
existence scientifically "beyond reasonable doubt."[871] His confidence in God's
existence was based on the cosmological argument (the conclusion that the existence of a creation proves the Creator), and the fact that no form of evolution,
including Neo-Darwinism, can account for the creation of either life or the cosmos.[872] Furthermore, as a philosopher, he concluded that belief in Christianity
is critical in developing a workable, humane system of ethics and morality.[873]

---

865 Quoted in Muck, 1990, p. 33.
866 Bergman, 1999 and Appendix B: One study found *five percent* of all scientists believed that "humans
were created in their current form less than 10,000 years ago" (Witham, 1997; Madigan 1997, p. 6-7).
Assuming this study is valid, this translates into close to 100,000 of the almost two million scientists working in academic and basic research or engineering being either creationists or ID advocates (Data from the
National Science Foundation, Division of Science Resource Studies, 1997).
867 For examples see Gordon Stein, 1982, p. 14; Muck, 1990, pp. 32-34; and Ravitch et al., 1983, pp. 377-411.
868 Adler, 1980, p. 19.
869 Adler, 1993, p. 210.
870 Quoted in Muck, 1990, p. 33.
871 Adler, 1980, p. 19; 1990, p. 107.
872 Adler, 1980, pp. 136–137.
873 Adler, 1970.

Ernst Chain: The Man Who Revolutionized Medicine

Ernst Chain and Howard Florey are responsible for "one of the greatest discoveries in medical science ever made" which happened to be in the field of antibiotics.[874] A little known fact is that Chain openly opposed Darwinism on the basis of his scientific research.

Ernst Boris Chain (June 19, 1906 – August 12, 1979) was born in Berlin, Germany, where he obtained his Ph.D. in biochemistry and physiology. A brilliant student, multilingual, and an accomplished concert pianist, Chain was most well known as a pioneering scientific researcher.[875] Although he became a highly respected scientist, as a Jew, he foresaw what was coming and left his homeland not long after Hitler came to power.[876] He moved to England where he worked as a research scientist—at both *Cambridge* and then *Oxford University*—until 1948.[877] While at Oxford, his wife, Anne Beloff, earned a Ph.D. in biochemistry from Oxford and then did scientific research at Harvard University.[878] Chain also completed a Ph.D. in biochemistry at Cambridge.

After Chain left Oxford, he worked in research and as a professor at several universities. The promise of better equipment than he was able to obtain in Great Britain lured Chain to Rome. The British science establishment and government, conscious of its loss, soon bribed Chain back by building him a new laboratory to continue his research in biochemistry.[879] His life-long work was "all about the mystery of life."[880] In his 40-year search to understand the mystery of life, Chain accomplished "amazingly diverse achievements."[881] He even achieved feats once considered to be impossible, such as the production of lysergic acid by the deep fermentation process.[882]

Chain's career epiphany came in 1938 when he stumbled across Fleming's 1928 paper on penicillin in the *British Journal of Experimental Pathology*, which he brought to the attention of his colleague Howard Florey.[883] Chain's

---

874   Masters, 1946, p. 7.
875   Lax, 2004, p. 59.
876   Asimov, 1972, p. 712.
877   Schlessinger and Schlessinger, 1986, p. 93.
878   McMurray, 1995, p. 335.
879   Asimov, 1972, p. 712.
880   Lax, 2004, p. 63.
881   Mansford, 1977, p. xxi.
882   Barton, 1977, p. xviii.
883   Lax, 2004, p. 79.

chief contribution to the research was both to isolate and purify penicillin. It was largely Chain's work on penicillin that earned him his numerous honors and awards, including a fellow of the Royal Society and numerous honorary degrees.[884] These include—besides a Nobel Prize—a knighthood in 1969, the Pasteur Medal, the Paul Ehrlich Centenary Prize, and the Berzelius Medal among other awards.[885] His Nobel was specifically for his research that demonstrated the structure of penicillin and for successfully isolating the active substance by freeze-drying the mold broth to make its use practical.[886] When Chain was doing his research 125 gallons of broth were required to produce enough penicillin powder for one tablet! Today, the same tablet is mass-produced for a few cents (of course, you might pay much more than that for it…).

An internationally respected scientist, Chain is now widely regarded as one of the major founders of the field of antibiotics. Aside from sanitation, developing the field of antibiotics was arguably one of the most important revolutions in modern medicine. Other important scientific work done by Chain included the study of snake venom, specifically the finding that its neurotoxic effects are caused by the destruction of an essential intracellular respiratory coenzyme.

In 1940 Chain also discovered penicillinase, an enzyme that catalyzes the destruction of penicillin. This discovery was important because penicillinase is used by bacteria to deactivate penicillin, negating its effectiveness.[887] Chain knew that bacteria could become resistant to the drug and had already started working on the problem in 1940.[888]

Chain's Doubts About Darwinism

One of Chain's life-long professional concerns was the validity of Darwinism. He concluded that Darwin's theory of evolution was a "very feeble attempt" to explain the origin of species based on assumptions so flimsy, "mainly of mor-

884   Lax, 2004, p. 253.
885   Curtis, 1993, p. 77-90.
886   McMurray, 1995, p. 334.
887   Barton, 1977, p. xxiii.
888   Barton, 1977, p. xxiii.

phological and anatomical nature," that "it can hardly be called a theory."[889] In his words, the main theory that has dominated biology

for almost a century is that of the Darwin-Wallace concepts of evolution and natural selection through the survival of the fittest. This mechanistic concept of the phenomena of life in its infinite varieties of manifestations which purports to ascribe the origin and development of all living species, animals, plants and micro-organisms, to the haphazard blind interplay of the forces of nature in the pursuance of one aim only, namely, that for the living systems to survive, is a typical product of the naive 19th century euphoric attitude to the potentialities of science which spread the belief that there were no secrets of nature which could not be solved by the scientific approach given only sufficient time. There exist people even today who hold such views, but on the whole the scientists, and in particular, the biologists of the 20th century are less optimistic than their colleagues of the 19th century.[890]

A major reason why he rejected evolution was because the idea was a

hypothesis based on no evidence and irreconcilable with the facts. These classic evolutionary theories are a gross over-simplification of an immensely complex and intricate mass of facts, and it amazes me that they are swallowed so uncritically and readily, and for such a long time, by so many scientists without a murmur of protest.[891]

Chain concluded that he "would rather believe in fairies than in such wild speculation" as Darwinism.[892] Chain's eldest son added that there

was no doubt that he did not like the theory of evolution by natural selection—he disliked theories ... especially when they assumed the form of dogma. He also felt that evolution was not really a part of science, since it was, for the most part, not amenable to experimentation—and he was, and is, by no means alone in this view.[893]

---

889   Quoted in Ronald Clark, 1985, p. 147.
890   Chain, 1970, pp. 24–25.
891   Chain, 1970, p. 25.
892   Quoted in Ronald Clark, 1985, p. 147.
893   Quoted in Ronald Clark, 1985, pp. 147–148.

Clark identified three factors that were important in "Chain's dismissal of Darwin's theory of evolution." The first one was Chain's dislike of theories that could not be experimentally verified. In Chain's words:

> "I cannot work up too much enthusiasm for any theory, knowing that theories are ephemeral and, as new facts are discovered, must be dramatically changed or discarded. In my view they have no absolute value, and their usefulness consists essentially in their capacity to stimulate new experiments. This is, at least, the criteria by which I judge them."[894]

To illustrate his point, Chain used an example from his own field of research: antibacterial therapeutic agent effectiveness, which was widely believed to be directly related to its color properties until Chain proved one antibacterial compound, namely sulfonamide, was the result of its colorless component. Another reason he did not consider evolution a scientific theory was because it is obvious that "living systems do not survive if they are not fit to survive"

> It is equally obvious that if in a given species chance mutations give rise to genetic variants which in a particular ecological surrounding have a better chance of survival than other members of the species this will give them an advantage in survival value over their less fit competitors.[895]

Chain recognized that the problem was not the survival of the fittest but the arrival of the fittest and that mutations do produce some variety:

> There is no doubt that such variants do arise in nature and that their emergence can and does make some limited contribution towards the evolution of species. The open question is the quantitative extent and significance of this contribution. To postulate, as the positivists of the end of the last century and their followers here have done, that the development and survival of the fittest is entirely a consequence of chance mutations, or even that nature carries out experiments by trial and error through mutations in order to create living systems better fitted to survive, seems to me a hypothesis based on no evidence and irreconcilable with the facts.[896]

---

894 Quoted in Ronald Clark, 1985, p. 147.
895 Chain, 1970, p. 25.
896 Chain, 1970, p. 25.

He added that evolution "willfully neglects the principle of teleological purpose which stares the biologist in the face wherever he looks, whether he be engaged in the study of different organs in one organism, or even of different subcellular compartments in relation to each other in a single cell, or whether he studies the interrelation and interactions of various species."[897]

Chain was especially aware of how the research in his own field caused evolution problems. In particular, Chain noted our modern knowledge of the genetic code and its function in transmitting genetic information is incompatible with classical Darwinian ideas of evolution.[898]

Another concern about evolution that Chain expressed was evolutions implications for morals. In a 1972 speech he presented in London he stated:

> It is easy to draw analogies between the behavior of apes and man, and draw conclusions from the behavior of birds and fishes on human ethical behavior, but ... this fact does not allow the development of ethical guidelines for human behavior. All attempts to do this, such as Lorenz' studies on aggression in animals, suffer from the failure to take into account the all important fact of man's capability to think and to be able to control his passions, and are therefore doomed to failure. ... It is the differences between animal and man, not the similarities, which concern us ... the various speculations on cosmology which are advanced from time to time, are nothing more than an amusing past time for those proposing them.[899]

Chain once wrote to a colleague who wanted him to pen a forward to a book that he was writing on evolution and the importance of belief in God, but Chain declined, adding, "I have said for years that speculations about the origin of life lead to no useful purpose as even the simplest living system is far too complex to be understood in terms of the extremely primitive chemistry scientists have used in their attempts to explain the unexplainable that happened billions of years ago. God cannot be explained away by such naive thoughts."[900]

In support of a paper written by Dr. R. E. Monro, Chain later wrote that Monro's paper was a valuable and timely essay on an important issue, namely, whether or not the "writings in the field commonly termed molecular biology

---

897   Chain, 1970, p. 25.
898   Chain, 1970, pp. 25–26.
899   Quoted in Ronald Clark, 1985, p. 148.
900   Quoted in Ronald Clark, 1985, p. 148.

strengthen the mechanistic concepts of life so popular during the last half of the past century, particularly after Darwin's ideas of evolution through natural selection" was developed.[901]

Chain added that Jacques Monod has "written a semi-philosophical book on the subject which has been much quoted; he and Crick are the main exponents of the positivistic-materialistic philosophy according to which all aspects of life are explainable in relatively simple physico-chemical forms. This approach has always seemed to me to demonstrate a great lack of knowledge of biology on the part of those proposing such primitive ideas."[902] He added that:

> In a lecture which Crick, who, together with Watson and Wilkins, discovered the bihelical structure of DNA, gave a couple of years ago to students at University College ... he said ... that it was ridiculous to base serious decisions on religious belief. This seems to me a very sweeping and dogmatic conclusion ... scientific theories, in whatever field, are ephemeral and ... may be even turned upside down by the discovery of one single new fact ... . This has happened time and again even in the exactest of sciences, physics and astronomy, and applies even more so to the biological field, where the concepts and theories are much less securely founded than in physics and are much more liable to be overthrown at a moment's notice.[903]

One might dismiss his views on Darwinism as simply the result of his faith, but Clark stresses how "directly such views were linked to his religious beliefs is open to endless argument."[904] Chain's eldest son wrote that his father's concerns about evolution were *not* based on religion, but rather on science. Chain, however, made it clear that he was very concerned about the effects of Darwinism on human behavior:

> any speculation and conclusions pertaining to human behavior drawn on the basis of Darwinian evolutionary theories ... must be treated with the greatest caution and reserve...a less discriminating section of the public may enjoy reading about comparisons between the behavior of apes and man, but this approach—which, by the way, is neither new nor original—does not really lead us very far. ... Apes, after all, unlike man, have not produced

---

901   Ronald Clark, 1985, p. 178.
902   Quoted in Ronald Clark, 1985, p. 178.
903   Chain, 1970, p. 25.
904   Clark,1985, p. 148.

great prophets, philosophers, mathematicians, writers, poets, composers, painters and scientists. They are not inspired by the divine spark which manifests itself so evidently in the spiritual creation of man and which differentiates man from animals.[905]

Chain stressed that humans have "left the apes behind in the evolutionary scale" because humans managed "to develop a bigger brain, is really no explanation at all; it is only a statement covering up ignorance by an ill-defined term."[906]

Chain wrote that scientists "looking for ultimate guidance in questions of moral responsibility" would do well to "turn, or return, to the fundamental and lasting values of the code of ethical behavior forming part of the divine message which man was uniquely privileged to receive through the intermediation of a few chosen individuals."[907]

The Importance of Ernst Chain's Work

Sir Derek Barton wrote that there are "few scientists who, by the application of their science, have made a greater contribution to human welfare than Sir Ernst Chain."[908] His work founded the field of antibiotics, which has saved the lives of multimillions of persons. Chain is only one of many modern scientists who concluded that modern Neo-Darwinism is not only scientifically bankrupt but also harmful to society. He also stands as an example of a creationist who produced significant scientific research for the betterment of mankind. This is an important point since many creationist and ID critics today make the false claim that "religion" renders one incapable of doing good science. I am in the process of compiling a list of Nobel laureates that were Darwin doubters.

Conclusions

As this chapter illustrates, it is possible to earn a degree and survive in secular academia or the scientific establishment as a Darwin skeptic. Unfortunately, such survivors generally must be of the highest caliber in their field, those

---

905   Chain, 1970, p. 26.
906   Chain, 1970, p. 26.
907   Chain, 1970, p. 26.
908   Barton, 1977, p. xxvii.

with less "rock star" status are likely to have a much more difficult time. Many of those who have survived achieved their success many years ago. Chain was employed in academia but his primarily work was as a research scientist. Adler, also an academic, spent most of his time writing. Dr. von Braun was a highly esteemed research scientist his entire life, thus less likely to have problems. Furthermore, all three of these men lived in the 20th century, a far more tolerant time for Darwin Doubters. If these three scientists were to enter graduate school today they might have never make it through a Ph.D. program in science. Even if they graduated, unless they were in the closet, they would likely not have advanced as far as they did in their careers in academia or scientific research.

Chapter 15: What Can Be Done?

The problems that Darwin Doubters of all stripes experience are directly related to the fact that religious discrimination in this nation is both a major problem in education and a shameful national crime.[909] The loss (often destruction) of careers as a result of exercising one's First Amendment rights should be vigorously opposed by all Americans. I have been hard-pressed to find a single recent case of an active, believing Darwin Doubter in secular academia who was open about his or her beliefs and has not experienced some type of discrimination. Job termination (or problems) due to religion is not yet a universal test of faith, but it is quickly becoming one of the most certain means of measuring it.

Furthermore, the problem is getting worse. A *University of Michigan* law school graduate wrote:

> [I]f you gingerly raise scientific questions about evolution you will be denounced as a creationist nut, your life will be turned upside down, and your employers will be hounded. You will probably be fired and certainly have to hire a lawyer. Now let's take a show of hands: Any Darwin skeptics? Good. Evolution has been proved again!"[910]

---

909   Black, 2004; Shortt, 2004; McQuaid, 2003.
910   Coulter, 2006, p. 255.

A cover story in *New Scientist* titled "The End of Reason: Intelligent Design's Ultimate Legacy,"[911] included sub-titles such as "A Battle for Science's Soul," predicting the end of science and life as we know it if the nefarious Darwin skeptics take over the world, which the article concluded is their evil intent. The article claimed that "if ID ever came to be accepted, it would stifle research."[912] The web site "Science Against Evolution" responded to this ridiculous suggestion by noting that

> A scientist who believes in evolution is likely to recognize that starfish and lizards both have the ability to re-grow lost body parts, so they must have evolved from a common ancestor. This could lead him to try to construct an ancestral tree to find this common ancestor. The speculative tree is published, and a bunch of other evolutionists spend lots of time arguing about whether the tree is correct or not. That's what we call "stifling research."[913]

This type of response is precisely what is needed to challenge every effort made by those who oppose Darwin Doubters with irresponsible claims. Blogs, web sites, and other forms of communication challenging the unsupported dogma of Darwinism is required if we are to ensure that freedom of expression and reason will prevail. As I have documented in this book, educators and students are now being *required* to subscribe to belief in evolution as a condition of employment, working on summer science projects, receiving a degree, or promotion. Vulgarity and name-calling against Darwin skeptics is open and rampant, especially on internet blogs. Calls for the removal of skeptics from academia and science are shrill, ubiquitous, and often include the notion of being well-deserved. What is the next step in the opposition of Darwin Doubters? Putting them in jail for promoting scientific sedition? Making it illegal to publish anything contrary to evolution? With the discrimination tactics already common, one can only wonder what the next escalation point might be.

In another striking example of recent discrimination, The *University of California*, one of the largest universities in the world, has now started to re-

---

911   Mackenzie, Debora, 2005.
912   Mackenzie, Debora, 2005, p. 5.
913   http://www.scienceagainstevolution.org/v9i11n.htm

ject the transfer of college credits for courses taught at Christian schools that have content in the textbooks used that question Darwinism. The Association of Christian Schools International (ACSI), which represents over 800 schools, are fighting back and have filed a federal lawsuit challenging the University of California's policy, which in effect prevents students taught from a conservative Christian viewpoint from being admitted to colleges in the UC system. ACSI says UC admissions officials have ruled that courses taught from a Christian perspective—including English, science, history, and social studies—no longer qualify for credit. An ACSI representative explained:

> The University of California objected to a "biased" English text because it emphasizes Christian themes in great literature through the years ... It has objected to a science text that teaches the standard course content, and then [also] teaches creation. It has objected to a history text that emphasizes the role of Christianity in history. It has objected to a social studies text that emphasizes the Christian heritage of America...[914]

The *Calvary Chapel Christian School* in Murrieta, California was informed that its courses were rejected for using textbooks published by the two major Christian textbook publishers, namely Bob Jones University Press in South Carolina and A Beka Books in Pensacola, Florida. *The Los Angeles Times* reports that:

> university officials described some of the courses using those texts as being "too narrow" to be accepted—and suggested the school "submit for UC approval a secular science curriculum with a text and course outline that addresses course content/knowledge generally accepted in the scientific community." Dr. Albert Mohler, Jr.—president of The Southern Baptist Theological Seminary in Louisville, Kentucky—sees the UC system's actions as an "unprecedented form of discrimination" against Christian schools, parents, churches, and students.[915]

Attorneys will argue in court that the UC policy violates the free-speech and religious-freedom rights of both Christian students and Christian schools, on the grounds that different schools have the right to teach from different perspectives:

---

914   Brown and Brown, 2005, p. 1.
915   Brown and Brown, 2005, p. 1.

That's a vital part of our freedom that's ensured by the First Amendment...
Essentially every First Amendment decision of the times past is a precedent
in our favor. California's action is, to my knowledge, unprecedented.[916]

The UC system, through spokeswoman Ravi Poorsina, defended their position by claiming that "the university has a right to set course requirements ... [to]
ensure that students who come here are fully prepared with broad knowledge and
the critical thinking skills necessary to succeed."[917]

This wrong-headed approach taken by the UC powers that side-steps what
the true measure of a student's basis for admission to their academic system *should*
be: how well students do on their LSATs and other admission tests. It should not
matter one whit whether the texts they used do not share what the UC conclude
the philosophical underpinnings of those texts should be – the proof is in the
results and can be resolved quite simply *by looking at how well students do on their
exams*. This should be the primary if not only criterion of concern to UC where
student ability is concerned. Suggestions that students might not come "fully prepared" and with the necessary "critical thinking skills" ise a thinly veiled smoke-
screen for yet another form of discrimination against believers, especially conservative Christians. Only by standing up and challenging UC claims will efforts to
impose secular worldview on religious groups be abated.

Tragically, the media and so-called "civil liberties" organizations are quite
often deafeningly silent on the problem of religious discrimination or worse,
support such discrimination by their failure to take a stand in the defense of
victims.

It is also clear that the problem is getting worse, especially with the development of Intelligent Design (ID) as a response to naturalistic materialism,
starting with publication of such works such as the 1967 book *Mathematical
Challenges to the Neo-Darwinian Interpretation of Evolution*.[918] Darwin Doubters
are increasingly being described as dangerous threats to our culture, a danger
to modern science, and much worse – all of which puts in motion ideas in our
young people that need to be contested if academic freedom is to survive.

---

916 Brown and Brown, 2005. p. 1
917 Brown and Brown, 2005, p. 1.
918 Moorhead and Kaplan. 1967

Bhattacharjee writes that "teaching the idea that a higher intelligence played a role in creating life on Earth ... sends chills down the spines of most Kansas scientists and educators[919] He concluded that teaching this idea "will make Kansas an undesirable location for high-tech companies, academics, and other knowledge-based workers ... introducing ID in school curricula would undermine a state-backed plan to invest $500 million over the next 10 years to boost Kansas's bioscience industry."[920]

No scientific research was cited to back up this claim—and the existing evidence contradicts it. Teaching students that a higher intelligence did not play a role in creating life on Earth will hardly make students smarter and better able to cope with the scientific demands of high-tech industries. This plays to the common false claims that atheists are smarter, more intellectually capable, able to think more critically, or better educated than theists. ID critics also claim that "ID does not foster analytical thinking because its arguments are faith-based."[921] Such claims illustrate just how desperate, arrogant and prejudiced the opponents of Darwin Doubters really are.

Censorship and tenure denial were not always a major problem in the recent past. A professor who had endured discrimination at one institution could usually find a position with little difficulty at another university. Generally, the religious reasons for the discrimination did not have to be revealed and, with this experience behind him, a creationist or ID professor then knew he might need to hide his beliefs, or at least be very careful. As a result, he was more likely to obtain tenure the second time around.

Today, however, it is a far more difficult situation because of both greater (and more open) hostility against religious educators in general, and Darwin Doubters in particular, at many universities, as well as a glut of Ph.D.'s in many fields. The Internet can be, and often has been, used to research a prospective employee to determine if there is any creationist or ID involvement in their background. Universities often appear to be "very keen on fostering 'diversity' as long as it is not ideological diversity."[922] Furthermore, the intolerance even extends to political party involvement. For example, one survey found fully 80

919   Bhattacharjee, 2005a, p. 627.
920   Bhattacharjee, 2005a, p. 627.
921   Bhattacharjee, 2005a, p. 627.
922   Holden, 2004, p. 1678.

percent of professors were Democrats and that Republicans were hardly any-where to be found. Some academics have suggested that we now need affirma-tive action programs for Republicans.

Many professors who were denied tenure for reasons of Darwin skepti-cism or alleged 'religious' beliefs are quite often blackballed and are *never* able to reenter their profession as an educator. I am aware of several Ph.D.'s denied tenure who have returned to school in an attempt to start over and earn a degree in another area (in many cases, law). The investment of time, talent, and money represented by the eight to ten years of schooling already sacrificed in prepara-tion for a profession unjustly closed to them is tragic. As Lionel Lewis notes:

> [M]ost academics who lose a job for whatever reason have difficulty finding "a regular teaching position at an academically respectable American college or university." In the best of times, dissidents or deviants of any stripe are not welcome. ... Potential sources of embarrassment are generally shunned. Others are not hospitable to those who might in any way be a burden. These individuals had been labeled as political undesirables.... This reality, more than their political beliefs or activities, may have occasioned the career problems they encountered. In other words, showing that they did not fit in well may have been as important in disqualifying them in the eyes of others as their putative political beliefs. For better or worse, academics are cau-tious, indeed, many are timid. Moreover, the academic world is small, and it does not take long for information and reputations to spread.[923]

Far-Reaching Effects

This issue is critical for America. The preservation of religious freedom and freedom of speech really does require eternal vigilance.[924] It is not an isolated problem, nor do the effects end with loss of employment for merely a few. The numbers of Darwin Doubters who are being discriminated against has steadily grown over the years and is increasing as the hostility against them continues to escalate.[925] And the controversy will not go away, because over 90 percent of the

---

923   Lionel S. Lewis, 1987, p. 50.
924   Staver, 2005.
925   For a remarkable list of Darwin Skeptics, please visit this site: http://www.rae.org/darwinskeptics.html

American population do not accept orthodox neo-Darwinism or naturalistic evolution.

It is difficult to openly and unemotionally deal with the controversy in a public forum in view of court rulings such as the controversial conclusion of Judge Jones in the *Kitzmiller* case. The common interpretation is the judge ruled that even criticism of Darwinism cannot be taught in the public schools, at least according to many ID critics.[926] The result is Darwinism has the protection of a legally enforced monopoly on education; dissenting ideas are not allowed to have a foot in the door because they are falsely and conveniently branded as necessarily "religious." *Columbia University* Law school graduate Pamela Winnick concluded from her survey of legal cases that Darwinians are clearly on a crusade against all opposition to their views, especially any philosophical premise advocating a Creator, as is true of Judaism, Christianity and Islam.[927] This monopoly of Darwinism threatens the freedom and rights of all Americans. Even those who are not creationists, ID advocates, or adherents of any of the creator-friendly religious views are beginning to experience problems, especially if they question any aspect of evolution and often simply because they are more "conservative" than the norm—meaning they take a stand on social issues often labeled conservative.

The late eminent astronomer and agnostic Fred Hoyle noted that "the Cambridge Clique" (of which he once was a part) was composed of "fanatical, extreme leftists or Marxists, and they couldn't stand having a conservative professor in their midst"[928] After being knighted in 1972, Hoyle decided that he had endured enough and left Cambridge. His only regret was that he did not leave Cambridge when he was forty, because if he had, he said, "I would have achieved so much more."

Even non-teachers who are only indirectly involved in ID can experience problems. At the invitation of the California State Board of Education, Dr. Vernon Grose wrote two short paragraphs for its science framework paper. One of the paragraphs dealt favorably with ID. For this offense, Dr. Grose experienced severe adverse treatment. In his words:

---

926 http://www.pamd.uscourts.gov/kitzmiller/kitzmiller_342.pdf. pp 1-2, 49, 56-57, 64, 70-139.
927 Winnick, 2005.
928 Overbyte, 1981. p. 71.

On 13 November 1969, the California State board of Education unanimously adopted two short paragraphs that I had written for them as an invited expert witness. They inserted those two paragraphs into an appendix of a document known as a 'science framework,' which was designed to set some guidelines for public school science instruction in kindergarten through the eighth grade.[929]

The reaction to Dr. Grose's remarks, which merely encouraged looking at both sides of the evolution controversy, was a battle that Gross summarizes in a 708-page book set in 8-point type.[930] In Grose's own words:

No one—not even screen writers for the wildest TV and movie fantasies—would have foreseen the bizarre happenings that resulted from that unanimous vote. It provoked Associated Press and United press International news releases for over three years. Nineteen Nobel laureates in science mobilized and signed a joint resolution to combat a position they erroneously believed was intended by my words. *The National Academy of Sciences*, for the first time in their 110-year history, passed a resolution to block what they erroneously thought the two paragraphs proposed. Johnny Carson even discussed the issue with William F. Buckley, Jr., on his "Tonight Show."

The impact on my personal life was also considerable. I was threatened by the Dean of the Graduate Division of the University of California. One prominent scientist organized a campaign to blackmail a publisher with whom I had a contract, thereby committing tortuous interference with a contractual relationship. Hate mail poured in.[931]

Dr. Grose's goal was merely to teach *about* origins in the classroom in such a way as to "open up alternatives where there was previously only dogma presented..." For this—because he did not come out squarely *against* Darwin Doubters—he suffered major repercussions for taking his position until he died.[932] The offensive paragraph, and the details of the debate that followed, are documented in Grose's 2006 book.

---

929   Grose, 1995, p. 16.
930   Grose, 2006.
931   Grose, 1995, p. 16.
932   Grose, 2006.

It is difficult to understand why anyone would be or even *could* be denied employment simply because of his or her religion, race, sex, nationality, or culture since we have laws in the U.S. protecting people against such forms of illegal discrimination. Yet, as I have documented in this book, it happens frequently. It also is difficult to understand how believing that life on this planet was created by an intelligent Creator is (as one Cambridge University professor claimed) is an incredibly "dangerous" idea.[933]

Persecution and discrimination of any type is often hard for rational and law abiding people to understand. Why, for example, would the old Soviet government want to viciously persecute its religious citizens?[934] As a group they were, for the most part, law-abiding and responsible contributors to their society. Most were not revolutionaries and typically did not make waves against their government -- by-and-large, they cooperated with the orderly functions of their society. Yet the trials of many religious people have been constant throughout modern Soviet history, varying in intensity but never ceasing.[935] Stalin closed most of Russia's places of worship, and decimated the clergy ranks by murder, prison, and exile. Nikita Khrushchev continued the attack, and boasted that he would "exhibit" the last Soviet Christian on television by 1965. Of course, he did not. Unfortunately, however, his attitude is not very far removed from that found in American academia today against Darwin Doubters.

The Problem Is Widespread Because Little Is Being Done to Stop It

I estimate, by examining data published by various professional societies that an average of about four hundred cases of religious firings or clear, blatant incidents of job discrimination occur annually in academia in America by people who merely question orthodox Darwinism. Almost none of these, unfortunately, end up in court, and those that do lose.[936] After examining the alternatives, many Christians realize that it is difficult to win a case against a university or school—the old story about fighting City Hall—and so they often do not try.

---

933   Proffitt, 2004 , p. 1894 – 1895.
934   Courtois et al., 1999.
935   Wurmbrand, 1986.
936   Tyner, 1984. pp. 4-6

Others find a position elsewhere (which, as I have noted, is becoming increasingly difficult in academia), and still others leave academia entirely.

The result is that an increasing majority of those with a non-theistic perspective remain within academia and in many of the life sciences professions. Ironically, many critics of Darwin skeptics argue as evidence for the rationality of evolution that the "vast majority" of scientists and educators accept evolution, while failing to mention one reason why—dissidents are kept from joining their ranks in the first place or are frequently eliminated once they are discovered.

Another creationist with a superior record of research and publications who taught in the biology department at a large state university was denied tenure. Because several major procedural violations occurred in his case (among other things, the university missed several crucial deadlines), if he had gone to court, he might well have won the case. However, he felt that it was wrong to take an employer (or anyone else) to court. He stressed that he was not opposing someone else's seeking redress through the courts, but that this was an unacceptable alternative for him. He has been unemployed for the last three years, and is still actively looking, but is extremely discouraged. Another creationist, a Harvard biology Ph.D., has been actively seeking a teaching position for the last decade. Previously to this, he was discharged from teaching posts several times, each time over his questioning Darwinism and related issues, and each time he did nothing to bring redress. Employers often know that many professors will not file a law suit, thus they seem to feel free to terminate. One employer spoke to me about a professor who questioned Darwinism on religious grounds:

> Frankly, I don't like fundamentalists, especially Baptist, Church of Christ types, Pentecostals or other 17th century retrogressives. If we find out we hired one, especially if they start talking to the other research scientists about their beliefs, I would terminate them within the month. Usually they leave without much of a protest. And I've never had one bring suit, even though firing on religious grounds is illegal, and I know that it is. But who cares—several guys I told straight out. "We don't want any creationists working in this lab, so if you don't turn in your resignation letter tomorrow, we will have to fire you. You better just find a position elsewhere." Besides, if they appeal to the EEOC and win, we'll just hire them back. No one has, so I'm not worried about it.[937]

---

937   Interview with a scientist who asked to remains anonymous.

Universities and corporations know that they have both time and money on their side. In an article about discrimination in general, Quilter quotes an executive who said to an employee that was fired quite openly because of illegal discriminatory reasons: "Take this $2,500 and jam it. We're a multimillion-dollar corporation, and if you sue us—even if you win—we can drag it out for years on appeal until you're dead and you'll never see a penny."[938]

In light of this, I feel strongly that the government is obligated to ensure enforcememt of discrimination laws, and should take great care to fulfill this responsibility on behalf of its citizens. When illegal discrimination occurs, it should be speedily rectified.

Nations that have more freedom of religion, speech, and the press are usually those that have religious minorities living within their borders to fight for these rights. Many of the rights that Americans have today exist *only* because of the perseverance of religious minorities in the courts.[939] This country was founded by religious minorities who had to leave their homelands, and both our Constitution and legal system were deliberately built by these religious minorities who sought to protect their freedom.[940] The First Amendment was designed in part to protect the expression of religious liberty in public life. As law professor and first amendment scholar William Marnell stated so effectively:

> The First Amendment, then, was not the product of indifference toward religion. It was not the product of the Deism which prevailed in the Enlightenment, however much of the spirit of Deism may have been present in certain of the Founding Fathers. Above all, it was not the product of secularism, and to translate the spirit of twentieth-century secularism back into eighteenth-century America is an outrage to history. The First Amendment was rather a logical outcome of the Protestant Reformation and its ensuing developments. It was so far removed from secularism as to be the product of its exact opposite, the deep-seated concern of a people whose religious faith had taken many forms, all of them active, all of them sincerely held. It was so far removed from indifference toward religion as to be the result of its antithesis, the American determination that the diversity of churches might survive the fact of political union.

---

938 Quilter, 1982, p. 36.
939 Buzzard, 1982 pp. .9-75.
940 Pfeffer, 1963.

The "wall of separation between Church and State" was not and could not be a Chinese Wall to separate the eternal and the temporal. The real relationship between Church and State, in America and in every country where religion is strong, is a thing of the spirit, the infusion of the spirit of religion into the ordering of the affairs of society. A wall of separation which would bar that spirit from making itself felt in secular concerns can never be built, because it would have to bisect the human heart.[941]

Responsibility alone compels us to require that employers be accountable to, and obey the law. Tenure proceedings do not trump the guaranteed freedoms of U.S. citizens, and all tenure rules need to conform to the constitutional rights of U.S. citizens. Religious discrimination is against the law, and a failure to challenge such discrimination is acquiescence to (and in some cases, partnership with) wrongdoing. The present deplorable state of affairs is, no doubt, in part due to the fact that Christians have not obeyed the clear New Testament teaching of the need to be ever-vigilant, ever fighting for the rights and concerns of the oppressed, the poor, and minorities in general (Matthew 25:34-35).

The Need to Become Involved

If slanderous remarks are made in a national magazine, or if a firing occurs and clear evidence of discrimination exists, but no action is taken—the freedom of *all* Americans is being violated. This is not something that happens to "other" people—when the freedoms of one group are threatened, it is a threat against us *all*. Which reminds me of the famous lament commonly attributed to Martin Niemoeller:

> They came after the Jews and I was not a Jew, so I did not object. They came after the Catholics and I was not a Catholic, so I did not object. They came after the trade unionists, and I was not a trade unionist, so I did not object. Then they came after me, and there was no one left to object.

---

941   Marnell, 1964, pp. xiii-xiv.

If the public rose up and demanded that our civil rights and guaranteed freedoms be upheld, discrimination would soon end.

Theists must do much more, and soon, if they hope to avert a growing cultural anti-theism among secular society, academia and the media. The situation, as described by the editors of *Context* is critical. In discussing the work of Princeton sociologist Robert Wuthnow, one of the editors noted that, as to the concept of living questions (those that are "inherently important"), Christianity, in effect

> sacralizes—makes sacred—the intellectual life. Part of the Christian gift is overlooked because it comes from Evangelicals. The dirty secret? "American higher education disdains evangelical Christians. Few groups are as despised a minority. Jews certainly are not. African Americans no longer are. Gays are not. Women are not. Roman Catholics once were, perhaps even very recently. But no groups arouse passions and prejudices more than Evangelicals and fundamentalists." Wuthnow has seen academic committees reject prospects as "not ready for Princeton" because they cite evangelicalism in their application autobiographies.[942]

The editor then asked rhetorically, "Why are not Evangelicals supprted by affirmative action programs, or efforts to promote greater tolerance?" The answer was that, unlike African Americans or women, the status of Evangelicals

> is assumed to have been adopted voluntarily rather than being an ascriptive identity. Christians ... can... repudiate Christianity... Even when they teach at Christian colleges, their true feelings are often kept closely guarded ... many of these Evangelicals are victims of social-class discrimination ... as usually white, often male ... they rarely qualify for aid. They remain disadvantaged.[943]

Dolliver observed that "religious liberty is a universal need," and should be advocated for every nation, as peace and justice are now.[944] The solution to this problem is best summarized by Christian leader Donald Wildman who, in his public presentations, said 20 years ago that he has been telling his audiences that

---

942   Editorial *Conext*. March 15, 1991, Vol. 23, pp. 2–3.
943   Editorial *Conext*. March 15, 1991, Vol. 23, , pp. 2–3.
944   Dolliver, quoted in Beck, 1986, p. 3.

unless the Christian community becomes involved in the struggle for [religious freedom] and does so quickly, that those being born today will be physically persecuted if they desire to practice their Christian faith. "I fully understand how radical this statement sounds, but it is an intellectually honest statement—not one to shock."[945]

Fighting the New Bigotry

The media, too, must become aware of their contribution to the New Bigotry. When prominent past writers such as H.L. Mencken call religious belief a "pathological" phenomenon, or highly revered intellectual leaders such as Freud call religion "mental illness," and towering intellectuals such as Marx called it the "opiate of the people," it is no wonder that such negative reactions exist, reactions that spill over to those who question Darwinism. It is open season on anyone whom the media can pin the now much abused and negative term "fundamentalist," which often includes almost anyone who takes their religion seriously. Respect for religious views needs to be cultivated, protected and honored rather than publicly derided.

The fact that religion is central in academia's war against creation and ID was noted by Michael McGehee, who wrote that many educators believe better science education will "combat creationism." He suggests: "This proposed remedy, however, treats symptoms and not causes. The best way to refute the ignorance represented by creationism is not by better science education but by better education in religious studies."[946]

It needs to be stressed that, even though the majority of those who currently support Intelligent Design and question or reject Darwin are Christians, agnostics who reject Darwinism also face the same problem—the persecution that this book focuses on is that rendered against doubting Darwin people *per se*, not just against Darwin Doubters who believe in God, or in Christ. Not all Darwin Doubters are theists. Among the agnostic Darwin Doubters include David Berlinski, Michael Denton, Periannan Senapathy, Chandra Wickramasinghe, Murray Eden, Marcel-Paul Schützenberger, Hubert Yockey, Stanley

945   Wildman, 1984, p. 22.
946   McGehee, 1987, p. 44.

Salthe, Christian Schwabe, Gerald A. Kerkut, Professor Lima-de-Faria, Pierre-P. Grasse', Soren Lovtrup, David Stove, Fred Hoyle, and many, many others.

Religion is not the only motive used to oppress Darwin Doubters. Another motive is the need to defend "methodological naturalism," or "sciencetism" in general. Acknowledging that challenges to evolution can not be easily refuted, many Darwinists advocate defending persecution and use of prevention rather than engagement, preferring to use ridicule and removing opposition rather than effectively addressing it.

Sometimes the motives of the opposition to Darwin Doubters springs from hatred of theism in general, or of fundamentalist Christianity in particular. In all cases, public education about religion, to help the public see that most evangelicals, fundamentalists, and other theists are not the idiots and demons they are made out to be, will greatly help to educate and alert the public to the unjustified stereotypes that many employers (including universities and scientific institutions) are laboring under. Fighting bigotry requires labeling it for what it is (bigotry), and working with the government, civil rights organizations, and churches to identify it when it crops up and then apply existing laws to properly deal with it.

Defend Intellectual Freedom

The need to protect intellectual freedom is a major concern in the area of not only science but also religion. The study of religion is a major tool to help us examine our life values and goals. Many people are not sure of their goals, and stumble through life because they have poorly defined goals and beliefs. In America, where most people profess to be Christians, many people who call themselves Christians have little understanding of Christianity aside from a few basics that could be summarized in a few paragraphs.

Surveys consistently find that a high percentage of Americans cannot name the synoptic gospels, do not know whether the Book of Proverbs is in the Hebrew or Greek scriptures, where the gospels are positioned, and are unsure which converted Jew wrote many books of the New Testament. In discussing these concerns with students, it is clear that their theological knowledge tends to be very limited.

This deplorable state of affairs could be because high schools today rarely offer courses in either religion or philosophy, and most college programs don't require study in this area, even though religion thoroughly dominates many world cultures. Surveys of my biology classes (mostly students preparing for a medical career) reveal that, while about ninety percent believe in some form of creationism (theistic evolution for some, although a majority are fiat creationists), many students know little about this topic beyond believing that God is responsible. Students usually want to discuss primarily the field into which they are planning on going into, and most have little interest in pursuing the subject of origins in much depth.

I perceive that it is imperative, for all these reasons, that all public school students complete at least a basic, objective religion survey course taught by a teacher who does not have an anti-theistic or anti-biblical bias. The purpose of such a class would not be "indoctrination," but to provide a basic education and appreciation for other views. In our emerging world economy, such instruction should be seen as necessary for successfully interacting with worldwide business partners, which many students of today will most certainly be engaged with as the business adults of tomorrow. Students who receive such training will be able to help produce the tolerance required to competently engage in the world of the future. It will also help us to better understand and appreciate religion rather than perceive it as something to avoid or disdain. Unfortunately, the broad bias found today among many secular science and academic professionals works directly against such a goal. Awareness of this problem is the first step in dealing with it. The next step is to work within the churches and the educational establishment to introduce programs that can help to educate the populace about religion. Release time for religious instruction is one of the most effective legal approaches. Discrimination in the workplace seminars would also be an effective way to educate people about how they can avoid violating the civil rights of their colleagues.

The Need for More Objective Scholarly Publications

Another important step in reducing prejudice is the publication of books and articles that deal with the controversy more accurately. The problem is not that there are too few books skeptical of Darwinism, but that too few scholarly books exist written in defense of a creation or ID world view produced by mainline publishers. I have in my library over 5,000 books that in some way deal with the creation/evolution controversy. Many of them cover much of the same ground, and most were written for non-scientists and published by religious presses. Few of them adequately cover the controversy itself, or review how the scientific debate intersects with science and the problem of theodicy. A market exists for this literature and talented capable scholars can do much to fill it. Unwarranted claims, such as "skeptics of Darwin are anti-science," need to be carefully critiqued with documentation.

Supporting the existing competent literature is also important. One of the better books in this field is *Where Darwin Meets the Bible: Creationists and Evolutionists in America* by Larry A. Witham.[947] This book has earned the endorsement of many academics, from Edward J. Larson (the Pulitzer-prize-winning author of two books on the controversy) to professor emeritus David M. Raup of the University of Chicago, and even anti-creationist Eugenie C. Scott (Executive Director for the *National Center for Science Education*).

Witham objectively evaluates the *conflict* between the two world views, helping the reader to understand the relevant issues, frequently by citing authorities on both sides of the conflict. Most important, he cuts through the propaganda so frequently encountered in this issue. Witham presents the facts, but it requires some discernment on the part of the reader to understand the *implications* of those facts. His well-documented research cuts through scores of false misconceptions, stereotypes, and deliberate misrepresentations that typify much of the writing coming from those in the Darwinist camp.

Witham notes that the problem in most all cases is not a debate over the facts. He gives this example: When the human genome sequencing was completed in June of 2000, Cal Tech president David Baltimore boldly stated that this effort "should be, but won't be, the end of creationism," whereas theists concluded that the enormous amount of information in the genome (that, and the fact it turned out to be more complex than once believed) raised new and major doubts about the ability of Darwinian mechanisms to produce such prodigious amounts of ordered information.[948] Support for organizations that critique Darwinism is a first start, as is inviting speakers to churches, schools,

---

947 Witham, 2002.
948 Witham, 1996, p. 269.

clubs and service organizations, such as Rotary International, to help support the production and dissemination of scholarly works that critically evaluate Darwinism.

The Free Speech Issue

Another result of the war against Darwin Doubters is that the free speech of everyone —especially students, teachers, and professors—has come under assault and has suffered tremendously:

> Take a look at the state of free speech on our school campuses. Teachers and students alike are watering down their remarks to the same muddy gray for fear of offending some sensitive soul.[949]

An example of lack of free speech on one campus is the following state-ment by a science student:

> As a biology major we get evolution on a daily basis, and to me that's an alternative religion. I've never seen a discussion of evolution and religion by students in a class. I just think there's a distinction between understanding the theory and believing it. You have to know the theory to have an intel-ligent discussion about it. This class is definitely hostile toward religion. The professor said that 'anyone with a brain can see evolution is true.' I've wanted to forget this. I know I've got a brain, and it bothers me that he would influence others this way.[950]

As the many case studies in this book document, educators are frequently being required to "believe" or "accept" the tenets of evolution as a condition of being qualified to teach it. This special and pernicious treatment is not applied to educators who teach other topics such as Marxism or other concept that students need to learn about. This requirement for a litmus test of "belief" also qualifies as blatant discrimination, since a similar requirement does not exist for educators who teach other topics. What qualifies an educator is how well he can present a topic to his students, regardless of whether he happens to subscribe to

---

949   Crier, 2002, p. 26.
950   Cherry et al., 2001, p. 71.

what he is teaching them. An economics teacher would be remiss in his duties if he failed to adequately acquaint his students with various investment strategies, and a marketing professor would likewise be less than helpful if he only taught his students one marketing tactic. Most people acknowledge this line of reasoning, yet, Darwin Doubters are treated differently. Why should it be a crime to present students with ideas that challenge evolution—especially at the university level? Why should an educator be required to hide from his students the fact that there *is* a controversy among scientists on this issue that has nothing directly to do with "religion" as many ID opponents claim?

Unfortunately, many science professors and activists are adamant that merely understanding evolution is *not* adequate grounds for functioning as a science educator. Some professors (such as Cailliet, Patterson, and Dini) have gone on record as actually *requiring acceptance of* evolution as grounds for academic advancement and eventual placement as a professional in the sciences, and that failure to categorically make such a statement of faith should result in severe penalties, sanctions, and restrictions. There is a need to oppose any such actions at every level possible.

Seek Enforcement of Existing Laws

The appropriate response to this problem is to bring the commonality and seriousness of the problem to the attention of both the public and the authorities whenever it occurs. We can do this by ensuring that the public insists that our government and constabularies enforce existing anti-discrimination laws. Religious and viewpoint discrimination is illegal, and vigorous efforts are obviously necessary to fight it, both on the part of those discriminated against and as well as the various law and policy enforcement officials. This is the only way that the existing laws will be taken seriously and enforced. Increased public awareness is immensely important in dealing with this problem. In addition, precedent-setting appellate court cases are important to reduce the likelihood that employers in the future will discriminate against Darwin skeptics.

Enforcement of anti-discrimination laws means that those who engage in illegal discrimination activities should suffer damages, lawyer's costs, etc.—if this occurred, most employers would think twice before discriminating. They currently perceive that the likelihood of a conviction in a religious discrimination case is extremely low, and for this reason they often do not hesitate to discriminate. They can easily cover their tracks, often have high-paid attorneys at their disposal, and are able to win cases by delay tactics or skirting the law.

To their credit, many individuals *are* concerned about the civil liberties and the rights of individuals, even those with whom they personally disagree. In reviewing several religious discrimination cases, I have discovered that it is not uncommon to find persons who are active in defending the rights of religious minorities clearly disagree with the beliefs of those whom they defended. Their support comes from their conviction that all persons have the right to hold a set of beliefs, even if unpopular, if they are sincerely held and are protected by law.

The anti-religious bias of certain segments of American society was vividly reflected in an exchange between the Supreme Court justices and the *Lamb's Chapel* attorneys. Statements by Supreme Court justices in the case are decidedly relevant to the creation-evolution issue. The church had requested school space to show a film titled *Turn Your Heart Towards Home* by child psychologist James Dobson to parents and other interested persons during after-school hours. The school censored the entire meeting because of the film's alleged "religious" content. When Supreme Court justice White questioned *why* the school objected, school attorney John Hoefling stated the film had religious overtones that would move the state toward "entanglement" with religion, adding that, "It was too close to proselytizing."[951]

The case was such a blatant an example of discrimination that even the *American Civil Liberties Union* and *Americans United for Separation of Church and State* filed an Amicus brief *in favor* of *Lamb's Chapel*, concluding that allowing the group to show the film is "unlikely to be perceived as a government endorsement of religion."[952] The Chapel's court brief concluded that since only non-school hours were involved, showing the film was denied "not because of the 'subject' it wanted to discuss—'the protecting and strengthening of family relationships'"—but because it discussed that subject *from a religious perspective.*

In view of Justice Brennan's ruling that "once the government permits discussion of certain subject matter, it may not impose restrictions that discriminate among viewpoints on those subjects," Justice Clarence Thomas asked the school's

---

951   McManus, 1993, p. 1.
952   McManus, 1993, p. 1.

attorney "What if there was to be a debate between a religious voter versus an atheist on the family?"[953] The school's attorney responded that the debate would be prohibited because an openly religious person is involved. Thomas then queried, "What if there were ten atheists debating one minister so the minister could not dominate the situation?" Hoefling indicated that this too would be disallowed because the religious world view—and *only* the religious world view—is to be totally excluded from the public schools, even in after-school activities.[954]

Jay Sekulow, the attorney for *Lamb's Chapel*, concluded that this position openly favors the nonreligious and discriminates against religious persons—and the Supreme Court justices agreed. Justice O'Connor even asked if it was really "neutral" to prohibit "only persons with a religious perspective"—while allowing the other side to present their views—and she openly asked, "But are anti-religious perspectives permitted?" The school's attorney replied, "Yes."

In response to this answer, she reiterated, "So is that neutral?" Justice Stevens went even further asking, "Are left-wingers neutral? What if communists and socialists wanted to speak?" Hoefling admitted that he had no objection to any of these views—the *only* views that were disallowed were those traditionally labeled religious (and evidently primarily Christian). This exchange motivated Sekulow to state, "Atheists are in. Agnostics are in. Communists are in. But, religious people are not in! Only one side of the debate can be heard."[955] The same is true in the creation-evolution controversy.

Justice Scalia also perceptively noted the hypocrisy of this position, stating that he felt it was widely accepted that "a lack of religious institutions" would result in "more people to mug me and rape my sister." In view of the dramatic increase of crime in the United States in the 1990s—we now have close to the highest crime rate of any country in the world—Scalia asked, "How is this new regime working?" The audience understood the point—the results of a society that has banished religious values and views from public life does not seem to have worked very well and "gales of laughter burst across the august colonnaded court chamber."[956]

Realizing that this is true, much can be done to deal with this problem. Churches can become involved as they did in the civil rights movement (and a

---

953 McManus, 1993, p. 19.
954 McManus, 1993, p. 19.
955 McManus, 1993, p. 19.
956 McManus, 1993, p. 19.

major reason for the success of the civil rights movement was due to the involvement of the churches). Another step is to invite your congressperson to your church or community organization and discuss their views on discrimination against Darwin skeptics. A more direct way is to circulate petitions to get the academic freedom issue on the ballot. Some other practical suggestions readers can undertake to help remedy the problems posed in this book include.

1. If possible write articles critical of Darwinism under a pseudonym.

2. Work to make the tenure review process fair and equable by changing the rules in academia for achieving tenure. The criteria should be standardized across the board and tenure voting results made public. Educators should be expected to meet certain *objective* criteria - and if they meet that criteria, tenure should be awarded. Personal dislike of a colleague or their (alleged or otherwise) 'religious' beliefs should not be sufficient to deny them tenure. A sliding scale could be applied to each category including teaching research and service, and extra credit applicable for stellar performance. It should *never* be possible for an educator to be denied tenure based solely on a faculty vote if all the other criteria have been met, and this is especially true if the tenure requirements have been exceeded.

3. Check out the academic freedom clauses in faculty contracts at local colleges and universities and make sure you agree with it. If none exists, then propose one or encourage your college or university to propose a fair one, then monitor how well they adhere to it.

4. Emeritus or senior professors need to take younger professors under their wing and leverage their influence whenever and wherever possible.

5. Take steps to make your voice heard in editorials, at school board meetings, etc. Become informed on the issues and take a stand with others who are in a position to lose their jobs or take heat because they are Darwin Doubters.

The Danger of Inaction

When I presented some of the concerns in this book to a tenured professor teaching science at a secular university, he felt I was overreacting. That there were many cases of religious discrimination, he was quite sure. How was one to know for certain that intolerance against Darwin Doubters was the main reason for termination? I assured him that in most all of the cases I had examined, I knew that this was the major reason for termination, denial of promotion, or withholding of awarding an earned degree. Even if one were to eliminate the questionable cases, we would still be left with many hundreds of terminations due to intolerance each year. The professor responded, "Well, that may be so, but I have excellent student ratings, a number of publications, and am in the upper quarter of our department in merit ratings for performance and productivity, so I am not worried."

A few weeks later I received a phone call from my friend. He told me that he had just been fired due to his doubts about Darwin. As Cal Thomas concluded over two decades ago:

> I have become convinced that Secular Humanism is not our greatest enemy. Our greatest enemy is the apathy of people of faith. We say we believe certain things. We memorize hundreds of Bible verses. We attend church three times a week. But we live as practical atheists.
>
> Our problem is that we have not extended our religious faith beyond the private areas of church and home and out into the culture as salt and light... Our religious life should touch all of our life or it isn't worth much...Do we write letters to the editor to express our viewpoints? Do we attend public school board meetings and voice our concerns? Are we intimidated when someone accuses us of violating church-state separation, or do we hand them a copy of the Constitution and say, "Please show me where that appears?" (It does appear in the old Soviet Constitution, by the way—article 124.)
>
> No, Secular Humanism isn't the ultimate enemy. We are. We could use a little less noise about the evil Secular Humanists and a lot more involvement by our own people in our own country. As our old comic strip friend Pogo once observed, "We have met the enemy and he is US"[957]

---

957   Cal Thomas, 1983, p. 20.

The issue of how we respond to Darwin Doubters in our culture is a flash-point for how well our culture is walking its talk of freedom. We can say we are a free country, that freedom of speech and freedom of religion are some of our most cherished ideals – but if we allow those who could care less about those freedoms to continue unchallenged in their illegal and what I consider to be unscrupulous practices, then it's just talk. When such people are attacked for exercising their freedoms, they need to be defended. What part will you play in their defense?

Conclusion

This chapter has tried to summarize the major findings of this study and offer some practical suggestions on what can be done to effectively address the problem of discrimination against Darwin Doubters. It is the beginning of a comprehensive effort to document the problem and work towards solving it. This book's website

http://www.slaughterofthedissidents.com

will further document this problem, add more practical suggestions, and include copies of original documents supporting many of the case studies included in this book (as well as new cases). If readers experience employment or other problems due to their doubts about Darwinism they may consult the website for help and more information.

Index

A

B

D

F

I

J

K

L

M

N

O

P

R

S

T

U

V

W

Y

BIBLIOGRAPHY

Updates to this bibliography will be posted periodically as a PDF document at:
www.slaughterofthedissidents.com/biblio/

<u>*Important note about internet references in this bibliography:*</u> Many times you will find internet sources are missing when you go to visit a web site using the reference we've listed below (information gets moved frequently on the internet). This is why we started adding the last date of successful access after most of them. With that date in hand, you can go back in time using the web site located at http://www.archive.org and nearly always access the cited information.

A.

Addicott, Jeffrey F. 2002. "Storm Clouds on the Horizon of Darwinism: Teaching the Anthropic Principle and Intelligent Design in the Public Schools." *Ohio State Law Journal,* Vol. 63: 1507.

ACLJ. 1999. "Biology Teacher Removed Due to Religious Beliefs." ACLJ *News Release.* June 1. http://findarticles.com/p/articles/mi_m0EIN/is_1999_June_1/ai_54767918 (as of 06/09/08)

———. 2000. "ACLJ Files Appeal in Case of Minnesota Biology Teacher Removed for Criticizing Darwin." July 24. http://findarticles.com/p/articles/mi_m0EIN/is_2000_July_24/ai_63633530 (as of 06/09/08)

Achenbach, Joel. 2001. "The World According to Wells." *Smithsonian,* 32(1):111–124. April.

Achtemeier, Gary L. 2000. "Small-School Snobbery?" *World Magazine,* March 3.

Ackerman, Paul. 1998. Letter from Paul Ackerman to Jerry Bergman, dated August 25.

American Association of University Women (AAUW). 2004. *Tenure Denied: Cases of Sex Discrimination in Academia.* AAUW Educational Foundation. http://www.aauw.org/research/tenuredenied.cfm (as of 04/11/08).

American Civil Liberties Union (ACLU). 1986. *A Special Two-Year Report on the ACLU's Defense of the Bill of Rights Against the Attack of the Reagan Administration and Its Allies.* October.

Adler, Jonathan. 2008. "Anti-Evolution Teaching as Academic Freedom." In The Volokh Conspiracy weblog, May 2. http://volokh.com/posts/1209736087.shtml (as of 05/17/08).

Adler, Mortimer J. 1940. *Problems for Thomists: The Problem of Species*. New York: Sheed and Ward.

———. 1957. *What Man Has Made of Man*. New York: Ungar.

———. 1967. *The Difference of Man and The Difference It Makes*. New York: Holt, Rinehart and Winston.

———. 1970. *The Time of Our Lives: The Ethics of Common Sense*. New York: Holt, Rinehart and Winston.

———. 1977. *Philosopher at Large: An Intellectual Autobiography 1902–1976*. New York: Collier-Macmillan

———. 1980. *How to Think about God: A Guide for the 20th-Century Pagan*. New York: Macmillan

———. 1990. *Truth in Religion: The Plurality of Religions and the Unity of Truth*. New York: Collier-Macmillan.

———. 1993. "A Philosopher's Religious Faith." *In Philosophers Who Believe: The Spiritual Journeys of 11 Leading Thinkers*, edited by Kelly James Clark, pp. 203-221. Downers Grove, IL: InterVarsity Press.

———, and V.J. McGill. 1963. "Darwin: The Origin of Species" and "Darwin: The Descent of Man." In *Biology, Psychology, and Medicine*, pp. 183–216 and 217–251. Chicago: Encyclopaedia Britannica.

Affannato, Frank E. 1986. "A Survey of Biology Teachers' Opinions About the Teaching of Evolutionary Theory and/or the Creation Model in the United States in Public and Private Schools." Ph.D. dissertation, University of Iowa.

Aguillard, D. 1999. "Evolution Education in Louisiana Public Schools: A Decade Following *Edwards v. Aguillard.*" *The American Biology Teacher*, 63(3):182–188.

Aldrich, K.J. 1999. "Teachers' Attitudes toward Evolution and Creationism in Kansas Biology Classrooms, 1991." *Kansas Biology Teacher*, 81(1):20–21.

Allen, Frederick. 2005. "They Made America." *Invention & Technology*, 20(3):26–35. Winter.

Aleksander, Igor. 1989. "Asking Questions." *Nature*, 342:310. Nov. 16.

Altemeyer, Bob, and Bruce Hunsberger. 1997. *Amazing Conversations: Why Some Turn to Faith and Others Abandon Religion*. Amherst, NY: Prometheus Books.

Aman, John. 2003. "Intelligent Design Theology Challenges Darwin in Schools." *Coral Ridge Ministries' IMPACT Newsletter*, August.

Anderberg, Clifford W. 1953. *The Impact of Evolution on Dewey's Theory of Knowledge and the Critics of Dewey.* Madison, WI: University of Wisconsin.

Anderson, Alan. 2003. Feedback. *New Scientist*, 179:56. August 30.

Anderson, David E. 1990. "Rulings Cause Alarm for Religious Officials." *Bryan Times*, July 13, p. 9.

Anderson, Jason and Hans Dieter-Sues, eds. 2007. *Major Transitions in Vertebrate Evolution.* Indianapolis, IN: Indiana University Press.

Anderson, Kirby. 1987. "Fundamentally Dangerous." *Today's Banner*, May, p. 12.

Andrew, E.R. 1980. "NMR Imaging of Intact Biological Systems". *Philosophy Transactions of the Royal Society of London*, 289:471–481.

Anonymous. 1980. Editorial. *Probe Ministries Newsletter*, January, pp. 1–2.

———. 1982. "Seeds of Terror." *Discover Magazine*, 3(3):81. March.

———. 1986. Editorial. *Fort Wayne Journal-Gazette*, Aug. 19, p. 4.

———. 1987. "Creationism at Issue: High School Teacher Fired." *Liberty Report*, Summer, pp. 1–4.

———. 1991. "Anti-abortionists File Lawsuit" *Fairfield Daily Ledger*, pp. 12–13.

———. 1992. "The Story of Dr. Raymond Damadian." *Decision Magazine*, Sept.

———. 1994a. "Creationism Costs Job." *The Tampa Tribune*, April 13.

———. 1994b. "Teacher Fired." *The Journal-Gazette*, April 13.

———. 1994c. "Teacher Defends Creationism." *The Toledo Blade*, April 15, p. 9.

———. 1995. Editorial. *Probe Ministries Newsletter*, pp. 1-2.

———. 1996. "Dr. Raymond Damadian: Insights from the Pioneer of the MRI." *Physician*, May/June.

———. 1999. "Science Evolves into Lawsuit: Teacher Says Assignment by School Violates His Religious Freedom." *The Blade* (Toledo, Ohio). Sunday, October 17, Section A, p. 21.

———. 2000a. "Anti-Creationists Threaten Another Teacher's Liberty." http://www.answersingenesis.org/docs2/4350news7-26-2000.asp (as of 04/11/08).

———. 2000b. "Pacific Northwest Heats Up with Evolution Controversies!" http://www.answersingenesis.org/docs/4227news2-25-2000.asp (as of 04/11/08).

———. 2001. "Feature: Evolution and Intelligent Design." *Religion & Ethics Newsweekly*, September 28, Episode 504. http://www.pbs.org/wnet/religionandethics/week504/feature.html (as of 04/11/08).

———. 2002a. "Christian Colleges: Give Us Liberty; Secular Educators Have It Backward: Faith Statements *Promote* Academic Freedom." *Christianity Today*, Editorial Section, 46(8):24–25.

———. 2002b. "Teaching the Curriculum or the Truth." *Creation Bulletin*. November. http://www.tccsa.tc/bulletins/200211 (as of 04/11/08).

———. 2003. *Project Steve*. National Center for Science Education. http://www.ncseweb.org/resources/articles/3541_project_steve_2_16_2003.asp

———. 2005. "Creationism Has No Place in Schools." *Bristol Herald Courier*, Sunday, June 12.

———. No date [A]. "Darwinism in Education." http://www.straight-talk.net/evolution/education.htm

———. No date [B]. "Science or Myth? A Documentation History of Events. The Burlington-Edison Committee for Science Education. Defeating the Discovery Institute—A Blow by Blow Account." http://www.scienceormyth.org/history.html (as of 04/11/08).

———. No date [C]. *Faculty Handbook*. Office of the Executive Vice President and Provost, Iowa State University. http://www.provost.iastate.edu/faculty/handbook/faculty_handbook/

Ankerberg, John, and John Weldon. 1998. *Darwin's Leap of Faith: Exposing the False Religion of Evolution*. Eugene, OR: Harvest House.

Answers in Genesis. 2003. "The Dark Side of 'Evolutionary Politics." 2 pp. http://www.answersingenesis.org/docs2003/0321uni_persecution.asp?vPrint=1 (as of 04/11/08).

Applebome, Peter. 1996. "Creationism Won't Die Out as Theory of Human Origin." *New York Times*, Sunday, March 10, p. A6

Asimakoupoulos, Greg. 2003. "Ben Carson: A Doctor in Patient Clothing." *Physician*, 15(4):4–6. July–August.

Asimov, Isaac. 1972. *Asimov's Biographical Encyclopedia of Science and Technology: The Lives and Achievements of 1195 Great Scientists from Ancient Times to the Present Chronologically Arranged*. New York: Doubleday.

———. 1982. "The Case Against Creation." *Humanist in Canada*, (15)1:2–4.

———. 1984. "Is Big Brother Watching?" *The Humanist*, 44(4):6–10. July–Aug.

Associated Press. 1981. "76% for Parallel Teaching of Creation Theories." *The San Diego Union*, Nov. 18, p. A15.

———. 2004. "Famous Atheist Now Believes in God." ABC News. http://www.simpletoremember.com/vitals/atheist_believes_in_god.htm (as of 06/09/08)

Ault, Larry. 1981. "State Witness Calls Overton Closed-minded." *Arkansas Democrat*, December 15.

Avalos, Hector. 2004. "The Flaws in Intelligent Design." *Iowa State Daily*, October 22.

———. 2008. Review of *The Privileged Planet: How Our Place in the Cosmos is Designed for Discovery*, by Guillermo Gonzalez and Jay W. Richards. http://www.talkreason.org/PrinterFriendly.cfm?article=/articles//Avalos.cfm

Axe, Doug, Brendan W. Dixon, Philip Lu. 2008. "*Stylus*: A System for Evolutionary Experimentation Based on a Protein/Proteome Model With Non-Arbitrary Functional Constraints." PLoS ONE, 3(6): e2246, June 4. http://www.plosone.org/article/info%3Adoi%2F10.1371%2Fjournal.pone.0002246

Ayala, Francisco. 1994. *Creative Evolution*. New York: James and Bartlett.

B.

Babinski, Edward, ed. 1995. *Leaving the Fold: Testimonies of Former Fundamentalists*. Amherst, NY: Prometheus.

Bainbridge, William Sims, and Rodney Stark. 1980. "Superstitions: Old and New." *Skeptical Inquirer*, 4(4):18–31.

Baker, Hunter. 2006. "Amazing Outrage: Baylor Denies Beckwith's Tenure." *The Reform Club*, Friday, March 24.

Baker, William R. 1994. "Evolution Theory is Just That." *News-Sun* Local/State Section, April 21, p. 15A.

Barker, Dan. 2003. *Losing Faith in Faith*. Madison, WI: Freedom from Religion Foundation

Barna, George. 1991. *What Americans Believe: An Annual Survey of Values and Religious Views in the United States*. Ventura, CA: Regal Books.

Bartlett, Thomas. 2006. "Still Fighting." *The Chronicle of Higher Education*, September 8, p. A5.

Barton, Sir Derek. 1977. "Introductory Remarks." In *Biologically Active Substances: Exploration and Exploitation*, edited by D.A. Hems. New York: John Wiley and Sons.

Bartz, Paul A. 1987a. "What Really Happened at the 'Latest Scopes Trial'?" *Bible Science Newsletter*, July, p. 2.

———. 1987b. "The Urgent Need to Fight Creationism." *Bible Science Newsletter*, 25(8):1,2,5. Aug.

Bartz, Paul A. 1983. Letter from Paul Bartz to Jerry Bergman, dated June 16.

Bass, Thomas. 1990. Interview with Richard Dawkins. *Omni*, 12(4):58–89.

Bates, Vernon Lee. 1976. *Christian Fundamentalism and the Theory of Evolution in Public School Education: A Study of the Creation Science Movement*. Los Angeles, CA: University of California.

Becard, Andre. 1982. "Creationism." *American Atheist*, May, p. 8.

Beck, Ray Howard. 1986. "Limits on Religious Liberty Widespread in 1985." *The United Methodists Review*, Jan. 10, p. 3.

Beckwith, Francis J. 2002. "A Liberty Not Fully Evolved? The Case of Rodney LeVake and the Right of Public School Teachers to Criticize Darwinism." *San Diego Law Review*, pp. 1311–1326. Fall. http://www.discovery.org/articleFiles/PDFs/Beckwith_on_ID_in_SDLR.pdf (as of 04/24/08)

———. 2003. *Law, Darwinism, and Public Education: The Establishment Clause and the Challenge of Intelligent Design*. Lanham, MD: Rowman and Littlefield Publishers.

———. 2005. "Letter to the Editor." *Academe*, May–June.

Begley, Sharon. 1996. "Heretics in the Laboratory: Can a Creationist Be a Good Scientist? And *vice versa*." *Newsweek*, September 16, p. 82.

Behle, J. Gregory. 1987. "Creationism and the Nature of Science." *The Chronicle of Higher Education*, Apr. 15, p. 49.

Bellah, Robert N., and Frederick E. Greenspahn, eds. 1987. *Uncivil Religion: Interreligious Hostility in America*. New York, NY: Crossroad.

Belloc, Hilaire. 1926a. *A Companion to Mr. Wells's "Outline of History."* London, Sheed and Ward.

———. 1926b. *Mr. Belloc Still Objects to Mr. Wells's "Outline of History."* London, Sheed and Ward.

Belz, Joel. 2001. "'Intimidation' or Invitation? University of GA Profs Slapped for After-Hours Faith and Science Talks." *World*, February 3, p. 8.

Ben-Maimon, Moses. 1946. *Guide of the Perplexed of Maimonides*. New York: Hebrew Publishing Co. Part II, Ch. 30.

Berg, Lyn. 1998. Letter from Lyn Berg to Jerry Bergman, dated September 9.

Bergaust, Erik. 1976. *Wernher von Braun*. Washington, DC: National Space Institute.

Berger, Peter L. 1970. *A Rumor of Angels: Modern Society and the Rediscovery of the Supernatural*. Garden City, NY: Anchor Books.

———, and Thomas Luckmann. 1990. *The Social Construction of Reality: A Treatise in the Sociology of Knowledge*. New York, NY: Anchor Books.

Bergin, Mark. 2005. "Mad Scientists." *World*, August 20, p. 23.

———. 2006. "Baylor Boot." *World*, 21(36):27. September 23.

———. 2007. "Publish and Perish: Iowa State Denies Tenure to an Intelligent Design Advocate with Impeccable Credentials." *World*, 22(19):24. May 26.

Bergman, G. Merle. 1985. "The Professor Who Lost His Job." *Liberty*, Vol. 80, No. 3, p. 28. May–June.

Bergman, Jerry. 1979. *Teaching About the Creation-Evolution Controversy*. Bloomington, Indiana: Phi Delta Kappa Educational Foundation.

———. 1980a. "Public Opinions Regarding Creation and Evolution." *Origins*, 7(1):42–44.

———. 1980b. "Peer Evaluation of University Faculty." *College Student Journal Monograph*, Vol. 4, No. 3. January.

———. 1981. "The Attitudes of College Students in Teacher Education Programs toward the Teaching of Evolution and Creation." *NACM Newsletter*, No. 22.

———. 1984a. "The New Minorities to Hate." *Contrast*, 3(2):1–5. Mar.–April.

———. 1984b. "Religious Discrimination in Academia." *Universitas*, Apr., p. 2.

———. 1984c. "Religious Discrimination in Academia." *Christians in Education*, Spring, p. 16.

———. 1984d. *The Criterion: Religious Discrimination in America*. Richfield, MN: Onesimus Pub. Co.

———. 1984e. Review of "Betrayers of Truth: Fraud and Deceit in the Halls of Science" by William Broad and Nicholas Wade. Published in *Creation Research Society Quarterly*, 21(2):89–91. Sept.

———. 1985a. Review of "History of Modern Creationism." *Journal of the American Scientific Affiliation*, 37(3):187–188. Sept.

———. 1985b. "Discrimination Against Creationists Is Becoming More Insidious." *The Christian News*, Feb. 4, p. 7.

———. 1986. "'Creation Science' in U.S. Supreme Court." *Academe*, Sept.–Oct., p. 4.

———. 1989. *Why the American Justice System Does Not and Cannot Work: An Evaluation of the Justice Administrative System.* Defiance, Ohio: Defiance College.

———. 1990. "The Ray Webster Case." *Contrast*, 9(1):1–4. Jan.–Feb.

———. 1993a. "Censorship in Secular Science: The Mims Case." *Journal of the American Scientific Affiliation*, 45(1):37–43. March.

———. 1993b. "Censorship in Academia: The Professor Richard H. Bube Case". *Contra Mundum*, 9:42–44.

———. 1994. "Arno A. Penzias: Astrophysicist, Nobel Laureate." *The Journal of the American Scientific Affiliation*, 46(3):183–187. Sept.

———. 1995a. "Wernher Von Braun: The Father of Modern Space Flight; A Christian and a Creationist." *Creation Research Society Quarterly*, 32(1):7–10. June.

———. 1995b. "A Study of Court Cases Related to Creationism." Unpublished manuscript.

———. 1996. "Religious Beliefs of Scientists: A Survey of the Research." *Free Inquiry*, 16(3):41–46,54. Summer.

———. 1999. "The Attitude of Various Populations Toward Teaching Creation and Evolution in Public Schools." *Creation Ex Nihilo Technical Journal*, 13(2):118–123.

———. 2001. "Homosexuality, Disease, and Creationism." *Creation Research Society Quarterly*, 38(2):68–74.

———. 2003. "The Galileo Myth and the Facts of History." *Creation Research Society Quarterly*, 39(4):226–235, March.

———. 2006a. Literature review in progress.

———. 2006b. Paper in preparation.

———. 2007a. "The Privileged Planet: Showdown at the Smithsonian." *Creation Matters*, 12(1)1,4–7. Jan–Feb.

———. 2007b. "Darwinism: Survival without Purpose." *Acts & Facts*, Nov., pp. 10–12.

———. 2007c "The Trilobite eye: A Wonder of Complex Design." *Creation Science Dialogue*, Vol. 34, No.3/4. December. http://www.create.ab.ca/articles/trilobite.html

———, and George Howe. 1990. *Vestigial Organs Are Fully Functional.* Terra Haute, IN: CRS Books.

———, and Kevin Wirth. In preparation. *The Creation/Evolution Controversy.* Annotated Bibliography. Vols. I and II. New York: Garland.

Berkman, Michael B., J.S. Pacheco, and E. Plutzer (2008). "Evolution and Creationism in America's Classrooms: A National Portrait." *PLoS Biol* 6(5): e124

Berman, Marshall. 2003. "Intelligent Design Creationism: A Threat to Society, Not Just Biology." *The American Biology Teacher*, 65(9):646–648. Nov–Dec.

Bernstein, David. 2003. *You Can't Say That! The Growing Threat to Civil Liberties from Antidiscrimination Laws*. Washington, DC: The Cato Institute.

Bernstein, Jeremy. 1979. "The Nobel Prize in Physics." In *The World of Science*, pp. 280–282. Woodbury, NY: Bobley.

———. 1984. *Three Degrees Above Zero: Bell Labs in the Information Age*. New York: Charles Scribner's.

Bethell, Tom. 1986. "Creationists and Authoritarians." *The Wall Street Journal*, Dec. 9, p. 32.

Beuttler, Fred W. 2001. "Why Can't We Be Sensible about Darwinism?" *Research News*, April, p. 12.

Beverley, James. 2005. "Thinking Straighter: Why the World's Most Famous Atheist Now Believes in God." *Christianity Today*, April, pp. 80–83.

Bevins, George M. 1983. *The Creationist Movement: Science, Religion and Ideology*. Western Michigan University. Unpublished Paper.

Beyak, Trudy. 1996a. "Is It Possible to Be a World-Class Scientist and a Creationist?" *Abbotsford & Mission News*, Saturday, Sept. 21.

———. 1996b. "Damadian's Dream Machine." *Abbotsford & Mission News*, Saturday, Sept. 21.

Bhattacharjee, Yudhijit. 2003. "Evolution Battle on Campus." *Science*, 300:247.

———. 2005a. "Kansas Gears Up for Another Battle Over Teaching Evolution." *Science*, 308:626. April 29.

———. 2005b. "Smithsonian Gives Grudging OK to Film Backing ID Argument." *Science*, 308:1526. June.

Bird, Wendell. 1978. "Freedom of Religion and Science Instruction in Public Schools." *The Yale Law Journal*, 87(3):575–570. Jan.

———. 1979. "Freedom from Establishment and Unneutrality in Public School Instruction and Religious School Regulation." *Harvard Journal of Law and Public Policy*, 2:125–205.

———. 1982. "Creation Science and Evolution Science in Public Schools: A Constitutional Defense under the First Amendment." *Northern Kentucky Law Review*, 9(2).

————. 1989. *The Origin of Species Revisited.* Two volumes. New York, NY: Philosophical Library.

Birney, D.S., G. Gonzalez, and D. Oesper. 2006. *Observational Astronomy.* 2nd edition. New York: Cambridge University Press.

Bishop v. Aaronov. 1990. 723 F. supp. 1562 (ND Ala).

Bishop, Phillip. 1991. Letter from Phillip Bishop to Jerry Bergman, dated October 25.

Bishop, Phillip A. v. O. H. Delchamps, Jr., et al. 1991. Brief submitted to the Supreme Court of the United States. Oct. term.

Bishop v. Delchamps, Jr., et al. 1991. U.S. Supreme Court. Oct. term. 1991. Case 91–286.

Black, Jim Nelson. 2004. *Freefall of the American University: How Our Colleges Are Corrupting the Minds and Morals of the Next Generation.* Thomas Nelson.

Bland, Aileen. 1984. "Biology Topics in Introductory Science Courses in Accredited Bible Colleges." Ed.D. dissertation, East Texas State University.

Blank, Lisa, and Hans O. Andersen. 1997. "Teaching Evolution: Coming to a Classroom Near You?" *National Center for Science Education Reports,* 17(3):10–13.

Blanshard, Paul. 1963. *Religion and the Schools: The Great Controversy.* Boston: Beacon Press.

Blanshard, Paul. 1976. "Religion and the Schools: The Great Controversy." *The Humanist,* Mar.–April.

Blinkhorn, Steve. 2001. "Yes, But What's It For? The Current State of Language Can Make It Difficult to Discuss Evolution in an Accurate Way." *Nature,* 412:771.

Bliss, Richard B. 1978. "A Comparison of Two Approaches to the Teaching of Origins of Living Things to High School Students in Racine, Wisconsin." Ed.D. dissertation, University of Sarasota [now Argosy University].

Bliss, Richard. 1982. Letter from Richard Bliss to Jerry Bergman, dated October 3.

Bloom, Allan. 1987. *The Closing of the American Mind: How Higher Education Has Failed Democracy and Impoverished the Souls of Today's Students.* New York, NY: Simon and Schuster.

Bohanon, Ceil. 2006. "Evangelicals Assert Right to Be Heard." *The Journal-Gazette,* May 2, p. 9A.

Bolyanatz, Alexander H. 1984. "The Creation/Evolutionary Controversy: More Heat Than Light." *Anthropology Newsletter,* 25(7):1–2.

Bork, Robert H. 1996. *Slouching Towards Gomorrah: Modern Liberalism and American Decline.* New York: Regan Books/Harper Collins.

Bottum, Joseph. 2006. "Down in Waco…" *First Things* blog archive, March 27. http://www.firstthings.com/onthesquare/?p=215 (as of 04/11/08).

Bowen, Ezra. 1985. "A Philosopher for Everyman." *Time*, May 6, p. 68.

———. 1987. "The Last Great Aristotelian." *Time*, 129(18):84–85. May 4.

Bowler, Peter. 1990. *Charles Darwin.* Cambridge, MA: Basil Blackwell.

Boyle, Alan. 2006. "Einstein and Darwin: A Tale of Two Theories." Interview with Neil deGrasse Tyson. MSNBC.com, May 2.

Bradley, Walter. 2005. "Letter to the Editor." *Academe*, May–June.

Bragg, Melvyn. 1998. *On Giants' Shoulders: Great Scientists and Their Discoveries— from Archimedes to DNA.* New York: Wiley.

Braun, Marcus. 1985. "Creation vs. Evolution." *Sword of the Lord*, Oct. 18, p. 14.

Brenner, M. Harvey. 1983. "Suicides Soar among Jobless." *Newslink of the American Society of Suicidology*, 9(1).

———. 1976. *Mental Health and the Economy.* Cambridge MA: Harvard University Press.

Bridgestock, Martin. 1985. "Creation Science: You've Got to Believe It to See It!" *Ideas in Education*, July.

Broad, William, and Nicholas Wade. 1982. *Betrayers of Truth: Fraud and Deceit in the Halls of Science.* New York: Simon and Schuster.

Brown, Andrew. 1999. *The Darwin Wars: The Scientific Battle for the Soul of Man.* New York: Simon and Schuster.

Brown, Harold O., ed. 1990. "And in the USSR?" *The Religion and Society Report*, 7(8). Aug.

Brown, Ira V. 1947. *Lyman Abbott, Christian Evolutionist: A Study in Religious Opinion.* Cambridge, MA: Harvard University Press.

Brown, Jim, and Ed Vitagliano. 2003. "Professor Dumped Over Evolution Beliefs." *AgapePress Christian News Service, Spring.* http://headlines. agapepress.org/archive/3/112003a.asp (as of 06/09/08)

Brown, Jim, and Jody Brown. 2005. "UC System Sued for Alleged Discrimination Against Christian-Based Education." *AgapePress*, August 31.

Browne, Malcolm. 1978. "Clues to the Universe's Origin Expected." *New York Times*, Mar. 12, p. 1.

———. 1979. "The Nobel Prize in Physics." In *The World of Science.* Woodbury, NY: Bobley Publishing Company.

Brumfiel, Geoff. 2005a. "Cast Out from Class: Intelligent Design– Who Has Designs on Your Students' Minds?" *Nature*, 434:1062–1065. April 28.

———. 2005b. "Evolutionist Row Makes Museum Ditch Donation." *Nature*, 435:725, June.

———. 2007. "Darwin Skeptic Says Views Cost Tenure." *Nature*, 447:364, May 24.

Bryson, Nancy. 2003. Interview of Nancy Bryson by Jerry Bergman.

———. 2004. Interview of Nancy Bryson by Jerry Bergman.

Bube, Richard. 1971. "We Believe in Creation." *Journal of the American Scientific Affiliation*, 23(4):121–122. Dec.

———. 1989. "Obtaining Approval for a Seminar on Science and Christianity in a Secular University: A Case Study." *Journal of the American Scientific Affiliation*, 41(4):206–212.

———. 1990. Interview of Richard Bube by Jerry Bergman.

Buckner, Edward M. 1983. *Professional and Political Socialization: High School Science Teacher Attitudes on Curriculum Decisions, in the Context of the "Scientific" Creationism Campaign.* Microfilm version of author's Ph.D. dissertation from Georgia State University. Ann Arbor, MI: *University Microfilms International.*

Buderi, Robert. 1989. "Small Changes, Big Fuss." *Nature*, 342:219. Nov. 16.

Budziszewski, J. 2002. "The Second Tablet Project." *First Things*, 124:23–31. June/July.

Buell, Jon. 1990. "Friend's Letter." *Foundation for Thought and Ethics Newsletter*, June, pp. 1–2.

Bunk, Steve. 1998. "In a Darwinian World, What Chance for Design?" *The Scientist*, 12(8):3.

Burdick, Clifford. 1979. "Documentation of Discrimination against Creationist Students." Unpublished manuscript, Tucson, AZ.

Business Wire. 2004. FOX News Channel Garners More Than Half of Cable News Audience During Second Quarter; FNC Captures Nine Out of Top Ten Cable News Shows. Released June 29, 2004. http://findarticles.com/p/articles/mi_m0EIN/is_2004_June_29/ai_n6087812 (as of 042808)

Butler, John A. 1958. *Science and Human Life.* New York: Basic Books.

Buzzard, Lynn, and Samuel Ericsson. 1982. T*he Battle for Religious Liberty.* Elgin, IL: David C. Cook.

Byers, Stacia. 2003. "Chemistry Teacher Resigns amid Persecution." *AIG Newsletter.*

Bytwork, Alvin. 1996. God's University Battles. Unpublished manuscript.

C.

Cahn, Robert W. 2000. "The Tree of Ignorance: Evolution Emerges Unscathed from the Battle of Creation." *Nature*, 406:935–936. August 31.

Cain, Cindy Wojdyla. 1988. "Teacher Defends Creation Science; Freedom of Speech is Issue: Webster." *Joliet Herald-News*, Sunday, Mar. 27, Section 1, p. 4.

Campbell, Bernard G. 1982. *Humankind Emerging*. Third edition. Boston: Little, Brown and Co.

Campbell, John, and Stephen Meyer. 2003. *Darwinism, Design, and Public Education*. East Lansing, MI: Michigan State University Press.

Campbell, Neil A., Lawrence G. Mitchell, and Jane Reece. 1994. *Biology: Concepts and Connections*. Redwood City, CA: Benjamin/Cummings Co.

Candisky, Catherine. 2005. "Evolution Debate Re-emerges: Doctoral Student's Work was Possibly Unethical, OSU Professors Argue." *Columbus Dispatch*, June 9, NEWS, p. 1C.

Carnes, Tony. 2000. "Design Interference: William Dembski fired from Baylor's Intelligent Design Center." *Christianity Today*, December 4.

Carr, Herman. 1993. "Sharper Images of MRI's Origins." *Physics Today*, 46(1):94. January.

―――. 2004. "Field Gradients in Early MRI" *Physics Today*, 57(7):83. July.

Carrier, Richard. 2004. "Antony Flew Considers God ... Sort Of." *The Secular Web*. http://www.secweb.org/asset.asp?AssetID=369 (as of 04/11/08).

Carson, Ben, with Gregg Lewis. 1999. *The Big Picture: Getting Perspective on What's Really Important in Life*. Grand Rapids, MI: Zondervan.

Carter, Stephen L. 1993. *The Culture of Disbelief: How American Law and Culture Trivialize Religious Devotion*. New York, NY: Basic Books.

Cashill, Jack. 2005. "Explosive Memo Reveals Darwinist Strategy for Kansas." *WorldNetDaily*, Friday, May 6.

Casti, John L., and Anders Karlqvist, eds. 1999. *Mission to Abisko: Stories and Myths in the Creation of Scientific "Truth."* Reading, MA: Perseus Books.

Catholic World News. 1999. "Teacher Sues after Being Removed for Religious Beliefs." http://www.cwnews.com/news/viewstory.cfm?recnum=10431 (as of 04/11/08).

Caudill, David Stanley. 1989. *Disclosing Tilt: Law, Belief and Criticism.* Amsterdam: Free University Press.

Caudill, Edward, ed. 1989. *Darwinism in the Press: The Evolution of an Idea.* Hillsdale, NY: Lawrence Erlbaum Assoc. Publishers.

————. 1997. *Darwinian Myths: The Legends and Misuses of a Theory.* Knoxville, TN: The University of Tennessee Press.

Cavanaugh, Michael Arthur. 1983. *A Sociological Account of Scientific Creationism: Science, True Science, Pseudoscience.* Pittsburgh, PA: University of Pittsburgh.

————. 1985. "Scientific Creationism and Rationality." *Nature,* 315:185. May 16.

Cawood, Hap. 1994. "WSU's Reasons for Firing Have Had Odd Evolution." *Dayton Daily News,* Editorial, April 16, p. 10A.

Caylor, Bob. 1997. "Creation or Evolution?" *The News Sentinel,* Jan 2, pp. 1A, 5A–6A.

Chain, Ernst. 1970. *Social Responsibility and The Scientist in Modern Western Society.* London: The Council of Christians and Jews.

Chain, Ernst, H. Florey and N. Heatley. 1949. *Antibiotics.* New York: Oxford University Press.

Chapman, C. 2002. "Earth's Attic." *Nature,* 419:791–794.

Chapman, Matthew. 2000. *Trials of the Monkey: An Accidental Memoir.* New York: Picador.

Chasan, Alice. n.d. "Intelligent Design *Is* Testable". *Beliefnet Blog* (Interview of Michael Behe). http://www.beliefnet.com/story/181/story_18157_1.html (as of 06/09/08)

Cherry, Conrad, Betty A. Deberg, and Amanda Porterfield. 2001. *Religion on Campus.* Chapel Hill, NC: The University of North Carolina Press. Assisted by William Durbin and John Schmalzbauer.

Choron, Jacques. 1972. *Suicide.* New York: Scribner's.

Christensen, Harold T., and Kenneth L. Cannon. 1978. "The Fundamentalist Emphasis at Brigham Young University: 1935–1973." *Journal for the Scientific Study of Religion,* 17(1):53–58. March.

Christian Legal Society. "CLS in the Supreme Court." *Briefly,* Sept. 1992, p. 2.

Chuvala, Bob. 1996. "Images of the Body. Reflections of the Soul." *Physician,* 8(3):4–7.

Clark, Edward L. 1953. "The Southern Baptist Reaction to the Darwinian Theory of Evolution." Ph.D. dissertation, Southwestern Baptist Theological Seminary.

Clark, Ronald W. 1985. *The Life of Ernst Chain: Penicillin and Beyond.* New York: St. Martin's Press.

Cleveland Plain Dealer. 2002. "Ohio Issue Poll." June.

Cohn, Frederick. 1907. *Evolutionism and Idealism in Ethics.* Lincoln, NB: University of Nebraska.

Cole, John. 1994. "Biology Firing Kills Academic Freedom." *The Guardian,* April 20, p.5.

Colson, Charles W. 2004. *Born Again.* Old Tappan, NJ: Chosen Books.

————, and Nancy Pearcey. 1999. *How Now Shall We Live?* Wheaton, IL: Tyndale.

Combs, Harry, with Martin Caidin. 1979. *Kill Devil Hill: Discovering the Secret of the Wright Brothers.* Boston, MA: Houghton Mifflin.

Combs, Roberta. 2007. "Washington Weekly Review." *Washington Weekly Review,* May 25.

Comfort, Nathaniel C. 2007. *The Panda's Black Box: Opening Up the Intelligent Design Controversy.* Baltimore, MD: The Johns Hopkins University Press.

Conklin, Paul. 1998. *When All the Gods Trembled: Darwinism, Scopes, and American Intellectuals.* Lanham, Maryland: Rowman, & Littlefield.

Connoley, Bonita. 1998. Letter from Bonita Connoley to Jerry Bergman, July 29.

Cook, Terry. 1983. "Creation-Evolution Battles." Portland, Oregon: Citizens for Public Education.

Coren, Michael. 1993. *The Invisible Man: The Life and Liberties of H. G. Wells.* New York: Atheneum.

Coughlin, Ellen. 1981. "Ironic Detachment of Religious Scholars." *The Chronicle of Higher Education,* December, p. 20.

Coulter, Ann. 2006. *Godless: The Church of Liberalism.* New York: Crown Forum.

Courtois, Stéphane, Nicolas Werth, Jean-Louis Panné, Andrzej Paczkowski, Karen Bartosek, and Jean-Louis Margolin. 1999. *The Black Book of Communism: Crimes, Terror, Repression.* Cambridge, MA: Harvard University Press.

Cowherd, David C. 1994. "WSU Doesn't Understand that Science is Independent of Religion." *News-Sun* Local/State Section, April 21, p. 15A.

Coyne, Jerry. 2001. "Creationism by Stealth." Review of Jonathan Wells's *Icons of Evolution: Science or Myth? Nature,* 410:745-46.

————. 2002. "Intergalactic Jesus." *London Review of Books,* 24(9):1–6. May.

————. 2003. "Gould and God." *Nature,* 422:813–814.

———. 2005. "Thanks to the Smithsonian, a Brushfire Is Out." *evoldir* (an evolutionary biology newsgroup), June 6.

Crawford, Elisabeth. 1984. The Beginnings of the Nobel Institution. The Science Prizes 1901–1915. New York: Cambridge University Press.

Craycraft, Kenneth. 1999. *The American Myth of Religious Freedom*. Dallas, Texas: Spence Publishing Company.

Crease, Robert. 1991. "Bell Labs: Shakeout Follows Break-up." *Science*, 252:1480–1482. June 14.

Crick, Francis. 1981. *Life Itself: Its Origin and Nature*. New York, NY: Simon and Schuster.

———. 1988. *What Mad Pursuit: A Personal View of Scientific Discovery*. New York: Basic Books.

———. 1990. "How I Got Inclined Towards Atheism." In *Atheist Centre Golden Jubilee: International Conference Souvenir*. http://www. positiveatheism.org/india/s1990a01.htm (as of 04/11/08).

———. 2003. Quoted by Matt Ridley in "Do Our Genes Reveal the Hand of God?" *The Telegraph*, March 20. http://www.telegraph.co.uk/connected/ main.jhtml?xml=/connected/2003/03/19/ecfgod19.xml (as of 04/11/08).

Crier, Catherine. 2002. *The Case against Lawyers*. New York: Broadway Books.

Crocker, Caroline. 2008. "Do ID Proponents Get Persecuted in the Academy?" *Salvo*, Issue 4 p. 84. Winter.

Crowther, Robert. 2006. "In Ohio Darwinist Admits Plan to Burn Evolution Critic." *Evolution News and Views*. January 10.

Culp, G. Richard. 1975. *Remember Thy Creator*. Grand Rapids, MI: Baker Book Co.

Cuozzo, Jack. 1998. *Buried Alive*. Green Forrest, AK: Master Books.

Curtis, Robert. 1993. *Great Lives: Medicine*. New York: Scribner's. pp. 77-90.

Cushman, Candy. 2001. "Heresy Trials: Is a Vocal Christian Inherently Unqualified to Teach Biology?" *World*, 16(31):18–21. August 18.

D.

Damadian, Raymond. 1971. "Tumor Detection by Nuclear Magnetic Resonance." *Science*, 151:1151–1153. March 19.

———. 1988. "FONAR; BETA-2000M Fixed-Site Magnetic Resonance Scanner." New York, NY: FONAR Corp.

———. 1994a. "The Story of MRI." *The Saturday Evening Post*, 266(3):54–57.

———. 1994b. "America's Forgotten Asset." *The Saturday Evening Post*, 266(3):58–77.

———, et al. 1976. "Field Focusing Nuclear Magnetic Resonance (FONAR): Visualization of a Tumor in a Live Animal." *Science*, 194(4272). Dec. 24.

———, M. Goldsmith, and L. Minkoff. 1977. "NMR in Cancer: XVI. Fonar Image of the Live Human Body." *Physiological Chemistry and Physics*, 9:97.

Davis, H. Francis. 1967. *A Catholic Dictionary of Theology*. London: Nelson.

Davis, Percival and Dean H. Kenyon/ 1989. *Of Pandas and People*. Richardson, TX: Foundation for Thought and Ethics. Sixth printing, 2005

Davison, John. 1984. "Semi-meiosis as an Evolutionary Mechanism." *Journal of Theoretical Biology*, 111:725-735.

———. 2005. "What It Means to Be an Anti-Darwinian at the University of Vermont" http://www.uvm.edu/~jdavison/uvm-antidarwinian.html

Darwin, Charles. 1871. *The Descent of Man*. London: John Murray.

Darwin, Charles. 1993. *The Correspondence of Charles Darwin*. Vol. 8. Edited by Frederick Burkhardt. New York: Cambridge University Press.

Dawkins, Richard. 1976. *The Selfish Gene*. New York: W. W. Norton.

———. 1986. *The Blind Watchmaker: Why the Evidence of Evolution Reveals a Universe without Design*. New York: W. W. Norton.

———. 1989. "Review of *Blueprints: Solving the Mystery of Evolution*." *New York Times*, Apr. 9, pp. 34–35, Section 7, Col. 2.

———. 1995. *River out of Eden*. New York: Basic Books.

———. 1999. "You Can't Have It Both Ways: Irreconcilable Differences?" *Skeptical Inquirer*, July/August, pp. 62–63.

———. 2003. *A Devil's Chaplain*. Boston: Houghton Mifflin.

Dean, Cornelia. 2007. "Believing Scripture but Playing by Science's Rules." *The New York Times*, February 12, pp. A1,A12.

DeHart, Roger. 2004. "My Story." Unpublished manuscript written by Roger DeHart and provided to Jerry Bergman. All contents and quotations attributed to DeHart in this chapter have been approved by DeHart.

Dembski, William A. 1996. "Teaching Intelligent Design as Religion or Science?" *The Princeton Theological Review*, April, pp. 14–18.

———. 1998. "Science and Design." *First Things*, 86:21-27. Oct. Found on *First Things* web site at http://www.firstthings.com/article.php3?id_article=3580 (as of 04/11/08).

————. 1999. "Is Intelligent Design Testable? A Response to Eugenie Scott. American Scientific Affiliation. With Eugenie's Response. http://www.asa3.org/ASA/topics/Apologetics/2001Dembsk1.html (as of 06/09/08)

————. 2000. Press release, October 19. http://www.texscience.org/files/ dembski-baylor.htm (as of 04/11/08).

————. 2001a. "Is Intelligent Design Testable?" ARN Website, January 24. http://www.arn.org/docs/dembski/wd_isidtestable.htm (as of 04/11/08).

————. 2001b. "Introduction." In *Signs of Intelligence*, edited by William A. Dembski and James M. Kushiner. Grand Rapids, MI: Brazos Press.

————. 2002. *No Free Lunch*. New York: Rowan & Littlefield.

————. 2004a. *The Design Revolution*. Downers Grove, IL: InterVarsity Press.

————. 2004b. Correspondence and personal interviews from William Dembski to Jerry Bergman, various dates.

————, and Jay Richards. 2001. *Unapologetic Apologetics*. Downers Grove, IL: InterVarsity Press.

————, and Jonathan Wells. 2008. *The Design of Life*. Dallas, TX: Foundation for Thought and Ethics.

Dennett, Daniel. 1995. *Darwin's Dangerous Idea*. New York: Simon and Schuster.

Denton, Michael. 1986. *Evolution: A Theory in Crisis*. Bethesda, MD: Adler and Adler.

————. 1998. *Nature's Destiny: How the Laws of Biology Reveal Purpose in the Universe*. New York: Free Press.

Dershowitz, Allen. 1995. "Sending Hate Anonymously." *Bryan Times*, May 13, p. 4.

Desmond, Adrian. 1997. *Huxley: From Devil's Disciple to Evolution's High Priest*. Reading, MA: Addison-Wesley.

Devine, Daniel. 2008. "Final Denial." *World*. March 8, 15, 2008.

Deyrup, Mark, and John MacDonald. 1982. "Countering the Creationists." *Bioscience*, 32(4):245.

DeWolf, David, John G. West, Casey Luskin, and Jonathan Witt. 2006. *Traipsing into Evolution: Intelligent Design and the Kitzmiller v. Dover Decision*. Seattle, WA: The Discovery Institute.

DeWolf, David K., Stephen C. Meyer, and Mark Edward DeForrest. 2000. "Teaching the Origins Controversy: Science, Or Religion, Or Speech?" *Utah Law Review*, Vol. 2000:39. http://www.arn.org/docs/dewolf/utah. pdf (as of 04/11/08).

DeYoung, Gerry. 1990. Letter from Gerry DeYoung to Jerry Bergman. n.d.

Diamond, Jared. 1985. "Voyage of the Overloaded Ark." *Discover*, 6(6):82–92.

———. 1996. "Daisy Gives An Evolutionary Answer." *Nature*, 380:103. March 14.

Dickman, Howard, ed. 1993. *The Imperiled Academy*. New Brunswick, NJ: Transaction.

Dickson-LaPrade, Daniel. 2008. "A Victory over 'Intelligent Design' in Oklahoma." *Reports of the National Center for Science Education* 27(5-6):7-8. September–December.

Discovery Staff. 2005. "Attack on OSU Graduate Student Endangers Academic Freedom." *Center for Science and Culture*, June 13. http://www.discovery.org/scripts/viewDB/index. php?command=view&id=2661 (as of 04/11/08).

DiSilvestro, Robert. 2005. "An 'Intelligent Design Thesis'?" *The Scientist*, August 29, p. 8.

Donohue, William A. 1985. *The Politics of the American Civil Liberties Union*. New Brunswick, NJ: Transaction.

———. 1994. "Culture Wars against the Boy Scouts." Society, 31(4): 59-68.

Donovan, Hedley. 1978. "An Echo from the Creation." *Time*, 112:108. Oct. 30.

Dose, Klaus, ed. 1974. *The Origin of Life and Evolutionary Biochemistry*. New York: Plenum Press.

Downey, Roger. 2002. "Not the Whole Truth." *Seattle Weekly*, May 16–22. http://www.seattleweekly.com/features/0220/news-downey.shtml (as of 04/11/08).

Draper, John William. 1875. *History of the Conflict between Religion and Science*. New York: D. Appleton and Company.

Dreher, Rod. 2006. "Baylor Wars, Again." *Dallas Morning Views*, March 24.

Dreifus, Claudia. 2002. "An Insatiably Curious Observer Looks Back on a Life in Evolution." *The New York Times*, Apr. 16, 2002.

Drinan, Robert. 1963. *Religion, the Courts, and Public Policy*. New York: McGraw-Hill.

DuCharme, Keith. 2004. "Science and Philosophy Merge in Professor's 'Privileged Planet.'" *Iowa State Daily*, March 25.

Duffy, Cathy. 1995. *Government Nannies*. Gresham, Oregon: Noble Publishing Association.

Duke, W.C. 1982. "The American Scientific Affiliation and the Creation Research Society: The Creation-Evolution Issue." Ph.D. dissertation, Southwestern Baptist Theological Seminary.

Duro, Carol and Peter. 1985. *You Don't Know My God*. Yorktown, NY: Emmanuel Christian Ministries.

Dwyer, Jim. 1993. "The Quirky Genius Who Is Changing Our World." *Parade Magazine*, Oct. 10, pp. 8,10.

E.

Easterbrook, Gregg. 1997a. "Science and God: A Warming Trend." *Science*, 277:890–893.

———. 1997b. "Of Genes and Meaninglessness." *Science*, 277:892. August 15.

Ecker, Ronald L. 1990. *Dictionary of Science and Creationism*. Buffalo, NY: Prometheus.

Edelman, Charles. 1984. "Freedom from Religion." *American Atheist*, Feb., p. 28.

Edelson, Ed. 1973. "How Scientists Are Detecting Cancer with Supermagnets." *Popular Science*, March, pp. 99–100,116.

Editors. 1991. "Report." *Context*, 23(9):1. May 1.

Edwards v. Aguillard. 1987. 482 U.S. 578.

Eglin, P.G. 1983. "Creationism versus Evolution: A Study of the Opinions of Georgia Teachers." Ph.D. dissertation, Georgia State University.

Egnor, Michael. 2008. "What Happens When You Write Positive Blogs about ID?" *Salvo*, Issue 4, pp. 85–86. Winter.

Eidsmoe, John. 1984. *God and Caesar*. Westchester, Ill.: Crossway Books.

Einstein, Albert. 1970. "Autobiographical Notes". Translated by Paul Schilpp. In *Albert Einstein: Philosopher-Scientist*. LaSalle, IL: Open Court.

Eldredge, Niles. 1982. *The Monkey Business: A Scientist Looks at Creationism*. New York, NY: Washington Square Press.

———. 1985. *Timeframes*. Princeton, NJ: Princeton University Press.

———. 1995. *Reinventing Darwin*. New York, NY: John Wiley & Sons.

———. 2000. *The Triumph of Evolution and the Failure of Evolution*. New York: Freeman.

Elgin, Paula Garrison. 1983. *Creationism vs. Evolution: A Study of the Opinions of Georgia Science Teachers*. Georgia State University.

Ellis, William E. 1986. "Creationism in Kentucky: The Response of High School Biology Teachers." In *Science and Creation: Biological, Theological and Educational Perspectives*, edited by W.R. Hanson, pp. 72–91. New York: Macmillan.

Ellwanger, Paul. 1984. *CFE Newsletter*, published occasionally.

———. 1983. Letter from Paul Ellwanger to Jerry Bergman, dated June.

Employment Practices Solutions. 2004. "But Could He Dissect a Frog? Suit Says Biology Teacher Treated Unfairly Because of Religious Views." *Employment Practices Solutions.*

Epstein, Helen. 1979. *Children of the Holocaust: Conversations with Sons and Daughters of Survivors.* New York, NY: G.P. Putnam's Sons.

Ericsson, Samuel. 1982. "Is Your Home Really Your Castle?" *Liberty*, 77(2):6. Mar.–Apr.

Etz, Don. 1994. "Questions Raised." *News-Sun* Local/State Section, April 21, p. 15A.

Evans, Harold. 2004. *They Made America: From the Steam Engine to the Search Engine.* New York: Doubleday.

Eve, Raymond A., and Francis B. Harold. 1991. *The Creationist Movement in Modern America.* Boston, MA: Twayre Publishing.

———. 1994. "Who are the Creationists? An Examination of a Conservative Christian Social Movement in International Perspective." *Population Review*, 38(1–2):65–76.

Ewing, Jania. 1994. "Adam, Eve Still Rate with Medical Students." *The Age* (Melbourne, Australia), April 11.

F.

Fair, Charles. 1994. "Shades of Big Brother." *News-Sun* Local/State Section. April 21, p. 15A.

Fairhurst, Alfred. 1923. *Atheism in our Universities.* Cincinnati, OH: The Standard Pub. Co.

Falwell, Jerry. 1982. Fund-raising letter dated July 10.

Fant, Kenne. 1993. *Alfred Nobel: A Biography.* New York: Arcade Publishing.

Farrar, Steve. 2003. "Overlooked Nobel Advertises His Plight." *Times Higher Education*, December 12, p. 1. http://www.timeshighereducation.co.uk/story.asp?storyCode=181826&sectioncode=26

Federal Register. Vol. 54, No. 213, 10-31-1980, pp. 72611–72615.

Feduccia, Alan. 1999. *The Origin and Evolution of Birds*. New Haven and London: Yale University Press.

Feldman, Amy. 1988. "Monkey See, Monkey Do." *Inside Chicago*, July–August, p. 17.

Ferris, Timothy. 1988. *Coming of Age in the Milky Way*. New York, NY: William Morrow

Feucht, Dennis. 1999. "Nobelist William Phillips Addresses ASA99 at John Brown University." *Newsletter of the American Scientific Affiliation*. 41(5):1,3.

Fezer, Karl D. 1983. "Competency and Controversy: Issues and Ethics on the University Pseudoscience Battlefield." *The Skeptical Inquirer*, 8(1):2–5.

———. 1984a. "Would You Hire a Creationist?" *Creation-Evolution Newsletter*, 4(3):22. May–June.

———. 1984b. "More from Kofahl." *Creation-Evolution Newsletter*, 4(4):22. July–Aug.

Filler, Aaron. 2004. *Do You Really Need Back Surgery?* New York: Oxford University Press.

Finniss, Gary M. 1985. "We're All Related to Apes." *USA Today*, Aug. 17, p. 7.

Fischer, Robert. 1981. *God Did It, But How?* LaMirada, CA: Cal Media.

Fisher, Mark. 1994a. "WSU Prof Creates Controversy." *Dayton Daily News*, April 12, pp. 1A, 8A.

———. 1994b. "Prof Failed to Prepare Students, WSU Says." *Dayton Daily News*, April 13, p. 2B.

———. 1994c. "Ousted Instructor Gains Support." *Dayton Daily News*, April 14, p. 1B.

———. 1994d. "Students Back Fired WSU Teacher." *Dayton Daily News*, April 15, pp. 1B–2B.

———. 1994e. "WSU Instructor Applauded; Creationism Controversy Overblown, Say Some Students." *Dayton Daily News*, April 15, p. 1B.

Fisher, Richard Taylor. 1989. *The Effects of Education on Creationist Beliefs among High School Science Teachers*. Arlington, TX: University of Texas.

Fix, William R. 1984. *The Bone Peddlers: Selling Evolution*. New York: Macmillan.

Flacks, William L. 1985. "The Professor Who Lost His Job." *Liberty*, 80(4):28. July–Aug.

Flanigan, Jackson, et al. 1995. "Pennsylvania vs. EEOC: Tenure Decision and Confidentiality." *The NEA Higher Education Journal*, 11(1):79–95. Spring.

Flank, Lenny, Jr. 2007. *Deception by Design: The Intelligent Design Movement in America*. St Petersburg, FL: Red and Black Publishers.

Fleming, Robert. 1990. "Artificial Intelligence." *Omni*, 12(4):28. Jan.

Flew, Antony. 1998. Interview. *Free Inquiry*, 18(1):22. Winter.

————, and Gary R. Habermas. 2005. "My Pilgrimage from Atheism to Theism: An Exclusive Interview with Former British Atheist Professor Antony Flew." *Philosophia Christi*, Winter.

Flood, Robert. 1986. *The Rebirth of America*. Philadelphia, PA: Arthur DeMoss Foundation.

Foley, Eileen. 2003. "The Fanatics Don't Get What Science is About." *Toledo Blade*, Sect. A, p. 11.

Folger, Janet. 2005. *The Criminalization of Christianity*. Sisters, OR: Multnomah Publishers.

Foreman, Chris. 1987. "Science, Censorship, and Omni Magazine." *Origins Research*, 10(1):1–2. Spring–Summer.

Forrest, Barbara, and Glenn Branch. 2005. "Wedging Creationism into the Science Academy." *Academe*, January–February.

Forrest, Barbara, and Paul R. Gross. 2004. *Creationism's Trojan Horse: The Wedge of Intelligent Design*. New York: Oxford University Press.

Forster, Arnold. 1970. *The Trouble Makers*. Westport, CT: Negro Universities Press.

Fort Wayne Newspapers. 2003. "MRI Pioneers Win Nobel Prize." *Journal-Gazette*, Oct. 7, 2003, p. A3.

Fortey, R.A., D.E.G. Briggs, and M.A. Wills. 1996. "The Cambrian Evolutionary "explosion":Decoupling cladogenesis from morphological disparity." *Biological Journal of the Linnean Society* 57:13–33

Foster, Julie. 2000a. "Unnatural Selection: Science Teachers Under Fire for Criticizing Evolutionary Theory." *WorldNetDaily*, March 3. http://www.worldnetdaily.com/news/article.asp?ARTICLE_ID=17819 (as of 04/11/08).

————. 2000b. "Biology Professor Forced Out. Pointed to Flaws in Theory of Evolution, Encouraged Critical Thinking." *WorldNetDaily*, Friday, April 14. http://www.wnd.com/news/article.asp?ARTICLE_ID=17856 (as of 06/09/08).

————. 2000c. "Teachers' Union Opposes Evolution Bill. Ohio Legislator Doesn't Want Theory Presented as 'Fact.'" *WorldNetDaily*, Sunday, May 7. http://www.worldnetdaily.com/news/printer-friendly.asp?ARTICLE_ID=17873 (as of 06/09/08).

———. 2000d. "Evolution Critic Censored. Teacher Punished for Pointing Out Flaws in Darwin's Theory." *WorldNetDaily*, Tuesday, July 25. http://www.worldnetdaily.com/news/printer-friendly.asp?ARTICLE_ID=17931 (as of 06/09/08).

Fox News Channel. 2002. "Supreme Court Won't Hear Case on Teaching Evolution." Tuesday, January 8.

Frair, Wayne. 1978. "Report of the 1978 Board of Directors Meeting." *Creation Research Society Quarterly*, 15(2):121–122. September.

———. 1998. Letter from Wayne Frair to Jerry Bergman, dated September 9.

———. 2005. Letter from Wayne Frair to Jerry Bergman.

———, and Percival Davis. 1983. *A Case for Creation*. Third edition. Chicago, IL: Moody Press

Francis, Daniel, and Brenda Francis. 1994. "WSU Is Too P.C." *News-Sun*, Local/State Section, April 21, p. 15A.

Freedomforum.org. June 3, 1999. "Teacher Claims Minnesota School District Won't Allow Him to Teach Biology." Associated Press. http://www.freedomforum.org/templates/document.asp?documentID=8700& printerfriendly=1 (as of 04/11/08).

———. May 9, 2001. "Minnesota Appeals Panel Rebuffs Teacher's Bid to Challenge Evolution in Classroom." Associated Press. http://www.freedomforum.org/templates/document.asp?documentID=13894 (as of 04/11/08).

Freeman, Steve. 1986. "Teacher Finds Hate for Creationism." *Aurora Beacon News*, April 6, p. 4.

Freund, Philip. 1965. *Myths of Creation*. New York: Washington Square Press.

Friedman, Robert Marc. 2001. *The Politics of Excellence: Behind the Nobel Prize in Science*. New York: Henry Holt (W. H. Freeman).

Frymire, Philip. 2000. *Impeaching Mere Creationism*. San Jose, CA: Writers Club Press.

Fuerst, Paul. 1984. "University Student Understanding of Evolutionary Biology's Place in the Creation/Evolution Controversy." *Ohio Journal of Science*, 84(5):218–228.

Fuller, Steve. 1996. "Does Science Put an End to History, or History to Science?" *Social Text*, Nos. 46/47, pp. 27–42. Spring–Summer.

Furst, Randy, and Kurt Chandler. 1986. "St. Cloud Teacher Argues Right to Teach Creationism." *Minneapolis Star and Tribune*, Dec. 11, pp. 1, 14.

Fung, William Y. 1944. *The Theory of Values in Emergent Evolution*. New York, NY: New York University.

Futuyma, Douglas. 1983. *Science on Trial.* New York: Pantheon Books.

———. 1986. *Evolutionary Biology.* Sunderland, MA: Sinauer.

G.

Gabler, James. 1982. "Creationists At Large." *Moody Monthly*, 89(9):50–55. May.

Gallup, George, Jr., and David Poling. 1980. *The Search for America's Faith.* Nashville, TN: Abingdon.

Gallup, George, Jr., ed. 1993. "Creationism Survey." *Gallup Poll Monthly*, Sept., p. 28.

———, and D. Michael Lindsay. 1999. *Surveying the Religious Landscape: Trends in U.S. Beliefs.* New York: Morehouse Publishing.

Gardner, Martin. 1957. *Fads and Fallacies in the Name of Science.* New York: Dover.

Garrison, Greg. 1991. "The Preachy Professor." *Liberty*, July–Aug, pp. 2–4.

Gatewood, Willard B. 1966. *Preachers, Pedagogues and Politicians.* Chapel Hill, NC: University of North Carolina Press.

———. 1969. *Controversy in the Twenties; Fundamentalism, Modernism, and Evolution.* Nashville, TN: Vanderbilt University Press.

Gentry, Robert V. 1986. *Creation's Tiny Mystery.* Knoxville, TN: Earth Science Associates.

Gentz, William, ed. 1986. *The Dictionary of the Bible and Religion.* Nashville, TN: Abingdon.

Gibeaut, John. 1999. "Science or Myth? Evolution of a Controversy." *American Bar Association Journal*, November, pp. 1–6.

Gilbert, Martin. 1985. *The Holocaust: A History of the Jews of Europe during the Second World War.* New York, NY: Holt, Rinehart and Winston.

Gilberti, Walter. 2005. "An Exchange on Science, Evolution and Intelligent Design." World Socialist Web Site. http://www.wsws.org/articles/2005/jul2005/evol-j16_prn.shtml

Gingerich, Owen. 2006. *God's Universe.* Cambridge, MA: Harvard University Press.

Gleick, James, guest ed., and Jesse Cohen, series ed. 2000. *The Best American Science Writing.* New York: The Ecco Press.

Glynn, Patrick. 1997. *God: The Evidence.* Rocklin, CA: Forum.

Goddard, Connie. 1990. "Court Says School May Bar Teaching Creationism." *Publishers Weekly*, 237(47):10. Nov. 23.

Goldberg, Louis P., and Eleanore Levenson. 1935. *Lawless Judges*. New York: Greenwood.

Goldhagen, Daniel Jonah. 1996. *Hitler's Willing Executioners: Ordinary Germans and the Holocaust*. New York: Alfred A. Knopf.

Goldman, Morris. 1970. "A Critical Review of Evolution." *A Science and Torah Reader*. New York: NY: Union of Orthodox Jewish Congregations of America.

Goldman, Steven, ed. 1989. *Science, Technology, and Social Progress*. Bethlehem: Lehigh University Press.

Goldschmidt, Richard Benedict. 1956. *The Golden Age of Zoology*. Seattle, WA: University of Washington Press.

———. 1960. *In and Out of the Ivory Tower: The Autobiography of Richard B. Goldschmidt*. Seattle, WA: University of Washington Press.

Goldsmith, Donald. 1985. *The Evolving Universe*. Menlo Park, CA: Benjamin Cummings.

Gomez, Gina V. 1994. "Scott Disputes University Claims." *Dayton Daily News*, April 15.

Gon III, S.M. 2007. "The question 'Where did Trilobites Come From' is not so simple to answer." Origins of Trilobites. December 29. http://www. trilobites.info/origins.htm (as of 06/14/08).

Gonzalez, Guillermo. 2005. "Misrepresenting Intelligent Design." *The Scientist*, August 29, p.8.

_____, and Jay W. Richards. 2004. *The Privileged Planet: How Our Place in the Cosmos is Designed for Discovery*. Washington, DC: Regnery Publishing.

_____, D. Brownlee, and P. Ward. 2001. "Refuges for Life in a Hostile Universe." *Scientific American*, 285:60–67.

Good, Carter, and Phi Delta Kappa, eds. 1945. *Dictionary of Education*. New York: McGraw-Hill.

Gordon, Bruce L. 2000. "The Polanyi Center Controversy at Baylor University: A Response." *Research News & Opportunities in Science and Theology*, 1(4). December.

Gordon, Larry. 1989. "School Won't Mix Science with Bible." *Los Angeles Times*, Jan. 20, p. 34.

Goss, Richard J. 1994. "The Riddle of the Religious Scientist." *The American Rationalist*, 39(1):105–107. May–June.

Gould, Stephen Jay. 1981. "Creationism." *The New Republic*, Apr. 4, p. 20.

————. 1983. "In Praise of Charles Darwin." In *Darwin's Legacy*, edited by Charles L. Hamrum. San Francisco: Harper & Row. This essay originally appeared in the February, 1982 issue of *Discover* magazine.

————. 1989. *Wonderful Life: The Burgess Shale and the Nature of Life*. NY: W.W. Norton.

————. 1992. "Impeaching a Self-Appointed Judge." *Scientific American*, 267(1):118-121. July.

————. 1997. "Unanswerable Questions." Chapter 3 of *A Glorious Accident*, edited by Wim Kayser, pp. 75–104. New York: W.H. Freeman.

————. 1999. *Rocks of Ages: Science and Religion in the Fullness of Life*. New York: Ballantine.

————. 2000. "What Does the Dreaded "E" Word Mean, Anyway?" *Natural History*, 109(1):28–44.

Gourlay, Walter E. 1962. *Picture Book of Today's Scientists*. New York: Sterling.

Graduate Student "X." 2006. "Tenure Denial as Revenge." *American Spectator Online*, March 27. www.spectator.org/dsp_article.asp?art_id=9583 (as of 04/11/08).

Graffin, Gregory. 2003. *Monism, Atheism, and the Naruralist Worldview: Perspectives from Evolutionary Biology.* PhD dissertation, Cornell University.

————, and William Provine, 2007. "Evolution, Religion and Free Will." *American Scientist*, 95(4):294-297.

Grant, John. 2007. *Corrupted Science: Fraud, Ideology and Politics in Science.* London: Artists and Photographers Press.

Graur, Dan. 2005. "Solidarity with the Flat-Earthers" *Nature*, 435:276. May 19.

Green, Jocelyn. 2008. "ID Tagged: Faculty Member at Iowa State University Denied Tenure for Supporting Intelligent Design." *Christianity Today*, 52(2):15-16.

Greene, Jay E., ed. 1966. *Modern Men of Science*. New York: McGraw-Hill Book Company.

Gregory, Isabella. 2005. www.randi.org/jr/052705a.html

Gregory, Jan, ed. 1993. *Punctuated Equilibrium: A Report of the Academic Freedom Committee; Executive Summary*. San Francisco: San Francisco State University.

Grine, Joanne Del Greco. 1985. *A Study of Creationist Pressure: Strategies against Evolution Instruction in the Public Schools*. Pittsburgh, PA: University of Pittsburgh.

Grose, Vernon. 1995. "Adversary Truth vs. Technical Truth." *Agora*, 3(3):16–21.

————. 2006. *Science but Not Scientists*. Bloomington, IN: Author House.

Grundmeier, Lucas. 2004a. "A Universal Debate." *Iowa State Daily*, October 12.

_____. 2004b. "Professors Question Intelligent Design Theory." *Iowa State Daily*, October 15.

Günther, Markus. 2006. "Did Humans Descend from Monkeys?" *Mannheimer Morgen*, May 10.

Guterman, Simeon L. 1971. *Religious Toleration and Persecution in Ancient Rome*. Westport, CT: Greenwood Press.

Gwynne, Peter. 1978. "Nobel Quartet." *Newsweek*, Vol. 92, pp. 105–106. Oct. 30.

H.

Haas, John. 1971. "Biogenesis: A Reviewed Interest in an Old Question." *Christian Scholar's Review*, 1(4):291–305.

Hafernik, John. 1993. Letter to Dean H. Kenyon, dated June 15.

Hall, Annie. 2005. "OSU Takes Closer Look at Graduate Student's Dissertation." *The Lantern*, June 23.

Hall, Varna. 1975. *The Christian History of the Constitution of the United States of America*. San Francisco, CA: Foundation for Christian Education.

Hammond, John Winthrop. 1924. *Charles Proteus Steinmetz: A Biography*. New York: The Century & Co.

Hamre, James S. 1991. "The Creationist-Evolutionist Debate and the Public Schools." *Journal of Church and State*, 33(4):765–784.

Hand, John Raymond. 1968. *Why I Accept the Genesis Record*. Lincoln, NE: Back to the Bible Broadcast.

Haney, Ken. 1985. "Academic Freedom's Double Standard." *Christian Times*, June 28, pp. 4, 12.

Hannah, James. 1994a. "Wright State Teacher Let Go for Creationist Views." *Springfield (OH) News-Sun*, April 13, p. 3.

_____. 1994b. "Creationism Flap Ignites Debate." *The Bellefontaine Examiner*, April 15, p. 4.

Hardaway, Gary. 2001. "Teacher Collides with ACLU, School World View. Defenders of Darwinism Suppress Data, Teach Falsehoods." *Lynden Tribune*, May 23.

Harlow, Caroline W. 2005. "Hate Crime Reported by Victims and Police." *Bureau of Justice Statistics* (U.S. Department of Justice), November, p. 3. This report presents an extensive breakdown of hate crime statistics. Also available at www.ojp.usdoj.gov/bjs/pub/pdf/hcrvp.pdf (as of 06/05/08).

Hartmann, 2007. "Rapid evolution in early trilobites fueled by high variation." *Geotimes*, July 27. http://www.geotimes.org/july07/article. html?id=WebExtra072707.html

Hartwig, Mark. 1996. "California's New Science Framework: How Firm a Foundation?" *Origins Research*, pp. 2, 8.

_____. 1991. "Christian Prof. Loses Free-Speech Case." In "Academic Freedom" column, *Moody Monthly*, June 24, p. 55.

———, and P.A. Nelson. 1992. *Invitation to conflict: A Retrospective Look at the California Science Framework*. Colorado Springs, CO: Access Research Network.

Hartzler, Harold H. 1991. *A Personal View of ASA*. Paper presented at the ASA conference in 1991. Wheaton, IL: Wheaton College.

Hastings, Tim. 1989. "Teacher Appeals for Freedom: School Provokes New Monkey Trial." In *Caleb: Issues and Answers*, p. 1.

Hauptman, John. 2007. "Rights Are Intact; Vote Turns on Question, 'What Is Science?'" *Des Moines Register*, June 2.

Hawking, Stephen. 1988. *A Brief History of Time; from the Big Bang to Black Holes*. New York: Bantam.

Hazen, Robert M. 1991. *Why My Kids Hate Science*. Newsweek, February 25, p. 7.

Hearn, Virginia, ed. 1974. *What They Did Right*. Wheaton, IL: Tyndale.

———. 1993. "Intelligent Design." *Newsletter of The American Scientific Affiliation*, 35(6): 1–3.

Hedtke, Randall. 2002. *The Great Evolution Curriculum Hoax*. Phoenix, AZ: ACW Press.

Heeren, Fred. 2000. "The Lynching of Bill Dembski." *The American Spectator*, Nov., p. 1.

Hefley, James C. 1976. *Textbooks on Trial*. Wheaton, IL: Victor Books.

Hegstead, Roland. 1980. "Biology Teacher's Job Jeopardized by Insistence of Creation Views." *Liberty*, 75(1):27. Jan–Feb.

Hemmerich, Larry G. 1994. "Word 'Religion' Being Misused." *News-Sun*, Local/State Section. April 21, p. 15A.

Hems, D.A., ed. 1977. *Biologically Active Substances: Exploration and Exploitation*. New York: John Wiley and Sons.

Henke, Kevin R. 2004. *Young Earth Creationists' Hypocrisy on Discrimination*. http://www.noanswersingenesis.org.au/aig_hypocrisy_henke.htm (as of 07/06/04)

Hensley, Dan. 1994. "Evolution Belief Requires Faith." *News-Sun* Local/State Section. April 21, p. 15A.

Herbert, David. 2004. *The Faces of Origins*. London, Ontario: D & I Herbert Publishing.

Herrmann, Robert A. 2003. "… My Book on Intelligent Design and the GGU-model, The General Theory of Everything." http://www. raherrmann.com (as of 04/11/08).

Hess. 2003. "Christian Speech Threatened in the Corporate World." *Citizen*, 17(12):9. December.

Hick, John. 1985. "A Liberal Christian View." *Free Inquiry*, 5(4):40–42.

Hiebert, Rick. 1996. "Darwin Wins Friends in Rome." *British Columbia Report*, Nov. 11, pp. 30–31.

Hill, Alexander, and Chi-Dooh Li. 1995. "Religious Speech in Schools: A Study in Contradictions." *Church and State*, 37(3):623-640.

Hillery, George. 1990. "Develop Research Agenda with Soviets." *Newsletter of Christian Sociological Society*, 17(3):6–7. June.

Hilts, Philip. 1981. Editorial. *Washington Post*, Dec. 3, p. 6.

Himmelfarb, Gertrude. 1962. *Darwin and the Darwinian Revolution*. New York: Norton.

Hinds, Catherine. 1983. "More Than 'A Couple of White Chicks Sitting' Around Talking." *Brown Alumni Monthly*, 83(9):25–29. June–July.

Hirschorn, Michael. 1987. "University Efforts to Censor Newspapers Are on the Increase, Student Editors Say." *The Chronicle of Higher Education*, Apr. 22, pp. 35–37.

Hitchens, Christopher. 2007. *God Is Not Great: How Religion Poisons Everything*. New York: Twelve Publishers.

Hites, Robert W. 1965. "Change in Religious Attitudes during Four Years of College." *Journal of Social Psychology*, 66:51–63.

Hitt, Jack. 1996. "On Earth as It Is in Heaven." *Harper's Magazine*, 293(1758):51–59. Nov.

Hoagland, Mahon, Bert Dodson, and Judith Hauck. 2001. *Exploring the Way Life Works: The Science of Biology*. Sudbury, MA: Jones and Bartlett.

Hodgson, Ronald, and Shu-ping Hodgson. 1994. "A Survey on University Students' Understanding of the Place of Evolutionary Biology in the Creation/Evolution Controversy." *Creation-Evolution*, 34(1):29–37. Summer.

Hofstadter, Richard. 1961. *Academic Freedom in the Age of the College*. New York: Columbia University Press.

Holden, Constance. 1988. "Japanese Views on Science Compared to U.S. Attitudes." *Science*, 240(4850):277.

———. 1993. "'Intelligent Design' at San Francisco State" *Science*, 262:1976–1977.

———. 1996. "Anti-Evolution Bill: Back to the Drawing Board." *Science*, 271:1501. March 15.

———. 2004. "Academia as 'One-Party' System." *Science*, 306:1678. December.

Holland, Earle. 1985. "Creation 'Science': A Survey of Student Attitudes." *Ohio State University Quest*, 7(3):1. Spring.

Holley, I.B., Jr. 1992. Review of "Intellect: Mind over Matter" by Mortimer Adler. *American Scientist*, 80(2):202–203.

Hollis, Donald P. 1987. *Abusing Cancer Science: The Truth about NMR and Cancer*. Chehalis, WA: Strawberry Fields Press.

Holmes, Jay. 1962. *America on the Moon: The Enterprise of the 60s*. Philadelphia, PA: J.B. Lippincott Co.

Hondros, Chris. 1994. "Firing Justified; Biology Class No Place for 'Scientific Creationism' Theory." *Dayton Daily News*, April 22, p. 4.

Hopkins, Andrea. 2007. "Dinosaurs, Humans Coexist in U.S. Creation Museum." *Reuters News Report*. January 15.

Hoppe, Richard. 2005. "ID vs. Academic Integrity: Gaming the System in Ohio." June 7. http://www.pandasthumb.org/pt-archives/001127.html (as of 04/11/08).

Horowitz, David. 2006. *The Professors: The 101 Most Dangerous Academics in America*. Washington, DC: Regnery.

Houppert, Karen. 2005. Professing Faith. *Mother Jones*. 30(7):36–77.

Hoyle, Fred. 1983. *The Intelligent Universe: A New View of Creation and Evolution*. New York: Holt, Rinehart and Winston.

———, and Chandra Wickramasinghe. 1981. *Evolution from Space*. New York, NY: Simon and Schuster.

Hubbard, L. Ron. 1950. *Dianetics*. Los Angeles, CA: The American St. Hill Organization.

Hubbard, Lyle. 2003. "Letters to Editor". *Reports of the National Center for Science Education*, 23(3–4):14. May–Aug.

Hudson, Kathi, ed. "Christian Biology Teacher John Peloza Loses First Round." *Education Newsline*, Apr.–May, 1992.

Hudson, R.P. 1978. "1978 Nobel Prize in Physics." *Science*, 202:962–963. December 1.

Hull, David. 1992. "God of the Galapagos." *Nature*, 352:485–486. August 8.

Hull, David L. 1994. "Science and the Modern World View." *The Quarterly Review of Biology*, Dec., pp. 491–493.

Hunsberger, Bruce. 1978. "Stability and Change during College." *Journal for the Scientific Study of Religion*, 17(2):159–164. June.

Hunter, James Davison. 1987. *Evangelicism: The Coming Generation*. Chicago: University of Chicago Press.

Hurley, Paul. 1970. "100 Years of Hilaire Belloc." *The Catholic Digest*, July, pp. 23–28.

Huxley, Aldous. 1937. *Ends and Means*. New York: Harper and Brothers.

Huxley, Julian. 1942. *Evolution: The Modern Synthesis*. London: Allen & Unwin.

———. 1955. "Evolution and Genetics." Chapter 8 in *What is Science?*, edited by James R. Newman. New York: Simon and Schuster.

Hylden, Jordan L., and John H. Jernigan. 2003. "Leaning Ivory Tower: The Most Troubling Bias among Academics is Not Political but Religious." *Harvard Political Review*, 30(2):13.

I.

ICR Midwest Center Newsletter. 1976. "University Students Hear Scientific Evidence Against Evolution."

Ikenson, Ben. 2004. Ingenious Inventions. New York: Black Dog and Leventhal Publishes

Indo, John. 1981. "Logic for Fundamentalists?" *Free Inquiry*, 2(1):3. Winter.

Industrial Chemist. 1988. "Readers Question Evolution." 9(2):47.

Ingraham, Richard. 1982. "Evolution in Context." *In San Jose Studies*, 8(3), Fall.

Irion, Robert. 2004. "Are Most Life-friendly Stars Older than the Sun?" *Science*, 303:27.

Irwin, James B., with William A. Emerson, Jr. 1973. *To Rule The Night: The Discovery Voyage of Astronaut Jim Irwin*. Philadelphia: A. J. Holman.

J.

Jackson, Wayne. 1981. "In the News." *Reason and Revelation*, Vol. 2, Feb. 1, p. 4.

Jacobs, Troy. 1983. "The Role of Recombinant Genetics in Humanism." *The Humanist*, 43(1):18–20.

Jacobson, Jennifer. 2004. "Conservatives in a Liberal Landscape." *The Chronicle of Higher Education*, LI(5):A8–A11, September 24.

Jacoby, Susan. 2004. *Freethinkers: A History of American Secularism*. New York: Metropolitan Books/Henry Holt.

Jakob, Peter. 1990. *Visions of a Flying Machine*. Washington, DC: Smithsonian Institution Press.

Jaschik, Scott. 1991. "Academic Freedom Could Be Limited by Court Ruling: U.S. Appeals Panel Opposed Action by U. of Alabama against Professor." *The Chronicle of Higher Education*, Apr. 17, p. A23.

———. 2005. "Not So Intelligently Designed Ph.D. Panel." *Inside Higher Ed.*, June 10. http://www.insidehighered.com/news/2005/06/10/osu (as of 04/11/08).

Jennings, Max. 1994. "Teaching Creationism Is Different than Pushing It." *Dayton Daily News*, Editorial, April 13 p. 10A.

Jinkins, J.R, J.S. Dworkin, C.A. Green, J.F. Greenhalgh, M. Gianni, M. Gelbien, R.B. Wolf, J. Damadian, and R.V. Damadian. 2003. "Upright, Weight-bearing, Dynamic-kinetic Magnetic Resonance Imaging of the Spine—Review of the First Clinical Results." *JHK Coll Radiology*, 6:55–74.

Johns, Warren L. 2001. "Darrow for Defense: The Flip Side of Deja Vu." http://creationdigest.com/archives/Archive_2005_Winter/FlipSideofDejaVu.htm

Johnson, Jeanette. 1971. "Basic Research Leads to Radio Signals From Cancer Tissue." *Downstate Reporter*, 2(2):1–4,16. Spring.

Johnson, Phillip E. 1990a. *Evolution as Dogma: The Establishment of Naturalism*. Richardson, TX: Haughton Publishing Company.

———. 1990b. "Unbelievers Unwelcome in the Science Lab; Evolution: Darwinists are Really Fundamentalists Who Would Use Their Enormous Clout to Exclude Creationists." *Commentary, Los Angeles Times*, Nov. 3, p. B7.

———. 1991. *Darwin on Trial*. Washington, DC: Regnery Gateway.

———. 1992. "The Creationist and the Sociobiologist: Two Stories about Illiberal Education." *California Law Review*, 80(4):1071–1090. July.

———. 1993. Letter to Editor. *The Wall Street Journal*, Dec. 15, 1993, p. A15.

———. 1994. "Is God Unconstitutional?" *The Real Issue*, 13(3):1,7–9.

———. 1995a. *Reason in the Balance: The Case against Naturalism in Science, Law, and Education*. Downers Grove, IL: InterVarsity Press.

————. 1995b. "Honesty is the Best Policy: Scientific Naturalism Excludes God from Reality." *The Scientist*, April 17, p. 12.

————. 1997. *Defeating Darwinism by Opening Minds*. Downers Grove, IL: InterVarsity.

————. 1998. *Objections Sustained: Subversive Essays on Evolution, Law and Culture*. Downers Grove, IL: InterVarsity.

————. 2000. *The Wedge of Truth*. Downers Grove, IL: InterVarsity.

————. 2001. "Evolution as Dogma: The Establishment of Naturalism." In *Intelligent Design Creationism and its Critics: Philosophical, Theological, and Scientific Perspectives*, edited by Robert T. Pennock. Cambridge, MA: MIT Press.

Jones, Bob. 1999. Editorial *World*, p. 21.

Jones, E. Michael. 1987. Letter from Michael Jones to Jerry Bergman, n.d.,

Jones, Orson P. 1987. Letter from Orson Jones to Jerry Bergman, dated April 5.

Jones, Steve. 2003. "View from the Lab: A Blast of Hot Air from Bruised Egos." *Daily Telegraph (London)*, October 29, p 18.

Jones, Steve, Robert Martin, and David Pilbeam, eds. 1992. *The Cambridge Encyclopedia of Human Evolution*. Cambridge University Press.

Jonsson, Kjell. 1999. "Einstein at the Amusement Park: The Public Story of Relativity in Swedish Culture." Chapter 7 in Casti and Karlqvist, pp. 101–120.

Joravsky, David. 1970. *The Lysenko Affair*. Cambridge, MA: Harvard University Press.

Judson, Horace Freeland. 1996. *The Eighth Day of Creation*. Cold Spring Harbor Press.

————. 2004. *The Great Betrayal: Fraud in Science*. Orlando, FL: Harcourt, Inc.

Jukes, Thomas. 1980. "Creationism." *BioScience*, Dec.

————. 1993. Letter to Editor. *The Wall Street Journal*, Dec. 15, 1993, p. A15.

————. 1996. "Flight from Reality." *Skeptical Inquirer*, 20(1):50–52. Jan–Feb.

Jungmann T. P. 1983. "Application of sodium dodecyl sulfate electrophoresis of hemolysate to the biochemical systematics of the rockfish sebastes." *Biochemical Systematics and Ecology*, vol. 11, no. 4, pp. 389-395.

K.

Kanengiser, Andy. 2003. "MUW Educator Returned to Post— Division Head to Remain After Row Over Controversial Removal." *Clarion Ledger*, March 15.

Kaplan, Marty. 1996. "Ambushed by Spirituality." *Time*, 147:62.

Kaufman, Matt. 2000. "Don't Challenge Evolution, Teacher Told." *Citizen*, Jan. 5.

Kay, Marshall, and Edwin H. Colbert. 1965. *Stratigraphy and Life History*. New York: Wiley.

Kayzer, Wim, ed. 1997. *A Glorious Accident*. New York: W.H. Freeman.

Kean, D.M., and M.A. Smith. 1986. *Magnetic Resonance Imaging: Principles and Applications*. Baltimore, MD: Williams & Wilkins.

Keith, Bill. 1982. *Creation vs. Evolution: Scopes II—The Great Debate*. Lafayette, LA: Huntington House.

———. 1984. "Rampant Persecution of Creationists Reaches Epidemic Proportions." *Creation*, July, pp. 10–11.

Keller, Julia C. 2003. "Texas Texts Reignite Evolution Debates." *Research News and Opportunities in Science and Theology*, 4(2):1,26–27.

Kelley, Delores Goodwin. 1977. *A Rhetorical Analysis of an 1884–1888 Controversy in American Religious Thought: Response within the Presbyterian Church in the United States to Evolutionism*. University of Maryland College Park.

Kelley, T. 1998. Unpublished document. May 30.

Kemp, Peter. 1982. *H. G. Wells and the Culminating Ape: Biological Themes and Imaginative Obsessions*. London: Macmillan.

Kemper, Steve. 2005. "Evolution on Trial." *Smithsonian*, 36(1):52–61. April.

Kenyon, Dean. 1996. Letter from Dean Kenyon to Jim Foley, dated February 6.

——— 1993. Interview of Dean Kenyon by Jerry Bergman, n.d.

Kevles, Bettyann Holtzmann. 1997. *Naked to the Bone: Medical Imaging in the Twentieth Century*. Reading, MA: Addison Wesley.

Key, Thomas D.S. 1985. "A Biologist Examines the Book of Mormon." *Journal of the American Scientific Affiliation*, 37(2):96–99. June.

Kiefer, Otto. 1971. *Sexual Life in Ancient Rome*. London, England: Abbey Library.

Kilpatrick, James J. 2001. "Case of Scientific Heresy is Doomed." *The Augusta Chronicle*, Sunday, December 21, p. A04— the James J. Kilpatrick column.

King-Hele, Desmond. 1963. *Erasmus Darwin*. New York, NY: Charles Scribner's Sons.

Kitchen, Sebastian. 2003. "Tech Professor's Evolution Policy Prompts Federal Inquiry", *Avalanche-Journal*, January 30.

Kitcher, Philip. 1982. *Abusing Science*. Cambridge, Mass.: The MIT Press.

Kitzmiller et al. vs. Dover. (Judge John E. Jones III – Kitzmiller Opinion rendered December 20, 2005, page 76-79). http://www.pamd.uscourts.gov/kitzmiller/kitzmiller_342.pdf

Kjelle, Marylou Morano. 2003. *Raymond Damadian and the Development of MRI*. Bear, Delaware: Mitchell Lane.

Kleinfield, Sonny. 1985. *A Machine Called Indomitable: The Remarkable Story of a Scientist's Inspiration, Invention, and Medical Breakthrough*. New York, NY: Times Brooks.

Klope, D.C. 1991. "The Rhetorical Constitution of the Creationist Movement." Ph.D. dissertation, University of Utah.

Klopfenstein, Ron. 1994. "Evolution Illogical." *The Journal-Gazette*, April 27.

Klugman, Craig, ed. 1994. "Jeers to Dan Scott..." Editorial, *The Journal-Gazette*, April 16.

Knight, David. 2005. "Dare to Dream." *New Scientist*, 187:52–53. August 13.

Knight, John. 1985. "Creation-Science, Evolution-Science, and Education: Anything Goes?" *The Australian Journal of Education*, 29(2):115–132. August.

———. 1986. "'Creation-Science' in Queensland: Some Fundamental Assumptions." *Social Alternatives*, 5(3):26–31. Sept.

———, Richard Smith, and Graham Maxwell. 1986. "The Right Side: 'Creation-Science' in Queensland, Australia." *New Zealand Sociology*, 1(2):88–103. Nov.

Koenig, Robert. 2001. "Creationism Takes Root Where Europe, Asia Meet." *Science*, 292:1286–1287.

Kofahl, Robert. 1982. Interview of Robert Kofahl by Jerry Bergman, December. n.d.

Kohli, Paul E. 2002. "Only Intelligent Designer Designs So Intelligently." Letter to the Editor. *The Columbus Dispatch*, Monday, March 11.

Koop, C. Everett. 1991. *Koop: The Memoirs of America's Family Doctor*. New York: Random House.

Kottak, Conrad. 2006. *Anthropology: Exploration of Human Diversity*. Boston: McGraw Hill.

Krane, Dan. 1994. Interviews of Dan Krane by Jerry Bergman, transcribed by Kathy Hern. Various dates.

Krannawitter, Thomas, and Daniel Palm. 2005. *A Nation under God? The ACLU and Religion in American Politics*. Lanham, MD: Rowman & Littlefield.

Kuhn, Thomas. 1970. *The Structure of Scientific Revolutions*. Chicago: University of Chicago Press.

Kulp, J. Lawrence. 1949. "Discussion of Dr. Monsma's Paper." *Journal of the American Scientific Affiliation*. 1(3):19–30.

———. 1950. "Flood Geology." *Journal of the American Scientific Affiliation*, 2(1):1–15.

Kupelian, David. 2005. "Censorship!" *Whistleblower*, 14(8):4–5. August.

Kurtz, Paul, ed. 1996. "Religious Belief in America: A New Poll." *Free Inquiry*, 16(3):34–40. Summer.

Kuznetsov, Dmitri. 1990. "An Open Letter to Bill Honig." *Acts & Facts*, 19(3):1–3.

L.

Laba, Estelle, and Eugene Gross. 1950. "Evolution Slighted in High School Biology." *Clearing House*, 24:396–399. March.

Lamb, Andrew. 2005. Letter from Andrew Lamb to Jerry Bergman, dated July 19.

Lamont, Ann. 1994. "Wernher von Braun, Pioneer of Space Exploration." *Creation Ex Nihilo*, 16(2):26–30. March–May.

Lang, Walter. 1964. "Persecution of a Creationist." *Bible Science Newsletter*, 2(1):1–2.

———, and Valena Lang. 1984. *Two Decades of Creationism*. Minneapolis, MN: Bible Science Association.

Langen, Tom A. 2004. "What is Right with 'Teaching the Controversy'?" *TRENDS in Ecology and Evolution*, 19(3):114.

LaNoue, George, and Barbara Lee. 1987. *Academics in Court: The Consequences of Faculty Discrimination Litigation*. Ann Arbor, MI The University of Michigan Press.

Larsen, David C., Jeffrey Wetheimer, Rutan & Tucker. 1992. John E. Peloza vs. Capistrano Unified School District, Board of Trustees of the Capistrano Unified School District...Memorandum of Points and Authorities in Opposition to Defendant's Motion to Dismiss Jan. 6, 1992.

Larson, Edward. J. 1984. "Public Science versus Popular Opinion: The Creation-Evolution Legal Controversy." Ph.D. dissertation, University of Wisconsin.

———. 1985. *Trial and Error: The American Controversy over Creation and Evolution*. New York: Oxford University Press.

————. 1997. *Summer for the Gods: The Scopes Trial and America's Continuing Debate over Science and Religion*. New York, NY: Basic Books.

————, and Larry Witham. 1997. "Scientists are Still Keeping the Faith." *Nature*, 386:435–436.

————, and Larry Witham. 1998. "Leading Scientists Still Reject God." *Nature*, 394:313.

————, and Larry Witham. 1999. "Scientists and Religion." *Scientific American*, 281(3):93.

Lassen, Peter Rygaard. 2003. "Magnetic Resonance Imaging and the Nobel Prize 2003." *Modern Physics*, November 18.

————. 2005. Letter from Peter Lassen to Jerry Bergman, n.d..

Lax, Eric. 2004. *The Mold in Dr. Florey's Coat*. New York: Henry Holt.

Leakey, Louis S. B. 1966. *White African: An Early Autobiography*. Cambridge, MA: Schenkman.

Leakey, Richard, and Roger Lewin. 1978. *Origins*. New York: E. P. Dutton.

Leap, Terry L. 1995. *Tenure, Discrimination, and the Courts*. Second edition. Ithaca, NY: Cornell University Press.

Lecler, Joseph, ed. 1966. *Religious Freedom*. New York: Paulist Press.

Lefler, Dion. 2005. "Evolution Debate Spawns a Saucy Monster." *The Wichita Eagle*, Sunday, August, 28, p. 1.

Leith, Brian. 1982. *The Descent of Darwinism*. London: Collins.

Leo, John. 2004a. "Liberal Media? I'm Shocked!" *U.S. News and World Report*, June 7, p. 12.

————. 2004b. "More Dancing in the Dark." *U.S. News and World Report*, June 28, p. 8.

Lerner, Eric J. 1991. *The Big Bang Never Happened*. New York: New York Times Books.

Leslie, Francis J., and John Greer. 1999. "Attitudes Towards Creationism and Evolutionary Theory: The Debate Among Secondary Pupils Attending Catholic and Protestant Schools in Northern Ireland." *Public Understanding of Science* (UK), 8:93–103.

Lessios, H.A. 2007. "Admission that Intelligent Design Is a Religious View." *Nature*, 448:15–22.

Leuba, James H. 1916. *Belief in God and Immortality: A Psychological, Anthropological and Statistical Study*. Boston: Sherman, French and Company.

LeVake, Rodney. 1999. "Is Evolution a Sacred Cow? Beware of Teaching the Controversy". http://creationdigest.com/archives/Archive_2003_Autumn/IsEvolutionaSacredCow.htm (as of 06/08/08).

Levine, Joseph S., and Kenneth R. Miller. 1994. *Biology: Discovering Life.* Second edition. Lexington, MA: D. C. Heath and Company.

Lewin, Roger. 1980. "Evolution Theory under Fire." *Science*, 210(21):883.

Lewis, C.S. 1962. *Mere Christianity.* New York: MacMillan.

Lewis, Jack P. 1989. "The Days of Creation: An Historical Survey of Interpretation." *Journal of the Evangelical Theological Society*, 32(4):433–455.

Lewis, Lionel S. 1987. Review of *No Ivory Tower: McCarthyism and the University*, by Ellen W. Schrecker. Academe, Jan.–Feb., pp. 48–50.

Lewis, Ralph. 1982. "The Creationists." *Michigan State News*, Jan. 6, p. 1.

Lewontin, Richard. 1971. "The Yahoos Ride Again." *Evolution*, 25(2):442.

———. 1981. "Evolution/Creation Debate: A Time for Truth." *BioScience*, 31(8):559.

———. 1997. "Billions and Billions of Demons." Review of "The Demon-Haunted World: Science as a Candle in the Dark," by Carl Sagan. *New York Review of Books*, January 9. pp. 28–32.

Lieberman, Myron. 1997. *The Teacher Unions: How the NEA and AFT Sabotage Reform and Hold Students, Parents, Teachers, and Taxpayers Hostage to Bureaucracy.* New York: The Free Press.

Lightcap, Joy. 2004. Unscientific Methods. *World*, 19(36):30–31. September 18.

Lightman, Bernard. 2007. Letter from Bernard Lightman to Jerry Bergman, dated April 6.

Limbaugh, David. 2003. *Persecution; How Liberals Are Waging War against Christianity.* Washington, DC: Regnery.

Lipps, Jere H., Philip W. Signor. 1992. *Origin and Early Evolution of the Metazoa.* Springer.http://books.google.com/books?id=gUQMKiJOj64C&dq=Trilobite%2Bevolution&source=gbs_summary_s&cad=0 (as of 06/14/08)

Little, David. 1990. "Ideological Discrimination and Persecution." *First Things*, 1(1). Jan.

Little, William. 1968. *The Shorter Oxford English Dictionary.* London: Oxford University Press.

Looy, Mark. 1990. "Top Soviet Scientist Now Conducting Creationist Research in Moscow— Surprised at Lack of Academic Freedom in California." ICR Press Release, Jan. 26, p. 2.

———. 1998. Letter from Mark Looy to Jerry Bergman, dated October 27.

_____. 2006. Cincinnati Post, "Flawed Editorial", Opinion page, August 14.

Lote, Christopher H. 1990. "Ungodly Thoughts." *Nature*, 346(5):10.

Lovtrup, Soren. 1987. *Darwinism: The Refutation of a Myth*. New York: Croom Helm.

M.

Macchia, R., J. Termine, and C. Buchen. 2003. "Raymond V. Damadian, M.D.: Magnetic Resonance Imaging and the Controversy of the 2003 Nobel Prize in Physiology or Medicine." *The Journal of Urology*, 178(3): 783–785.

Macaulay, David. 1979. *Motel of the Mysteries*. Boston, MA: Houghton Mifflin Co.

MacIver, Robert M. 1955. *Academic Freedom in Our Time*. New York: Columbia University Press.

Mackenzie, Debora. 2005. "The End of Reason: Intelligent Design's Ultimate Legacy" New Scientist, July 9-15.

Mackenzie, Norman, and Jeanne Mackenzie. 1973. *H. G. Wells: A Biography by Norman and Jeanne Mackenzie*. New York: Simon and Schuster.

Mackinney, Betty. 1997. Letter from Betty Mackinney to Jerry Bergman, dated February 7.

Maddox, John. 1998. *What Remains to Be Discovered*. New York: Free Press.

_____. 1999. "News and Views: Obituary— Thomas Hughes Jukes (1906–1999)." *Nature*, 402:478.

Madigan, Timothy, ed. 1997. "Faith Steady Among Scientists— Or Is It?" *Free Inquiry*, 17(3):7–8. Summer.

Mallowe, Mike. 1982. "Portrait: Dr. C. Everett Koop." *Life*, April, pp. 27–28.

Manheim, Frank T. 1993. "Advocating Tolerance." *Geotimes* 38(4):4. Apr.

Mansfield, Paul, and P.K. Grannell. 1973. "NMR 'Diffraction' in Solids?" *Journal of Physical Chemistry: Solid State Physics*, 6:L442–L446.

Mansford, K.R.L. 1977. "Profile of Sir Ernst Chain." In *Biologically Active Substances: Exploration and Exploitation*, edited by D.A. Hems. New York: John Wiley and Sons.

Marnell, William. 1964. *The First Amendment: The History of Religious Freedom in America*. Garden City, NY: Doubleday.

Marrus, Michael R. 1987. *The Holocaust in History*. Hanover, PA: University Press of New England.

Marsden, George M. 1993. "Religious Professors are the Last Taboo." *Wall Street Journal*, December 22, p. A12.

———. 1994. *The Soul of the American University: From Protestant Establishment to Established Nonbelief.* NY: Oxford University Press.

———. 1997. *The Outrageous Idea of Christian Scholarship.* New York: Oxford University Press.

Marsh, Frank Lewis. 1963. *Evolution or Special Creation.* Washington, DC: Review and Herald.

Martin, Blair. 2000a. "BU Science-Religion Center Draws Critics: Polanyi Center's Views May Hurt Department Reputations, Some Fear." *The Baylor Lariat*, April 6. http://www3.baylor.edu/Lariat/Archives/2000/20000406/art-front01.html (as of 04/11/08).

———. 2000b. "Outgoing Prof Says Sloan is Discouraging Comment on Issue." *The Baylor Lariat*, April 12.

———. 2000c. "Professors Continue to Clash in Wake of Recent Conference." *The Baylor Lariat*, April 18.

———. 2000d. "Polanyi Official's E-mail Concerns Some Faculty." *The Baylor Lariat*, October 19.

———. 2000e. "Professors Debate Legitimacy of Polanyi: Outgoing Professor Says Sloan is Discouraging Comment on Issue." Unpublished paper.

Masters, David. 1946. *Miracle Drug: The Inner History of Penicillin.* London: Eyre and Spottiswoode.

Mathews, Jay. 1989. "California Proposal Could Alter Teaching of Evolution Nationwide." *Washington Post*, Nov. 7, p. A7.

Matsuno, Koichiro, ed. 1984. *Molecular Evolution and Protobiology.* New York: Springer.

Mattson, James, and Merrill Simon. 1996. *The Pioneers of NMR and Magnetic Resonance in Medicine: The Story of MRI.* New York: Bar-Ilan University Press.

Mawyr, Martin. 1982. "Are We Losing Our Religious Freedom?" *Moody Monthly*, May, pp. 36–39.

Mayer, William. 1982. "The Legacy of Darwin." *Free Inquiry*, 2(3):28–31.

Maynard, Roy. 1997. "Poison Ivy?" *World*, 12(26):12–15. Nov. 15.

Mayr, Ernst. 1988. *Toward a New Philosophy of Biology.* Cambridge, MA: Harvard University Press.

———. 2000. "Darwin's Influence on Modern Thought." *Scientific American*, 283(1):78–83.

McAuliffe, Kathleen. 1987. "The Inventor. (Raymond Damadian, Successful Inventor)." *U.S. News and World Report*, 102:66. Jan. 26.

McCabe, Joseph, and Thaddeus Burr Wakeman. 1911. *The Answer of Ernst Haeckel to the Falsehoods of the Jesuits*. New York: The Truth Seeker Company.

McConkey, Dale and Peter Augustine Lawler. 2000. *Social,Structurres, Social Capital, and Personal Freedom*. Westport, CT: Greenwood Publishing Group. This book contains a chapter entitled "Academic Freedom for Religious Academics" (Chapter 8, pp. 131-140) and provides excellent insight into the case of Dr. Philip Bishop and the subject of academic freedom. Portions of this book can be previewed online at: http://books.google.com/books?id=9I0WFRMuMB0C&pg=PA13 7&lpg=PA138&vq=%22Academic+freedom+is+essential+to+these+ purposes+and+applies+to+both+teaching+and+research.+Freedom+ in+research+is+fundamental+to%22&sig=TF07YUNPniqsVi3NU eZq9OMSJkM#PPA133,M1 (as of 04/16/08)

McCool, Grant. 2003. "Doctor Makes Rare Protest Over Nobel Prize." *U.S. National-Reuters Newsletter*, October 10.

McDonald, Don. 1999. "The Hidden Cost of a Ph.D.: One Man's Journey through a Loss of Faith, and Back." *The Real Issue*, 18(1):6–9.

McDonald, Kim. 1986. "Pervasive Belief in Creation-Science Dismays and Perplexes Researchers." *The Chronicle of Higher Education*, Dec. 10, pp. 6–10.

McDowell, Josh, and Bob Hostetler. 1998. *The New Tolerance: How a Cultural Movement Threatens to Destroy You, Your Faith, and Your Children*. Wheaton, IL: Tyndale House.

McFarland, Steven T. 1991. Letter from Steven McFarland to Jerry Bergman, dated Aug. 1.

———. 1992. "Free Speech and Academic Censorship." *Briefly* (Christian Legal Society), Apr., p. 2.

McGehee, Michael. 1987. "Creationism." *The Chronicle of Higher Education*, Jan. 7, p. 44.

McGuigan, Patrick. 1984. "Creationist Scholar Fights for Liberty." *Conservative Digest*, October, p. 41.

McIver, Thomas. 1988. *Anti-Evolution: An Annotated Bibliography*. Jefferson, NC: McFarland and Company.

———. 1989. *Creationism: Intellectual Origins, Cultural Context, and Theoretical Diversity*. Los Angeles, CA: University of California.

McManus, Mike. 1993. "Time for Common Sense on Church-State Issues?" *Lodi News Sentinel*, February 27, p. 19.

McMillen, Liz. 1987a. "The Residue from Academics' Lawsuits: Often Anguish for Everyone Involved." *Chronicle of Higher Education*, Apr. 1.

———. 1987b. "U. of Calif. Professors Launch a Drive to Give Tenure Candidates Access to Files." *The Chronicle of Higher Education*, Mar. 18.

McMurray, Emily. 1995. *Notable Twentieth-Century Scientists*. New York: Gale Research Inc.

McMurtrie, Beth. 2000. "Baylor U. Faculty Senate Seeks Closure of Center Created to Study Religion and Science." *Chronicle of Higher Education*, Wednesday, April 19.

McQuaid, Elwood. 2003. *Persecuted: Exposing the Growing Intolerance Toward Christianity*. Eugene, OR: Harvest House Publishers.

McQueen, David. n.d.. Letter from David McQueen to Jerry Bergman.

McRobbie, Donald, Elizabeth Moore, Martin Graves, and Martin Prince. 2003. *MRI: From Picture to Proton*. New York: Cambridge University Press.

McWhirter, Cameron. 1994. "Crossing Bible with Biology Creates Fuss at Wright State." *The Cincinnati Enquirer*, May 1, pp. A1, A8.

Meikle, William. 1985. Letter from William Meikle to Jerry Bergman, dated January 10.

Meldrim, Harmon. 1994. "What about Academic Freedom?" *News-Sun*, Local/State Section. April 21, p. 15A.

Melnick, James A. 1982. "A Reply to 'Creationism Is Not a Science.'" *Newsletter on Intellectual Freedom*, 31(3):75–76,109. May.

Melnick, James A. 1983. Interview of James Melnick by Jerry Bergman, n.d.

Melton, J. Gordon. 2003. *The Encyclopedia of American Religions*. Detroit: Thompson-Gale.

Mendez, Juan. 1987. "Annual Report." *Amnesty International USA*, New York, 1987.

Menzie, Kathy. 2006. "Academic Freedom: Illusions, Allusions, and Conclusions." *Democratic Communique*, 20:69-104.

Metzger, Walter. 1955. *Academic Freedom in the Age of the University*. New York: Columbia University Press.

Meyer, Stephen C. 1993a. "A Scopes Trial for the '90s." *The Wall Street Journal*, Dec. 6, p. A14.

———. 1993b. "Scientific Correctness in San Francisco: A Tale of Two Deans." Unpublished paper.

———. 1994. "Open the Debate on Life's Origins." *Insight*, February 21, pp. 26–28.

Midgley, Mary. 2002. *Evolution as a Religion*. Revised edition. Routledge. Originally published in 1985.

Miller, Jon D. 1987. "Scientific Literacy in the United States." *In Communicating Science to the Public*, edited by D. Evered and M. O'Connor, pp. 19–40. New York: Wiley.

Miller, Kenneth R. 1982. "Answers to the Standard Creationist Arguments." *Creation/Evolution*, 3(1):1–13. Winter Issue.

————. 1999. *Finding Darwin's God: A Scientist's Search for Common Ground between God and Evolution*. New York: Cliff Street Books (HarperCollins).

Milner, Richard. 1990. *The Encyclopedia of Evolution*. New York, NY: Facts on File.

Mills, David. 2003. *Atheist Universe: Why God Didn't Have a Thing To Do with It*. New York, Libris Corp.

Mims, Forrest. 1993. Letter to Editor. *The Wall Street Journal*, Dec. 15, 1993, p. A15.

Minch, Aaron. 1994. "Professors Should Teach Just the Facts; Individuals Should Develop Own Opinions." *The Guardian*, April 20, p. 5.

Minkoff, Eli, and Pamela Baker. 2001. *Biology Today: An Issues Approach*. New York: Garland Science.

Mitchell, Charles. 2005. "The Search for Truth— So Long as It Doesn't Offend My Sensibilities!" *The Torch*, June 13. http://www.thefire.org/index.php/article/5723.html/print (as of 04/11/08).

Mohler, Albert. 2004. Press release dated September, 17.

Molén, Mats. 2004. "Skapelstroende fick inte Nobelpriset!" *Genesis*, No. 1, 2004, pp. 10–11.

Monastersky, Richard. 2007. "Intelligent Design vs. Tenure: Was It Antireligious Bias When Iowa State Took a Pass on a Scientist with Controversial Views?" *The Chronicle*, 53(39), p. A9.

Montgomery, David. 2003. "In a Funk over the No-Nobel Prize." *Washington Post*, October 10, p. C01.

Montgomery, Homer. 2003. *Syllabus* for Geology 3332. Dated January 21, 2003. University of Texas at Dallas.

Mooney, Carolyn J. 1994. "Devout Professors on the Offensive: Some Academics Say It Is Time to Acknowledge the Role Religion Plays in Their Scholarship." *The Chronicle of Higher Education*, May 4, A18, A21–A22.

Moore, Art. 2002. "Brave New Schools: College Rejected for Teaching Creationism. Accrediting Group: 'Biblical Worldview' Inhibits 'Basic Knowledge.'" *WorldNetDaily*, May 10.

Moore, James R. 1979. *The Post-Darwinian Controversies: A Study of the Protestant Struggle to Come to Terms with Darwin in Great Britain and America.* Cambridge, MA: Cambridge University Press.

Moore, John. 1983. *How to Teach Origins (without ACLU Interference).* Milford, MI: Mott Media.

Moore, John N. 1982. Interview of John N. Moore by Jerry Bergman, June 3.

Moore, Randy. 2001. "Educational Malpractice: Why Do So Many Biology Teachers Endorse Creationism?" *Skeptical Inquirer*, November/December, pp. 38–42.

Moore, Raymond C., Cecil G. Lalicker, Alfred G. Fischer. 1952. *Invertebrate Fossils.* NY: McGraw-Hill.

Moore, Robert A. 1983. "The Impossible Voyage of Noah's Ark." *Creation/Evolution*, Issue XI. Winter.

Moorhead, Paul and Martin Kaplan. 1967. *Mathematical Challenges to the Neo-Darwinian Interpretation of Evolution.* Philadelphia: The Wistar Institute.

Morell, Virginia. 1995. *Ancestral Passions: The Leakey Family and the Quest for Humankind's Beginnings.* New York: Simon and Schuster.

Morgan, Edward William. 1983. "A Biblical and Theological Critique of Scientific Creationism." Ph.D. dissertation, Southern Baptist Theological Seminary.

Morgan, Richard. 1972. *The Supreme Court and Religion.* New York: The Free Press.

Moritz, Charles. 1985. *Current Biography Yearbook.* New York: H. W. Wilson Co., pp. 328–331.

Morris, Henry M. 1980. "Scopes Trial in Reverse: Teacher Dismissed for His Creationist Views." *Acts and Facts*, 9(10):1–2,6–7. October.

———. 1981. "Ruling in 'Reversed Scopes Trial' Goes Against Creationist Teacher." *Acts and Facts*, 10(1):4,6. January.

———. 1988. *Men of Science: Men of God Great Scientists Who Believed the Bible.* Green Forest, AK: Master Books.

———. 1989a. *The Long War against God: The History and Impact of the Creation/Evolution Conflict.* Grand Rapids, MI: Baker Book House.

———. 1989b. "A History of Religious Freedom Being Denied at ICR." *Impact* Insert.

———. 1990. "ICR Scientists Visit Russia." *Acts and Facts*, 19(7):1–4. July.

————. 1991. "Internal Creation Conference in Korea." *Acts and Facts*, 20(10):1–2.

————. 1993. *History of Modern Creationism*. 2nd edition. Santee, CA: Institute for Creation Research.

————. 1997. *That Their Words May Be Used Against Them*. Green Forrest, AR: Master Books.

Morris, John. 1998. Letter from John Morris to Jerry Bergman, dated August 1.

Morris, Richard. 1999. *Artificial Worlds: Computers, Complexity, and the Riddle of Life*. New York: Plenum.

————. 2001. *The Evolutionists: The Struggle for Darwin's Soul*. New York: W.H. Freeman.

Morrison, John Lee. 1951. *A History of American Catholic Opinion on the Theory of Evolution, 1859–1950*. Columbia, Missouri: University of Missouri.

Morrow, Scott. 1996. Letter from Scott Morrow to Jerry Bergman, dated November.

Moy, Timothy. 2001. "Science, Religion, and the Galileo Affair." *Skeptical Inquirer*, 25(5): 43-49. Sept.–Oct.

Moyers, Bill D. 1990. *A World of Ideas II: Public Opinions from Private Citizens*. New York: Doubleday.

MSNBC.com. 2005. "Teacher Told to Revise Creationism Lesson Plan: For 15 Years, VA Teacher had Offered Bonus Work on Creationism." *The Associated Press*, June 10.

Muck, Terry C. 1990. "Truth's Intrepid Ambassador." *Christianity Today*, 34(17):32–34. Nov. 19.

Muller, Hermann J. 1959. "One Hundred Years Without Darwin Are Enough." *The Humanist*, 19:139.

Muller, Steven. 1987. "Note" *The Humanist*, Vol. 47, p. 67.

Mullis, Kary. 1998. *Dancing Naked in the Mind Field*. New York: Pantheon Books.

Munday, Dave. 1979. "Iowa State Students Protest Bias." *Liberty*, Washington DC: Religious Library Association of America, Sept.–Oct., pp. 24–25.

Murphy, William P. 1963. "Academic Freedom: An Emerging Constitutional Right." *Law and Contemporary Problems* 28(3):447-486. Summer.

Murray, N., B. Hansen, M. Holman, and S. Tremaine. 1998. "Migrating Planets." *Science*, 279:69.

Myers, Ellen. 1998. Letter from Ellen Myers to Jerry Bergman, dated August 25.

Myers, John. 1992a. "U.S. Supreme Court Denies Review of Bishop: Academic Freedom Stumbles in Wake of 11th Circuit Court Ruling." *The Real Issue*, 11(3):1–2,8. Oct.

―――. 1992b. "Experts Respond to the Recent Restrictions on Faculty Freedoms: 11th Circuit Court Ruling Sparks Debate on Freedom of Expression." *The Real Issue*, 11(4):4. Dec.

―――. 1994. "An 'Agenda of Intolerance': Professor Claims He was Denied Due Process." *The Real Issue*, 13(2):1–4. March–April.

Myers, P.Z. 2005a. "James Randi on the Smithsonian/ID Business." Post on *Pharyngula*. June 3.

―――. 2005b. "More on Bryan Leonard." Post on *Pharyngula*. June 10. http://pharyngula.org/index/weblog/print/2404 (as of 04/11/08).

―――. 2005c. "While We're at It, Let's Also Fire the Math Teachers Who Can't Do Algebra." *Pharyngula*, August 1.

―――. 2006. "Heck Yeah—Caroline Crocker Should Have Been Fired." *Pharyngula*, Feb. 5. http://scienceblogs.com/pharyngula/2006/02/heck_yeahcaroline_crocker_shou.php (as of 06/06/08).

―――. 2008. "Tainted by its Authorship." *Pharyngula*, June 12. http://scienceblogs.com/pharyngula/2008/06/tainted_by_its_authorship.php

N.

Nahigian, Kenneth. 1992. "Evolutionists vs. Creationists." *The Sacramento Union*, Sat., Mar. 21.

Narlikar, Jayant. 1981. "Was There a Big Bang?" *New Scientist*, Vol. 91, pp. 19–21. July 2.

―――. 1991. "What If the Big Bang Didn't Happen?" *New Scientist*, Vol. 129, pp. 48–52. March 2.

National Academy of Sciences (NAS). 1998. T*eaching about Evolution and the Nature of Science.* Washington, DC: National Academy Press.

National Education Association. 1988. *Entering the Profession: Advice for the Untenured.* Booklet

Neal. 2005. "What's the World Coming To?" June 10. http://neal2028.blogspot.com/2005_06_01_neal2028_archive.html (as of 04/11/08).

Nelkin, Dorothy. 1976. "The Science-Textbook Controversies." *Scientific American*, 234(4):33–39.

————. 1977. *Science Textbook Controversies and the Politics of Equal Time.* Cambridge: MIT University Press.

————. 1982. *The Creation Controversy: The Science of Scripture in the Schools.* New York:: W.W. Norton.

Nelson, Anita. 1982. Letter from Anita Nelson to Jerry Bergman, dated July 5.

Nelson, Paul. 2001. "Unfit for Survival." In *Signs of Intelligence*, edited by William A. Dembski and James M. Kushiner, pp. 128-144. Grand Rapids, MI: Brazos Press.

Neuhaus, Richard John. 2005. "Stifling Intellectual Inquiry." *First Things*, 152:59–60. April.

Neville, Robert C. 1963. "A Theory of Divine Creation." Ph.D. dissertation, Yale University.

Newberry, Mike. 1964. *The Yahoos*. New York: Marzanie and Munsell.

Nguyen, Tommy. 2005. "Smithsonian Distances Itself from Controversial Film." *Washington Post*, Thursday, June 2; p. C1.

Nickels, M.K., and B.A. Drummond. 1985. "Creation/Evolution: Results of a Survey Conducted at the 1983 ISTA Convention." *Creation/Evolution Newsletter*, 5(6):2–15.

Nickerson, Raymond S. 1998. "Confirmation Bias: A Ubiquitous Phenomenon in Many Guises." *Review of General Psychology*, Vol. 2., No. 2., 175-220. http://psy2.ucsd.edu/~mckenzie/nickersonConfirmationBias.pdf (as of 07/15/08)

Nissimov, Ron. 2000a. "Baylor Professors Concerned that Research Center is Front for Promoting Creationism in Classroom." *The Houston Chronicle*, June 2.

————. 2000b. "Intelligent Design Leader Demoted." *The Houston Chronicle*, October 20, p. A31.

NLJ Online Religious Freedom. 2000. "Teacher Dismissed for Challenging Darwinism." Sept.

Northe, Gail. 1993. *God is Evolution, Evolution is God*. Cohasset, MA: Vedanta Centre.

Novak, Michael. 1985. "Religion in Politics." *ADL Bulletin*, 42(1):3–4,10–12. January.

Numbers, Ronald L. 1982. "Creationism in 20th-Century America." *Science*, 218(5):538–544.

————. 1988. "George Frederick Wright: From Christian Darwinist to Fundamentalist." *ISIS*, 79:624–645.

————. 1991. "Creationism." *The Encyclopedia Americana*. Danbury, CT: Grolier.

————. 1992. *The Creationists: The Evolution of Scientific Creationism*. New York: Alfred A Knopf.

————. 1992. Letter from Ronald Numbers to Jerry Bergman, n.d.,

————. 1998. *Darwinism Comes to America*. Cambridge, MA: Harvard University Press.

————. 2006. *The Creationists: The Evolution of Scientific Creationism*. Cambridge, MA: Harvard University Press.

O.

Odenwald, Sten, and Richard Fienberg. 1993. "Galaxy Redshifts Reconsidered." *Sky and Telescope*, February, pp. 31–35.

Oelschlägel, Bernd. 2005. "Science and the Bible Helped Me Find the Meaning of Life." *Awake*, November 22, pp. 12–15.

Olasky, Marvin. 1997. "Fundies Need Not Apply: Academic Bigotry Is Just Another Front in the Cultural War." *World*, May 31, p. 30.

————. 2003. "Arrogance and Ignorance: Darwinian Texas Tech Professor is going against Basic Professorial Ethics." *World*, February 15, p. 36.

O'Leary, Denyse. 2004. *By Design or by Chance?* Kitchener, Ontario: Castle Quay Books.

————. 2005a. "Privileged Planet Shown at University of Toronto, Without Controversy." Christianity.ca, posted July 6. http:www.christianity.ca/faith/weblog/2005/7.06.html

————. 2005b. "Design Film Sparks Angst: Under Fire, Smithsonian Disavows Presentation on Intelligent Design." *Christianity Today*, 49(8):22, August.

————. 2005c. "With Materialistic Science, You Can't Go Wrong or Right Either." Unpublished paper. 3 pp.

————. 2005. Letter from Denyse O'Leary to Jerry Bergman, n.d..

Olson, Ross. 2001. "Doubting Darwin." Letter sent Aug. 20 to the Editor of the *Star Tribune*. http://www.rossolson.org/letters/doubting_darwin.html

Olsen, Ted Webb. 2003. "Did Nobel Committee Ignore MRI Creator Because of Creationism?" *Christianity Today*, Oct. 6, p. 9.

Oltman, Brian. 2005. "Film Based on Professor's Book Showing at Smithsonian: Professor's Ideas Gain Recognition in Film." *Iowa State Daily*, June 7.

O'Toole, Christopher. 1944. "The Philosophical Theory of Creation in the Writings of St. Augustine." Ph.D. dissertation, Catholic University of America.

Overman, Richard Hinson. 1966. "Evolutionary Theory and the Christian Doctrine of Creation: A Whiteheadian Interpretation." Ph.D. dissertation, Claremont Graduate School.

Overman, Richard L., and Steve Deckard. 1997. "Origins Beliefs Among NSTA Members." *Impact*, 292:1–4. Oct.

P.

Pagel, Mark, ed. 2002. *Encyclopedia of Evolution*. New York: Oxford University. Vol. 1.

Parkinson, James. 1982. Interview of James Parkinson by Jerry Bergman, n.d..

Parr, Marina. 2001. "Burlington Reassigns Biology Teacher: DeHart at Center of Debate over Evolution vs. Creation." *Skagit Valley Herald*, August 21.

Parsons, Keith M. 2004. *The Great Dinosaur Controversy: A Guide to the Debates*. Santa Barbara, CA: ABC–CLIO, p. ix.

Patterson, James, and Peter Kim. 1991. *The Day America Told the Truth*. New York: Prentice-Hall.

Patterson, John. 1984. "Do Scientists and Scholars Discriminate Unfairly Against Creationists?" *Creation-Evolution Newsletter*, 4(3):19–20. May–June.

———. 1984. Letter from John Patterson to Kevin Wirth, dated February 7.

Paul, Gregory. 2005. "Cross-National Correlations of Quantifiable Societal Health with Popular Religiosity and Secularism in the Prosperous Democracies." *Journal of Religion & Society*, 7:1–17.

Peachy, David. 1981. Letter to Editor. *Next*, 2(3):4.

Peacocke, Arthur. 1990. *Theology for a Scientific Age: Being and Becoming–Natural and Divine*. Cambridge, MA: Oxford University Press.

Pearcey, Nancy R. 1989. "Journey from Evolution." *Contrast*, 8(8):1–4.

———. 2000a. "Creation Mythology: Defenders of Darwinism Resort to Suppressing Data and Teaching Outright Falsehoods." *World Magazine*, 15(25):23.

———. 2000b. "Don't Question Authority: Diverse Probe into Darwinism is Met with Intolerance at Baptist Baylor." *World Magazine*, May 27, p. 12.

Peloza, John. 1991. "Teacher Stands Up Against Censorship: John Peloza Fights to Teach Good Science." *Education Newsline*, May–June.

Peloza v. Capistrano. 1994. 37 F.3d 517 (9th Circuit).

Pennock, Robert. 1999. *Tower of Babel: The Evidence against the New Creationism*. Cambridge, MA: MIT Press.

Perakh, Mark and Matt Young. 2006. "Is Intelligent Design Science?" In *Why Intelligent Design Fails*, edited by Matt Young and Tanner Edis, pp. 185-196. New Brunswick, NJ: Rutgers University Press.

Petto, Andrew. 1996. "Short Takes." *National Center For Science Education Reports*, 16(4):10. Winter.

Pfeffer, Leo. 1963. *The Liberties of an American*. Boston: Beacon Press.

Phelps, M.E., E.J. Hoffman, and M.M. Ter-Pogossian. 1975. "Attenuation Coefficients of Various Body Tissues, Fluids, and Lesions at Photon Energies of 18 to 136 keV." *Radiology*, 117(3Pt1):573–583.

Pilkington, G.W., P.K. Poppleton, and G. Robertshaw. 1965. "Changes in Religious Attitudes and Practices among Students During University Degree Courses." *British Journal of Educational Psychology*, 35:150–157.

Pique, Charles. 2001. "Evolution Can Be Supported by Fact." *Charleston Gazette*, April 24, p. 3.

Plaut, Steven. 2006. "The PC Inquisition Comes to Baylor University."

Postman, Neil. 1992. *Technopoly: The Surrender of Culture to Technology*. New York: Alfred A. Knopf.

Pozarzycki, Lottie. 1994. "Teacher's Censure Perplexing." Letter to Editor. *The Toledo Blade*, April 30, p. 8.

Prager, Dennis. 1994. "Word Abuse: A Lexicon." *Wall Street Journal*, January 21.

Prasad, Amit. 2007. "The (Amorphous) Anatomy of an Invention: The Case of Magnetic Resonance Imaging (MRI)." *Social Studies of Science*, 37(4):533-560.

Press, Frank, ed. 1984. *Science and Creationism: A View from the National Academy of Sciences*. Washington, DC: National Academy Press.

Price, George McCready. 1917. *Q.E.D.* New York, NY: Fleming H. Revell.

Prince, R.W. 1985. "An Examination of Henry M. Morris' Interpretation of Biblical Creation." Ph.D. dissertation, Southern Baptist Theological Seminary.

Proffitt, Fiona. 2004. "In Defense of Darwin and a Former Icon of Evolution." *Science*, 304:1894–1895.

Provine, William. 1987. "Trial and Error: The American Controversy over Creation and Evolution." *Academe*, Jan.–Feb., pp. 50–52.

————. 1989. "Evolution and the Foundation of Ethics." In *Science, Technology, and Social Progress*, edited by Steven Goldman, pp. 253–267. Bethlehem: Lehigh University Press.

————. 1993. "Response to Johnson Review." *Creation-Evolution*, Issue No. 32, pp. 62–63. Summer.

————. 1999. "No Free Will." *Isis*, 90:S117–S132.

Q.

Quammen, David. 2004. "Was Darwin Wrong?" *National Geographic*, 206(5):2–31. Nov.

Quilter, Deborah. 1982. "You're Fired Because You're Old." *S. F. Focus*, Oct., p. 36.

R.

Rabinowitz, Dorothy. 1980. *About the Holocaust; What We Know and How We Know It*. New York, NY: Institute of Human Relations Press, 2nd printing.

————. 2004. "A Heretic in Academia." *The Wall Street Journal*, Thursday, March 18, p. A16.

Rafferty, Kate. 1987. "Fidel Castro Speaks Out on Prayer, Salvation and Hell." *Today's Banner*, May, p. 14.

Rank, Scott. 2004. "Is Intelligent Design Science or Creationism." *Iowa State Daily*, October 18.

Rasmussen, Brent. 2005. "Creationism's Damaged Fruit." *DarkSyde*, Thursday, June 23. http://www.dailykos.com/story/2005/6/23/16213/2331 (as of 04/11/08).

Ravitch, Diane, Ronald E. Gwiazda, Floretta Dukes McKenzie, Mary Francis Berry, Martin Carnoy, Steven M. Cahn, and Mortimer J. Adler. 1983. "Symposium: The Paideia Proposal." *Harvard Educational Review*, 53(4):377–411, November.

Rawlings, Hunter, III. 2005. State of the University Address. Cornell University. Oct. 21. http://www.cornell.edu/president/announcement_2005_1021.cfm (as of 04/11/08).

Raymo, Chet. 1998. *Skeptics and True Believers*. New York, NY: Walker.

Reapsome, James. 1980. "Religious Values: Reflection of Age and Education." *Christianity Today*, May 2, pp. 23–25.

Reeder, Diane. 1984. "University Creationists Speak." *Christian News Herald*, Mar., p. 3.

Reeser, Jan. 1998. Letter from Jan Reeser to Jerry Bergman, dated September 10.

Reidinger, Paul. 1987. "Creationism and the First Amendment." *American Bar Association Journal*, Jan. 1, p. 35.

Reke, Daniel R. 1994. "Identical to Monkey Trial." *News-Sun*, Local/State Section, April 21, p. 15A.

Rennie, John. 2002. "15 Answers to Creationist Nonsense." *Scientific American*, July, pp. 78–85.

Rice, Fredric. 2004. "Unaccredited Creationist Cult—The Skeptic Tank." http://www.skeptictank.org/flist026.htm (as of 04/11/08).

Richards, Jay Wesley. 2001. "Proud Obstacles and a Reasonable Hope." In *Signs of Intelligence*, edited by William A. Dembski and James M. Kushiner, pp. 51-59. Grand Rapids, MI: Brazos Press.

———. 2004. "Reality & Reluctant Science: Old Science Confronts a Formidable Challenge in the Scientific ID Movement." *Touchstone*, July–August, pp. 46–52.

———. 2005. Response to William Tucker's "Are We a Privileged Planet?" *The American Enterprise*, June 10.

Richards, Roger. 2003. Letter from Roger Richards to Jerry Bergman, dated October 22.

Riley, Richard. 1998. "Secretary's Statement on Religious Expression." U.S. Department of Education Report.

Roach, Erin. 2006. "Baylor Denies Tenure to Highly Regarded Beckwith." *(BP) News*, March 31.

Roberts, John E. 1985. "Bigots Attack Fundamentalists." *Pulse*, March.

Roberts, Ron, and Robert Marsh Kloss. 1979. *Social Movements*. St. Louis: C. V. Mosby.

Robertson, Ian. 1987. *Sociology*. Third edition. New York, NY: Worth Publishers.

Foust, Michael, 2001. "Phillip Johnson: Evolution Battles at Baylor, Kan. Could Have Been Won." *The Southern Baptist Theological Seminary News and Resources*. 3 pp. http://www.jodkowski.pl/ip/PJohnson004.html#Foust1 (as of 06/09/08)

Robinson, Jeff.. 2004. "Seminary Appoints Dembski to Lead New Center for Science and Theology." *Towers Online*, September 16. http://www.towersonline.net/story.php?grp=news&id=211 (as of 06/09/08)

Robinson, R.W. 1991. "The Preachy Professor." Letter to Editor. *Liberty*, Sept–Oct., p. 28.

Roots, Kimberly. 2004. "Dembski to Head Seminary's Faith-and-Science Center." *Science and Theology News*, Nov., p. 34.

Rörsch, A. 1999. "Mutation Research Frontiers: Challenges to Evolution Theory." *Mutation Research*, 423:F3–F19.

Rose, Jerry D. 1982. *Outbreaks: The Sociology of Collective Behavior*. New York, NY: The Free Press.

Rosenberg, Morris. 1979. *Conceiving the Self.* New York: Basic Books.

Ross, Marcus. 2005. "Who Believes What? Clearing Up the Confusion over Intelligent Design and Young-Earth Creationism." *Journal of Geoscience Education*. 53(3):319–323.

Ross, Susan Dente. 2004. *Deciding Communication Law: Key Cases in Context.* Mahwah, New Jersey: Lawrence Erlbaum Associates.

Rothe, Anna, and Evelyn Lohr, eds. 1952. *Current Biography.* New York: H. W. Wilson Co.

Roy, Pat. 1998. Letter from Pat Roy to Jerry Bergman, dated December 3.

Rusch, Wilbert. 1983. *A Brief Statement of the History and Aims of the CRS,* Ann Arbor, MI: published by the author.

Ruse, Michael. 1982. *Darwinism Defended.* Reading, Mass: Addison-Wesley.

———. 1993. *The New Antievolutionism.* Transcript of a presentation at the American Association of the Advancement of Science in Boston, on February 13.

———. 2000. "How Evolution Became a Religion: Darwinians Wrongly Mix Science with Morality, Politics." *National Post*, Saturday, May 13.

———. 2001. *Can a Darwinist Be a Christian?* New York: Cambridge University Press.

———. 2003a. Letters to Editor. *Reports of the National Center for Science Education*, 23(3–4):14. May–Aug.

———. 2003b. "Is Evolution a Secular Religion?" *Science*, 299:1523–1524.

———. 2004. "Controversy over the Nobel Prize in Medicine." *Metanexus Salus*, March 16. http://metanexus.net/metanexus_online/show_article. asp?8759 (as of 04/11/08).

Rutan & Tucker, David C. Larsen, Jeffrey Wertheimer. 1991. John E. Peloza vs. Capistrano Unified School District, Board of Trustees of the Capistrano Unified School District… Memorandum of Points and Authorities in Support of Defendant's Motion to Dismiss, Dec., 16.

Rutherford, Adam. 2007. Wrong by Design. *Guardian Unlimited*, Comment Is Free, July 11. http://commentisfree.guardian.co.uk/adam_ rutherford/2007/07/wrong_by_design.html

Rutledge, Margo. 1994. "Teacher Believes His Firing Is Unfair." *Springfield (OH) News-Sun*, April 14, p. 4.

S.

Sack, Dave. 2003. Letter from Dave Sack to Jerry Bergman, dated May 19.

Sagan, Carl. 1977. "An Analysis of *Worlds in Collision*." In *Scientists Confront Velikovsky*, ed. by Donald Goldsmith, pp. 41-104. Ithaca, NY: Cornell University Press.

———. 1979. *Broca's Brain*. New York: Random House.

———. 1980. *Cosmos*. New York: Random House.

Salem Press, eds. 1994. "Nuclear Magnetic Resonance Produces Images of the Brain." In *Great Scientific Achievements: The Twentieth Century*, Vol. 9, pp. 964–966. Salem Press.

Santillanes, Valerie. 1996. "Leeway for Creationism in Class Nets Support: Poll: Many Support Inclusion of Creationism." *Albuquerque Journal*, Sept. 13, pp. A1–A2.

Santorum, Rick. 2004. "Antireligious Courts." *Crisis*, 20(5):61. May.

Savoye, Craig. 2000. "Whose 'Science'?" *Christian Science Monitor*, February 8.

Schadewald, Robert. 1985. "The Missionary of Creationism." *The Skeptical Inquirer*, 9(3):290–293.

Schaeffer, Francis. 1981. *A Christian Manifesto*. Westchester, IL: Crossway.

———. 1985. *How Should We Then Live: The Rise and Decline of Western Thought and Culture*. Wheaton, IL: Crossway Books.

Schaeffer, Franky. 1982. *A Time for Anger*. Westchester, IL: Good News.

Schlessinger, Bernard, and June A. Schlessinger. 1986. *The Who's Who of Nobel Prize Winners*. Phoenix, AZ: Oryx Press.

Schmidt, Peter. 2004. "'Report Card' Spurs Calls for Change in Academia." *The Chronicle of Higher Education*, Volume LI, Number 5, September 24.

Schmidt, William. 1983. "Religious Students." *Newsweek on Campus*, Nov., p. 2.

Schneeberger, Gary. 2005. "Court Says No to Religious Gifts in School." John Jay Institute for Judicial Interpretation. http://www.libertyparkusafd. org/lp/Jay/Journal/2003/Court%20Says%20No%20to%20Religious%2 0Gifts%20in%20School.htm (as of 06/10/08)

Schneider, David. 2003. "Science Observer: First in Flight?" *American Scientist*, 91:501–502.

Schrecker, Ellen. 1986. *No Ivory Tower: McCarthyism and the Universities*. New York: Oxford University Press.

Schultz, Duane P. 1982. *Psychology and Industry Today: An Introduction to Industrial and Organizational Psychology*. 3rd edition. New York: Macmillan.

Schwartz, John. 2005. "Smithsonian to Screen a Movie that Makes a Case Against Evolution." *The New York Times*, May 28, p. A8.

Schwarzschild, Bertram. 2003. "Lauterbur and Mansfield Awarded Nobel Medicine Prize for Magnetic Resonance Imaging." *Physics Today*, 56(12):24–27. December.

Science News. 1978. "Nobel Prizes: Research with an Impact." Vol. 114, Oct. 21, p. 276.

Scott, Dan. 1994a. Memo to Barbara Hull dated March 29.

———. 1994b. Memo from Dan Scott to Barbara Hull dated April 7, 1994.

———. 1994. Letter from Dan Scott to Jerry Bergman, dated April 13.

———. 1994. Letter from Dan Scott to Jerry Bergman, dated April 16.

———. 1994. Letter from Dan Scott to Jerry Bergman, dated April 17.

Scott, Eugenie. 1994. "Dean Kenyon and 'Intelligent Design Theory' at San Francisco State U." *National Center for Science Education Reports*, 14(1):13,15.

———. 1996. "Monkey Business: Rebuffed In The Courts, Anti Evolutionists Are Seeking A New Niche In The Schools, One Classroom at a Time." *The Sciences*, 36(1):20–25. Jan–Feb.

———. 1999. "*Just When You Thought It Was Safe to Teach Evolution.*" Speech delivered on July 31, 1999 at the Northern California FFRE Mini-Convention, Holiday Inn Civic Center, San Francisco. http://ffrf.org/fttoday/2000/jan_feb2000/scott.html (as of 042808)

———. 2000. "Just When You Thought It Was Safe to Teach Evolution." *Freethought Today*, 17(1):4–9. January/February.

———. 2002. Quoted from "A Conversation with Eugenie Scott." *Research News and Opportunities in Science and Theology*, 2(8):3,16.

———. 2004a. "A Solution to the Dangers of Teaching Evolution in Public Schools: The Creation-Evolution Continuum." *Skeptic*, 10(4):48–49.

———. 2004b. "The Creation-Evolution Continuum: How To Avoid Classroom Conflicts." *Skeptic*, 10(4):50–54.

———. 2004c. *Evolution vs. Creationism*. Berkeley, CA: University of California Press.

———. 2006. *Not In Our Classrooms: Why Intelligent Design Is Wrong for Our Schools*. Boston: Beacon Press.

———, and Glenn Branch. 2004. "Teaching the Controversy: Response to Langen and to Meyer." *TRENDS in Ecology and Evolution*, 19(3):116.

———, and Henry P. Cole. 1992. "Peloza Lawsuit Dismissed by Federal Judge: Called "Loose Cannon" by Judge." *BASIS*, 11(3):1. March.

Seachord, Daniel Edward. 1984. "Human Evolution as Myth: A Discussion of Certain Quasi-Religious Features Found in Models of Human Evolution." Ph.D. dissertation, Washington State University.

Seagraves, Kelly. 1973. *Jesus Christ Creator*. San Diego, CA: Creation-Science Research Center.

Sears, Alan, and Craig Osten. 2005. *The ACLU vs America: Exposing the Agenda to Redefine Moral Values*. Nashville, TN: Broadman & Holman.

Serrell, Paul. 2002. "Legal Battle: Christian College Fights to Teach Creation." *CBN News Headlines*, Tuesday, June 18.

Seung-Han Yang, Paul. 1998. "Creation Science and Caring for the Creation in Korea." *The Journal of the American Scientific Affiliation*, 50(4):279–283.

Shallis, M. 1984. "In the Eye of a Storm." *New Scientist*, January 19, pp. 42–43.

Shallit, Jeffrey. 2007. Review of *A Jealous God: Science's Crusade Against Religion*. In *Reports of the National Center for Science Education*, 27:5–6: 50–51.

Shankar, Ganga. 1989. "Analysis of Factors Influencing the Teaching of Evolution and Creationism in Texas Public High School Biology Classes." Ed.D. dissertation, Texas Technical University.

Shanks, Niall. 2004. *God, the Devil, and Darwin: A Critique of Intelligent Design Theory*. Oxford, NY: Oxford University Press.

Shapiro, Ben. 2004. *Brainwashed: How Universities Indoctrinate America's Youth*. Nashville, TN: WND Books. Foreword by David Limbaugh.

Shapiro, Robert. 1986. *Origins: A Skeptic's Guide to the Creation of Life on Earth*. New York: Summit Books.

Sheppard, Pam. 2005. "The Smithsonian Institution Makes 'Intelligent' Decision: Agrees to Co-Sponsor Film Premiere That Supports Design Theory." *Answers in Genesis*, May 30. http://www.answersingenesis.org/docs2005/0530Smithsonian.asp?vPrint=1

Shermer, Michael. 1997. *Why People Believe Weird Things*. New York: W. H. Freeman.

————. 2000. *How We Believe: The Search for God in an Age of Science*. New York: W.H. Freeman.

Shipka, Thomas. 1987. "The Crisis in Peer Review." *NEA Advocate*, April–May, pp. 6–7.

Shipley, Maynard. 1927. *The War on Modern Science: A Short History of the Fundamentalist Attacks on Evolution and Modernism*. New York, NY: Alfred A. Knopf.

Shipman, Pat. 2005. "Being Stalked by Intelligent Design." *American Scientist*, 93(6):500–502.

Shively, Michael, and Carrie F. Mulford. 2007. "Hate Crime in America: The Debate Continues". *NIJ Journal*, No. 257 (June). Washington, DC: National Institute of Justice. http://www.ojp.usdoj.gov/nij/journals/257/hate-crime.html (as of 04/11/08).

Shofstahl, Charles. 1985. "Professor Persecuted for His Faith." *Christian Inquirer*, February, p. 26.

Shoppy. 1987. "Biology Department Not Open to Creationist View." *The Hillsdale Collegian*, April 15, p. 5.

Shortt, Bruce N. 2004. *The Harsh Truth about Public Schools*. Vallecito, CA: Chalcedon Foundation.

Shrotri, Anupama. 2004. "God of the Gaffes." *New Scientist*, December 25, p. 31.

Simmons, Geoffrey. 2007. *Billions of Missing Links*. Eugene, OR: Harvest House.

Simmons, John. 2002. *Doctors and Discoveries: Lives that Created Today's Medicine*. Boston, MA: Houghton Mifflin.

Simonds, Robert. 1983. Letter from Robert Simonds to Jerry Bergman, dated June 17.

Simpson, George Gaylord. 1965. "Micro-Evolution, Macro-Evolution, and Mega-Evolution." Chapter III of *Tempo and Mode in Evolution*, edited by L.C. Dunn. New York: Hafner Publishing Company, Inc.

————. 1970. *The Meaning of Evolution*. New Haven, CT: Yale University Press.

Simpson, James Y. 1926. Landmarks in the Struggle between Science and Religion. New York, NY: George H. Doran.

Singer, Peter. 2001. "Heavy Petting." *Nerve*, March. http://www.nerve.com/Opinions/Singer/heavyPetting/main.asp (as of 04/15/08).

Sisson, Edward. 2004. "Teaching the Flaws in Neo-Darwinism" In *Uncommon Dissent*, edited by William A. Dembski, pp. 75-97. Wilmington, DE: ISI Books.

Smith, Anika. 2008. "Science Lab Explores New Intelligent Design Research". *ID the Future Podcast*, May 5. http://intelligentdesign.podomatic.com/entry/eg/2008-05-05T10_07_03-07_00

Smith, Bardwell. 1973. The Tenure Debate. San Francisco, CA: Jossey-Bass.

Smith, F. LaGard. 1996. ACLU— *The Devil's Advocate: The Seduction of Civil Liberties in America*. Colorado Springs, CO: Marcon Publishers.

Smith, E. Norbert. 1986. Interview of E. Norbert Smith by Jerry Bergman, October.

————. 2005. Letter from E. Norbert Smith to Jerry Bergman, dated July 24.

Smith, Page. 1990. *Killing the Spirit: Higher Education in America*. New York: Viking.

Smith, Richard. 1982. "Shaky Compromises and Shady Deals." *American Atheist*, 24(5):3–5.

Smith, Robert F. 1980. "Origins of Civil Liberties." *Creation Social Science and Humanities Quarterly*, 3(2):23–27. Winter.

Smout, Kary Doyle. 1998. *The Creation/Evolution Controversy: A Battle for Cultural Power*. Westport, CT: Praeger.

Spencer, Wayne. 1988. "Origins Survey Report." Wichita KS: Wichita State University.

Spong, John Shelby. 1991. *Rescuing the Bible from Fundamentalism*. San Francisco: Harper.

Stahl, Barbara. 1974. *Vertebrate History: Problems in Evolution*. New York: Dover Publications

Stambaugh, James S. 1991. "Hugh Ross, ICR, and Facts of Science." *Impact*, August.

Stanciu, T.L. 1995. "On the Wall Ruling." *Rutherford Institute News*, 4(8):4. Aug.

Stark, J. 1938. "The Pragmatic and the Dogmatic Spirit in Physics." *Nature*, 141:770–772. April 30.

Stark, Rodney. 2003. *For the Glory of God*. Princeton, NJ: Princeton University Press.

State of Minnesota In Court of Appeals C8-00-1613 Rodney LeVake, Appellant, vs. Independent School District #656; Keith Dixon Superintendent; Dave Johnson, Principal; and Cheryl Freund, Curriculum Director, Respondents. Filed May 8, 2001. Affirmed. Foley, Judge. 6 pp. http://www.lawlibrary.state.mn.us/archive/ctappub/0105/c8001613.htm (as of 04/11/08).

Staver, Mathew D. 2005. *Eternal Vigilance: Knowing and Protecting Your Religious Freedom*. Nashville, TN: Broadman & Holman.

Stein, Gordon. 1982. Review of "The Angels and Us" by Mortimer J. Adler. *The American Rationalist*, 27(1):14

Stein, Jess, ed. 1988. *The Random House College Dictionary, Revised Edition*. New York: Random House.

Steinberg, Alvin, ed. 1984. "A Youth for Christ Problem." *Community*, 1(4):9. Feb.

Steiner, Duane. 2005. Personal Communication from Duane Steiner to Jerry Bergman, June 2, 2005.

Sterelny, Kim. 2001. *Dawkins vs. Gould: Survival of the Fittest*. Cambridge, UK: Icon Books.

Stewart, William, ed. 1987. *Science and Engineering Indicators—1987*. Washington DC: U.S. Government Printing Office.

Stokes, Charles. 1987. "Creationism and the Nature of True Science." *The Chronicle of Higher Education*, 33(31):49. Apr. 15.

Stokes, Trevor. 2005. "Pro-Intelligent Design Thesis Stalls ... and Smithsonian Has ID Troubles." *The Scientist*, July 4, pp. 12–13.

Stone, Richard. 1992. "Could Creationism Be Evolving?" *Science*, 255:282.

Stowell, Joseph M. 1987. "News Feature." *Moody Monthly*, 88(1):93. Sept.

Stracher, Cameron. 2002. "Scan and Deliver: The Duel Over Who Should Get Credit for the Original MRI." *Opinion Journal*, June 14, pp. 1–3.

Stringer, Christopher, and Robin McKie. 1996. *African Exodus: The Origins of Modern Humanity*. New York: Henry Holt.

Strobel, Lee. 2000. *The Case for Faith*. Grand Rapids, MI: HarperCollins/Zondervan.

———. 2004. *The Case for a Creator*. Grand Rapids, MI: Zondervan.

Strong, Leslie. 1994. "How Does Editor Know Proper Science?" *The Journal-Gazette*, April 25, p. 6.

Sullivan, Dale L. 2000. "Keeping the Rhetoric Orthodox: Forum Control in Science." *Technical Communication Quarterly*, 9(2):125–146. Spring.

Sunderland, Luther D. 1983. "First Amendment Free Exercise Guarantees Are A Joke." *Contrast*, 2(4):1–4. Sept.–Oct.

Suurkula, Jaan. 1997. "Junk DNA." May. http://www.psrast.org/junkdna.htm (as of 04/11/08).

Swancara, Frank. 1969. *Thomas Jefferson vs. Religious Oppression*. New York: New York University Books.

Swanson, Angela. 2000. "Dembski Removed as Director of Baylor's Polanyi Center: Baylor President accuses Intelligent Design Leader of "Uncollegial" Behavior." *Research News & Opportunities in Science and Theology*, 1(4):35. December.

Sweet, Frederick. 2005. "Creationist Terror in American Classrooms." *Intervention Magazine*, Feb. 4, p. 1.

Sykes, Charles J. 1988. *Prof Scam: Professors and the Demise of Higher Education*. Washington, DC: Regnery Gateway.

T.

Tannahill, Reay. 1980. *Sex in History*. New York, NY: Stein and Day.

Tatina, Robert. 1989. "South Dakota High School Biology Teachers & the Teaching of Evolution." *American Biology Teacher*, 51(5):275–280. May.

Taylor, Arch B. 1995. "The Bible, and What It Means to Me." In *Leaving the Fold: Testimonies of Former Fundamentalists*, edited by Edward Babinski, pp. 152–168. Amherst, NY: Prometheus.

Taylor, G. Rattray. 1954. *Sex in History*. New York, NY: Vanguard Press.

Taylor, Larry. 2003. "Biology Professor Alters Evolution Statement for Recommendations; Justice Ends Probe." *Skeptical Inquirer*, 27(4):6.

Taylor, LaTonya. 2002. "Christian College Denied Accreditation." *Christianity Today*, 46(8):16.

Teeple, Howard. 1995. "I Started to Be a Minister." In *Leaving the Fold: Testimonies of Former Fundamentalists*, edited by Edward Babinski, pp. 347–357. Amherst, NY: Prometheus.

Templeton, Charles. 1996. *Farewell to God*. Toronto: McClelland and Stewart.

Templeton, John. 1996. *Who's Who in Theology and Science*. New York: Continuum.

Tevlin, Jon. 2000. "Teacher Awaits Appeal on Evolution Education in Fairbault: The Question Is Whether Darwin Can Be Criticized, He Says." *Minneapolis Star-Tribune*, August 14.

Than, Ker. 2005. "Intelligent Design: The Death of Science." *Live Science*, September 23. http://www.livescience.com/strangenews/050923_ID_science.html (as of 06/09/08)

Thomas, Cal. 1983. *Book Burning*. Westchester, IL: Crossway Books.

———. 1983. "Meet the Enemy." *Fundamentalist Journal*, December.

Thompson, Bert. 2000. *Creation Compromises*. Montgomery, AL: Apologetics Press.

————, and Brad Harrub. 2002. "Quick, Let's Discriminate Against Creationists!" *R&R Resources*, 1(12):45. http://www.apologeticspress. org/articles/2504 (as of 04/11/08).

Thomson, Keith Stewart. 1982. "The Meaning of Evolution" *American Scientist*, September.70(5): 529-531.

Thwaites, William. 1993. Letter to Editor. *The Wall Street Journal*, Dec. 15, p. A17.

Tipler, Frank J. 2004. "Refereed Journals: Do they Insure Quality or Enforce Orthodoxy?" In *Uncommon Dissent*, edited by William A. Dembski, pp. 115–130. Wilmington, DE: ISI Books.

Toalston, Art. 2000. "Intelligent Design Controversy Continues to Fester at Baylor." *Current Baptist Press News*, Oct. 24.

Tosaw, Donald. 2003. Letter from Donald Tosaw to Jerry Bergman, dated January 18.

Totheroh, Gailon. 2004. "Ohio Education War: Evolution, Media and Intelligent Design." CBN.com report dated March 28, 2004.

Toumey, Christopher P. 1987. "The Social Context of Scientific Creationism." Ph.D. dissertation, University of North Carolina.

————. 1994. *God's Own Scientists: Creationists in a Secular World*. New Brunswick, NJ: Rutgers University Press.

Trager, Robert, and Donna L. Dickerson. 1999. *Freedom of Expression in the 21st Century*. Thousand Oaks, London, New Delhi: Pine Forge Press.

Troost, C. John. 1966. "An Analysis of Factors Influencing the Teaching of Evolution in the Secondary Schools of Indiana." Ed.D. dissertation, Indiana University.

Tucker, William. 2005a. "Are We a Privileged Planet?" *The American Enterprise*, June 9.

————. 2005b. "God Is in the Details." *The American Enterprise*, June 15.

Tushnet, Mark. 1999. *Taking the Constitution Away from the Courts*. Princeton, NJ: Princeton University Press.

Tyner, Mitchell. 1984. "The Professor Who Lost His Job." *Liberty*, 80(1):4–6,26. Jan.–Feb.

Tyrangiel, Josh. 2000. "The Science of Dissent." *Time*, 156(2):60. July 10.

Tyrrell, R. Emmett. 1986. "Free Speech Isn't in College Curriculum." *Detroit News*, Oct. 1, p. 4.

U.

U.S. Court of Appeals. 1994. *Peloza v. Capistrano*. 37 F.3d 517 (9th Circuit).

U.S. Dept. of Health and Human Services. On-line biography of C. Everett Koop. http://www.surgeongeneral.gov/library/history/biokoop.htm (as of 04/11/08).

U.S. District Court. 1992. *John E. Peloza v. Capistrano Unified School District, et al.* Memorandum No. CV 91-5268-DWW (Bx), Jan 16, 1992.

U.S. District Court. 1992. *John E. Peloza v. Capistrano Unified School District, et al.* Order Granting Attorneys' Fees and Costs to Prevailing Party, No. CV 91-5268-DWW (Bx), Apr. 14, 1992.

U.S. Supreme Court. 1987. *Edwards v. Aguillard*. 482 U.S. 578. Edwards, Governor of Louisiana, et al. v. Aguillard et al. Appeal from the United States Court of Appeals for the Fifth Circuit. No. 85–1513. Argued December 10, 1986—. Decided June 19, 1987.

V.

Valentine, James.W. 2004. *On the Origin of PHYLA*. Chicago and London: University of Chicago Press.

————, Awramik, S.M., Signor, P.W., and Sadler, P.M. 1991. "The Biological Explosion at the Precambrian-Cambrian Boundary" *Evolutionary Biology*, Vol. 25, Max K. Hecht, editor. New York and London: Plenum Press.

Vanderveen, Beth C. 1999. Letter from Beth C. VanderVeen to Roger DeHart, dated July.

Vedantam, Shankar. 2006. "Eden and Evolution." *Washington Post*, February 5, p. W8.

Veith, Gene Edward. 1997. "Academic Respectability: Christian Colleges that Strive After It Can Expect Intellectual Mediocrity." *World*, 12(11):26. June 28.

————. 2000. "The Galileo Treatment: Baylor Jumps to the Wrong Side of a Scientific Revolution." *World*, November 18, p. 13.

————. 2004. "Flew the Coop." *World*, Dec. 25, p. 22.

————. 2006. "New Tenor on Tenure: Baylor Can't Shake Faculty Flirtations with Secularism." *World*, April 15, p. 30.

Verbrugge, Magnus. 1984. *Alive: An Enquiry into the Origin and Meaning of Life*. Vallecito, CA: Ross House Books.

Vermeij, Geerat. 1997. *Privileged Hands: A Remarkable Scientific Life*. New York: W. H. Freeman.

Vickers, G.D. 1987. Letter to Raymond Damadian, January 7.

Vincent, Lynn. 2004. "Unscientific Methods. Does Freedom of Speech End at the Classroom Door?" *World*, 19(36):30–31. September 18.

Vitz, Paul. 1986. *Censorship: Evidence of Bias in our Children's Textbooks*. Ann Arbor, MI: Servant Books.

Viviano, Frank. 1981. "The Crucifixion of Evolution." *Mother Jones*, 6(8):2–6.

Vogel, Gretchen. 2003. "2003 Nobel Prizes: Physicists Honored for Their Medical Insights." *Science*, 302:382–383.

Von Braun, Wernher. 1971. *Space Frontier*. New York: Holt, Rinehart and Winston.

W.

Wach, Joachim. 1964. *Sociology of Religion*. Chicago: The University of Chicago Press.

Wagner, Dennis. 1982. "Evolutionists Confront Creationists at AAS Symposium: An Analysis." *Students for Origins Research Newsletter*, 5(2):1,4–6.

———. 1992. Interview of Dennis Wagner by Jerry Bergman, January.

Wagner, Donald. 2000. "Academic Freedom for Religious Academics in Public Universities: The Case of Philip Bishop." Chapter 8 of *Social Structures, Social Capital, and Personal Freedom*, edited by Dale McConkey and Peter Lawler, pp. 131–140. Westport, CT: Praeger.

Walker, Samuel. 1999. "In Defense of American Liberties: A History of the ACLU." Carbondale, IL: Southern Illinois University Press.

Walters, Tracy W. 1985. Review of *Scientists Confront Creationism* by Lori R. Godfrey. In Origins Research, 8(2):5. Fall–Winter.

Ward, Bob. 2005. *Dr. Space: The Life of Wernher von Braun*. Annapolis, MD: Naval Institute Press.

Ward, Peter D., and Donald Brownlee. 2000. *Rare Earth: Why Complex Life Is Uncommon in the Universe*. New York, NY: Copernicus.

Warriner, David. 1975. *What is Man?* Cape Girardeav, MO: Challenge Press.

Washington Post. "Dissing Darwin." *Op-Ed*. June, 3, 2005. p. A22.

Wasley, Paula. 2006. "Tenure Denied." *The Chronicle of Higher Education*, April 14, p. A8.

Watanabe, Teresa. 2001a. "Enlisting Science to Find the Fingerprints of a Creator." *Los Angeles Times*, March 25. http://www.arn.org/docs/news/fingerprints032501.htm

———. 2001b. "Seeking Science to Support Teaching of a Created World." *Los Angeles Times*, August 25, p. 1.

Watson, James D. 1996. *The Double Helix*. New York: Scribner Classics.

———. 2002. *Genes, Girls, and Gamov*. New York: Knopf.

———. 2003. Quoted in "Do Our Genes Reveal the Hand of God?" *The Telegraph*, March 20. http://www.telegraph.co.uk/connected/main.jhtml?xml=/connected/2003/03/19/ecfgod19.xml (as of 04/11/08).

Watson, Wilbur. 1982. *Aging and Social Behavior*, Monterey, CA.

Weaver, Linda. 1987. "Creation-Evolution Debate Examines Beliefs." *The Hillsdale Collegian*, April 16, p. 7.

Webb, Jeremy. 2005. "Evolution's Greatest Inventions." *New Scientist*, 186(2494):27–35. April 9.

Webber, Robert L. 1980. *Pioneers of Science: Nobel Prize Winners in Physics*. Bristol: The Institute of Physics.

Weber, Karl A. 1994. Letter from Karl Weber to Jerry Bergman, dated May 7.

Weed, William Speed. 2003. "The Way We Live Now: Questions for Raymond Damadian." *The New York Times*, Section 6, p. 37.

Wehrli, Felix W. 1992. "The Origins and Future of Nuclear Magnetic Resonance Imaging." *Physics Today*, 45(6):34–42. June.

Weikart, Richard, 2004. *From Darwin to Hitler*. New York: Palgrave Macmillan.

Weinberg, Steven. 1992. *Dreams of a Final Theory*. New York: Pantheon Books.

———. 1977. *The First Three Minutes: A Modern View of the Origin of the Universe*. New York: Basic Books.

———. 2000. "A Designer Universe?" In *The Best American Science Writing*, edited by James Gleick and Jessie Cohen, pp. 241–248. The ECCO Press.

Weiner, J.S. 1955. *The Piltdown Forgery*. London: Oxford University Press.

Weisberg, Jacob. 2005. "Evolution vs. Religion – Quit Pretending They're Compatible." Posted Wednesday, Aug. 10, 2005, at 12:30 p.m. http://www.slate.com/id/2124297/nav/tap1/ (as of 04/11/08).

Weiss, Rick. 2003. "Prize Fight." *Smithsonian*, 34(9):35–38. December.

Wells, George. 1981. "Censorship Charge Not Supported, Judge Complains." *Arkansas Gazette*, December 15.

Wells, H.G. 1934. *Experiment in Autobiography*. Boston: Little Brown.

———. 1979. *The Complete Science Fiction Treasury of H. G. Wells*. New York: Crown.

Wells, J. 1982. "Creationists." *American Atheist*, July, p. 57. [Note: This author is to be distinguished from Jonathan Wells of the Discovery Institute, below.]

Wells, Jonathan. 2000. *Icons of Evolution: Science or Myth?* Washington, DC: Regnery-Gateway.

Welsh, John. 2003. "Next Up: Science and Social Studies. Education Officials Tackle More Standards." *Pioneer Press*, June 19.

West, Anthony. 1984. H. G. *Wells: Aspects of a Life*. London: Hutchinson.

West, John W., Jr. 2001. "The Regeneration of Science and Culture." In *Signs of Intelligence*, edited by William A. Dembski and James M. Kushiner, pp. 60-69. Grand Rapids, MI: Brazos Press.

———. 2007. "Two Astronomers at Iowa State Tied to Statement Denouncing Intelligent Design as 'Creationist Pseudoscience.'" *Evolution News & Views*, Discovery Institute. http://www.evolutionnews. org/2007/05/two_astronomers_at_iowa_state.html

Westacott, Michael J., and John F. Ashton, eds. 2005. *The Big Argument: Twenty-Four Scholars Explore Why Science, Archaeology and Philosophy Haven't Disproved God*. Sydney: Strand Publishing.

Wheeler, T. Arthur. 1994. "Creationism Classroom Invasion Causes a Pseudo-science Controversy." *Dayton Daily News*, April 23.

White, Andrew D. 1955. *A History of the Warfare of Science with Theology in Christendom*. New York: George Braziller. [Original 1896]

White, Chuck. 1994. "Wright State Removes Professor for Teaching Creationism!" *Xenia Daily Gazette*, April 19.

Whitehead, John W. 1982. *The Second American Revolution*. Elgin, IL: David C. Cook.

———. 1983. *The Freedom of Religious Expression in the Public High School*, Westchester, IL: Crossway.

———. 1986. "Priorities and Resistance." In *The Rebirth of America*, edited by Nancy Leigh DeMoss, pp. 197–204. New York: The Arthur S. DeMoss Foundation.

———. 1995. *Politically Correct: Censorship in American Culture*. Chicago, IL: Moody Press.

———, and John Conlan. 1978. "The Establishment of the Religion of Secular Humanism and Its First Amendment Implications." *Texas Tech Law Review*, 10(1):1–66. Winter.

Wieland, Carl. 1998. "Twenty Years of Creation Magazine." *Creation*, 20(3):25.

———. 2004. "The Not-so-Nobel Decision." *Creation*, 26(4):40–42.

Wiester, John L. 1990. Letter to Editor. *Wall Street Journal*, Nov. 9.

———. 1991. "Evolution and Creation." *The Scientist*, 5(5):12. Mar. 4.

Wilder-Smith, A.E. 1987. *The Scientific Alternative to Neo-Darwinian Evolutionary Theory: Information Sources and Structures*. Costa Mesa, CA: TWFT Publishers.

———. 1986. Interview of A.E. Wilder-Smith by Jerry Bergman, October.

Wildman, Don. 1984. "Creationist Educators Suffer Persecution." *NFD Journal*, October, pp. 22–23.

Williams, Alton. 2004. "Why I Believe the Bible: A Nuclear Scientist Tells His Story." *Awake!*, 85(2):19–23. January 22.

Williams, Precious. 2000. "King of the Dinosaurs." *The Independent*, Sunday, March 26, pp. 4–6.

Williams, R.M. 1970. *American Society*. Third edition. New York, NY: Alfred A Knopf.

Wills, Garry. 1990. *Under God*. New York: Simon and Schuster.

Wilson, A.N. 1984. *Hilaire Belloc: A Biography*. New York: Atheneum.

———. 1999. *God's Funeral*. New York: W. W. Norton.

Wilson, Edward. O. 1978. *On Human Nature*. Cambridge, MA: Harvard University Press.

———. 1998. "Edward O. Wilson." *Free Inquiry*, 18(1):19. Winter 1997–1998.

Wilson, John. 2000a. "Baylor University's Polanyi Center Comes Under Fire from the University's Faculty." *Christianity Today*, April 24.

———. 2000b. "Baylor's Dismissal of Polanyi Center Director Dembski was not a Smart Move." *Christianity Today*, October 23.

Winder, Gordon. 1984. Letter from Gordon Winder to Jerry Bergman, n.d.

Winnick, Pamela. 2005. *A Jealous God: Science's Crusade Against Religion*. Nashville, TN: Nelson Current.

Wirth, Kevin. 1982. "Science Education: Only the Best Ad-Hoc Will Do." *Origins Research*, 5(2):2.

———. 1984. "A Call for Dialogue." *Origins Research*, 7(9):2. Fall–Winter.

———. 2002. Interview of Kevin Wirth by Jerry Bergman, December.

————. 2008. Unpublished manucript. "Case Study of Religious Discrimination Against a Creationist—The Thomas Jungmann Incident."

Witham, Larry. 1997. "Many Scientists See God's Hand in Evolution." *Washington Times*, April 11, p. A8.

————. 2002. *Where Darwin Meets the Bible: Creationists and Evolutionists in America*. New York: Oxford University Press.

Wolf, Larry W. 1991. "The Preachy Professor." Letter to Editor. *Liberty*, Nov–Dec., p. 30.

Wolfe, Alan. 1973. *The Seamy Side of Democracy: Repression in America*. New York: David McKay.

Wonderly, Daniel. 1990. *Why Was the Anti-Creationism Movement Able to Arise So Rapidly Following the Creation Arkansas Trial?* Paper presented at the 1990 ASA conference at Grantham, PA: Messiah College.

Wood, James. 1992. "Notes on Church-State Affairs." *Journal of Church and State*, 34(4):658. Autumn.

Wood, James L., and Maurice Jackson. 1982. *Social Movements*. Belmont, CA: Wadsworth.

Woods, Jim. 1994. "Creationism Talk Blamed for Firing: A Wright State Biology Teacher Says Telling Students His Views on the Topic Spurred His Dismissal." *The Columbus Dispatch*, April 17, p. 2D.

Woodward, Thomas. 2003. *Doubts about Darwin*. Grand Rapids, MI: Baker Books.

World Net Daily. 2005. "Smithsonian Backs Off Intelligent Design Film." June, 4.

Wright, Elinor. 1987. "On Creationism." *Free Inquiry*, Spring, pp. 3–4.

Wright, Robert. 1988. *Three Scientists and Their Gods: Looking for Meaning in an Age of Information*. New York: Times Books.

Wurmbrand, Richard. 1986. *Marx and Satan*. Bartlesville, OK: Living Sacrifice Book Company.

Wycoff, Mick. 1992. "Evolution: It's Not Just a Single Theory, It's a Lot of Theories." *The Scientist*, March 30, p. 15.

Y.

Yahoo! 1999. "Biology Teacher Removed Due to Religious Beliefs." June 1. http://groups.yahoo.com/group/writing-for-the-wall/message/246 (as of 04/11/08).

Yam, Phillip. 2003. "The Nobel Prizes for 2003." *Scientific American*, December, p. 42.

Yankelovich, Daniel. 2000. "2000 Evolution and Creationism in Public Education: An In-Depth Reading of Public Opinion." *People for the American Way Foundation*, March.

Yant, Martin. 1991. *Presumed Guilty: When Innocent People Are Wrongly Convicted*. New York: Prometheus Books.

York, Frank. 2000. "No Admittance: Critical Thinking Is Where It's At, Right? Not If the Topic is Evolution." *Teachers in Focus*, March 12, pp 4–7.

Z.

Zal, Cyrus. 1992. "Summary of the John Peloza Case." Unpublished manuscript.

————. John E. Peloza vs. Capistrano Unified School District, Board of Trustees of the Capistrano Unified School District. Opening Brief for Appellant Case No. 92-552228 Appeal.

————. John E. Peloza vs. Capistrano Unified School District, Board of Trustees of the Capistrano Unified School District...Memorandum of Points and Authorities in Opposition to Defendant's Motion for Attorneys' Fees, Apr. 6, 1992.

————. John E. Peloza vs. Capistrano Unified School District, Board of Trustees of the Capistrano Unified School District...Memorandum of Points and Authorities in Opposition to Defendant's Motion to Dismiss Jan. 6, 1992.

Zimmerman, Michael. 1987a "Creationists' Appeal for Freedom of Speech Diverts Attention from Their Anti-Science Views." *The Chronicle of Higher Education*, April, 1. pp. 42–43.

————. 1987b. "The Evolution-Creation Controversy: Opinions of Ohio High School Biology Teachers." *Ohio Journal of Science*, 87(4):115–125.

————. 1988. "Ohio School Boards' President's Views on the Evolution-Creation Controversy." *Newsletter of the Ohio Center for Science Education*, Oct 1987 and Jan 1988.

Zindler, Frank. 1995. "Frank R. Zindler: Biography." In *Leaving the Fold: Testimonies of Former Fundamentalists*, edited by Edward Babinski, pp. 358–363. Amherst, NY: Prometheus.

Zuidema, Henry. 1984. "How to Rock a Campus without Hiring." *Liberty*, 79(6):16–18. Nov.

————. 1985. "Teaching Scientific Creationism on Campus: Is the Controversy Cooling?" *Liberty*, 80(1):7–9. Jan–Feb.

Jerry Bergman PhD has taught biology, genetics, chemistry, biochemistry, anthropology, geology, and microbiology at the college level for over 35 years. He has taught at the Medical College of Ohio where he was a research associate in the department of experimental pathology, 6 years at the University of Toledo, and 7 years at Bowling Green State University. Dr Bergman is a graduate of the Medical College of Ohio, Wayne State University in Detroit, The University of Toledo, and Bowling Green State University. He has also completed 40 graduate hours in the department of chemistry Miami University in Oxford Ohio, and has studied geology, philosophy, nutrition, and chemistry at the University of Wisconsin, Madison, Wisconsin. So far he has earned 9 degrees, all in the sciences.

He has written over 800 publications, mostly in the science area, which have appeared in 12 languages in over 22 books and monographs. His work includes a monograph on peer evaluation published by the College Student Journal Press, a Fastback on the creation-evolution controversy published by Phi Delta Kappa, a book on vestigial organs with Dr George Howe, a book on religious discrimination published by Onesimus Press, and a book on mental health published by Claudius Verlag in München, Germany. He has also published a college textbook on measurement and evaluation (Boston, Houghton Mifflin Co.), and has contributed to dozens of other textbooks. Other works have been published by Greenwood press, Syracuse University Press, Prometheus Books, and the State University of New York University Press. He was also a consultant for over 20 science textbooks, mostly in the area of biology and biochemistry.

Dr Bergman has presented over one hundred scientific papers at professional and community meetings in the United States, Canada, and Europe. To discuss his research, he has been a featured speaker on many college campuses throughout the United States and Europe, and is a frequent guest on radio and television programs. His research has made the front page in newspapers throughout the country, has been featured on the Paul Harvey Show several times, and has been discussed by David Brinkley, Chuck Colson, and other nationally known commentators on national television.

He is listed in *Marquis Who's Who in the Midwest*, since 1992 *Marquis Who's Who in America* since 2000; and in *Marquis Who's Who in Education* since the 6th Edition, and *Marquis Who's Who in Science and Engineering* since the 8th edition, *Marquis Who's Who in Medicine and Health Care* since 2005, and *Who's Who in Theology and Science*, and *Who's Who in America*. He was selected by his students for *Who's Who Among America's Teachers* for the years 2000 and 2005.

Printed in the United States
122844LV00002B/1-27/P